Ezra Pound's Eriugena

Historicizing Modernism

Historicizing Modernism challenges traditional literary interpretations by taking an
empirical approach to modernist writing: a direct response to new documentary
sources made available over the last decade.

Informed by archival research, and working beyond the usual
European/American avant-garde 1900-45 parameters, this series reassesses
established readings of modernist writers by developing fresh views of
intellectual contexts and working methods.

Ezra Pound's Eriugena

Mark Byron

Bloomsbury Academic
An imprint of Bloomsbury Publishing Plc

B L O O M S B U R Y
LONDON · OXFORD · NEW YORK · NEW DELHI · SYDNEY

Bloomsbury Academic

An imprint of Bloomsbury Publishing Plc

50 Bedford Square	1385 Broadway
London	New York
WC1B 3DP	NY 10018
UK	USA

www.bloomsbury.com

BLOOMSBURY and the Diana logo are trademarks of Bloomsbury Publishing Plc

First published 2014
Paperback edition first published 2016

British Library Cataloguing-in-Publication Data
A catalogue record for this book is available from the British Library.

ISBN: HB: 978-14411-3954-2
PB: 978-14742-7564-4
ePDF: 978-14411-1262-0
ePub: 978-14411-7927-2

Library of Congress Cataloging-in-Publication Data
A catalog record for this book is available from the Library of Congress.

Series: Historicizing Modernism

Typeset by Integra Software Services Pvt. Ltd.

Contents

Series Editor's Preface   vi

Acknowledgements   vii

Abbreviations   x

Archival Materials   xii

Francesco Fiorentino   xiii

Notes on the Text   xiv

Preface   xv

Introduction   1

1   Pound's Eriugena: Neoplatonist and Heretic   15

2   John Scottus Eriugena: The Meeting of Athens and
Rome in Gaul   51

3   The Missing Book of the Trilogy   113

4   The Poetics of Exile: Laon to Changsha   207

Appendices

A   Francesco Fiorentino at Brunnenburg:
An Annotated Transcription of Pound's Reading in Eriugena   259

B   YCAL MSS 53 Series II, Box 29 Folder 627
Cantos LXXIV–LXXXIV, Typescript Drafts in Italian   267

Bibliography   270

Index of Works by Pound   288

Index of Works by Eriugena   289

General Index   290

Series Editor's Preface

Historicizing Modernism

This book series is devoted to the analysis of late-nineteenth- to twentieth-century literary Modernism within its historical context. *Historicizing Modernism* thus stresses empirical accuracy and the value of primary sources (such as letters, diaries, notes, drafts, marginalia or other archival deposits) in developing monographs, scholarly editions and edited collections on Modernist authors and their texts. This may take a number of forms, such as manuscript study and annotated volumes; archival editions and genetic criticism; as well as mappings of interrelated historical milieus or ideas. To date, no book series has laid claim to this interdisciplinary, source-based territory for modern literature. Correspondingly, one burgeoning sub-discipline of Modernism, Beckett Studies, features heavily here as a metonymy for the opportunities presented by manuscript research more widely. While an additional range of 'canonical' authors will be covered here, this series also highlights the centrality of supposedly 'minor' or occluded figures, not least in helping to establish broader intellectual genealogies of Modernist writing. Furthermore, while the series will be weighted towards the English-speaking world, studies of non-Anglophone Modernists whose writings are ripe for archivally based exploration shall also be included here.

A key aim of such historicizing is to reach beyond the familiar rhetoric of intellectual and artistic 'autonomy' employed by many Modernists and their critical commentators. Such rhetorical moves can and should themselves be historically situated and reintegrated into the complex continuum of individual literary practices. This emphasis upon the contested self-definitions of Modernist writers, thinkers and critics may, in turn, prompt various reconsiderations of the boundaries delimiting the concept 'Modernism' itself. Similarly, the very notion of 'historicizing' Modernism remains debatable, and this series by no means discourages more theoretically informed approaches. On the contrary, the editors believe that the historical specificity encouraged by *Historicizing Modernism* may inspire a range of fundamental critiques along the way.

Matthew Feldman
Erik Tonning

Acknowledgements

While I take great pleasure in acknowledging my many debts incurred throughout the long life of this book project, the range and extent of those debts are formidable. This project germinated from a short section of my doctoral dissertation concerning the function of light imagery in *The Pisan Cantos*. It is with relief and a sense of belatedness that I can finally give public thanks to my doctoral supervisor at Cambridge University, J. H. Prynne. It is true that my intellectual trajectory would not nearly resemble its present form without his unique insights, astonishing generosity and timely *hilaritas*, not least my sense of the way Pound assimilated his views on Chinese writing and Confucian thought with his study of Neoplatonism and Aristotelian ontology within his poetics. My deepest thanks also go to Andrew Burns, whose work on the twelfth-century reception of Eriugena comprises an important aspect of Eriugena Studies. As students we were lucky to participate in Peter Dronke's final seminar series, on the *Periphyseon*, before his retirement. It was truly an early medieval experience. Indirectly, John Marenbon also deeply influenced my understanding of Eriugena's thought, especially his absorption of the *Categoriae Decem*.

The gradual assimilation of the themes upon which this monograph is built was a process that took shape in several key locations, and with the insightful support of individuals and a variety of institutions. Foremost, I want to thank Mary de Rachewiltz for allowing me to consult many of Pound's books during visits to Schloss Brunnenburg in Dorf Tyrol, not least the several volumes of Francesco Fiorentino. Mary's hospitality is legendary: she has actively facilitated – and made possible – a large number of intellectual projects on Pound and modern poetry, without which the field would be immeasurably poorer. My preliminary research during a visit to Brunnenburg in July 2006 was supported by a Travelling Fellowship from the Australian Academy of the Humanities. Besides Brunnenburg, the other key research institution in my project is the Beinecke Rare Book and Manuscript Library at Yale University. I began work in earnest on Pound's Cavalcanti notebooks with the assistance of a Donald C. Gallup Fellowship in January 2006, and was greatly assisted by the generosity of Patricia C. Willis, Curator of the American Literature Collection, and Nancy Kuhl, her formidable successor. The Beinecke is blessed with a truly extraordinary staff, whose deep knowledge of the collections is matched by a spirit of generosity and hospitality. Too many people to name individually extended their assistance to me in visits in 2006, 2012 and 2013. I would like to thank especially both Naomi Saito and Ann Marie Menta for their considerable help in matters of accessing the collection and obtaining crucial reproductions.

The development of the final manuscript of this book was enabled by funding entailed in an Australian Research Council Discovery Project, the subject of which was scholarly editorial methods in Modernist Studies (2011–2013). Whilst the present book represents a slight tangent from the central premise of that project, it nonetheless forms a critical element of the bigger picture, especially with regard to Modernist manuscript studies. The early medieval subject matter that so powerfully drew Pound's attention suggests the rich potential Medieval Studies presents to Modernist scholars. I was able to air aspects of this project in a number of conference presentations, principally at the Ezra Pound International Conference in London (2011) and Dublin (2013), as well as at Modernism, Christianity and Apocalypse, expertly convened by Erik Tonning at Solstrand, Norway, in 2012. A brief teaching fellowship at Rikkyo University, Tokyo, in 2011 also allowed me to present aspects of Chapter 4 to audiences at Rikkyo University, Tokyo Woman's Christian University, and Nagoya University. My warmest thanks to Dorsey Kleitz, David Ewick, Tateo Imamura and Akitoshi Nagahata for their kind hospitality, and to Yoshiko Kita for making the fellowship possible.

One section of Chapter 4 has been published in a different form as 'In a Station of the *Cantos*: Ezra Pound's 'Seven Lakes' Canto and the Shō-Shō Hakkei Tekagami', *Literature and Aesthetics* 22.2 (2012): 138–52; another related part has been published as 'Ezra Pound's 'Seven Lakes' Canto: Poetry and Painting, From East to West', *Eibei-Bungaku / The Rikkyo Review* 73 (March 2013): 121–42. Short sections of Chapter 1 and Chapter 4 will appear as 'Ezra Pound's Eriugena: Eschatology in the *Periphyseon* and *The Cantos*', in *Modernism, Christianity and Apocalypse*, ed. Matthew Feldman and Erik Tonning (Brill), currently in press.

It is especially gratifying to be able to thank so many colleagues in Pound Studies, especially those with whom I have built friendships over many iterations of the biennial Ezra Pound International Conference. The many conversations, suggestions, helpful references and general camaraderie all provide the essential elements of a vibrant intellectual community, for which I am truly grateful. I would like to thank in particular: John Gery (EPIC secretary), Ron Bush, Ira Nadel, David Moody, David Ten Eyck, Anderson Araujo, Biljana Obradovic, Sean Pryor, Réka Mihálka, David Ewick, Dorsey Kleitz, Paul Rossiter, Shinji

Watanabe, Miho Takahashi, Yoshiko Kita, Akitoshi Nagahata, Peter Liebregts, Aaron Jaffe, Giuliana Ferreccio, Massimo Bacigalupo, Lucille Dumont and Demetres Tryphonopoulos.

Continuum Press, now a part of the Bloomsbury fold, deserves all the thanks and praise I can muster, not least for showing belief in what at first sight perhaps appeared to be an unlikely topic. The Historicizing Modernism series has two fine editors in Erik Tonning and Matthew Feldman, who have shown great patience and enthusiasm over the long gestation of the book manuscript of *Ezra Pound's Eriugena* and unwavering belief in its potential. It is a privilege to count myself among their colleagues. Many thanks also to Mark Richardson, whose patience stood the tests I inadvertently presented, and whose aid in seeing the manuscript to print is very much appreciated.

Andrea Yapp has shown much grace throughout the writing process during which this book took shape, and embodied the perfect combination of interest and patience. Andrea, this book is my bonbon to you. Finally, my thanks to Boo, without whose constant company this would have been a much lonelier writing project. She is surely the only cat in Sydney who has been both homeless in Seattle and a customer of Alaskan Airlines.

Abbreviations

Works by Pound

All citations from *The Cantos* are from the fifteenth printing of the 1993 New Directions edition, and take the form of canto number in Roman numerals followed by page number in Arabic numerals: thus Canto LXXIV page 449 is (LXXIV / 449).

Other primary works are abbreviated as follows:

ABCR	*ABC of Reading*. London: Faber, 1961.
CON	*Confucius: The Great Digest, The Unwobbling Pivot, The Analects*. New York: New Directions, 1969.
E&DP	*Ezra and Dorothy Pound: Letters in Captivity, 1945–1946*, ed. Omar Pound and Robert Spoo. New York: Oxford UP, 1999.
EP&JL	*Ezra Pound and James Laughlin: Selected Letters*, ed. David M. Gordon. New York: Norton, 1994.
EPS	*'Ezra Pound Speaking': Radio Speeches of World War II*, ed. Leonard Doob. Westport and London: Greenwood, 1978.
GK	*Guide to Kulchur*. London: Faber, 1938.
Impact	*Impact: Essays on Ignorance and the Decline of American Civilization*, ed. Noel Stock. Chicago: Henry Regnery, 1960.
LE	*Literary Essays of Ezra Pound*, ed. T. S. Eliot. London: Faber, 1954.
MIN	*Make It New*. London: Faber, 1934.
P&D	*Pavannes and Divagations*. Norfolk, CT: New Directions, 1958.
P / L	*Pound / Lewis: The Letters of Ezra Pound and Wyndham Lewis*, ed. Timothy Materer. London: Faber, 1985.
SL	*Selected Letters: 1907–1941*, ed. D. D. Paige. London: Faber, 1950.
SP	*Selected Prose 1909–1965*, ed. and intro. William Cookson. London: Faber, 1973.
SR	*The Spirit of Romance*. 1910; New York: New Directions, 1968.
T	*The Translations of Ezra Pound*, intro. Hugh Kenner. 1953; London: Faber, 1970.

Works by Eriugena

PL 122	*Joannis Scoti Opera*, ed. Henry Joseph Floss, Patrologia Latina Volume 122, second series, gen. ed. Jacques-Paul Migne (Paris, 1853).
Ambig. S. Max.	*Versio Ambiguorum S. Maximi*, PL 122, pp. 1193–222
Eccl. Hier.	Pseudo-Dionysius, *De caelesti Ierarchia*, PL 122, pp. 1035–68.
Epi. Cel. Hier.	*Epigramma in beatum Dionysium de caelesti Ierarchia*, PL 122, pp. 1037–38.
Exp. Cel. Hier.	*Expositiones Super Ierarchian Caelestiam S. Dionysii*, PL 122, pp. 126–264.
Exp. Myst. Theol.	*Expositiones in Mysticam Theologiam S. Dionysii*, PL 122, pp. 267–84.
Herren	Michael W. Herren, ed., *Iohannis Scotti Erivgenae: Carmina*, Scriptores Latini Hiberniae XII (Dublin: Dublin Institute of Advanced Studies, 1993).
Peri.	*Periphyseon / De Divisione naturae*, PL 122, pp. 439–1022
Versus	*Versus*, PL 122, pp. 1221–42.

Archival Materials

Three major sets of archival materials are treated in this study, from the Ezra Pound Collection (YCAL MSS 43) or the Ezra Pound Addition (YCAL MSS 53), the Beinecke Rare Book and Manuscript Library, Yale University:

1. YCAL MSS 43, Box 76, Folder 3383: a 26-page set of autograph manuscript notes on Eriugena, composed some time from early 1940.
2. YCAL MSS 43, Box 77, Folder 3406: a 38-page set of autograph manuscript notes on Eriugena, lodged within a more extensive set of manuscript canto drafts in Italian, composed 1941–1945.
3. YCAL MSS 53, Series II, Box 29, Folder 627: a two-page typescript digression on Eriugena in English and Italian, interleaved within an extensive sequence of canto drafts towards prospective Cantos LXXIV and LXXV in Italian. Note the tone of these pages is one of informality, if not scurrility, giving the notes a distinctive edge. They are transcribed in Appendix B.

All other quoted primary material is from the Ezra Pound Collection, The Beinecke Rare Book and Manuscript Library, Yale University, and is cited in the form: YCAL MSS 43, followed by Box and Folder number.

Francesco Fiorentino

There are five volumes of Francesco Fiorentino in Pound's library at Brunnenburg, listed below. Appendix A comprises an annotated transcription of 'Capitolo IX. Prima età della Scolastica. – Giovanni Scoto Eriugena', in Fiorentino's *Manuale di Storia della Filosofia*, a cura di Giuseppe Monticelli, vol. 1. Filosofia Antica e medioevale. Torino: G. B. Paravia, 1921, pp. 216–21.

The five volumes are:

(1921), *Manuale di Storia della Filosofia*, a cura di Giuseppe Monticelli, vol. 1. Filosofia Antica e medioevale. Torino: G. B. Paravia. [EP no 577a]

(1924), *Compendio di Storia della Filosofia*, a cura di Armando Carlini, terza edizione, vol. 1. Filosofia Antica e Filosofia del Medio evo e del Rinascimento. Firenze: Vallecchi Editore. [EP no 574]

(1929a), *Compendio di Storia della Filosofia*, a cura di Armando Carlini, terza edizione, vol. 2, parte prima (Parte III – La filosofia contemporanea [Bacon to Spencer]). Firenze: Vallecchi Editore. [EP no 575] [HB]

(1929b), *Compendio di Storia della Filosofia*, a cura di Armando Carlini, terza edizione, vol. 2, parte prima (Parte III – La filosofia contemporanea [Bacon to Spencer]). Firenze: Vallecchi Editore. [EP no 577] [SB]

(1929c), *Compendio di Storia della Filosofia*, a cura di Armando Carlini, terza edizione, vol. 2, parte seconda (Parte III – La filosofia contemporanea [Wundt to Bergson]). Firenze: Vallecchi Editore. [EP no 576]

Note that Fiorentino 1929a and 1929b are identical volumes. Each volume above is followed by its Brunnenburg accession number.

Notes on the Text

In all cases where Pound's manuscripts or typescripts are quoted, no attempt has been made to standardise spelling or punctuation and the abbreviation *sic* has not been used. In instances where Pound's handwriting is difficult to decipher, leaving some doubt as to the appropriate reading, the text in question has been placed in square brackets with three suspension points.

All translations from foreign languages are those of the author unless otherwise specified.

Preface

*Research [學 (xue)] without thought is a mere net and entanglement;
thought without gathering data [學 (xue)], a peril.*
        – *Analects* II.15.1 (*CON* 199)

The less we know, the longer the explanations.
        – 'Cavalcanti: Partial Explanation' (*MIN* 356)

Ezra Pound's literary career is distinctively singular for several reasons: his reinventions of poetic form, his ability to marshal his own resources and those of his peers to advance a variety of literary innovations, his drawing on history and politics to inform and shape his work, and his attempt to write a modern epic in the lineage of Homer and Dante. The engine driving each of these imperatives to innovate is Pound's irrepressible desire to learn from an impressive range of literary, philosophical, artistic and cultural traditions. He sought out 'the best which has been thought and said in the world' as guides to his own poetic creativity, and ventured across the European tradition from classical Greece and Rome to the early and high Middle Ages, as well as the Renaissance and the Enlightenment Age. Pound also found in the poetry of China and Japanese Noh drama two immensely rich traditions, offering entirely new ways of thinking about language and aesthetic representation to a Western audience. They only had to be properly understood and absorbed into artistic practice. Pound's efforts to unearth such varied funds of creative insight were not in every instance made *in vacuo*, but he is principally responsible for a range of innovations and resources available to poets today.

Pound's encyclopaedic imperative also led him to question intellectual orthodoxies, and to seek out and understand ideas and texts that ran counter to the received narratives of literary and cultural history. One prominent figure in Pound's counter-tradition is the ninth-century Irish theologian, scholar and poet Johannes Scottus Eriugena. This figure came to prominence in the court of Charles the Bald, two generations after Charles's grandfather, Charlemagne, had initiated the Carolingian Renaissance by establishing a new centre of learning at Aachen. Pound saw in Eriugena a strikingly original and courageous thinker, willing to endure ecclesiastical opprobrium in his pursuit of systematic theology, and an intellectually adventurous scholar who sought to advance Greek learning in Western Europe at a time of its near-eclipse. Pound was prescient in his support of Eriugena's importance in intellectual history, made the more striking by the fact that it is only in recent decades that his contributions to theology, poetics and dialectics have received the scholarly attention they deserve.

The two major phases of Pound's research into Eriugena's life and works were shaped by his limited access to source materials: the first phase, in the early 1930s, was shaped by Francesco Fiorentino's philosophy textbooks intended for secondary school students; and the second phase, in 1939–1940, was enabled by volume 122 of the Patrologia Latina containing Henry Joseph Floss's Latin edition of Eriugena's complete works. This second phase also saw Pound compose two series of notes on his reading. These notes have received only passing scholarly attention, but are important documents in Pound's developing philological sensibility. He draws on his previous work in the 1920s and 30s on the manuscripts of Guido Cavalcanti, as well as emulating some of the scribal habits of the early medieval monastic schools: habits of annotation, glossing and the production of florilegia. Despite the limited availability of source material, Pound discerned the intellectual magnitude of Eriugena's work decades before its context within the Carolingian Renaissance could be properly assessed. Pound's initial focus rested upon the various controversies with which Eriugena's name was associated: the Trinitarian and Predestination controversies in the ninth century, and the Averroist controversies at the University of Paris in the thirteenth century. He also saw in Eriugena's statement, 'Authority comes from right reason, never the other way on', a motto of intellectual autonomy worth championing. Pound's focus changed in the second phase of his research to matters of Eriugena's metaphysics, and particularly that of light associated elsewhere with Robert Grosseteste and the medieval Islamic commentators on Aristotle. Pound also saw in Eriugena's courtly poetry and 'Greek tags' a demonstration of *hilaritas*, a mode of *gentilezza* enabled by his proximity to and familiarity with his king, Charles the Bald. Eriugena served multiple intertwined functions for Pound: he was an intellectual sphinx, arising out of the desert wastes of early medieval thought as an alternative to scholastic narrow-mindedness; his embroilment in various controversies demonstrated that he was prepared to stand for his beliefs counter to a bull-headed ecclesiastical hierarchy, and for which he earned the loyalty and protection of his royal patron; and in the composition of courtly poetry in Greek, Eriugena serves Pound as a model for his own cosmopolitan, polyglot, experimental poetics. Pound drew

Eriugena into his own private textual community[1] in the months during which he composed *The Pisan Cantos*, as company for his own *vox clamantis in deserto*.

The limited extent to which Pound adapted his Eriugenian materials suggests a missed opportunity to exploit poetic and philosophical work with which he felt much sympathy. His knowledge was limited by material conditions of wartime access to adequate texts, as well as by the emergent state of Eriugenian scholarship. The potential significance of this thinker for Pound's project can be better estimated with a degree of hindsight, now that a comprehensive scholarly effort to edit and analyze Eriugena's texts has advanced. The *De Praedestinatione*, commissioned by Charles and Hincmar, Archbishop of Reims, sets out a reading of Augustine on doctrinal matters of predestination, from which Eriugena appears to arrive close to a Pelagian view that rejects any form of predestination. His translations of and commentaries on the writings of the Greek Neoplatonist writer Pseudo-Dionysius were also commissioned by Charles, and represent the earliest competent attempt to harmonize Eastern patristic thought with that of the Latin West. Eriugena's poetry also stands tall in Carolingian letters, not least as the most distinguished examples of Greek poetics for centuries either side of Eriugena's years of known activity or *floruit*. Yet the most significant achievement of this rare thinker was the *Periphyseon* (*De Divisione Naturae*), a cosmography in four books that comprises a treatise on dialectics; an *hexaemeron* (after Augustine) on the six days of creation; and an eschatology in which the originary *processio* of creation turns to a *reditus*, a return to the divine. Pound glossed this astonishing work in its entirety, but his notes make clear he had only begun to understand its greater significance for his project 'to write paradise'.

This study does not pretend to be the last word on Pound's Eriugena. Rather, in firmly establishing the nature of Eriugena's continuing historical, philosophical and aesthetic significance, this study clears the way for more comprehensive thinking about Pound's use of early medieval sources, and his emulation of their textual strategies. Pound's poetry, especially *The Cantos*, has been well served by generations of astute critical readers. His intertextual strategies have received sustained critical attention, such as his use of subject rhymes, his modes of citation and allusion by way of the 'ideogrammic method', and other techniques. *The Cantos* also incorporates some of the material aspects of different script traditions and variations within specific traditions with which it engages: this is most visibly in evidence in the incorporation of Chinese ideograms or their proxies, but there are more subtle practices in evidence that are central to traditions of manuscript studies and scholarly annotation, and having been absorbed as such, are not always so readily visible. This study hopes to show that Pound's engagement with the textual practices implicit in his Eriugenian source materials are intended to bear hermeneutic weight in a dialectical relationship with their prosodic and rhetorical features: that is, by his emulation of the late classical and early medieval practices of glossing, marginalia, abbreviation, the compilation of florilegia, matters of palaeography evident in Eriugena's texts and commentaries on them, Pound brings a distinctly medieval textual awareness into modern poetry. These textual innovations function as material support for intersecting conceptual and philosophical interests in the transmission of knowledge and insight into the possibility of a *paradiso terrestre*. In emulating and incorporating the textual practices and the techniques and ideas of his chosen authors, often without explicit intention to do so, Pound establishes an integral textual community that might survive even the most challenging social and psychological attenuations, and that preserves its provenance in the process and methods of its articulation.

Note

1 Brian Stock uses the term textual community to describe the sociality of *textual dissemination* in the context of eleventh-century heresy and reform: 'The term is used in a descriptive rather than a technical sense; it is intended not to convey a new methodology but a more intensive use of traditional methods, and, in particular, their use by groups hitherto dependent on oral participation in religion' (90). The presence of a written text was not essential to the community, but rather the presence of an individual who had mastered it for the purpose of reforming the group's thought.

Introduction

*What is the earliest date you cd. print a prose book? I want the 'Mencius,'
and as Jas [James Laughlin] keeps selling the Ta Hio regular. [...] It would
be about the same size. Or a trilogy: Ta Hio, 'Mencius' and a note on
Erigena. Probably about twice the size, depends on date.*

                – Ezra Pound to T. S. Eliot, 18 January 1940 (*SL* 335)

In a letter to his British publisher, Ezra Pound alludes to the ninth-century
Hibernian Greek-speaking theologian and poet Johannes Scottus Eriugena in
the company of two of the Four Books of Confucianism. What were the strategic
purposes in deploying this enigmatic figure – member of the court of Charles
the Bald and teacher in the Palatine school, a formidable theologian, translator
of Greek patristic texts and composer of Greek and Latin poetry – in such
company? This implied textual community seems an unlikely combination:
Eriugena had been nearly completely occluded from the mainstream Anglophone
philosophical tradition for centuries, but is placed alongside canonical texts of
one of the longest unbroken philosophical traditions. Pound developed intensive
research interests in Eriugena's life and thought from the late 1920s to the mid-
1930s and then in 1939–1940. What particular purposes did these interests serve
with regard to his other interests at the time? Reference to Eriugena's life and
writings occur at focal points in *The Cantos*, most notably in Canto XXXVI,
following the translation of Guido Cavalcanti's canzone 'Donna mi prega', and
in the first and penultimate cantos of *The Pisan Cantos*. How might this focus
on Eriugena accord with the themes of *Eleven New Cantos* and *The Pisan Cantos*
and the intervening intensive focus on economics, political liberty (the Adams
Cantos) and the orders linking state, family and individual (the China Cantos)?
What sense can be made of the sporadic, but strategic citation of Eriugena's
life, work and mythology, and Pound's renewed focus on Eriugena in *The
Pisan Cantos*? What significance abides in Pound's citation of different facets of
Eriugena's thought and work at different points in his letters and essays?

    Ezra Pound's oeuvre is renowned for its display of eclectic intellectual interests
ranging across a wide variety of languages, literary and artistic traditions,
philosophical and theological frameworks, and economic and cultural theories

and practices. Pound exerted significant energy in his attempts to come to grips with the Greek and Latin classics; Anglo-Saxon, Provençal and medieval Tuscan poetics; and ancient, medieval and early modern philosophy. He also invested considerable energy in working through the history and literary heritage of China and the rich complexities of its written script, the Japanese Noh drama, as well as the evolutions of political and economic principles in Europe and North America and their manifest transformations of the social (and artistic) sphere. This energy was at its base motivated by a critical curiosity, a sense of exploratory optimism and a willingness to apprehend materials and ideas well outside of his professed areas of expertise. Evidence of this temperament is found in Pound's extensive prose writings and letters, but finds its most eloquent and indicative expression in his epic poem, *The Cantos*. This text rehearses a kind of encyclopaedic performance at several levels: as a poetic appraisal of the ideas that inform its subject matter, it also engages with those ideas by innovations in poetic form and in complex modes of citation; patterns of imagery and allusion present a declarative but often gnomic text surface, prompting the reader to verify or dispute poetic assertion and to engage with the poetic image dialectically. The text both radiates out to a constellation of sources and influences, either by direct citation or through the lens of translation, annotation and paraphrase, and it gathers fragments or entire textual swathes into its poetic framework.

The role of culturally dominant influences upon Pound's aesthetic and on *The Cantos* is well documented in the critical commentary. He engages with two cornerstones of European culture – Homer's *Odyssey* and Dante's *Divina commedia* – in terms of their prosody and intellectual content, as well as in their formal architecture, as scholars have long observed. A converse tendency in Pound's work is also evident: his championing of important intellectual figures either unjustly maligned or inexplicably overlooked in the diverse cultural heritage upon which he draws for his poetic material. Pound seeks to retrieve such figures as Apollonius of Tyana, Ocellus, Guido Cavalcanti, Gemisthus Plethon and even such contemporaries as John Penrose Angold from unjust obscurity, and to bring them into the light of informed critical and cultural discourse. Often Pound will retrieve a 'minor' figure from the desiccated shadows of culture to make a specific discursive point or to illustrate a forgotten aesthetic. On occasion, the local force of these types of citation can be extrapolated as examples of a general principle – to illustrate the struggle for dominance in the ecosystem of ideas, to revive a wrongfully disregarded theory or poetics, or as an example of politically motivated marginalization. In a few cases, however, these apparently local, minor citations trace out a much greater significance.

In the case of Eriugena, these citations occur at strategic points in Pound's poem, documenting the poet's evolving approach to the possibility of writing his paradise.

Scholars have long identified how Pound deploys the 'ideogrammic method' to produce subject rhymes and argument by association, the 'ply over ply' enfolding aspects of a developing theme across the text, often outside the bounds and strictures of logic and dialectic. Associative logic, suggestion-by-citation and apotropaic gestures are, of course, nothing new: they are the bread and butter of literary composition. Yet the specific way Pound reconfigures poetic argument in *The Cantos* is akin to something like an archival impulse – an 'extended mind' that keeps the text evolving beyond its reification in print and its separation from its sources, including the most proximate sources in Pound's essays and the poem's physical archive of texts and manuscripts.[1] Even the most translucent or fragmented vestiges of culture and memory can be traced back to their originating moments and historical transmission by carefully following the mode and logic of their citation. Pound's Eriugena offers a telling opportunity to explore this textual logic in *The Cantos*, and to see how even dispersed and very fine threads of citation and allusion can tighten the textual fabric, and give this sprawling poem a focus or logic that might not necessarily register with the reader initially engaging with the text surface.

Pound engaged in two major phases of research and thinking on Eriugena. The first was from the late 1920s to the mid-1930s, a phase of philosophical autodidacticism, when Pound was reading the philosophy textbooks of Francesco Fiorentino, Étienne Gilson's *La Philosophie au Moyen-âge*, and other source texts. Pound's marginal notes in the Fiorentino volumes – which are housed in Schloss Brunnenburg, Tirolo di Merano – illuminate the kinds of questions in which Pound was most deeply entrenched at the time, especially the source and reach of religious and political authority in the European Middle Ages, from Britain to Byzantium. Given the historical framework of his reading, it is perhaps not surprising that Pound identified with some of the more lurid – and foggy – aspects of Eriugena's life, thought and reception, not least the matter of his various Papal condemnations and the book-burnings and academic censure at the University of Paris in the thirteenth century. Pound fixes on Eriugena's statement '*Auctoritas ex vera ratione processi ratio vero nequaquam ex auctoritate*' (Fiorentino 1921, 217) as a defining intellectual principle, in which reason guides intellect and philosophical/theological inquiry rather than deference or blind adherence to (church) authority. Pound clearly saw in Eriugena an intellect worth championing, and sought to reinstate him to a rightful place in the pantheon of medieval thinkers. Excepting Fiorentino and Étienne Gilson, Pound's sources were not always entirely adequate or accurate. Pound was aware of the limited value of such sources as the 'prete' C. B. Schlueter's Preface to the *Periphyseon*, which comes in for especially heavy criticism. The nature of these sources may account for certain misconceptions of Carolingian intellectual life on Pound's part, and may also represent a number of lost opportunities to widen and deepen his resource base in issues of wrongful ecclesiastical condemnation and theological dispute, both in the ninth and thirteenth centuries. Matters of historical accuracy are of particular importance, as Pound applies such themes of doctrinal dispute as analogues to historical events and personal circumstances elsewhere in *The Cantos*. Pound mentions Eriugena in letters and prose works at this time – in the 1934 essay 'Ecclesiastical History' and variously in *Guide to Kulchur* – but his major treatment occurs in Canto XXXVI, immediately following the last of Pound's several translations of Guido Cavalcanti's canzone 'Donna mi prega'. A complex network of medieval philosophical sources converges in this conflation of Guido and Scottus. It is an unlikely combination, *prima facie*, especially given Pound's enthusiastic reading of Robert Grosseteste's enormously influential treatise *De Luce*, but Pound's poem telescopes a complex discourse of the Arab and medieval interpretations of Aristotle (especially *De Anima*) culminating in the series of condemnations in Paris in the thirteenth century, in which Eriugena's texts were also embroiled.

The second phase of Pound's research into Eriugena follows the frenetic composition of the Adams and China cantos and the intensive schedule of essays and books in the later 1930s, such as *Jefferson and/or Mussolini* in 1935 and *Guide to Kulchur* in 1937. As Pound revived his interest in Eriugena, he moved from textbook excerpts in Fiorentino to the most authoritative editions he could find. A sequence of letters to T. S. Eliot, Étienne Gilson and Otto Bird recounts Pound's attempts to locate the Henry Joseph Floss edition of Eriugena's works, collated into Volume 122 of Jacques-Paul Migne's magisterial Patrologia Latina. Pound located a copy in the Biblioteca Marciana in Venice in 1939, following which Ubaldi degli Uberti acquired a copy for him from the Genoese municipal library in early 1940. Pound drew on this edited source to compose two sequences of notes annotating and indexing Eriugena's works – including the *Periphyseon*, Eriugena's translation of the Pseudo-Dionysian *Celestial Hierarchy* and his commentary on that text, and the Greek elements of Eriugena's own poetic compositions. One set of notes is interleaved with canto compositions in Italian that were to comprise the opening cantos of Pound's *paradiso* before the events of the war culminated in his imprisonment in May 1945. He subsequently composed *The Pisan Cantos* in English, in which the first and penultimate poems make numerous references to Eriugena. The second set of notes appears to be the groundwork for the proposed book on Eriugena, to which Pound refers in his letter to Eliot of 18 January 1940. Pound's attention had shifted from matters of ecclesiastical controversy that shaded Eriugena's texts – the Trinitarian and Predestination disputes of the ninth century, and the charges of pantheism in the thirteenth – to Eriugena's masterpiece, the *Periphyseon* or *De divisone naturae*; his translation of and commentary on the Pseudo-Dionysian *Celestial Hierarchy*; as well as to the poems Eriugena composed whilst serving in the palace for his king Charles the Bald.

The *Periphyseon* is a complex and brilliant work. Its Latin is of unusually complex grammatical structure and its argumentation shows an originality completely counter to the imitative style that characterized philosophy for centuries either side of its composition. It combines a kind of textbook on dialectical method in Book I with the *hexaemeron* of Books II–V, an extended meditation on the first verses of Genesis dealing with the six days of creation. The dialogue is carried out between a Master (Nutritor) and his pupil (Alumnus), in which the four divisions of nature are explicated as testimony to the divine scheme of the creation (*exitus* from the godhead) and eschatology (*reditus* or return to divine unity). This text, dealing as it does with the end of days, is fitting material for incorporation into Pound's *canti del carcere*, written under the long shadow of his looming extradition to the United States on the capital charge of treason. Eriugena's poetry, on the other hand, is treated as evidence of its author's significant facility in Greek, and his sometimes light-hearted relationship with his royal sponsor, exhibiting the virtue of *hilaritas* or robust moral vigour. The role of court poet in politically unstable times is one that would have resonated with Pound, given his attempts to interest Mussolini in his poetry before the war. Pound returns to Eriugena in later cantos, notably *Rock-Drill* and *Thrones*, rehearsing and reprising these themes as tokens of a certain intellectual afterglow. Eriugena abides as evidence for Pound of the persistence of culture despite the transnational war-machine's best efforts to wipe it all out.

A number of scholars – most notably William Tay, Peter Makin, A. David Moody, Walter Benn Michaels, Ronald Bush, and Peter Liebregts – have situated Pound's interests in Eriugena's life and thought within the larger project of his thinking through the Neoplatonic tradition and the classical inheritance more generally, as well as drawing connections with Pound's sustained interests in Confucian thought. Scholarly analysis has largely focused upon explicating this philosophical historical context. Eriugena lived during a crucial moment in the history of Western Europe, but it would be fair to say that the circumstances of his life and the milieu in which he operated were not terribly clear at the time of Pound's most intensive interest in Eriugena, nor even at the time of the earliest critical commentaries on Pound's Eriugena in the early 1970s. Since then, Eriugena Studies has undergone something of a renaissance, inducing a major phase of historical, philosophical and textual scholarship. There have been several major attempts to produce translations and adequate scholarly editions, with mixed results, but the general field of Carolingian history and philosophy, and the specific intellectual networks and circumstances of Eriugena's life are now more fully understood. Whilst Pound's prophetic gesture in reclaiming Eriugena was not completely isolated – Henry Bett (1925) and Dom Maïeul Cappuyns (1933) produced critically important studies of Eriugena in the years preceding Pound's most intensive study, and several lesser studies were also in circulation – he preceded a good portion of the highest quality scholarship on the subject. It is now the time to take a renewed look at the themes and issues with which Pound was engaged, and to consider them in the light of the present state of Eriugena Studies.

The flourishing of significant scholarship in recent decades provides a new focus for Pound's own aspirations in deploying Eriugena in his epic poem and in his prose writings. What did he hope to achieve in choosing this figure to accompany Cavalcanti in Canto XXXVI, or to bookend *The Pisan Cantos* in Cantos LXXIV and LXXXIII (Canto LXXXIV having been added belatedly, on the news of Angold's death reaching the Pisan Detention Training Center), or to function as a cipher of *hilaritas* and Greek learning in the Latin West? Pound homes in on the trope of stitching – Irmintrude, the Carolingian queen, stitches the king's vestments as John stitches 'Greek tags' into his verses – which functions also at the dimension of textual transmission. Annotation and glossing are recognized as vital components of Carolingian textual culture; they provide modern scholars with critical evidence by which to understand learned networks, the activity of scriptoria and the serial ownership of books amongst masters, monks and the cathedral and Palatine schools, which were the precursors to the first medieval European universities. Pound, fittingly, takes up an analogous kind of stitching in his own annotative activities, both in the marginal notes in his editions of Fiorentino and the Patrologia Latina and in his suites of glosses and notes keyed to the *Periphyseon*, as well as to Eriugena's translations of and commentaries on Pseudo-Dionysius. These materials demand close examination, in order to understand Pound's own annotative method, and to ascertain the patterns of citation of Eriugena's works. Impressive studies by

John Nolde and David Ten Eyck examine the ways Pound marshals his sources in Chinese history and in the diaries of John Adams. A complementary study of Pound's extensive annotative glosses of Eriugena's texts, whilst not concentrated into a single decad of *The Cantos*, sheds new light on the significance of this thinker for Pound in manifold ways across a number of texts and at strategic points in his epic poem. This study aims to illuminate how the poet apprehended his source texts, and to clarify how, and why, Pound installs specific techniques of reference and allusion in his poetry. Careful analysis of Pound's manuscript notes can illuminate at the dimension of form and technique as much as at the dimension of intellectual content and discursive thematics.

Pound's book on Eriugena remained unwritten, but the poetic intersections with Eriugena are sufficiently numerous and significant to present a case for the wider implications for major themes in his poetry, and to function as a guide to how Pound negotiates his sources and assembles his own draft materials. The two phases of Pound's research into Eriugena's thought differ in focus: the earlier phase is coloured by a sense of curiosity and intrigue towards Eriugena as a potentially heretical figure, unfairly anathematized by a conservative clergy in the Carolingian age and subsequently in the early history of the University of Paris, more than three hundred years after his death. The later phase raises the intensity of metaphysical speculation, especially concerning the philosophy of light, as well as matters of consolation (*hilaritas* emblematized by the Greek verses). Pound also turns to matters of eschatology in the *reditus* of Book V of the *Periphyseon*, resonant with the personal apocalypse in the Pisan DTC. By deploying Eriugena at these pivotal points in his poem, Pound navigates a series of topics within his general poetics: a deeper understanding of Carolingian political history; the nature of theological speculation in the context of Neoplatonism; and the place of early scholasticism in the traditions passed down via the Islamic commentators on Aristotle, to Aquinas, and beyond. In Eriugena, Pound glimpsed a maligned tyro to champion but he might equally have missed other cognate opportunities for redemption, such as the deeply problematic figure of Gottschalk of Orbais (God's servant), with whom Eriugena debated matters of predestination in his first public composition, or the ill-fated Amaury (Amalric) de Bene, who suffered the ultimate price for his alleged heresy in early thirteenth-century Paris. The gravitational pull towards the works of Confucius and Mencius come into sharper focus in *The Pisan Cantos*: the Confucian texts function as guides to the comportment of the self; the itinerary of the soul; and the relation of the individual agent to society, political rule and metaphysical fruition. Pound establishes the Confucian combination of ethics, politics and metaphysics as cognate to Eriugena's thought – proof of the translatability of the best in thought and action across history and between separate spheres of civilization.

Situating the specific uses to which Pound puts Eriugena's texts is a crucial first step in understanding the significance of this figure in Pound's poetics more generally, and this in turn requires careful framing within the current state of scholarship in Carolingian history and theology. Once these filiations are established as clearly as current knowledge allows, the question arises as to how might the subtle networks of allusion and citation embodied in Pound's Eriugena inflect other dimensions of his epic poem. These references abide amid the variegated surface of *The Cantos*, where extended sequences of transposed prose, typographic icons, dialogue and lyric tableaux arise among a multitude of other textual forms. To take one prominent example: Canto XLIX, the famous 'Seven Lakes' canto, provides a surprising node in the Eriugenian network running slightly beneath the surface of the poem. In this canto, the affinities of theme and mood; the complex interactions of scripts, word and image; and cited text recombine Pound's own poetic material, plainly harmonizing with Eriugenian themes of temporal power and metaphysical consolation. But this is more than the inevitable recursion of poetic tropes in an epic poem: manuscript drafts of Canto XLIX comprise direct allusions to Eriugena in the orientation of these short lyrics. The 'Eight Views' of the Xaio and Xaing rivers – a classic *topos* of Chinese painting given ekphrastic treatment in Canto XLIX – might seem a long distance from the Palatine School of Laon, or the University of Paris in 1209, but these locales all function within the same network, integrated by the theme of rustication. The contemplative dimension of Eriugena's thought combines with the landscape traditions of Chinese poetry and painting to produce an intensely political and pedagogical vision, against which is set the apparent consolation of the natural world. This theme famously arises again in *The Pisan Cantos*, where Pound calls upon a resource he has already developed – in Canto XLIX and elsewhere – subtly threading Eriugena and China together into a cosmos he hopes can sustain the purgatorial burdens of poetry and life. Pound's Eriugena is a kind of *avatar* of a more expansive text and poem – threading between themes, poetic forms, languages of composition and contemplation, visual and decorative arts, glossatory and annotative modes of poetic composition, and ultimately, modes of critical reading.

* * *

This study attempts to demonstrate how Pound understood Eriugena's thought at different points in his writing career: this process, begun in the late 1920s, evolved during the later 1930s and was reprised in later decads of *The Cantos*. Pound's sense of Eriugena's significance thus bears the complexities attendant upon an increasingly nuanced understanding of historical and philosophical material over the span of three decades, and is reflected in the ways in which his modes of annotation, citation and allusion evolve. Pound's intensive study during the later 1930s grappled with Eriugena's texts roughly in the order in which they were written. My examination will progress in a likewise (roughly) chronological fashion, both with regard to Pound's career and his shaping role in Modernism, on the one hand, and to how Eriugena and Carolingian intellectual history have been understood by scholars, on the other.

Chapter 1 discusses the first phase of Pound's research into Eriugena's thought and its manifestation in his writing: it takes as its focus the Predestination controversy of 859–60 in which Eriugena's treatise *De praedestinatione* (his first text to enter the public record) played a central role, first as a rebuttal to the alleged heresies of Gottschalk of Orbais, and then as an object of ecclesiastical scrutiny and condemnation. Pound principally relies upon Francesco Fiorentino's textbooks, evident in the way he refers to Eriugena in *Guide to Kulchur* and several essays of the later 1930s. Pound's annotations to those textbooks provide critical primary material towards an understanding of the role Eriugena initially served for Pound. Canto XXXVI combines Pound's preferred translation of Cavalcanti's canzone 'Donna mi prega', with selected details of Eriugena's thought and posthumous reputation as they were known to him at the time: his latter-day status as heretic consequent to the Predestination controversy, and as victim of the book-bannings at the University of Paris in the thirteenth century.

Chapter 2 revisits the scholarly assessment of Eriugena's work, addressing the rapidly evolving historical and palaeographical understanding of his texts, as well as the milieu in the court and kingdom of Charles the Bald. Considerable advances in Carolingian studies in recent decades have substantially clarified many of the issues surrounding Eriugena's roles at court and in the Palatine school, his relationship with the cathedral school at Laon and also the precise constitution of an Irish 'colony' in Charles's kingdom. Recent scholarship has thrown considerable light on the specific details and consequences of the Predestination controversy in which Eriugena was embroiled, especially the relevant doctrinal and ecclesiastical issues, and the roles of other actors in the controversies such as the monk Gottschalk of Orbais and Hincmar, Archbishop of Reims. Eriugena's reliance upon patristic authority, especially that of Augustine, is in marked contradiction with Pound's favourite epithet: 'Authority comes from right reason, never the other way on.' This restores a dimension of discretion and subtlety to Eriugena's historical portrait, replacing the stridency of such appeal to Pound with a more complex character study. Pound's suggestive link between ninth-century ecclesiastical controversies and those of thirteenth-century Paris in Canto XXXVI requires careful attention: especially the reception of Aristotle's theory of the soul in *De Anima* by scholars in Paris and their attempts to assimilate the Islamic philosophical renaissance of Avicenna and Averroes with orthodox Neoplatonic ideas.

Chapter 3 shifts the focus to the way Pound apprehends Eriugena's translations of and commentaries on Pseudo-Dionysius; his court poetry (especially in the context of its Greek learning); and his masterwork of theophany and eschatology, the *Periphyseon*. These texts were made available to Pound via the copy of Patrologia Latina 122 he sourced first at the Biblioteca Marciana in Venice in 1939, and that he then was able to 'wheedle' out of the Genoese library in the first weeks of 1940. Pound's two extensive suites of notes were to inform his new Italian cantos. The Italian cantos 74 and 75 remained in draft form, and were ultimately omitted from his composition regime: they are preserved, with most of the draft material for *The Cantos*, in the Ezra Pound Collection at the Beinecke Library at Yale University, and have received comprehensive scholarly treatment by Ronald Bush (1997 and 2010). Pound's notes and transcriptions pertaining to Eriugena hold a prominent place in the first and penultimate poems in *The Pisan Cantos*, especially concerning the *Periphyseon* and Eriugena's poetry. These notes are transcribed and annotated in Chapter 3, charting their direct and indirect relation to Pound's poem, both in the Pisan suite and afterwards. A poetic fragment on an Eriugenian theme (in both English and Italian) is also transcribed and annotated in Appendix B. The two transcriptions in Chapter 3 are presented with scholarly apparatus to allow a careful examination of Pound's working methods – his note-taking, glossing and transliterating from his Latin (and Greek) sources. These methods reveal a range of scholarly interests and aptitudes that correlate surprisingly closely with those of his sources. Pound's philological skills were considerable, if not altogether consistent, providing a platform from which he was able to assay a reading of Eriugena's texts in Latin at the end of the decade. His intermittent work on the literary manuscripts of Guido Cavalcanti had reached a critical intensity in 1929–1932 with his scrupulous preparation for the bilingual (and ultimately unpublished) London Aquila edition in 1929 and the Genovese Marsano edition in 1932. This work functioned as a form of preparation for subsequent work on the Latin texts in Patrologia Latina 122. The unpublished notes bear evidence of wide-ranging thought on the subject of Eriugena's intellectual interests, although the notes also show that Pound spent much more time and attention on certain texts (the translations of the works of Pseudo-Dionysius as well as the *Carmina*) over others (the gospel commentaries, *De praedestinatione*, the *Periphyseon*). Close examination of the historical context of the production and circulation of Eriugena's texts, as well as their reception in later periods, affords an insight into the reasons why Pound was so drawn to this figure during the mid- and late 1930s. The notes also provide documentary evidence from which to develop a critical evaluation of what Eriugena meant for Pound, and how this evolved from his earlier contact with the Carolingian thinker and poet.

Chapter 4 situates Pound's Eriugena within his larger intellectual and poetic vision, principally in *The Cantos*. Pound's work on Eriugena intersects with the Neoplatonic themes appearing throughout *The Cantos*, and also intersects very deliberately with Pound's development of Confucian themes throughout the 1930s and 1940s. By viewing how and when Pound draws on his Eriugenian sources, it is possible to recalibrate the way historical, aesthetic and philosophical themes are deployed in his writing. The role of Eriugena in *The Pisan Cantos* demands close scrutiny: in terms of classical tropes of light and Neoplatonic light philosophy; as a thread linking that tradition with Confucian thought by way of textual transmission and scribal practices of glossing and calligraphic form; and Eriugena's courtly persona as the exemplar of *hilaritas* in the context of political, doctrinal and existential threats. Further associations with Chinese philosophy, particularly Pound's efforts to translate the foundational texts of Confucianism, bring the network of ideas pertaining to metaphysics and good government into tighter focus, and provide additional coherence to Pound's preoccupations from the Leopoldine cantos through the 1930s and into his wartime writings. Careful attention to specific aspects of *The Cantos* more generally reveals a deeply complicit network of ideas in which Eriugena is fundamentally implicated. This occurs most prominently in his mediation of the Chinese poetic and artistic figure of the *literatus* in the 'Seven Lakes' canto. Analysis of this composite poem and selected primary materials extends the study of Pound's Eriugena into zones of thematic resonance, buttressed by surprising analogies of physical form, the visual image, and philological and poetic technique. Pound's patterns of thought, at times erratic and inconsistent, provide in this canto exemplars of that intellectual adventurousness in which the reader is enjoined to understand and contest the ways various traditions and intellectual lineages are brought into conversation: a model and blueprint for thinking through civilization.

A clearer understanding of Eriugena in his time and intellectual context is an essential first phase in assimilating his thought into the larger structures of

Pound's Neoplatonism, as well as the conceptual networks he draws between Neoplatonism and Confucian texts, Chinese, American and European political history, and the political and social circumstances in which he was embroiled during the Second World War. The admirable but necessarily circumscribed studies of Pound and Eriugena from the 1970s – principally Makin, Michaels and Tay – are complemented by more recent work situating Eriugena within Neoplatonic thought more generally (Moody, Liebregts and Bush). This study does not attempt simply to recapitulate this impressive work, but instead to focus on the specific understanding of Eriugena's texts and context, and the implications of Pound's reading practices and notation for a view of the potential significance for Pound's paradisal vision. This study will attempt to provide a rigorous, if non-specialist, analysis of and commentary on Pound's Eriugenian materials. Once a clear picture has been established – one that has long warranted this kind of close attention – I suggest several modes of reading 'Pound's Eriugena' in relation to some conspicuously related episodes in *The Cantos*, as well as some less obvious networks of ideas that run through and beneath the surface of that text. Only then can a fuller account of Eriugena's role in Pound's Neoplatonism be contemplated: that complex task promises to recalibrate the nature of Pound's paradisal vision for *The Cantos* – a vision deferred in his wartime activities (not the least of which was an intensive career in radio)[2] and then critically disabled in the events leading up to his detention at Pisa and extradition to the United States in 1945: paradise swapped for *purgatorio*.

   Pound Studies is endowed with a large body of excellent scholarship and exegesis: from the careful documentary studies of the way Pound deploys specific sources to the impressive catalogue of studies that attempt syncretic evaluations of Pound's work, whether *The Cantos* or his writing in its entirety. I refer specifically to those studies that attempt to make sense of Pound's interests in theology – Makin, Bacigalupo, Liebregts, Tryphonopoulos, Surette, and others – all of which have greatly informed and clarified my thinking in Pound's Eriugenian deployments. This study sets out to clarify the precise nature of Pound's interest in Eriugena: how he annotates his source texts, and how he engages this material in his prose and in *The Cantos*. It sets the groundwork by which to assimilate such focused bibliographical and hermeneutic work into an overall assessment of Pound's thinking on the sacred, by examining the physical evidence of the way Pound interrogates his sources, Eriugenian and otherwise, how he reads and annotates, and how the nature of his source material shapes his own practices and compositional processes. The late classical and early medieval texts at issue – by Augustine, Maximus the Confessor, Pseudo-

Dionysius, Boethius and, of course, by Eriugena himself – embody their own traditions of annotative practice and textual transmission. Modern scholarship has also developed practices designed specifically for such texts and their historical contingencies – for example, methods by which to read Carolingian annotations, glossaries and florilegia. A reading of Pound's Eriugena requires a facility in reading Eriugena through, and with, late classical, early medieval and modern scholarly reading practices.[3] This kind of methodological attention brings Pound's sources into sharp focus, as it does his absorption of them into his own work. Thus the reader may better understand what is at stake in Pound's dealings with these sources, and what he hoped to achieve.

Pound had some expertise in the disciplines of codicology and palaeography, not least through his intensive work on the poetic manuscripts of various Provençal poets and his attempts to produce a scholarly edition of the poetry of Guido Cavalcanti. Numerous scholars – David Anderson and Peter Makin foremost among them – have carefully assessed these efforts and have made astute observations on Pound's scholarly virtues, his occasional technical and interpretive errors and the historical contexts of Pound's own formal training in medieval philology. This study develops a fuller view of the relationship between the bibliographical constitution of Pound's source texts and his methods of dealing with them. This kind of 'philological realism' is evident even in the first canto, where the *ego scriptor* makes careful note, in a deceptively casual aside, of the precise edition of the *Odyssey* from which he silently quotes ('Lie quiet, Divus'). This sensibility is everywhere in Pound: it is most evident in his published work on Cavalcanti (especially the essay of that title in *Make It New*) and the Troubadours, and it is evident, if not well known, in the annotative practices contained and preserved in Pound's working notes and in his personal library. This study refers to a number of Pound's books and his annotative methods – principally his editions of Francesco Fiorentino housed at Brunnenburg. A solid sample of Pound's manuscript material has received scholarly attention, resulting in published volumes of correspondence, as well as editions such as Richard Sieburth's exemplary production of Pound's notebooks composed during his 1912 walking tour of Troubadour country in southern France. But there is scope for a much larger study of Pound's library and his annotations therein. Such a study may provide vital documentary support for scholarly arguments concerning Pound's rationale and working methods in using such texts. It may also overturn or provide additional nuance to some long-held assumptions about Pound's motives, and his relative expertise or otherwise in matters philological, philosophical and bibliographical.

Notes

1 The 'extended mind' is an apposite and alluring term for the processes of literary composition that exceed conventional parameters of textual genesis: where manuscript drafts and decidedly contingent published texts interact beyond a teleological mode of accretive bibliographical facticity. The term was adapted from the cognitive sciences to the study of literary manuscripts by Dirk Van Hulle: I first heard of its use in this context at Van Hulle's keynote lecture on 7 March 2013 at the Society for Textual Scholarship 17th Biennial Conference at Loyola University, Chicago, titled 'The Stuff of Fiction: Digital Editing, Multiple Drafts, and the Extended Mind'. See Van Hulle 2011 and 2013.

2 Matthew Feldman has written on the considerable archival material yet to be fully examined – and some of it only recently rediscovered – pertaining to Pound's active wartime radio experiences, which has been vastly underestimated in the scholarship to date. Pound composed a significant cache of speeches under his own name or pseudonymously, some of which he delivered, some by other radio broadcasters and some apparently not delivered at all. These are variously located in the Beinecke Library at Yale, the British War Offices Archives in London, the archives of the Federal Bureau of Investigation, the US Department of Justice, and elsewhere. See Feldman 2012.

3 Rosamond McKitterick writes a brilliant scholarly overview of the innovations in Carolingian textual practices, including the production of florilegia and glossary chrystomathies as indicative of 'a collective statement of cultural affiliation' with their Latin sources (2012, 75). In this context, the cognate ancestral and intellectual filiations of Irish scribes in Francia with the author of the *Periphyseon* are hardly surprising. For a cathedral library to possess a manuscript bearing glosses of Eriugena's works, or better, direct transcriptions of key passages, was a significant indicator of its legitimacy in the later ninth and early tenth centuries.

1

Pound's Eriugena: Neoplatonist and Heretic

Among the extraordinary range of intellectual and historical sources upon which Pound drew in the course of his writing career, his strategic citation of the ninth-century Irish philosopher and theologian Johannes Scottus Eriugena demands special attention. For Pound, Eriugena embodied the nexus between aesthetics, pedagogy and political engagement in his role as court poet to Charles the Bald and scholar of Greek in the Palatine school.[1] Pound's eclectic interests in medieval poetry, philosophy and theology were reinforced in his study of Eriugena by a reflective awareness of the techniques of citation and allusion in his source materials, and their potential hermeneutic implications. His treatment of Eriugena's thought is thus conditioned by the specific ways in which those texts manifest themselves – in the form of early medieval manuscripts, later manuscript transcriptions and in glosses and florilegia. Pound demonstrates prescient awareness of this textual condition in ways that intersect directly with his own poetics.[2] In these textual and thematic respects, Eriugena becomes not merely relevant but is an acutely forceful exemplar of the new kind of poetry Pound develops in *The Cantos*. Scholars have long studied Pound's technique of clustering ideas into 'ideograms' or associative networks in his poetry (and prose); close attention to how he understands Eriugena's texts and their conditions illuminates not only how Pound deploys his materials thematically, but also how he emulates a kind of thinking manifested textually in the transition from the late classical to the early medieval era. This engagement with textual form produces a kind of archival trace at the level of allusion or citation, from which textual filiation may be drawn, and which forms the basis for conventions of intertextual reference still evident in the modern era.

In his essay 'Date Line', Pound famously referred to his modern epic, composed over the course of half a century, as 'a poem including history' (*MIN* 19). The poem spans an impressive range of literary, artistic, cultural and historical material: from the ancient, medieval and modern West to the dynastic history of

China, the Revolutionary era and early Republican history of the United States, as well as aperçus of sub-Saharan Africa, the ancient eastern Mediterranean, the Kimberley region of Western Australia, and elsewhere. It ranges across numerous literary forms and more than a dozen languages, as well as such genres as lyric, elegy, prose narrative, imperial decree, historical document, musical score and epistle. In this poem, Pound integrates his earlier poetic investments in literary experimentation and the critical recalibration of historically grounded poetic genres – Troubadour lyric forms, Greek and Latin classics (*Homage to Sextus Propertius*), Anglo-Saxon poetry (*The Seafarer, The Wanderer*), Dante and his great contemporary Guido Cavalcanti, and Chinese and Japanese genres and forms, to name only the most prominent of his non-Anglophone poetic sources. Excerpts from significant documents and texts are often provided by way of partial or full citations, glosses and annotations, bestowing a heightened emphasis to the texts and physical documents constellating around Pound's poem and interleaved within it.

Such aspiring encyclopaedism is indicative of Pound's predisposition towards totalizing, and even eschatological systems. Primary among the models for the structure of his *Cantos* is Dante's *Divine Comedy*, with its teleological movement to transcendence and unity with the divine. The narrative impulse of νόστος (*nostos* or homecoming) of the *Odyssey* also profoundly informs Pound's epic. His stated aim was to write a poem that celebrated what he saw as the best social and cultural achievements throughout history, as well as to adumbrate the most egregious impediments to historical and economic progress, all in aid of a redemptive vision of human social and spiritual capability. From its beginning the poem is oriented towards a vision of a *paradiso terrestre*, and from the 1930s it becomes increasingly grounded in an anti-capitalist poetics which occasionally becomes overtly Fascist. But this sense of totality is mediated by the fragmentary, the partial and the occluded, and this is represented not only in his choice of thematic source material but also in its physical and textual composition. Pound's sense of curiosity and contrariness also saw him disposed towards figures he regarded as intellectually eminent but unfairly marginalized in mainstream history. His major prose works of the 1930s such as *Make It New* (1934) and *Guide to Kulchur* (1937) exert substantial intellectual energy in buttressing such counter-traditions and in championing their guiding lights.

John Scottus Eriugena is now considered to have been perhaps the most important Neoplatonist in Christian Europe between Proclus, Boethius and Pseudo-Dionysius in the fifth and sixth centuries and the School of Chartres in the eleventh and twelfth centuries, or even Gemisthus Plethon and Marsilio

Ficino in the fifteenth century. He began his career in Charles's court as a *grammaticus* (grammarian) before turning his attention to Greek theology (Moran 46). Eriugena translated the complete works of Pseudo-Dionysius and wrote an influential commentary on *The Celestial Hierarchy*.[3] He was commissioned by Charles to produce a refutation of Gottschalk's argument for predestination.[4] His most significant work is the monumental *hexaemeron* and eschatology, the *Periphyseon* or *De divisione naturae*. This work inflects a Christian cosmogony with a distinct Neoplatonic sensibility: the *exitus* of all things from the godhead and the *reditus* or return at the last judgement, reflected in the dialectical argumentation of *divisio* and *resolutio* (Carabine 2000, 15–16). This text negotiates, dialectically, an Aristotelian/Augustinian ontology of the Categories, especially the first Category of *ousia* (often problematically translated as 'essence' or 'substance'). Eriugena also served as court poet to Charles the Bald, and composed verse in Greek as well as Latin at a time when Greek learning in Western Europe was confined to a modest number of mostly Irish scholars and their students. His work suffered ecclesiastical condemnations, especially in the ninth, thirteenth and sixteenth centuries,[5] and was placed on the Vatican's Index Librorum Prohibitorum Sanctissimi. Eriugena's Neoplatonist theology was inflected in particular by the thinking of the Cappadocian Fathers (Basil the Great, Gregory of Nyssa and Gregory Nazianzus), but was overshadowed by a scholastic philosophy dominated especially by the Aristotelian disposition of Thomas Aquinas. Between the sixteenth and twentieth centuries his work had fallen out of favour in Anglophone philosophy curricula, and even recent attempts to produce adequate translated editions of the *Periphyseon* remain incomplete.[6] But Pound's championing of Eriugena extended beyond that of rectifying a curricular oversight: he saw in this figure a profound inheritance of Platonic thought also found in medieval Islamic philosophers such as Avicenna, Averroes and Al-Farabi, passed on via the scholastic philosophers to (in Pound's estimation) the Troubadours and Guido Cavalcanti. By keeping alight the Neoplatonic flame, Pound saw in Eriugena a European forebear of its efflorescence in the Italian Renaissance, and an early proponent of the light philosophy deployed at thematically significant points in *The Cantos*.

The strategic importance of Eriugena for Pound is evident in the way his name arises at specific points in Pound's poetry and prose, coinciding with two major phases of research into Eriugena's writings and thought. Pound first read of Eriugena some time before 1928, in the 1921 reprint of the 1879 edition of Francesco Fiorentino's philosophy textbook, *Manuale di Storia della Filosofia*, edited by Giuseppe Monticelli. He then began to integrate Eriugena properly into his writing in the 1930s in the context of heresy and Troubadour poetry.[7] Pound's second phase of research began in earnest in late 1939, to which he made reference in letters to T. S. Eliot, George Santayana and Otto Bird. He consulted Volume 122 of the Patrologia Latina containing Eriugena's texts and translations in the Biblioteca Marciana in Venice in 1939 before returning to Rapallo to work from another copy sourced in Genoa later that year.[8] This second phase of Pound's research is concerned principally with Eriugena's Neoplatonic light philosophy, evident in his Latin translation of and commentary on *The Celestial Hierarchy* of Pseudo-Dionysius, and in his masterwork the *Periphyseon*. Citations of Eriugena in later decads of *The Cantos* such as *Rock-Drill* (1955) and *Thrones* (1959) recapitulate or simply cite the earlier, more extensive meditations. Pound's interests in various aspects of Eriugena's life and work deepened and became more nuanced along with his knowledge of the texts and their relation to ecclesiastical history. Naturally, the aesthetic and topical uses to which he put Eriugena also shifted over time, and can be divided roughly into two phases: before and after his acquiring Volume 122 of the Patrologia Latina in 1939. Each phase demands separate examination, and its manifestation in essays, letters and poetry also requires careful consideration. This chapter provides an overview of Pound's exploration of Eriugena's life and works prior to his acquisition of Patrologia Latina 122, and requires intermittent reference to more recent Eriugenian scholarship. Chapter 2 sets out in more complete form the current state of scholarship regarding the major events and texts. Before such a study takes place, though, it will serve well to set out some preliminary context with which to better understand Pound's Eriugenian preoccupations.

Eriugena's life and works: Preliminaries

Very little is known of Eriugena's life before or after his service in the court of Charles the Bald and the Palatine school. He was born, probably in Ireland, in the first quarter of the ninth century, and left before 847 for the continent: this date was the year in which Prudentius became Bishop of Troyes. In a letter to Eriugena concerning the composition of *De praedestinatione*, Prudentius makes reference to their friendship prior to his consecration (*Periphyseon*, Vol. 1, ed. Sheldon-Williams in Eriugena 1968, 2). The reason for Eriugena's departure from his homeland is not clear, but Cappuyns (57–8) and others have suggested that the viking raids of the time may have contributed to his decision to seek scholarly and corporal refuge elsewhere. This would be ironic, if true, as Charles's kingdom suffered similarly during Eriugena's tenure from viking attacks reaching far up the Seine and Oise rivers. It is likely that his preliminary education in Greek took place in Ireland – a leading light in transmitting the Greek language during the early Middle Ages – but may have continued on the continent, either in northern Francia or in the Rhine valley, and possibly by way of the strong network of Irish scholars that had steadily grown since the missionary work of Columbanus in the late sixth century.

This paucity of biographical fact is compounded by the ambiguities of Eriugena's name. Known variously as John Scottus, Iohannes Scottus Ierugena, Johannes Scottigena and by several other formulations during his lifetime, any of these appellations could equally have referred to other figures of the time or earlier: scholars in the nineteenth century frequently confused him with figures who lived even two centuries prior to his lifetime. Eriugena self-refers as John Scottus in most of the manuscripts attributed to his hand or that of his chief assistants (known as i^1 and i^2) and it is only in the translations of Pseudo-Dionysius in which he refers to himself as John Scottus Eriugena, although this carries considerable authority given that it is preserved in a ninth-century manuscript. The cognomen Eriugena indicates Ireland as the land of origin, and Scottus identifies the bearer as a member of the Scotti, or Irish. This doubling is not necessarily redundant as one could be of the Scotti but born outside of Ireland, in a colony such as that of Mainz or Liège. Thomas Gale, Eriugena's first translator and editor in English, referred to him as Erigena, a form he drew from the twelfth-century catalogue of Cluny and the thirteenth-century manuscript of Lilienfeld, which was adopted by Henry Bett in his landmark 1925 study and subsequently by Pound. Sheldon-Williams contentiously (and, to my mind, incorrectly) maintains that '[t]o attach the name Eriugena to works other than the Dionysian translations is not strictly correct', noting that '[Henry] Floss removed it from his edition in the Patrologia Latina' (2). To add to this confusion, a Saint-Pons-de-Tomières catalogue of 1276 employs the form Herigene. Floss preferred the form Ierugena, and Migne used Floss's text as the copy-text for the Patrologia Latina 122 edition. Pound's early reading on Eriugena was in French, Latin and Italian as well as English, widening the choice of name: Jean Scot or Erigène in French, Giovanni Scoto in Italian, Johannes Scottus in German. Pound, writing in the 1930s and in the first months of 1940, used the then-standard Anglophone form of Erigena (since superseded by Eriugena), but was sensitive to spelling variation as his essay 'Ecclesiastical History' makes evident: 'Scotus Erigena (spelled in Fr. Fiorentino's present edition with an extra *u*) said "authority comes from right reason"' (*SP* 61). The present study uses the commonly accepted form Eriugena as the primary mode of reference.

Eriugena's reputation in modern scholarship as 'the man who is widely regarded as the brightest light of the early Middle Ages and [...] sometimes viewed as the founder of medieval scholasticism' (Herren 1993, 1) reflects the authority he bore in his own time. He was given the honorific of *scholasticus et eruditus* at the royal court (Flori Diaconi, *Joannis Scoti Erigenæ Erroneas Definitiones*, PL 119, 103A). Prudentius, Bishop of Troyes, refers to him as *nullis ecclesiasticis gradibus insignitus*, indicating he was neither monk nor priest (Sheldon-Williams in Eriugena 1968, 3). *Pace* Sheldon-Williams, Eriugena and Martinus Hiberniensis were not 'principals of what almost amounted to a university' in Laon (3), and despite the standing of both figures, it is far from certain that they had any significant personal interaction: Eriugena was occupied largely at court or at the Palatine School, and Martin was master of the cathedral school of Laon. They were, however, part of a significant intellectual network of Irish scholars, each possessing some facility in Greek.

Eriugena first enters the historical record as the author of *De praedestinatione*: on the request of Charles the Bald and Hincmar, Archbishop of Reims in 851, Eriugena attempted a refutation of the thesis of double predestination posited by Gottschalk of Orbais, which resulted in the condemnation of his own text at the Councils of Valence in January 855 and Langres in May 859 (Herren 1993, 3). Following his translations from Greek specially commissioned by Charles – the corpus of Pseudo-Dionysius in c.860–62 (*The Celestial Hierarchy*, *The Divine Names*, *The Ecclesiastical Hierarchy* and *The Mystical Theology*), the *First Ambigua* and *Quaestiones ad Thalassium* of Maximus the Confessor, *De hominis opificio* of Gregory of Nyssa, the *Ancoratus* of Epiphanius and the *Solutiones ad Chosroem* of Priscianus Lydius – Eriugena's confidence in the texts and thought of the Eastern Fathers informed his work in the *Periphyseon*: 'The Platonic tradition which had flowed more purely and more richly through the teaching of the Eastern than of the Western Fathers liberated him from the confines of logic and dialectic and opened up wider fields of speculation' (4). Eriugena also produced *scholia* (critical commentaries) upon several principal Latin works: commentaries on Martianus Capella's *De nuptiis Mercurii et Philologiae* and Priscian's *Institutiones grammaticae*, and there is evidence to suggest he wrote commentaries on sections of Boethius's *De consolatione philosophiae* and Book VI of the *Aeneid* (7). His scriptural studies include commentaries on the Gospel of John and glosses on all the books of the Old Testament including the apocrypha, some of which provide important palaeographical information: 'The Old Irish glosses to the Old Testament works show that John continued to use his native language in teaching his compatriots' (Herren 1993, 9; see also ONéill 1986, 287–97). Sheldon-Williams notes the contents of *Periphyseon* Book I indicate an early attempt to compose a work in dialectic, on the Aristotelian Categories, which then became (from *Reims 875*, c.864–70) the five-book structure in which Books II-V bear upon the descent of the soul into the works of creation and the return of all creation to God, in the form of an *hexaemeron* (5–6). While there are signs of stylistic and thematic development from Book I, this view of a fundamental change of direction is no longer widely accepted in modern scholarship. The *Periphyseon* also engages with a singular anthropological meditation on the role of humanity in creation by which all things come into being and are turned again toward the divine in the *reditus*. Eriugena explores divinity by way of the twofold hermeneutics of *apophasis* (negative theology) and *kataphasis* (understanding through metaphor). Eriugena's brilliant work of meontology – the study of the non-existent – also demands close analysis, undertaken in Chapter 2.

Eriugena's warm relationship with Charles the Bald extended to his appointment as principal court poet from 859 to 870, 'although he complained of his patron's parsimony in several poems' (Herren 1993, 3). Following the condemnations of the 850s he spent significant time at Saint-Médard de Soissons under royal protection: Wulfad, Eriugena's former student and later abbot of Saint-Médard, is the dedicatee of the *Periphyseon*. Although not part of the cathedral school, Eriugena often travelled to Laon with Charles and mingled with the prominent Irish community, led by the school's master, Martin Hiberniensis. Eriugena's contacts with other Irish scholars extended to Fergus of Laon, Sedulius Scottus of Liège (whose proficiency in Greek rivalled Eriugena's) and the pupils Heiric of Auxerre, Wicbald and Hucbald of Saint-Amand. These contacts partly obviate a (now-redundant) historical view absorbed by Pound: 'Eriugena was not the isolated figure he was often made out to be by earlier scholarship that was wont to portray him as a lonely man ahead of his times' (Herren 1993, 5). Although nothing is known of Eriugena's life after c.870, a myth developed in which Eriugena left Charles's kingdom and assumed a teaching career in Britain. William of Malmesbury, who came into possession of a manuscript of the *Periphyseon*, subsequently owned by Thomas Gale and donated to Trinity College Library, Cambridge, was the chief proponent of this claim. William provided Eriugena with a tragicomic death at the hands of his students: 'Won over by [King Alfred's] generosity and, as I have learned from

Alfred's writings, holding the high position of teacher of the king, he settled at *Meldunum*, only to die there some years later, run through by the styli of the boys he was teaching.'[9] In Canto CV (771) Pound anticipates the apocryphal first-hand motive Sheldon-Williams ascribes to the disgruntled students: 'because he forced us to think' (Eriugena 1968, 5).

Phase one (1928–1938): Eriugena among the Neoplatonists

Pound's initial reading in Eriugena's life was mediated by general sources in medieval philosophy – principally Étienne Gilson's *La philosophie au moyen-âge* (1922) and five separate volumes of Francesco Fiorentino's *Compendio di Storia della Filosofia* and *Manuale di Storia della Filosofia*, but also more specific works such as Robert Grosseteste's *De Luce* and Ernest Renan's *Averroès et l'Averroïsme* (1852). As one scholar has noted: 'It is curious then that along side the "*Donna mi prega*" in Canto XXXVI we find not the Bishop of Lincoln and the generation of light but Scotus Erigena and authority and right reason' (Michaels 1972, 40). Further, Eriugena and Grosseteste are often mentioned together in Pound's catalogues of the 'conspiracy of intelligence' (*GK* 263) or 'the definition of words' (*ABCR* 90). This reliance upon secondary sources, compounded by the then-nascent state of Carolingian Studies, meant that Pound's historical information was incomplete and not altogether reliable, transmitted to him in texts largely lacking in sustained codicological analysis. Pound's interest in Eriugena's ethics and his supposed influence upon the Albigensian heresy saw him adopt the formula '*Auctoritas ex vera ratione processi ratio vero nequaquam ex auctoritate*' from his source (Fiorentino 1921, 217), which he translates as 'Authority comes from right reason/never the other way on' (XXXVI/179). Elsewhere he provides a shorthand version as 'authority comes from right reason' (*SP* 61; *GK* 74, 164, 333). As will become evident, this forthright defence of reason is not sustained unilaterally in Eriugena's writings, some of which rely very heavily on patristic sources for the authority of their arguments, and which regularly assert the properly dialectical relationship between authority and reason.[10]

Pound's initial interests in Eriugena derive from Fiorentino's chapter on Eriugena in the *Manuale* (transcribed with commentary in Appendix A): Fiorentino provides the basic contours of Eriugena's life, but his principal aims were to explicate the four divisions of nature in the *Periphyseon*, Eriugena's formulation of a positive and negative theology, and his Neoplatonic schema in general. Fiorentino also draws attention to Eriugena's biblical hermeneutics, by which the Bible presents theological concepts in terms the audience could understand: 'La Scrittura, per lui, è scritta in servigio de' nostri sensi rozzi ed infantili; bisogna che la ragione sappia intenderla: ci si vede una reliquiae dell'allegoria alessandrina' (Scripture, for Eriugena, is written in the service of our rude and infantile senses; one requires reason in order to understand it as intended: here we see a relic of Alexandrian allegory) (Fiorentino 1921, 216).[11] Pound's marginal annotations show he was searching for potential links with the thought of Arnaut Daniel; he also seized upon the condemnation by Pope Honorius III in 1225 on the grounds that Eriugena's thought carried influence with Cathar heretics (Fiorentino 1921, 221). The Troubadour link became a measure, for Pound, of the way Eriugena's thought had been unjustly misrepresented in history. He defends Eriugena from this allegation as early as 1931–1932 in his essay 'Terra Italica':

> The best scholars do not believe there were any Manichaeans left in Europe at the time of the Albigensian Crusade. If there were any in Provence they have at any rate left no trace in troubadour art. (*SP* 59)

Later in the decade, Pound argues that Eriugena's views on authority were not heretical, as they 'wd. have been *orthon logon* in greek, not *doxy*' (*GK* 333). He concurs with C. B. Schlueter – the 'prete' (LXXXIII/528) who edited Eriugena's *De divisione naturae* in 1818 – that Eriugena's worst crime was to have been misunderstood in his time, and to have been read by some Albigensians 300 years after his death (Michaels 1972, 43). Pound evidently draws from Henry Bett and Étienne Gilson in raising the recurrence of Eriugena's thought in the philosophy of the twelfth and thirteenth centuries. Not having considered the history in detail, Pound speculates on the 'real' reasons for the condemnation by Pope Honorius III in 1225: 'Was he cast out for talking nonsense on some other issue, or was it a frame-up, committed in the storm of political passion?' (*GK* 333). This question turns out to be more prescient than Pound could have known – if not in the context of the later condemnations, then certainly with respect to Eriugena's original doctrinal complications. Eriugena's dispute with Gottschalk was initiated by royal invitation, and with archepiscopal backing. The show of support for Gottschalk by important ecclesiastical figures in the kingdom (Prudentius of Troyes, Ratramnus of Corbie, Lupus of Ferrières) turned the dispute into a major lightning rod for ecclesiastical dissent. The condemnation by Honorius III three centuries later bore different political hues, being bound up in the suppression of the Cathars in Langue d'Oc, in the

Albigensian Crusade. Eriugena's texts were implicated in other condemnations at the University of Paris in 1210 and 1270: it is not clear whether Pound also has these events in mind in his earliest references to Papal condemnation. His initial interest in Eriugena was more polemical than philosophical: he was a writer neglected by the 'tradition' and vilified for his unorthodox views. Eriugena provided a vigorous alternative to the Aquinian reception of Aristotle (which itself entertained much scrutiny and suffered condemnation), and was read by Amalric of Bene[12] when the condemnation of 1210 took place at the University of Paris (Makin 1973, 61).

Pound introduces Eriugena in Canto XXXVI immediately following his translation of Cavalcanti's canzone 'Donna mi prega'. This first reference in *The Cantos* engages with matters of Papal condemnation that Pound first encountered in his reading of Fiorentino, as well as Eriugena's belated 'exhumation'. This is evident in Pound's spelling of Eriugena's name 'with an extra u' ('Ecclesiastical History', *SP* 61), which follows Fiorentino's convention in the *Manuale di Storia della Filosofia*. Following the translation of 'Donna mi prega', Canto XXXVI gives a brief history of Erigena's troubled reception in the time of the Troubadours. His teaching was associated with the Albigensian heresy and was condemned by Pope Honorius III in 1225:

> Eriugena was not understood in his time
> 'which explains, perhaps, the delay in condemning him'
> And they went looking for Manicheans
> And found, so far as I can make out, no Manicheans
> So they dug for, and damned Scotus Eriugena
> 'Authority comes from right reason
>   never the other way on'
> Hence the delay in condemning him (XXXVI/179)

The passage deserves close attention in the context of the canto as a whole, and is considered in this context below. But it remains to be considered how exhumation is a factor in Pound's introduction of Eriugena into his poem. The rhetoric of the passage is elliptical: why would his contemporaries' failure to understand him delay his condemnation? Could it be due to the fact that the true meaning of an heretical or counter-orthodox matter was not immediately apparent? Why would his formulation of reason over authority delay his condemnation instead of acting as a precipitating agent, as a direct challenge to the Church hierarchy? Further to this, Eriugena's writings were in fact condemned twice in the early years of his employment in Charles's court, at the Councils of Valence (855) and Langres (859), after which the court functioned as a sanctuary or royally sponsored asylum from ecclesiastical authority. Pound implies here that the matter of condemnation is linked directly to the Albigensian heresy, which might account for the decree by Pope Honorius III but neglects the many other decrees levelled at Eriugena in the intervening 300 years. The failure to find 'Manicheans' (Cathars) shifts attention to Eriugena as the object of the crusaders' attention. Pound uses the language of exhumation to describe this renewed attention: does he mean this literally, or metaphorically, as a way of figuring violence visited upon Eriugena's texts and reputation? In order to answer this question we need to look ahead to *The Pisan Cantos* where exhumation is mentioned twice more. In Canto LXXIV, Eriugena's influence upon the Albigensian Heresy is again noted: 'and they dug him up out of sepulture/soi disantly looking for Manichaeans./ Les Albigeois a problem of history' (LXXIV/429). The penultimate canto in the series concludes a catalogue of Eriugena's doctrines with the note: 'so they dug up his bones in the time of De Montfort/(Simon)' (LXXXIII/528). Yet none of the three condemnations – of 855, 859 and 1225 – led to his being exhumed, nor has the location of his grave ever been established. Pound might use florid imagery for rhetorical effect, rather than as historic assertion, but the confusing references to exhumation suggest ambiguities in his sources, or in his reading of them.

According to several Pound scholars, the 'exhumation' in Canto XXXVI refers to the decree of the Council of Paris in 1210 to have all copies of the *Periphyseon* burned. Alternately, the reference in Canto LXXIV is considered to be literal: that is, the reference is not referring to Eriugena's books or reputation but rather to his physical remains. The reference is considered to be a mistake in historical fact on Pound's part, in that Eriugena's remains have never suffered exhumation (Michaels 1972, 43; Makin 1973, 63; Kenner 1975, 451; Terrell 1984, 143). According to this line of thinking, Pound follows Fiorentino's *Manuale*, which makes reference to the exhumation of Amalric of Bene in 1210, but he mistakenly takes the subject of exhumation to be Eriugena: 'That Pound fused the two philosophers in his imagination is not unnatural; they are discussed almost in the same breath by Fiorentino' (Michaels 1972, 43); Amalric was a revivalist of Eriugena's doctrines (Bett 1925, 177), thus heightening the possibility of confusion. Yet this critical consensus is not entirely correct: Pound, when writing Canto XXXVI, had access to the third edition (1921) of Fiorentino's *Manuale di Storia della Filosofia* and to the third edition (1924) of the revised and enlarged *Compendio di Storia della Filosofia*. The 1921 *Manuale* sets out Amalric's posthumous condemnation (he died in 1206 or 1207) as the result of his perceived pantheism – the identification of the divine creator with the objects of creation in a condition of theophany – and the consequent action taken by virtue of Amalric's influence on David of Dinant[13]:

> Un concilio provincialea Parigi condannò la empietà di Almarico [sic], ne fece disotterrare e scomunicare il cadavere; perseguitò i seguaci, alcuni fece punier col rogo: a Davide di Dinant fu proibito l'insegnamento, e poichè inspiritori di queste eresie furon creduti i libri fisici di Aristotele, e quelli di Scoto Eriugena, pur questi furonö abbruciati e proibiti. (Fiorentino 1921, 243)
>
> [A Parisian provincial council condemned the impieties of Amalric, they did not disinter nor excommunicate his corpse; however they pursued his followers, taking other measures: David of Dinant was prohibited from teaching, the inspirations for his heresies were attributed to the physical texts of Aristotle and also those of Eriugena, which were thenceforth burned and prohibited.]

David Moody comments on the short chapter on Amalric in the 1924 *Compendio*, in which Amalric's exhumation and excommunication is mentioned in the same passage as the condemning and burning of both Aristotle's and Eriugena's books by the Council of Paris in 1210 (Moody 1996, 244). The prevailing critical ambiguity rests in reading literally the 'digging up' of Eriugena, when only Canto LXXXIII may be read this way. There is no mistaking Eriugena's and Amalric's bones in *The Pisan Cantos*: rather, according to Moody and *pace* Michaels, the mistake is in Pound's imperfect recollection of 'poichè la seppe diseppellita per la ricerche che si facevano contro lo Albigese' (the research unearthing the accusations made against the Albigensian) in Fiorentino's *Compendio* –a simple grammatical slip referring to Eriugena the man, instead of his works (244). The mention of Amalric in this context is thus entirely unnecessary.[14]

In these early investigations, Pound is attempting to make sense of complex theological debates and their consequences, untangling various condemnations occurring at different times and in different philosophical and ecclesiastical contexts. That he was reliant on Italian philosophical textbooks only seemed to heighten the chances of his confusing the identities of Amalric and Eriugena, or perpetrating a slippage between metaphor (digging up Eriugena's works) and the literal exhumation of his corpse. The enthusiasm with which Pound embarked upon untangling the knotty history of Eriugena's thought is tempered by the reliability of his sources and of the historical record. A closer examination of his own reading and annotating practices – particularly the Fiorentino volumes – sheds light on some of the questions he asked of his sources and the lines of interest he followed in this earlier phase of his research. Much of Pound's philosophical library, including the five

Fiorentino volumes, resides at Schloss Brunnenburg: the present commentary concerns Pound's annotations on the relevant chapter in the 1921 *Manuale* 'La Prima età della Scolastica: Giovanni Scoto Eriugena' (pp. 216–21), which is transcribed and annotated as Appendix A.

Fiorentino's account of Eriugena provides the bare facts of his life, centred upon his tenure in the court of Charles the Bald. He is lauded for his originality, especially in drawing on Eastern patristic sources and adapting them to a Western Christian context. Fiorentino frames his account of Eriugena's thought with the motto '*Auctoritas ex vera ratione processit, ratio vero nequaquam ex auctoritate*' (217), indicating Eriugena was first a philosopher and then a theologian. Fiorentino's chapter is distinctive in that it deals with the four divisions of nature in some depth, presenting the argument in the *Periphyseon* by way of Eriugena's positive and negative theologies, drawn explicitly from Pseudo-Dionysius. Pound's annotations indicate his attraction to the second division – that which is created (by God) and creates (the phenomena of the world of material existence) – which encompasses the realm of the Aristotelian Categories. This division is where (following Aristotle's *De Anima*) the Islamic philosophers Avicenna and Averroes locate the active intellect as the outermost of the ten emanations and the one that may 'graze' the possible intellect of a receptive human agent.[15] Pound of course sees Cavalcanti's exposition of *amor* as functioning in precisely this ontological zone. His reading of Fiorentino precisely coincides with his work on the 1929 Aquila Press edition of Cavalcanti's *Rime*. The concept of *divina ignorantia* (the notion from negative theology that God, being neither finite nor comprehensible, is not known even to Himself) also receives close attention in Fiorentino (218). Pound is drawn to this idea in the context of the theophany of Book III of the *Periphyseon* and the *reditus* of Book V, as well as its subsequent transformation into the notion of *docta ignorantia* (learned ignorance) in Nicholas of Cusa.

Fiorentino's discussion adumbrates other elements of the *Periphyseon* steeped in Neoplatonic thought, such as the correlation of the Trinity with the three Hypostases – 'Il processo divino si scorge nella triplicità delle sue energie: egli è Noo, è Logo, è Dianoia, come Iddio è Padre, è Figlio, è Spirito santo' (219). Discussion extends to the relation between orders of existence and propositions for the movement between them: this expression of a Neoplatonist 'Chain of Being' appealed to Pound in the context of Arnaut Daniel, as his marginal notes indicate (218 and 219). In the most general terms, these themes inform some of the intellectual background of Dante's *Divina commedia*, which Pound adapts for *The Cantos* into a quasi-Gnostic process of sublimation for the elect.

This sense of exclusivity transforms Eriugena's marginalization into a powerful expression of his insight, where his perceived threat to ecclesiastical agency is evident in his serial condemnations.

Fiorentino concludes by noting the way Eriugena's thought was overshadowed in subsequent scholastic philosophy, having incurred the disapproval of Pope Nicholas I, and then in 1225, drawing the ire of Honorius III in the (erroneous) context of its revival among the Albigensians (221). Fiorentino's favourable and nuanced account of Eriugena's thought, and his fair-minded appraisal of unwarranted Papal condemnation, clearly motivated Pound to seek out and champion Eriugena's thought, and to revive his reputation from its doctrinal-political fate. Pound articulates this agenda in the essay 'Ecclesiastical History' in 1934, where the learned and linguistically adept Eriugena is a victim of benighted ignorance, in '[a] time when, so far as we know, the Church authorities BELIEVED what they taught or were still searching for the truth' (*SP* 61). In 'Immediate Need of Confucius' published in the journal *Aryan Path* in 1937, Pound pursues the consequences for later philosophy in the besmirching of Eriugena's reputation and the occlusion of his significant philosophical contributions: 'I, personally, want a revision of the trial of Scotus Erigena. If "authority comes from right reason" the shindy between Leibniz and Bossuet was unnecessary' (*SP* 92). Pound persisted in this line of thinking for several years, putting forth a series of questions that demonstrate the generally inchoate understanding of Eriugena's indiscretions:

> The 'general' church threw out Scotus Erigena several centuries after his death. We have not sufficiently investigated the matter. Erigena did not, I think, consider himself a schismatic. 'Authority comes from right reason', that wd. have been *orthon logon* in greek, not *doxy*. It seems unlikely that he was heretical in this view. Was he cast out for talking nonsense on some other issue, or was it a frame-up, committed in the storm of political passion? Until we know this, we shall not know whether Bossuet and Leibniz were at loggerheads, one from stupidity and both from ignorance of the tradition (general). (*GK* 333)

There were condemnations during and after Eriugena's lifetime, but he did not present himself for anything resembling a trial, unlike his adversary in the Predestination controversy, Gottschalk of Orbais. The emphasis on 'right reason' becomes for Pound an abiding concern (*GK* 74), although it must be said that Eriugena relied upon authority as much as any other theologian of his time or for long after (as will be discussed in the next chapter). Pound draws this concept together with figures of the early Church – 'Given Erigena, given St Ambrose and St Antonino, plus time, patience and genius you cd. erect inside the fabric something modern man cd. believe' (*GK* 76) – as well as with figures of the Enlightenment: 'Civilized Christianity has never stood higher than in Erigena's "Authority comes from right reason". That is Xtianity which Leibniz cd. have accepted' (*GK* 164).[16] But Pound shows awareness of the dangers of anachronism:

> Even Erigena's dictum can be examined. Authority can in material or savage world come from accumulated prestige based on intuition. We have trust in a man because we have come to regard him (in his entirety) as sapient and well-balanced. We play his hunch. We make an act of faith. But this is not what Erigena meant, and in any case it does not act in contradiction to his statement, but only as an extension of it. (*GK* 165)

This is a curious and gnomic statement: Pound seems to suggest that faith in a person's authority is vested in the consistency of character and precedent stemming from past actions. In the context of the historical moment in which Pound famously composed *Guide to Kulchur* (in a matter of weeks in 1938), he seems to have his sights set on Mussolini at least implicitly as the model agent of authority, duly inflected with Confucian overtones. At the same time, he separates this portrait of 'good sense' from Eriugena's statement in which the basis of authority derives in the strength of argument: for Eriugena this means the practice of dialectic, and for Pound this takes the more generalized form of logical argument or in 'natural demonstration.'

The association of Eriugena's writings with Neoplatonism and Gnostic thought culminates for Pound in his yoking Eriugena's fate to Cavalcanti's canzone 'Donna mi prega', examined in some detail below. Pound also seeks out the cultural sources of the human-divine dialectic, a history in which the cult of Eleusis will 'shed a good deal of light on various passages of theology or of natural philosophy re the active and passive intellect (*possibile intelleto*, etc.)' (*GK* 59). This focus on precision in language – expressed elsewhere in Pound's work as a kind of secular incarnation of the Second Person of God or *verbum perfectum* – places Eriugena with other august figures at the intellectual peak of religious thought: 'Catholicism led Europe as long as Erigena, Grosseteste and their fellows struggled for definitions of words' ('Immediate Need of Confucius', *SP* 90). Indeed Pound goes further in *Guide to Kulchur*, assembling an entire intellectual lineage for vital thought occluded from the mainstream of church orthodoxy:

> A conspiracy of intelligence outlasted the hash of the political map. Avicenna, Scotus Erigena in Provence, Grosseteste in Lincoln, the Sorbonne, fat faced Frankie Petrarch, Gemisto, the splendour of the XVth century, Valla, the

over-boomed Pico, the florentine collectors and conservers...even if mere Serendipity hunters. (*GK* 263)[17]

At this point in his studies, Pound had yet to read any of Eriugena's texts directly. He was dependent upon secondary sources, particularly Fiorentino, but had already identified a number of ideas to which he felt a measure of solidarity. The formula 'Authority from right reason' rather than doxological precedent stands out among these ideas as that which Pound (via Fiorentino) associates with the condemnations suffered by Eriugena. This erroneous assumption neglects the fact that the matter of condemnation firstly centred upon Eriugena's text *De praedestinatione*, and in his rebuttal of Gottschalk's notion of double predestination (to sin and perdition, as well as to God's grace and paradise) Eriugena was seen to express a dangerous thesis of radical free will in humanity. Later condemnations in Paris were more to do with his theory of participation (interpreted as a form of pantheism), in which divinity dwells in each person as each makes manifest God's creation. The theology behind this idea is elaborated in the *Periphyseon*, to which Pound did not have access until the last months of the decade. But he discovered in Patrologia Latina 122 and Eriugena's corpus, an intellectual structure of the most impressive kind. How this shaped Pound's thinking on Eriugena as an emblem of specific ideas – on light as a kataphatic expression of divinity; on the celestial hierarchy; on the flame of civilization kept alive in the transmission of Greek in the Carolingian Age – becomes evident in Pound's two sets of notes on Eriugena, transcribed and edited in Chapter 3. Pound's conception of Eriugena and his historical context was manifest in the questions concerning his alleged apostasy and heretical status. This portrait, partial though it was, drew Pound to include Eriugena at the centre of his thinking on the precarious transmission of sacred knowledge. Pound saw fit to combine his translation of 'Donna mi prega' with his speculations on Eriugena's doxological status in Canto XXXVI, drawing together a complex and partially submerged constellation of ideas concerning the human-divine nexus that buttresses the entire poetic project of *The Cantos* – from hell and through *purgatorio*, towards *paradiso*.

Canto XXXVI and Cavalcanti's '*Donna mi prega*'

A better understanding of Eriugena's historical context clarifies precisely how Canto XXXVI combines Pound's translation of Cavalcanti's famously esoteric canzone with the first extended reference to Eriugena in *The Cantos*. Located midway through *Eleven New Cantos* (1934), Pound's use of source materials is decisive in determining the canto's significance. The four previous cantos in *Eleven New Cantos* concern the establishment of the American Republic, and dwell upon the extensive correspondence between Thomas Jefferson and John Adams in particular, as well as the activities of other major actors in the Revolution and the Continental Congress, such as James Madison, James Monroe and Benjamin Franklin. In the cantos immediately following XXXVI, Pound's 'poem including history' returns to the early years of the American Republic, comparing the terms of governance and, especially, the role of money in national politics and international relations to other times and places, such as eighteenth-century Italy and France. The poem then turns to contemporary economics centred on the arms trade and what Pound saw as the economic basis of the First World War, before a brief Homeric diversion to the island of Circe in Canto XXXIX, an abridged translation of Hanno's *Periplus* in Canto XL,[18] and a final panegyric to Mussolini in the final canto of the sequence. Pound actually begins Canto XLI with Mussolini's fabled response to Pound's poetry: 'Ma questo', said the Boss, 'è divertente'. Pound took this comment – 'Most diverting!' – to signify a deeper appreciation of his poetry on behalf of Il Duce than was probably intended.[19] Pound's prose at this time had turned decisively to matters of politics and economics, measuring Mussolini's Italy against Revolutionary and early Republican America. Pound's desire to draw an analogy between these political systems is evident in the publication of *Jefferson and/or Mussolini* in the following year (1935).

The historical and thematic textures of *Eleven New Cantos* raises the question: why Cavalcanti at this point in *The Cantos*, and why Eriugena? As a modern epic poem, *The Cantos* draws on several large-scale structuring devices, not least its emulation of Homeric and Dantean narrative frames. In a letter to his father of 11 April 1927, Pound provides an account of the meta-structure of the poem:

> A. A. Live man goes down into world of dead.
> C. B. 'The repeat in history'.
> B. C. The 'magic moment' or moment of metamorphosis, bust through from quotidian into 'divine or permanent world'. Gods, etc. (*SL* 210)

This structure of a descent to the underworld – *nekuyia*, or *katabasis* – followed by metamorphosis and transcendence, applies to Pound's vision for *The Cantos* as a whole. It also occurs at the level of the poetic decad, including *Eleven New*

Cantos. Pound's narrator, having navigated through the perils of American revolutionary aspiration and international politics, enters into a mystical zone of contemplation, seeking out what is permanent amidst the diurnal. This is one of several glimpses of the poem's *paradiso* from the viewpoint of *purgatorio*. Cavalcanti's famously difficult canzone serves this function in providing a meditation on the nature of Love, or *amor*, and especially its interactions with the faculty of reason and perceptive experience. His poem is replete with an hermetic vocabulary, inspiring a range of tendentious schematic readings. Pound sees in Cavalcanti's poem a thread of esoteric knowledge conveyed by a kind of Gnostic vocabulary directed to an elect audience, and which draws out the more speculative elements of both ancient fertility rites as well as Neoplatonism, conserving mystery in an otherwise quotidian zone of being. This mode of engagement might be considered to be roughly analogous to reading Beatrice as an allegory of divine Love in Dante's poem, except that in Pound's translation of Cavalcanti, the masculine *amor* is the active subject and vehicle of mystical knowledge. Pound draws a sharp distinction between the two Florentine poets: 'Dante's "heresies" are due to feeling, annoyance with Popes and so forth, rather than to intellectual hunger, or to his feeling cramped in the Aquinian universe' (*MIN* 357). In the cosmos of 'Donna mi prega', *amor* is conveyed to its 'knowers' in a schematic conceptual system of *virtù* (the disporting of human agency in alignment with the metaphysical category of the good), the *diafan* of light (the medium by which human agents can perceive the categories) and the *intellect possible* (the human faculty cognate with the tenth emanation, or active intellect). Pound also discerns Cavalcanti's familiarity – direct or otherwise – with medieval Islamic commentators on Aristotle and their European counterparts. The Averroist interpretation of Aristotle is of particular relevance at this point, as the controversy at the University of Paris over these precise matters occurred during Cavalcanti's lifetime. This provides a discursive entry point for Eriugena into the conceptual framework of Cavalcanti's poem as well as into *The Cantos*.

    Pound first encountered Cavalcanti's poem in his undergraduate studies at the University of Pennsylvania and Hamilton College, and he returned to it many times in subsequent years. His graduate research at Pennsylvania eventuated in his short monograph *The Spirit of Romance* (1910). Pound studied and attempted translations of the poem at different points in his adult life, including his 'traduction' published in *The Dial* in 1928. He tried to publish a critical edition of Cavalcanti's poems with facing-page translations on at least three occasions with different presses: *Sonnets and Ballate of Guido Cavalcanti*

(Boston: Small, Maynard 1912); *Complete Works of Guido Cavalcanti* (London: Aquila 1929), aborted when the Aquila Press declared bankruptcy; and *Guido Cavalcanti Rime* (Genoa: Marsano 1932). Pound's critical apparatus and commentary, published variously in journals during the 1910s, also appeared within the essay 'Cavalcanti' in *Make It New* (1934).[20] Cavalcanti's poem is crucial to Pound as an emblem of enduring truth, of *amor* understood as contemplation rather than emotion, symbolized in light and represented in a language of hermetic iconicity. For Pound, 'the whole poem is a scholastic definition in form', in contrast to what he saw as the lifeless scholasticism of Aquinas.[21] Pound emulates Cavalcanti's highly inflected vocabulary, extending Neoplatonist themes from earlier cantos that will recur later in *The Pisan Cantos*, *Rock-Drill* and *Thrones*.

The history and provenance of Pound's translation is of critical relevance to the meaning of Canto XXXVI. Pound was acutely aware of the compromised manuscript transmission of the poem, having visited several archives in Rome, Florence, Modena, Siena and elsewhere. He made detailed notes[22] of textual variants, corruptions and potential stemmatic relationships in an attempt to produce a comprehensive record: 'There are certain definite impasses, for definite philological reasons. The copyists simply did not know, and we are unlikely to find out any more or anterior manuscripts' (*MIN* 362). By virtue of the poem's problematic transmission, Pound cautions against ascribing evidence to Cavalcanti's membership of any cabalistic or esoteric tradition (*MIN* 378–79). The canto comprises two segments following 'Donna mi prega': the first concerning Eriugena and the Papal condemnations to which he was subject; and a final segment concerning the thirteenth-century Mantuan troubadour Sordello da Goito (a figure already familiar from the strident opening of Canto II) and the mercantile and political matters in which he was embroiled. The relation of these segments to each other anchors Canto XXXVI within Pound's epic as a whole.

Cavalcanti's poem represents a shift in poetic sensibility in thirteenth-century Italy, to the 'sweet new style'. The poets of the *dolce stil novo* had common poetic aims that reached their apogee in Cavalcanti's canzone:

> They were members of a new intellectual and urban élite, and wrote their lyrics for this society, for the cultivated young women in it, but even more perhaps for one another; they seemed convinced that their poetry would be scarcely fathomable by the rest of humankind. This comes out particularly in the songs in which these poets try to define the essence of love, songs that at times presuppose a range of intellectual reference such as no earlier lyric poet had counted on. (Dronke 2002, 157–58)[23]

Cavalcanti's didactic, philosophical poem represents a union of prosodic dexterity and rhetorical complexity. Pound retains the formal structure of the canzone in his translation of Cavalcanti in Canto XXXVI. This poetic genre developed in the Sicilian court of Federico Barbarossa in the thirteenth century, and was prized for its exacting formal requirements: the hendecasyllabic line (11 syllables); stanzas of dense internal rhyme (52 of 154 syllables rhyme in each stanza); and, peculiar to Cavalcanti's example, a dense and abstruse rhetorical and philosophical argument. Pound retains many of these features, as well as the envoi that completes the poem, following which the canto moves into the two extra stanzas dealing, respectively, with Eriugena and Sordello. Cavalcanti's poem is considered to be a response to Guido Orlandi's sonnet, 'Onde si move e done nasce Amore' (Say what is Love, and whence doth he start) (*MIN* 348). Pound cleverly combines the poetic dexterity of the canzone with the philosophical force of the *trobar clus* (closed form), a poetic mode taken from Provençal and the Troubadour tradition of poetic composition for initiated readers. This form provided a means by which to fuse love poetry with more abstruse concerns, freeing the poet to exercise his linguistic and conceptual dexterity. The influence of Cavalcanti's immediate predecessor Guido Guinizelli is evident in his playful, witty and contemplative lyrics, especially 'Al cor gentil rimpaira sempre amore':

> This experience of moving in serene harmony with the beloved has something more than human about it – in this the lovers are like the angels of the spheres, whose harmonious movement expresses their oneness with God. It is this wonderful conception of love that enables Guido [Guinizelli] confidently to argue, at the end of his canzone, that human love cannot be incompatible with love of God. (Dronke 2002, 158)

For Pound, Cavalcanti's aesthetic requires human *inventio*, 'an interactive force: the *virtu* in short' (*MIN* 348) in which bodily passions play a central part, rather than receding into asceticism or monasticism. The body, experiencing Love, is the vehicle by which is recalled 'the radiant world where one thought cuts through another with clean edge, a world of moving energies "*mezzo oscuro rade*", "*risplende in sè perpetuale effecto*", magnetisms that take form, that are seen, or that border the visible' (351). Ronald Bush formulates the central problematic of Pound's translation as: 'a medieval synthesis of two apparently disparate philosophical systems – Aristotle's rigorous definition of substance, matter, and form, in which memory plays a key role in the soul's acquisition of enduring and impersonal forms of knowledge, and the Neoplatonists' understanding of the emanation and return of divine intelligence (*nous*), in which memory helps the soul re-ascend to its divine home' (Bush 2010, 670–71). Cavalcanti's poem places Love in the Aristotelian realm of accident, not substance or category, making it an event of the senses, and then lodging it in the possible intellect where it awaits pleasurable fulfilment in the discovery of a matching temperament. His argument, conveyed in a schematic scholastic vocabulary, superficially resembles poetic arguments for *gentilezza* (the predisposition to love) associated with Guido Guinizzelli (Usher 1996, 24). But it adverts to the genre of *dimonstratio* in its terminology and dialectical movement: '[Cavalcanti] claims that his dialectic is a "demonstration" in the field of natural philosophy, and indeed this song came to be treated as a *quaestio disputato* and was furnished with learned Latin commentaries' (Dronke 2002, 158). Pound's essay appeals to this scholarly tradition, where the canzone is glossed rigorously and accompanied by extensive annotations. Further, his analysis of the poem in *Make It New* is cognizant of the valency of natural philosophy: 'It is not so much what Guido says in the poem, as the familiarity that he shows with dangerous thinking: *natural demonstration* and the proof by experience or (?) experiment' (*MIN* 356). Behind these contemporary influences, Pound finds evidence of medieval Islamic philosophy in Cavalcanti's vocabulary. The poem telescopes an entire history of reception of and commentary on Aristotle's physical theories, especially the Averroist perspectives on *De Anima* that precipitated the numerous book-bannings and condemnations in thirteenth-century Paris. The poem also engages Neoplatonic notions of emanations, partly stemming from Avicenna and Averroes, but equally suggesting a preliminary link with Eriugena via *The Celestial Hierarchy* of Pseudo-Dionysius.

Rhetorically, the canzone is a response to a question concerning the nature of *amor*: what is Love, and how can its truth be known to human agents? This disarmingly simple premise combines with Pound's careful internal rhymes and alliteration to produce a serene, poetic surface in the first stanza that belies the intensity of its philosophical vocabulary: 'reason', 'affect', 'knowers', 'natural demonstration', 'proof', 'power', 'being' and so on.

A lady asks me
        I speak in season
She seeks reason for an affect, wild often
That is so proud he hath Love for a name
Who denys it can hear the truth now
Wherefore I speak to the present knowers
Having no hope that low-hearted
        Can bring sight to such reason

> Be there not natural demonstration
>   I have no will to try proof-bringing
> Or say where it hath birth
> What is its virtu and power
> Its being and every moving
> Or delight whereby 'tis called "to love"
> Or if man can show it to sight. (XXXVI/177)

This vocabulary indicates a complex philosophical discourse at work in the poem, absorbing a range of responses to Aristotle's admittedly vague prescriptions in *De Anima* on the possible intellect (νοῦς δυνάμει) and the active intellect (νοῦς ποιητικός): human capacity for thought, and the source of that power. The Islamic commentators provide a range of views on whether the possible intellect partakes of the active intellect or merely reflects it, but agree in seeing the active intellect as an emanation from the supreme being (resonating with the model put forward in *The Celestial Hierarchy*) and which inspires thought in the possible intellect in the human subject by way of 'conjunction' (Davidson 1992, 4). For Alfarabi, Avicenna and Averroes, the supreme being consists in pure thought, giving rise to emanations or intelligences that keep the celestial spheres in motion. The tenth and outermost emanation is the active intellect, which is separate from the possible intellect but inspires human thought by motivating a 'eudaemonic state called conjunction' (4). This is a decisive element of Cavalcanti's thinking for Pound. Images from the active intellect 'graze' against the human possible intellect, making it aware of the divine through sensory experience. This is both empirical and esoteric, although Pound is careful to distinguish his formulation of the 'magic moment' as distinct from such Gnostic theories as articulated by Luigi Valli in *Il Linguaggio segreto di Dante e dei 'Fideli d'Amore'* (1928), who receives forthright criticism in Pound's essay 'Cavalcanti' (*MIN* 375–76).

Pound's translation of 'Donna mi prega' mostly adheres to the prosodic conventions of the canzone genre. He retains only a minimal rhyme scheme, but includes opportune instances of internal rhyme (season/reason in the opening lines, and delight/sight in the final lines of the first strophe, for example). The prosodic burden rests instead on repetition of words and assonantal and alliterative devices ('Having no hope', 'leave his true likeness', 'Disjunct in mid darkness'). Word-repetition accentuates the philosophical register of the poem – the transcendental concepts of *amor*, 'virtu', 'intellect possible' and their basis in human experience. Pound supplements his complex argument for the influence of Avicenna and Averroes upon Cavalcanti with medieval light philosophy: 'Grosseteste derives from Arabic treatises on perspective. It is too much to say that Guido had, perforce, read the Bishop of Lincoln, but certainly that is the *sort* of thing he had read' (*MIN* 360). In his own commentary on 'Donna mi prega' (360), Pound quotes from Baur's edition of Grosseteste's *De Luce*: 'Lux enim per se in omnem partem si ipsam diffundit...' (Baur 1912, 51) (For light of its very nature diffuses itself in every direction...(Grosseteste 1942, 10)). Pound asserts the incendiary nature of Cavalcanti's poem: 'We may trace [Guido's] ideas to Averroes, Avicenna; he does not definitely proclaim any heresy, but he shows leanings toward not only the proof by reason, but toward the proof by experiment' (*MIN* 345) and natural demonstration (356), where the whole poem is an extended definition of *l'accidente* and 'a sort of metaphor on the generation of light' (360). Already the affinities with Eriugena are in evidence, in whose theology light assumes the mantle of the dominant kataphatic gesture to divinity.

As a meditation on the nature of Love, the poem is, rhetorically, a response to its initial question: 'A lady asks me/I speak in season' (XXXVI/177). The first strophe sets out the terms of the problem: the lady 'seeks a reason for an affect' that goes by the name of *amor* or 'Love'. The nature of this affect immediately drills down into complex philosophical strata, where entire traditions of commentary, such as the Islamic inheritance of Neoplatonic theories of emanation and the Aristotelian categories are distilled into a few words. Pound is acutely aware of the premium placed on the definitions of words: 'What we need is not so much a commentator as a lexicon' (*MIN* 361). The 'truth' of Love can only be conveyed to 'present knowers', implying a kind of Gnostic or esoteric dimension to this phenomenon, open only to an elect few. The emphasis on vision – 'Having no hope that low-hearted/Can bring sight to such reason' – has the speaker disavow 'natural demonstration' and 'proof-bringing' before the uninitiated, perhaps as a measure of self-preservation. However, there exists a kind of sight perfectly suited to observing the essence of this affect, tied up in matters of the active and possible intellects. The provenance of Love, 'where it hath birth', is beyond the ken of material conception, as are 'its virtu and power/Its being and every moving' – that is, its strength, its source, its identity and its agency. The problem lies in ascribing a place for Love in a metaphysical hierarchy: it is both part of human experience and divine, and the nature of its transmission is the concept at issue.

The second strophe is an elaboration upon the kind of proof required to properly define *amor*: Pound sees Cavalcanti navigating a way between the Scylla of proof by authority and the Charybdis of base materialism, attesting that ' "*dove sta memoria*" is Platonism' (*MIN* 357). Thus the opening phrase, 'Where memory liveth', situates love as the lynchpin between the transcendent active intellect and human knowledge. The following lines develop a complex and subtle argument concerning the animation of human thought: in effect, an epitome of the entire Neoplatonist and medieval Islamic response to Aristotle's *De Anima*. Love is infused into human experience the same way that light enters a dark zone and brings the potential for colour into actuality: 'Formed like a diafan from light on shade'. The term *diafan* admits a technical meaning here, deriving from Albertus Magnus's commentary on *De Anima* (II.3.viii): 'we see light not by itself but in a certain subject, and this is the diaphane' (qtd in Liebregts 2004, 205). The play of positive and negative attributes bears directly upon Pound's interest in Eriugena, with respect to his Pseudo-Dionysian translations and commentaries:

> Love 'lacks colour' – it cannot be physically perceived; it is 'cut off from being': it is not a substance but an accident, a quality inhering in the sensitive part of the soul, which is dark, which lacks the light of reason. And yet, Guido affirms, flaunting a final paradox, it is precisely out of this darkness that something beautiful, love's reward, is born. (159)

Pound had not yet read Eriugena on divine darkness – the apophatic theology drawn from Gregory of Nyssa and Pseudo-Dionysius – but his fascination with this trope is evident in his commentary: 'I take it that the *Amor* moves with the light in darkness, never touching it and never a hair's breadth from it' (*MIN* 395).[24] Just as light makes its presence known by what it illuminates, Love transmits from the higher realms (νους) to the human realm ('of Mars') in which it takes on 'seen form', in the present case, in the beauty of a woman. Love, 'which being understood/Taketh locus and remaining in the intellect possible', must be experienced in the sensible world, but in so doing, it provides a conduit back to the divine intelligence, and by registering in the 'intellect possible', installs its image within human memory. It is crucial to note that Love is transcendent – with 'neither weight nor still-standing' – but like light, 'shineth out/Himself his own effect unendingly'. Love is impassive – identified as stillness or 'being aware'– and depositing 'his true likeness' in precisely the correct locus. This analogy between light and Love makes clear the Neoplatonic register Pound wishes to overlay upon Cavalcanti's philosophy of Love, sidelining the Aristotelian scholastic elements of Cavalcanti's poem in order to enlist this trope in the general theme of the possibility of a human *paradiso terrestre*.

The third strophe elaborates on the transcendental nature of Love: being 'not vertu but comes of that perfection', Love emanates from the Neoplatonist hypostasis, Nous, and is activated into human awareness not by reason but by experience. The role of the human agent realizes this insight into the divine realm through Love: 'the attainment of Love and hence of insight into the divine depend on one's active desire and will' (Liebregts 2004, 211); conversely, those without the requisite attributes are denied such insights.[25] This takes the form of a falsely negative projection onto Love itself, appearing to the unenlightened as 'Poor in discernment, being thus weakness' friend'. The following line asserts the life-giving powers of Love, whose power 'cometh on death in the end', and functions as a kind of counterweight, reinforced in the 'friend/end' rhyme. Love is not a 'natural opposite' to death but is an emissary from the divine. It does not emerge from 'chance' even if the human memory is insufficiently strong to retain the experience. Pound embellishes the notion of an elect audience being open to the light of the divine denied to others who lack the requisite faculties of the possible intellect and the locus of memory.

The fourth strophe explores the precise mechanisms at work when Love registers its impact upon the human intelligence. The wording of the initial lines might seem to suggest that Love is created out of human emotion – 'Cometh he to be/when the will/From overplus/Twisteth out of natural measure'. Love is experienced in human terms, and enters into the possible intellect as a consequence of its acting upon the receptive will. This point is confirmed by a continued association with light imagery: 'Moveth he changing colour/Either to laugh or weep/Contorting the face with fear'. A careful reading reveals that the poet addresses the physical effects of Love, 'that shall ye see of him'. Pound therefore presents something of a proof by 'natural demonstration' in this strophe. Love is experienced by the receptive human intelligence – 'folk who deserve him' – and is made manifest in the 'colours' of human emotion made visible by his 'light'. It reposes in human memory, conducive to further reception: 'his strange quality sets sighs to move/Willing man look into that forméd trace in his mind'. Pound inverts the conventional image of the inflamed lover to depict a human receptivity to divine experience as 'uneasiness that rouseth the flame'. The strophe moves into a kind of negative demonstration (perhaps kindling Pound's awareness of the negative theology of Pseudo-Dionysius and Eriugena), whereby the 'Unskilled can not form his image'. Love is essentially still, a dimension of divine experience, and one which 'Neither turneth about to seek his delight' nor seeks to measure its dimensions, 'Be it so great or so small'. The vocabulary of this strophe is less technical than the earlier sections of the poem (with the significant exception of 'forméd trace') but the hermeneutic challenges remain. The generalized, even vague, expressions of the process of

Love entering into human intellect are compounded by archaisms that feature prominently: 'resteth', 'rouseth', 'turneth' and 'moveth' (twice). These active verbs shift the rhetorical focus of Cavalcanti's argument (and Pound's mediation of it) from matters of definition of the divine realm – mere consolations of theological argument more in keeping with a bloodless Aquinian theology – to the reception of Love and the potential thread from human experience to the 'divine or permanent world' (*L* 210), the active pursuit of *paradiso*.

The final strophe of the poem describes the way in which Love, as an emanation of Nous, can function separately from it and persist in human affairs. The first six lines establish a model of affinity between Love and its natural exemplars: 'He draweth likeness and hue from like nature'. The phenomena of this world set to display Love are themselves images of Beauty, and thus share a likeness, drawing the sensitive to follow 'Deserving spirit, that pierceth'. This notion of likeness reminds the reader of Eriugena's second and third divisions of nature: the categories which are created and create, and the substantial objects of the world created by the categories but that themselves do not create. 'Likeness' also recalls the long-standing controversy surrounding Augustine's distinction between humanity being made in God's image (an immutable condition) and receiving God's likeness (which is diminished in the course of sin), a topic taken up in Eriugena's *De praedestinatione*, but upon which Cavalcanti remains silent.[26] Pound enlists Cavalcanti's canzone into his 'Great Chain of Being' alongside both the Neoplatonic and Islamic-Aristotelian heritage. Whilst Pound alludes to the stereotype of Eros/Cupid and his 'darts', this strategy only emboldens his schematic divergence from the model of Love as the compelled intoxication of an unsuspecting subject. Instead it poses a state of awareness of the divine thread joining Beauty to Nous. The vocabulary returns to a technical register, where the 'face' of Love is unknowable, enshrouded in the 'white light that is allness' – a clear reference to Grosseteste's *De Luce*. The human intellect disposed to receiving Love 'heareth, seeth not form' but its status as divine emanation functions as a kind of magnetism and guides the receptive subject. The philosophical discussion turns to the nature of emanation, repeating the earlier suggestion that the way Love inspires an image in the possible intellect is akin to the way light realizes the potential colour in things: 'Being divided, set out from colour,/Disjunct in mid darkness/Grazeth the light'. The verb 'to graze' is decisive (Pound's translation of the Italian *raser*) as the action by which the magic moment is activated: 'a moment of "grazing" or "shining" becomes the initiating figure for Pound's representation of "Elisio" – Elysium, or Paradise' (Bush 2010, 682). In its function as an accident emanating from the active intellect, making contact with the realm of the senses, Love is the most potent vehicle for human insight into the divine. This is captured in its grammatical inflections, as Pound makes clear in his commentary (*MIN* 377): 'the ideal (represented by the noun *amore*) must be received in its abstract form from the "universal intellect" and stored in the memory, which is part of the sensitive soul; it is then brought into being with the aid of the senses, to culminate in the individual physicalized experience (represented in the poem by the verb *amare*)' (Fisher 2002, 151).

The coda assumes a familiar poetic formula of envoi, or leave-taking, where the poem is a diplomatic emissary for Love's comprehension, aimed only at the elect who are receptive to the experience and understanding of Love. This reflects Pound's Neoplatonic focus in the link between *amor* and the hypostases of *nous*, *logos* and *dianoia*, and mediated by the tenth emanation of the active intellect. The canzone asserts the prerogative to wander freely, confident in its ornate art 'that thy reasons/Shall be praised from thy understanders' while the rest lack the 'will' to make meaningful commerce. These lines reinforce this association of Love and aesthetic Beauty in the elevated register, and the use of archaic pronouns and phrasal inversions characteristic of formal speech. At this point the reader might pause to consider the singular oddity of this rhetorical exercise: Pound has produced a translated poem that seeks to convince a Lady of the nature of Love, in which the speaker gives a philosophically adept and abstruse account of its function as an emanation from Nous, and its ability to 'graze' receptive human intellect into a recognition of its form, reflected in (recognized) Beauty and kept 'Where memory liveth'. The poem speaks exclusively, utterly unconcerned that those not adept at receiving such missives from the divine may simply pass by, oblivious. For Pound, this schema of hermetic wisdom also abides in the Troubadour poets: they speak a language of love and beauty conveyed through a vocabulary of precise definition. This bears direct consequences for the final section of Canto XXXVI.

Pound's translation of Cavalcanti's poem adumbrates the process where a sequence of light imagery – 'a diafan from light on shade', 'shadow cometh of Mars', 'Decendeth not by quality but shineth out' – represents the way *amor* embodies a thread from earthly experience to the divine realm. Cavalcanti also locates this in the sensitive soul, in a zone of darkness. The emphasis on 'natural demonstration' and reason by way of experience mitigates any temptation to figure *amor* as abstract or purely transcendent. Love installs itself in the human subject just as light rouses the potential for colour in objects: 'Being divided, set out from colour,/Disjunct in mid darkness/Grazeth the light'. The register and ingrained philosophical impetus of the poem lends it an hermetic allure, intended for the 'knowers' to whom the words register like light, or the way love grazes the possible intellect.

Pound bridges his translation of 'Donna mi prega' and a consideration of Eriugena's potential heresy by reference to the Thrones of Dante's *Paradiso*, 'Sù sono specchi, voi dicete Troni,/onde refulge a noi Dio giudicante':[27]

'Called thrones, balascio or topaze'
Eriugena was not understood in his time
'which explains, perhaps, the delay in condemning him'
And they went looking for Manicheans
And found, so far as I can make out, no Manicheans
So they dug for, and damned Scotus Eriugena
'Authority comes from right reason,
          never the other way on'
Hence the delay in condemning him
Aquinas head down in a vacuum,
          Aristotle which way in a vacuum? (XXXVI/179)

Dante refers to the celestial hierarchy – a tradition stemming from Pseudo-Dionysius (whose corpus Eriugena translated) and Pope Gregory the Great to Thomas Aquinas's *Summa Theologica* – a neat parallel to the theory of emanations Pound draws upon in Avicenna and Averroes. This motif of divine-human intercession links Cavalcanti's poem with the papal condemnations of Eriugena. Pound draws an association between the hermetic vocabulary and contemplative truth of Cavalcanti's poem and the unjust besmirching of Eriugena's reputation following his death. The critical focus given to the question of exhumation in this passage[28] is a function of Pound's apparent conflation of Eriugena with Amalric, who was indeed exhumed during the Aristotelian controversy of 1210. Pound's mention of exhumation again in *The Pisan Cantos* – 'and they dug him up out of sepulture' (LXXIV/449); 'so they dug up his bones in the time of De Montfort' (LXXXIII/548) – is likely a function of the constraints of composition in the Pisan DTC, and the absence of source material by which to verify historical events. The Council of Paris in 1210 decreed that copies of Eriugena's *Periphyseon* were to be burned along with those of Aristotle. The mention of Aquinas and Aristotle toward the end of this verse paragraph in Canto XXXVI might seem to imply a connection with Amalric: at the very least, it installs Pound's conception of Eriugena as a counterweight to what he considered to be the straitened scholastic logic of Aquinas.

Pound was reading deeply in medieval Islamic philosophy at the time he composed *Eleven New Cantos*, so it is not surprising that the diaphanous light imagery associated with Neoplatonism should appear at this point in his poem, and further, that direct associations should be drawn with Cavalcanti's canzone. Pound was also reading Robert Grossesteste, whose treatise *De Luce et de Icohatione Formarum* was an enormously influential cosmogony in the early thirteenth century, and through which Pound was exposed to the great Islamic philosophical tradition. That Pound cites Eriugena in the canto, instead of Avicenna, Averroes, Alfarabi or Grosseteste, is telling: at the time Pound had only read Eriugena second-hand in Italian high school philosophy textbooks, and was not to consult the relevant volume (122) of Migne's Patrologia Latina until several years later in 1939–1940. Pound's translation from Francesco Fiorentino's *Manuale di Storia della Filosofia* in Canto XXXVI ('Authority comes from right reason/never the other way on') becomes Eriugena's formula of political as well as ecclesiastical discourse for Pound.[29] Given the intensifying political context of his epic poem at the time of *Eleven New Cantos* – American Revolutionary history and Italian Fascism in the shadow of modern warfare and its economic underpinnings – Pound saw Eriugena as an appropriately sacrificial figure in formulating a radically bold but equally misunderstood Neoplatonist system of thought. Pound provides a neat bridge between the parts of this canto, proclaiming Cavalcanti's poem 'alive with Eriugenian vigour' (*MIN* 381). This connection is consolidated in Pound's mind when he eventually does read the *Periphyseon*, quoting Eriugena's phrase 'onmia quae sunt lumina sunt' in both Latin and English ('all things that are are lights') in his prose, in *The Pisan Cantos* and beyond. Eriugena functions as a kind of synecdoche for the so-called 'conspiracy of intelligence' beyond orthodox intellectual networks. Pound's admiration was magnified by his impression that Eriugena had performed as a kind of *vox sola* (or even a *vox clamantis in deserto*), without the support of a structured intellectual network such as the School of Chartres for William of Conches and John of Salisbury in the twelfth century, or Marsilio Ficino's Platonic Academy in Quattrocento Florence. In Eriugena, Pound saw a formidable intellect creating his own intellectual and textual community.

The third section of Canto XXXVI begins with an adapted Latin formula of Pound's invention – 'Sacrum, sacrum, inluminatio coitu' (the sacred, the sacred, illumination in coitus). This functions as a Latinate analogue to the Eleusinian Mysteries cited elsewhere in *The Cantos* (XLV, LI, LIII, *et passim*), which culminate in the *hieros gamos* (ἱερὸς γάμος), or 'the shower of the sacred', the sexual union of the high priestess and the hierophant. The thread of divine illumination by way of 'natural demonstration' unites this line with the erotic potential of 'Donna mi prega'. Pound connects the antecedent Troubadour poetic tradition to Cavalcanti and Dante by introducing the figure of Sordello in the following line – 'Lo Sordels si fo di Mantovana' – Sordello having spent time in exile in Provence. Rather than focus on the erotic mysteries Pound saw at work in Troubadour lyric (although Sordello's affair with Cunizza da Romano neatly ties in with the 'lady' of Cavalcanti's poem, and indeed Cunizza spent some time late in life at the residence of Cavalcante de' Cavalcanti), these lines swerve into a dynamic dialogical account of Sordello's economic and political affairs. Sordello da Goita (fl. 1220–1269), Italian by birth, came into his fortune as repayment for military service to Charles of Anjou, King of Sicily and Naples. Sordello's abrupt rise to power ('Five castles!') over several villages, including one famous for its textiles, establishes him as an active agent in his world, as well as poet. Pound quotes from the Latin document bestowing ownership of these properties – 'castra Montis Odorisii […]' – as well as from the letter Pope Clement IV sent to Charles, which ended Sordello's time in prison – '…way you treat your men is a scandal…'

Pound's splicing of (mediated, translated) primary material into his own poetic material forms a long-standing pattern across *The Cantos*, and here it can be seen to reflect and compound the preceding imagery: just as Cavalcanti promotes a process of 'natural demonstration' to illuminate the transit of Love from νους to the human possible intellect, Pound provides his own empirical example of the human agent receptive both to the divine, and to terrestrial experience that opens the way to the *paradiso terrestre*.[30] This culminates in the final line of Canto XXXVI – 'Quan ben m'albir e mon ric pensamen' (When I consider well in my fine thoughts) – taken from a poem in which Sordello meditates on the location of his experience of Love in the memory. Pound endorses a view of Sordello as one who willingly abdicates material wealth for the metaphysical illuminations of Love and the effulgence it bestows upon the poetic imagination. In this way, Canto XXXVI is a repository for such thinking, and physically frames Pound's iterative translations of Cavalcanti's subtle canzone. The canto comprises a zone apart, a 'shut garden' (Pryor 2011, 124–34): it is a still point amidst the statecraft, diplomacy and economy of Europe and the new American Republic of *Eleven New Cantos*.

Eriugena functions in Canto XXXVI as an emblem of persecution. He is an embodiment (an 'exhumed' one at that) of the way terrestrial power is abused in suppressing vital knowledge of the nature of *amor*: the divine thread joining sense perception and intellection in the memory. This is consistent with the way Eriugena is mediated for Pound in his sources: principally Fiorentino, but also Ernest Renan and Étienne Gilson. Pound reads sensitively the intellectual traditions in which Eriugena is situated by these authors, but as his reading deepens to include Eriugena's texts in Patrologia Latina 122, he becomes aware of the totalizing nature of divine illumination and the status of *paradiso* for Eriugena. The experience of *amor* is thus a first step to divine unification: for Eriugena, following Gregory of Nyssa, unification is a total *apocatastasis* (a return of all creation to God), including even sinners and the ignorant: 'paradise is human nature in its divine aspect – as it was originally and as it will be again in the return' (Dronke 1990, 218).[31] In Canto XXXVI, meanwhile, Pound enlists his philological skills, recently honed in the attempts to produce a scholarly edition of Cavalcanti's *Rime*, to adumbrate the Tuscan's most difficult poem, perhaps the most difficult poem in all of medieval literature. In his various commentaries, glosses and analyses, composed over many years and collected in the essay 'Cavalcanti', Pound draws together the threads of Islamic commentaries on Aristotle, Neoplatonic light philosophy, and the language of esoterism and election. In Canto XXXVI he augments this scholarly work in poetic translation, and resituates the entire framework of the poem in light of the mediated figure of Eriugena, who is full of promise as a neglected avatar of the metaphysical, ethical and political *paradiso* he attempts in the later *Cantos*.

Notes

1   During the Carolingian Age, the Palatine school would accompany the court as it moved around different locations in the Holy Roman Empire. Charlemagne's preferred residency was at Aachen, but Charles the Bald moved between Laon, Corbie and other locations, with a preference for Soissons, where he celebrated Easter more often than anywhere else. The certainty with which to posit the existence of a Palatine school as a formal structure facilitating a coherent program of study and disputation is more easily done with reference to the time of Charlemagne than to the time of Charles the Bald. For a careful account of the evidence see McKitterick 1981.

2   Several scholars have addressed Pound's intermittent citation of medieval textual practices, although not systematically. For an early example, in the first number of *Paideuma*, see Chase.

3   These texts were attributed for centuries to Dionysius the Areopagite, the Athenian converted to Christianity by Saint Paul and referred to in Acts 17. An unknown Syrian author composed these texts some time in the fifth century, who was later conflated with Saint Denis, patron saint of Paris (and thus of significance to Charles, King of Francia). (See Rorem 1993 for a comprehensive commentary on the texts; Rorem 1995 for a study of Eriugena's commentary on *The Celestial Hierarchy*; and Luibheid 1987 for translations of the texts.)

4   See the Introduction to Johannis Scotti Eriugenae, *Periphyseon (De divisione naturae)*, Book 1 (Sheldon-Williams in Eriugena 1968, 1–10).

5   Eriugena's *Periphyseon* was banned at the University of Paris in the condemnation of 1210 among other texts and teachings implicated in the Amalrician heresy considered to exhibit shades of pantheism: Amalric's view of divinity was seen 'to imply that Nature is a vast and sacred theophany [... in which] the body of God is quite literally everywhere: *corpus Domini est ubique*' (Davenport 6). Eriugena's work was again swept up in the condemnation of 1270, in which aspects of Aristotle's natural philosophy were at issue, especially the Averroist commentaries on *De Anima*. See Pederson 1997, 280–86.

6   Édouard Jeauneau has produced an authoritative five-volume Latin edition of the *Periphyseon* in the Brepols series Corpus Christianorum Continuatio Medievalis (1996–2003).

7   See his essay 'Ecclesiastical History,' in *SP* 61–3; this essay was first published in *The New English Weekly*, 5 July 1934.

8   Pound wrote to Otto Bird on 9 January 1938 to request information from Bird or Étienne Gilson regarding Eriugena's serial condemnations. He wrote to Santayana on 8 December 1939 and 16 January 1940, and to Otto Bird on 12 January 1940. Pound's letter to Eliot of 18 January 1940 from Rapallo suggests his possession of Patrologia Latina 122 on his return from Venice. According to Tim Redman it was Ubaldo degli Uberti, editor of the journal *Marina Repubblicana*, who located the volume for Pound (195). See *SL* 304–05 and 330–35. Two sets of notes, pertaining to research in Venice and Rapallo respectively, are located in the Beinecke Library Ezra Pound Collection: YCAL MSS 43 Box 77, Folder 3383 and Box 77, Folder 3406. I am grateful to Professor Ronald Bush for kindly permitting me access to a draft version of an essay, now published, in which he establishes and describes the incorporation of these materials into early drafts of unpublished cantos, especially the Italian drafts of early 1945, which are pivotal documents in the textual genesis of *The Pisan Cantos* (Bush 2013). This history will form part of the Critical Edition of Ezra Pound's *Pisan Cantos* (Oxford University Press) under the direction of Ronald Bush and David Ten Eyck.

9   '*Ubi post aliquot annos, a pueris quos decobat grafiis foratus, animam exuit.*' William of Malmesbury, *Gesta Pontificam Anglorum*, 240.7–8, fo. 92r, 588–89. Note that William's twelfth-century copy of the *Periphyseon* [*Cambridge Trin. Coll. O.5.20*] eventually passed down to Thomas Gale, whose seventeenth-century edition of the text was the basis for all subsequent editions until the mid-twentieth century. The probable source for William's claim was that he 'seems to have identified John the Scot with "John my priest" named by King Alfred in his prologue to the translation of Gregory's *Pastoral Care*' (Thompson 2007, 291).

10   Peter Dronke claims that '[w]hen putting forward some of his most original thought, Eriugena felt he needed an *auctoritas*' (1990, 219) and provides as an

example *Periphyseon* IV, 822A where Eriugena attributes his notion of paradise ('human nature in its divine aspect') to Gregory of Nyssa: 'where he is ostensibly just following Gregory, he is also quietly radicalizing him' (219). Édouard Jeauneau provides other examples in Eriugena's theory of sexual differentiation, also curiously attributed by him to Gregory of Nyssa (1987, 347).

11 Fiorentino refers here to the Alexandrian tradition of biblical hermeneutics, which saw allegory as a principal tool for exegesis. This tradition usually centres upon Origen and his homilies on the Old Testament, especially his *Homilies on Leviticus*.

12 Amalric of Bene taught philosophy and theology at the University of Paris in the first decade of the thirteenth century. He taught that all are from God and thus of God, echoing Eriugena's doctrine of participation. This was considered heretically pantheistic and was first condemned by the university in 1206 – its first documented case of academic censure – and then by Pope Innocent III in 1210. Following his death, ten of his followers were burnt outside the city gates: for a detailed account of the trial and punishment, see Dickson (1987 and 1989). Amalric was excommunicated and his body was exhumed and reburied in unconsecrated ground (Thijssen 1996, 43; Maccagnolo 1992, 435). His doctrines were formally condemned at the Fourth Lateran Council of 1215 alongside those of Joachim of Fiore in Canon 2. His name is given variously as Amaury de Bène (French), Amalricus/Almaricus (Latin), Amalrico di Bena (Italian, i.e. in Fiorentino), and Amalric of Bene (English): the latter form is used henceforth.

13 The order to excommunicate and disinter Amalric also ordered a ban on the works of David of Dinant. See Théry (15) for the Latin text and Thorndike (26–7) and Thijssen (1996, 44–5) for English translations. See also Maccagnolo for a comprehensive treatment of David's wrongful implication in the controversy. Far from courting ecclesiastical ire, David was in good standing with the Church: he served as papal chaplain to Innocent III in 1205–1206 (Thijssen 1996, 43).

14 Paolo Lucentini corroborates Moody's conclusion by independent means: he shows that the first time Eriugena and Amalric are mentioned together is in 1271, in Enrico Susa's *Lectura in quinque libros decretalium*, more than 60 years *after* the condemnation of 1210 (174). Susa asserts three 'errors' of the *Periphyseon*, namely: that all things are God; that the primordial cause is both created and creates; and that the *reditus* entails the unification of the sexes. To these errors Martino di Troppau adds others in his redaction of the *Chronicon pontificum et imperatorum* of 1271–1272 (Lucentini 175). Enrico's and Martino's false affiliations of Eriugena with Amalric are compounded by the lack of familiarity with any Eriugenian doctrinal matter in their texts. Further, Alberico di Trois-Fontaines is the first to link Eriugena with the Albigensian heresy in his *Chronica* of 1230–1235 (Lucentini 186–87): thus Eriugena's condemnation in 1225 is neither initiated by the Amalrician crisis of 1206–1210, nor by direct implication with Cathar beliefs. However Dronke (1990, 225) notes that the Amalrician belief that hell is not a place

but a state of ignorance, confessed in the trial of 1210, strongly resembles Eriugena's view in *De praedestinatione*. See also d'Alverny 333.

15 The terms 'active' and 'possible' intellect enter philosophical discourse in the West only with the reintroduction of Aristotle's *De Anima* in 1220 in the Arabo-Latin version of Michael Scot (McInerny x). As Moran points out, however, Eriugena's notion of mind as a self-manifestation out of a hidden unknowing bears a striking analogy, and thus might explain how Eriugena came to be confused with the Latin Averroist interpretations of Aristotle in the thirteenth century (286).

16 Pound does not mention the direct influence Eriugena had on Hegel, who was especially taken with Eriugena's argument from 'right reason' as an expression of the idealist priority of intellect over the understanding (see Beierwaltes 1973, 190–98). Moran considers Eriugena's corpus as a deconstruction of Latin ontotheology generally, and more specifically a rejection of the Augustinian equation of *esse* with 'I Am Who I Am' of Exodus 3.14 (99–102). This view resonates with the Heideggerian project of dismantling Western metaphysics and ontotheology. Eriugena also understands the Greek sense of *physis* as a structure of concealing and revealing, but adapts its parameters of *chronos* (time) and *peras* (limit) to *apeiron* (infinite) and timelessness (Moran 244).

17 Pound mentions Eriugena and Grosseteste several times as members of an occluded tradition, although he was likely unaware of the extent of their intellectual affiliations, including shared influences in Latin (Augustine, Boethius, Macrobius) and Greek (Basil of Caesarea, Gregory of Nyssa). Grosseteste also composed an *Hexaemeron*, translated the four treatises of Pseudo-Dionysius in the years 1239–43 with the aid of Eriugena's translations, and elsewhere made use of Eriugena's commentary on *The Celestial Hierarchy* (McEvoy 1987, 201; see also Callus 1945 and 1955, 1–69).

18 This abridgement is Pound's adaptation from Wilfred A Schoff's translation of *The Periplus of Hanno* (Terrell 1984, 165).

19 Although it seems that several of Pound's cantos were discovered among Mussolini's papers after his death (Feldman 2012, 96, n.12, citing Eastman 1979b).

20 The version of 'Donna mi prega' in Canto XXXVI is distinctive in that it was not intended for facing-page comparison with an edited version of Cavalcanti's text. For further details of this textual history, see Anderson 1983, passim.

21 See Ezra Pound, 'Cavalcanti' (*MIN* 360). Note that Pound makes no account of the probable influence of Averroes on the thought of Aquinas, not to mention the potential influence of Eriugena himself.

22 Pound's notebooks documenting his archival and philological work towards an edition of Cavalcanti's *Rime* are housed within the Ezra Pound Collection at the Beinecke Library, Yale University. (Their numbers and running titles in the

Bibliography reflect the Beinecke's accession information; see also de Rachewiltz 1980 for further information.)

23 It should be noted that the poetry of the *trobairitz* or female troubadours has since become a rigorous field of study in medieval lyric. For a selection of edited texts and analysis, see: Dronke 1984; Bogin 1980; and Bruckner 1985.

24 Pound shows uncanny judgement in his combining Cavalcanti's trope of light with the dialectic of Eriugena rather than that of Grosseteste in this canto. As Moran notes of the *Periphyseon*, a text that Pound had yet to read when composing Canto XXXVI: 'Given this recognition of the impenetrable darkness of the Divinity, and the utter reliance of human intellects on the divine power and illuminating grace, the participants [Alumnus and Nutritor, in the *Periphyseon*] firmly place their trust in true reason (*recta ratio*) to steer their course' (73). Moran also points out that *recta ratio* and *vera ratio* were favourite phrases of Augustine's.

25 This mode of election bears a distinct affinity to Augustine's doctrine of predestination, where free will must be augmented by divine grace in order to achieve salvation: free will alone is not sufficient. See Augustine, *De libero arbitrio* 3.18.51; see also Stump 130–33.

26 In his commentary on Peter Lombard's *Sententiae*, Aquinas also makes the distinction between the active or agent intellect, which takes the form of intelligible light, and the possible intellect of the receptive human mind, in which intelligible light abstracts forms from sense perceptions or phantasmata. Thus knowledge for Aquinas is strictly *per similitudinem*, in contrast to Eriugena's epistemology wherein the theophanic vision is God presenting himself by way of kataphasis. See Dominic J. O'Meara (1987).

27 'Above there are mirrors, you call them/Thrones, and from them God's judging shines to us' (Canto IX, ll. 61–2), qtd. in Dante Alighieri, *The Divine Comedy*, *Paradiso* (2011, 190–91).

28 See Kenner 1975, 451; Liebregts 2004, 203–23; Makin 1973, 60–83; Michael 1972, 37–54; and Moody 1996, 241–47.

29 See 'Ecclesiastical History,' *SP* 61 and *GK* 74, 168, and 333.

30 Peter Dronke (1990, 214) finds a telling exegetical symmetry between Eriugena and such thirteenth-century Aristotelians as Siger of Brabant and Boethius of Dacia: where Eriugena attempts to harmonize the antithetical views of Augustine and the Greek Fathers in exegesis, the Parisian Aristotelians expound arguments of Aristotle and Averroes impartially, without judging their truth-claims. For Dronke this is a defensive gesture, but its eminent relevance to Pound's recuperative views of Cavalcanti's thought is plain, as it is in Pound's own pursuit of 'right reason'.

31 See *Periphyseon* IV 822A: 'Quisquis diligenter praefati theologi uerba perspexerit, nil aliud, ut opinor, in eis reperiet suaderi quam humanam naturam ad imaginem

dei factam paradisi uocabulo, figuratae locutionis modo, a diuina scriptura
significari' ('Whoever looks closely into the words of this theologian [Gregory of
Nyssa] will find that his teaching is none other than the word Paradise is a mere
figure of speech by which Holy Scripture signifies the human nature that was made
in the image of God' [Sheldon-Williams in Eriugena 1995, 189]).

2

John Scottus Eriugena:
The Meeting of Athens and Rome in Gaul

Pound came to Eriugena by reading philosophical textbooks on classical, medieval Islamic and European philosophy. The medieval philosophers and theologians with whom Pound became most fascinated during these years – Robert Grosseteste, Richard of St Victor, Michael Psellus, Gemisthus Plethon, Avicenna, Averroes – were active centuries after Eriugena, by which time the world that produced him had faded from view. This relative historical isolation presents a temptation to bracket Eriugena from Pound's main line of thought on matters of the Trinity, mystical contemplation and the νοῦς; and other matters concentrating in the Neoplatonic tradition and its intersections with Christianity. Yet it would be equally ill-advised to read Eriugena's significance complacently or ahistorically, as though he is contemporaneous with these later thinkers. The task is rather to take his writing in its historical context, to be sensitive to the cultural moment in which it formed and was distributed, and the techniques by which it was disseminated: in the teaching heritage of the cathedral schools of Laon, Reims and Corbie as well as in textual glosses and florilegia contained in their libraries. Eriugena's significance as an original thinker is also shaped by how he deploys his primary influences: those of the western European tradition such as Augustine, Boethius, Martianus Capella and the known texts of Aristotle, and those from the eastern Christian tradition such as Maximus the Confessor, Pseudo-Dionysius and the Cappodocian Fathers, Basil of Caesarea, Gregory of Nyssa and Gregory Nazianzus.

This chapter surveys Eriugena's intellectual and historical milieu, his patronage in the court of Charles the Bald, the controversies in which he was enlisted and implicated, and the means by which his work survived and was subsequently transmitted to students and scholars. The following material is an exhaustive analysis neither of his oeuvre nor of the scholarly field that has grown around his work: the limits of space preclude such a detailed study, not to mention the formidable scholarly and philological expertise required to do it justice. However, rapid gains in scholarship over the last generation – both in Eriugena Studies and in Carolingian history – informs much of the discussion to follow. This chapter will assess elements of the works that attracted Pound's eye most acutely: the doctrinal, ecclesiastical and courtly implications of the Predestination controversy of 859–60; Eriugena's translation of and commentary on *The Celestial Hierarchy* of Pseudo-Dionysius; elements of the *Periphyseon* (*De divisione naturae*) concerning apophatic and kataphatic theology as well as the divine cycle of *processio* and *reditus*; and Eriugena's devotional and courtly poetry, the *Carmina*. These elements must be understood within the context of Eriugena's thought more generally: his dialectical understanding of reason and authority as tools of scholarly disputation; the tropological significance of light as an expression of theophany, including its absence or 'dark' superabundance; Eriugena's sophisticated meontology (the study of that which does not exist) which functions perspectivally; and his anthropology, in which humanity plays a central role as the agent through which all creation is manifested and through which the *reditus* is initiated. These aspects of Eriugena's thought occupy extended portions of his principal texts, and are considered *inter alia* in the following account of his major texts and life events. Although Pound did not progress beyond a transient familiarity with these texts and ideas, he discerned their potential significance for his own work. Close attention to Carolingian textual practices (glossing, annotation, florilegia) also affirms the surprisingly extensive material affinities between Eriugena's texts and Pound's textual experiments in *The Cantos*: the use of ideograms, epistolary material, poetic space, annotation and the splicing of historical documents and other texts into his poetry. Some of these topics will be explored in the context of *The Pisan Cantos* in the final chapter, especially the use of ideograms and the strong affinities Pound draws between Eriugena's thought and that of the Confucian tradition, the central texts of which Pound had translated during and after his second phase of research into Eriugena's thought. But here it remains to sketch out the primary concepts and disputes that drew Pound's attention, and the texts and historical contexts in which they arise.

Nemo Intrat in Caelum nisi per Philosophiam: The world of Eriugena

In *The Pisan Cantos* Pound serially makes mention of Eriugena's easy relations with his patron, Charles the Bald: they trade poetic phrases and exchange witticisms across the dining table whilst Charles's queen knits his socks. These light-hearted exchanges belie the severe difficulties Charles faced during his tenure as king, and eventually as Holy Roman Emperor (he was crowned in 875). They also silently pass over the intense interest Charles took in doctrinal matters, as well as the state of learning in his kingdom. Charles commissioned Eriugena to translate the works of Pseudo-Dionysius, unhappy with the state of the translation by Hilduin (Abbot of St Denis in Paris) from the copy presented by the Byzantine Emperor, Michael the Stammerer, to his father Louis the Pious in 827 (Marenbon 1988, 59). Charles reigned in a confraternal arrangement with his much older half-brothers, Louis the German and Lothar. This uneasy government inherited from Louis the Pious precipitated the gradual fragmentation of the territories of Charlemagne and a general onset of political instability. Indeed Lothar took control of the Empire whilst his father was still alive, and at one point had him imprisoned as a penitent. Charles has been portrayed as a weak and ineffective leader, but more recent scholarship shows his reputation was more one of a canny and able ruler, working within difficult parameters (see Nelson 1992). France has appropriated Charles as the first ruler of the first properly recognizable French nation: his grandfather as Holy Roman Emperor was ruler of territories that are now as German as they are French. Nelson quotes the epigraphic inscription on the obelisk at Fontenoy-en-Puisaye, the site of Charles's military victory with his brother Louis over Lothar (who was at that point the Holy Roman Emperor): 'La victoire de Charles-le-Chauve sépara la France de l'empire d'Occident et fonda l'indépendance de la nation français' (The victory of Charles the Bald annexed France from the Eastern Empire and founded the independent French nation) (Nelson 1992, 1; my translation). However, Charles's reign was threatened most directly by his half-brother Louis, following the death of the Emperor Lothar in 855. Charles's territories were twice invaded, and Louis's longevity meant that the two kingdoms were intertwined politically and fraternally; Louis died only a year earlier than Charles, who was 17 years his junior. Pound ignores this fraternal context, although in all fairness Nelson makes the same complaint of recent British Carolingian scholars. Charles's emulation of Theodosius and Justinian in his *capitularies* (legislative acts) resonates with Pound's interest in Procopius, whose *Secret History* portrays Emperor Justinian as a weak ruler, deceived by the connivances of Empress Theodora. Eriugena may represent learning and theological disputation, but he entered a world replete with vigorous forms of territorial dispute. His activity in the royal court would have lent him some insight into the challenges of maintaining territorial integrity and economic security, whilst negotiating matters of doctrine with members of a divisive and outspoken ecclesiastical hierarchy.[1] This latter issue would impinge upon Eriugena directly in the Predestination controversy, shaping his activities in Charles's kingdom thereafter.

Charles's capacity to rule unimpeded was complicated by the active role of ecclesiastical figures in Carolingian political life. Charles inherited this situation from the reign of his father Louis the Pious, during which the Frankish episcopate grew in influence (McKeon 1978, 7), but this process was a feature of the Carolingian age from the beginning. Charlemagne's father, Pepin the Short, initiated the identification of Church and Empire in 751 by enlisting papal support for the legitimacy of his ascent to the Frankish throne. His restoration of the ecclesiastical hierarchy saw his son gain the benefit of being crowned Holy Roman Emperor by Pope Leo III on Christmas Day in the year 800. The newly powerful ecclesiastical class shared an interest in the preservation of imperial political structures: 'in the reign of Charles' successors this group came to be involved more and more prominently in the workings of the empire, as events in the forty years following Charles' death necessitated rapid reinterpretation of that entity' (McKeon 1974, 437). The long-term consequences of this association was that 'if it could be argued in the north that the Frankish episcopate figured the empire, papal authority might well be used with at least equal force by an emperor seeking to assert his rule' (445–46).

The singular circumstances of Charles the Bald's reign – as an embattled and much younger half-brother to Lothar and Louis the German – were anticipated by the interference of Ebbo, Archbishop of Reims, in the affairs of Charles's father, Louis the Pious. Louis married Charles's mother, Judith, only four months after the death of his first wife Irmingarde (mother to Lothar, Louis the German and Pepin of Aquitaine). Judith was seen to exert undue influence on Louis, especially following the birth of Charles in 823, to whom royal preference was given from an early age. The political circumstances that consumed Louis's kingdom included viking raids, as well as the various intrigues of Lothar (named co-Emperor in 817), Louis the German and Pepin – most notably, the 832 plot to overthrow Louis, which culminated in 833 with the aid of Lothar. The general tone of filial disloyalty was only exacerbated by Louis's apparent diffidence. Ebbo remained loyal to the deposed Emperor when the latter was held captive at Saint-Médard de Soissons, convincing him to make a public confession and receive punishment as a penitent. Louis renounced the throne rather than face deposition. Ebbo changed sides to support Lothar, whose own rule failed: Lothar fled to Italy, and Ebbo was detained at Fulda on attempting to flee into Danish territory (443). Ebbo then fronted a *conventus* (an ecclesiastical hearing) of 40 bishops where Louis's deposition was deemed improper, upon which he was restored to the throne: 'On 28 February the assembly met in the cathedral of Saint Stephen at Metz, where the effects of Louis's resignation at Saint Médard were reversed when he received his crown back from the hands of the bishops' (443). Ebbo resigned his post and returned to Fulda. Following Louis's death in 840, Lothar's quarrel with Louis the German and young Charles over the right to rule was complicated by Ebbo's fate, which raised questions of his right to determine ecclesiastical matters, and therefore to endorse the legitimacy of rule. The Treaty of Verdun in 843 established the divided rule of the northern lands between Lothar, Louis and Charles: 'the western episcopate evolved a new formula for imperial rule, one founded not upon unitary rule but rather in a program of fraternal concord under Episcopal supervision' (444). Charles resisted Lothar's negotiations with the new Pope Sergius, and Hincmar, having displaced Ebbo, began his long episcopate in 845 at the council of Beauvais. Thus Charles's coming into power was ordained by reversals in ecclesiastical fortunes, as well as political fortunes of kings, all of which were presumed to have been temporal expressions of the will of God. It is worth noting that Gottschalk was protégé to Ebbo at Reims, foreshadowing his later troubles with Hincmar. Ebbo didn't contest any of this, choosing at first to remain in Italy, then moving to Hildesheim where he saw out his days as bishop in the years 846–51. Thus the twin threads of political rule and ecclesiastical exercise of temporal power fundamentally shaped the world of Eriugena: Pound may not have been aware of how profoundly entwined these entities actually were, but the theme resonates with his own interests expressed throughout *The Cantos*.

Irish in Frankish lands

The long history of Irish monastic scholarship in Western Europe takes hold with the figure of Columbanus in the late sixth century. Charlemagne recruited the Irish scholars Dungal and Dicuil along with Alcuin of York and the Lombard Paul the Deacon (Moran 8). From the mid-ninth century, Irish monks and pilgrims travelled through Laon territories. Péronne for example was the site of Perrona Scottorum, a seventh-century ecclesiastical foundation and the site of Saint Fursa's tomb (Contreni 1978, 81). The Carolingian familiarity with Irish scholars and monks is evident in the efforts to retain the infrastructure of pilgrimage: 'The Council of Meaux in 845 condemned the alienation of the *hospitalia scottorum*, shelters and way-stations for Irish pilgrims, and asked the help of Charles the Bald in restoring the hospices to the Irishmen' (82). In addition to their presence at court or on pilgrimage routes throughout the kingdom, the Irish were also to be found in the cathedral schools: 'At Cambrai, Bishop Albericus (763–90) had a collection of Irish canons copied in his scriptorium [the *Collectio canonum Hiberniensis*]' (82). The scholar Dunshad at Saint Remigius taught the texts of Martianus Capella, helping to initiate the seven liberal arts as the core curriculum in the kingdom. Sedulius Scottus was master at Liège and oversaw a fledgeling Irish community. His arrival on the continent has been 'plausibly associated with a record in the Frankish court annals of an embassy from the King of the Irish to Charles the Bald in 848, announcing Irish victories over the vikings and requesting safe passage for the king to make a pilgrimage to Rome' (Byrne 1984, xix; qtd in Ahlqvist 1988, 197). The remarkably persistent myth of the so-called 'Irish colony' at Laon is founded on two traditional but erroneous assumptions: 'that John Scottus himself taught at Laon and that Laon was the site of Charles the Bald's palace school' (Contreni 1978, 83). There is no evidence for Eriugena having taught at the cathedral school, although he is known to have had some contact with Martin Hiberniensis, for which there is documentary evidence.

Eriugena's intellectual life centred instead on the court and the Palatine school, such as it was, but he maintained contact with the cathedral school. Its cosmopolitanism was typical of the schools and scriptoria at the time: 'Copying centers, such as the one created at Reims by Archbishop Hincmar, had to be in touch with the whole Christian world in order to have access to the texts that they were commissioned to copy' (Tavard 1996, 17). If no 'Irish colony' existed at Laon, a strong Irish element could be found in nearby monastic centres. As Contreni notes, the relationship with the school was peripheral, with the exception of Martin Hiberniensis. Rather, '[t]heir relationship with Laon *and* with other centers permits us to view ninth-century intellectual activity in a dynamic setting and to underscore the contacts Laon had with other centers' (Contreni 1978, 79). In this context, Eriugena is first mentioned in the letter from Bishop Pardulus of Laon to the church at Lyons in 851 or 852 during the Predestination controversy (Moran 27). Contreni speculates that Eriugena may have spent his early years on the continent, probably in the Rhine valley, based on his letter lamenting the separation from Winibertus of Strasbourg, with whom he was working on a commentary of Martianus Capella at the time (Contreni 1978, 86). His tenure at court entailed appreciable time at Laon, evident in his friendship with Wulfad of Reims to whom he dedicated the *Periphyseon* and who later became abbot of Saint-Médard de Soissons, and eventually Archbishop of Bourges.

> Laon was also within the orb of John's activities as the letter of Pardulus suggests. Martin Hiberniensis drew on John's poetry for his Greek-Latin glossary and grammar. The same manuscript [444] contains a reference by Martin to Dionysius the Areopagite, a reference which reflects the translation of John Scottus. (86)

Eriugena's only student recorded with any certainty is Bishop Wicbald of Auxerre. His circle of Irish contacts would have included Fergus at Laon, who in turn extended the network to Sedulius Scottus and his circle at Liège, who refers to Fergus affectionately in a poem (89).

Further documentary evidence for the Irish diaspora in Western Europe includes the Irish manuscript *Bern Burgerbibliothek 363* dating from the last quarter of the ninth century:

> The manuscript is especially interesting for its marginalia which make numerous references to various ninth-century figures. Sedulius is mentioned more than 200 times. John Scottus is also frequently mentioned in marginal notes. Fergus also occurs, but less frequently. In addition to these three Irishmen there are: Dubthach, Suadbar, Comgan, Dungal, Colgu, Cormac, Macc Longain, Mac Ciallain, Taircheltach, Robartaich, Brigit (the saint), and Cathasach. (91–2)

Further evidence may be found in the use of Irish words in contemporary biblical glosses, suggesting that Eriugena taught a number of Irish scholars at least partly in their native language (93). Laon Manuscript 444 embodies crucial evidence for the intellectual networks in Laon and in locations elsewhere with which the cathedral school had contact. Contreni contends that it was copied under Martin's supervision at Laon, but its erroneous placement of various Old Irish quire signatures suggests that it was copied from an Irish source text, 'either a manuscript copied in Ireland or a continental manuscript copied under Irish supervision' (58). Palaeographical analysis has determined that Martin copied part of the manuscript and added a table of contents: as master of the cathedral school, this suggests that he employed the manuscript as a scholarly and teaching tool. His glossary reveals the kinds of materials to which students had access in the school – Macrobius, Priscian, Theophrastus, Martianus Capella – but also several poems by Eriugena, various prayers, grammatical notes and dialogues in Greek, as well as the *De declineationes grecorum* (70). It has been called 'the most important repository of Greek paradigms, word-lists, and textual excerpts that survives from the Carolingian age' (6). The cathedral library also possessed

Eriugena's commentary on the Gospel of John and his commentary on *The Celestial Hierarchy* of Pseudo-Dionysius, as well as several poems.[2]

Advances in recent decades in interpreting codicological and palaeographical evidence (textual glosses, the provenance of various scripts in florilegia and grammars) have aided the identification of various scholarly practices and even of individual scholars in the Carolingian centres of learning. Yet Contreni notes as recently as 1978 the paucity of specific historical information concerning Laon, despite its emblematic role in Carolingian intellectual life in Greek studies and as a centre for copyists. Two important commentaries of Matianus Capella's *De nuptiis Philologiae et Mercurii* are attributed to Laon, representative of its authoritative presence in this renewed scholarly paradigm. Despite its most famous scholarly products, the school's 'masters, students, books, and the nature and extent of the school's influence are hardly known' (1). The first generation in the golden age of the cathedral school at Laon was organized around Martin Hiberniensis (c. 819–75). Manuscripts such as Laon 444 provide evidence of Eriugena's scholarly contacts with Laon, direct or otherwise, but Contreni notes that neither Martin nor Eriugena are mentioned in the cathedral records, the *Annales Laudunenses et sancti Vincentii Mettensis breves*. Martin is known to have read the *Periphyseon*, and Marenbon contends that manuscript evidence suggests his familarity with the *Categoriae Decem* (the 'Ten Categories' derived from Aristotle). Despite this, their mutual influence is thought to have been limited by differences in temperament (Marenbon 1981, 111). The Laon cathedral school bore the distinction of its Imperial provenance: when Remigius – Archbishop of Reims – baptized Clovis on Christmas Day in 496, he was rewarded with an enlarged estate and the power to establish his own diocese. This founding connection with Reims continued in the form of a prayer association, wherein monks in each centre would trade in prayers of intercession (12). The royal connection in Laon was consolidated by Salaberga's founding of the female monastic foundation, Notre Dame-la-Profonde, in 640, attracting wives and widows of Merovingian royalty (15).

The distinctive Irish complexion of learning at Laon did not reach a level of ubiquity sufficient to realize the claim of an Irish 'school'. However, Laon was the Carolingian centre of learning in the latter half of the ninth century, inheriting at least some of its Hibernian hues from Irish monasteries in the Rhine valley. Irish figures at Laon such as Fergus and Cathasach were also associated with Sedulius Scottus at Liège. Martin Hiberniensis shows tendencies in his manuscripts that derive from the Rhine region, suggesting a link with Probus of Mainz (Marenbon 1981, 165). The indisputable Irish strength in Greek studies may have derived from these monasteries in Germanic lands as much as from Ireland itself: 'It seems certain that [Martin] received his education in Greek on the Continent from Irishmen' (165). The strength in grammatical instruction in the Carolingian renaissance is significant as a specific hermeneutic approach to scripture, in which the interpretation of words was a way to grapple with the nature of reality. Interpretive variation generated 'a dynamism born of contradiction and a tireless effort to understand better the Word' (167). The pedagogical context is striking in its affinities with the kinds of inquiry most valued by Pound: the precise definition of words as the starting principle for any philosophical investigation, whether in the Confucian, classical, Neoplatonist or modern philosophical domain; the importance of grammar as a propaedeutic towards hermeneutic study of texts; and the intensive priority placed on the proper representation of textual material to insure the sustained transmission of valuable cultural or theological knowledge. Perhaps largely unbeknownst to him, Pound's intellectual interests intersect with those of the Carolingian scholarly domain. More importantly, the methods by which he furthered those interests show a profound sensitivity to late antique and early medieval scholarly methods.

The political influence of Laon in the ninth and tenth centuries functioned inversely with the strength of the Carolingian monarchy: a weak centre of imperial power would raise the profile of its leading ecclesiastical figures, much as the example of Ebbo, Archbishop of Reims demonstrates. The rule of Charles the Bald raised the profile of the local bishops, perhaps most floridly illustrated in the power struggle between Hincmar, Archbishop of Reims, and his nephew, Hincmar, Bishop of Laon, in which Eriugena was indirectly implicated by virtue of the doctrinal consequences of the Predestination controversy of the 850s. Hincmar of Laon rejected the patronage of both his uncle and Charles, resulting in his deposition and blinding as punishment for transgressing temporal and ecclesiastical powers and therefore contravening the principle of divine right (Contreni 1978, 21). Hincmar presents a fascinating portrait in the realpolitik consequences of advancing an argument from reason rather than acceding to authority: an ideological position with which Pound would express much sympathy in the case of Eriugena and others. Following Charles's troubled hold on power, Laon became a political centre of the rapidly crumbling Carolingian realm (18). The scholarly centre of activity shifted from Laon to Auxerre during this time, however, having imported the scholarly texts and habits of learning from Martin and Eriugena. Heiric of Auxerre cites the *Periphyseon* in his *Life of Saint Germanus* and in glosses attributed to him in a number of important manuscripts,[3] especially those derived from Greek philosophy. His pupil Remigius 'wrote a commentary of the *De nuptiis* of Martianus Capella which is a skillful amalgam of the commentaries of John Scottus and the anonymous commentary sometimes attributed to Martin' (141–42). Both Bernard of Laon and Adelelm – the latter was master at Laon after Martin and Heiric, at the time when the links between Laon and Auxerre were at their strongest – donated many books once owned by Martin to the library at Laon. This continuity of learning operates in stark distinction from the changing fortunes of ecclesiastical and imperial power in the Carolingian realm.

The sacred nectar of the Greeks

The efflorescence of Greek in the ninth century was intimately tied to the presence of Irish scholars in the Carolingian kingdom. Heiric of Auxerre praised Charles's wisdom in his patronage of Greek learning on presenting his *Life* of Saint Germanus to the king: 'he wrote to Charles that even Greece was envious because its learning had been transferred to the kingdom of Charles' (Contreni 1978, 81). The Irish facility for Greek precedes this epoch, however: 'Bède affirme avoir encore connu des disciples de Théodore « qui parlaient le latin et le grec comme leur langue maternelle »' (Bede is said to have known the disciples of Theodore [of Canterbury, who taught in Ireland] "who speak Latin and Greek like it's their mother tongue") (Gilson 1922, 11; my translation). Eriugena's knowledge of Greek was 'unrivalled in the transalpine West in his time and for more than two centuries afterwards' (Contreni 5–6). The German medievalist Ludwig Traube notes 'that all knowledge of Greek in the Frankish dominions in the middle of the ninth century appears to have had an Irish source' (Kenny 1966, 572). This phenomenon arises in the context of a long-standing antagonism between the Carolingian world and Byzantium going back to Charlemagne and the anti-Greek polemics of the *Libri Carolini*,[4] a response to the Second Council of Nicaea of 787 (Meyendorff 52). The antagonism was newly inflamed in the 850s when Pope Nicholas I objected to the deposition of Ignatius from the Constantinopolitan Patriarchate by Photios in 857, just when Eriugena was translating Pseudo-Dionysius. Frakes notes that '[i]n most essential respects continental scholarship of this period [the latter half of the ninth century] could be characterized as dominate by the Irish, and thereafter by their students (among whom Remigius and his teacher Heiric are, of course, also to be numbered)' (Frakes 1988, 240).

Eriugena and Sedulius have come to epitomize the shift in scholarly method 'away from grammatical studies towards commentary on what were to become "school authors"' (Frakes 240). It was in this scholarly environment where Irish scholars began to borrow from antique grammarians, and to produce compendia, a textual form by which the *accessus ad auctores* developed: this genre comprised a prefatory account of the vital facts of an author's life and work, from the simple formula of *persona, locus, tempus, causa scribendi* to the seven-fold *circumstantiae* formula of *quis, quid, cur, quomodo, quando, ubi, quibus facultatibus* (229). Eriugena produces a variant of the *accessus* in Book I of the *Periphyseon* in his catalogue of the Aristotelian Categories, in both Greek and Latin. Frakes attributes the *circumstantiae* formula of the *accessus* to Eriugena:

> it seems only fitting that this rhetorical formula, which was most directly transmitted to the Middle Ages by the primary mediator of Greco-Latin culture of late antiquity – Boethius – was revived and recast as a Greco-Latin formula of *accessus* pre-eminently by Irish scholars and their continental students during the ninth and tenth centuries, especially by the prime representative of the theologico-philosophical branch of this group of scholars, Eriugena. (245)

The persistent myth of Eriugena as an isolated genius ushering Greek Neoplatonism into Western Europe often relies upon assertions of his near-unique linguistic facility in Greek. As long ago as 1933, Dom Maïeul Cappuyns provided an antidote to this febrile notion, showing that Eriugena was deeply entrenched in the context of his times, and in his own networks; more recently such scholars as Édouard Jeauneau and John Contreni have provided further evidence for these networks. John Marenbon assembles documentary evidence to show: 'historically, that so far from being isolated, John was a thinker whose work was read eagerly by a sizable band of followers, and whose ideas were copied, developed or distorted with enthusiasm by his contemporaries; and that, moreover, even John's more recondite Greek sources were used by other members of his circle' (Marenbon 1981, 10). Moreover, this program of learning was in evidence over three generations of the Carolingian Empire. Charlemagne's efforts to gather together leading scholars and to build up a comprehensive library preserved a great deal of Latin knowledge: 'The revival of interest in classical learning and in the great patristic writings of the fourth and fifth centuries is due to his far-sighted policy and the enthusiasm of his chosen helpers, chief of whom was Alcuin of York' (Laistner 178).[5] Greek learning, whilst not widespread in the Carolingian world, was an accomplishment found in the larger cathedral schools.[6] Hincmar of Laon read John Chrystostom, and the Eastern Fathers generally were highly valued at Laon (Contreni 1978, 34). Martin Hiberniensis added a Greek and Latin grammar to the Greek-Latin glossary in *Laon 444*, a manuscript that formed a central pillar of Greek instruction at Laon in the later ninth century (38). The library at Laon during the tenure of Adelelm was largely a result of Martin's bequeathment of this and other manuscripts. *Laon 444* also contains a letter copied by Martin from Lupus, Abbot of Ferrières (also known as Servatus Lupus), to Gottschalk in response to a request for the definition of Greek words: Martin was by this point Lupus's consultant in matters of Greek (108). The letter 'not only provides valuable evidence for the intellectual activity of the Carolingian humanist [Lupus], but it also affords a rare index of the influence of Martin Hiberniensis' (109).

It remains unclear how much instruction in Greek, if any, occurred in Ireland for Eriugena, Martin and their contemporaries, but a myth had grown up concerning the scholarly practices of the Irish. A typical formulation of this myth occurs in Ambroise Firmin-Didot's *Alde Manuce et l'Hellénisme à Venise* (Paris 1875):

> Le mysticisme qui constitutuait le fond du caractère irlandais, les rendit enclins aux reveries philosophiques, ce qui explique leur ardeur pour les doctrines de Platon. L'étude de la langue grecque formait donc l'une des bases de leur enseignement.
>
> (The mysticism which constitutes the basis of the Irish character disposes them to philosophical reveries, which explains their ardor for the doctrines of Plato. The study of the Greek language was thus one of the foundations of their education.) (Firmin-Didot 1875, xvii; qtd in Berschin 1988, 95)

This is a typical expression of 'le miracle irlandais', which required adjustment from its over-estimation of fragmented Greek script found in Ireland from the sixth to eighth centuries, a time when such material was found almost nowhere else in Western Europe. These discoveries may represent a more generalized competence, but it is more likely that Irish monks and scholars excerpted words and phrases from the popular sources of the time – Macrobius, Jerome, Boethius, Priscian, Isidore – rather than becoming sufficiently fluent to read and study full texts. However, 'on the Continent, the *Scotti peregrini* had a scholarly advantage simply because of their greater receptiveness for languages, especially Greek; and in the ninth-century cultural realm of the Carolingians, with its better resources, it was again possible for an *Irishman* to translate texts into Latin from Greek' (Berschin 98).

Eriugena and Carolingian textual culture

A fuller picture of Eriugena's place in intellectual history has become available in the modern scholarly understanding of Carolingian textual transmission. A good deal of early medieval thought is found primarily in commentaries and glosses rather than in the composition of original works, although prominent examples of the latter include such texts as the *Periphyseon*. Assumptions of textual authority, especially regarding theological or doctrinal matters, deeply inhere in the ways texts were understood, and in the methods monastic scribes and commentators dealt with the texts of the Church Fathers and the ancient philosophers. Whilst some of his choices of authority may have been unusual for his time and place, Eriugena certainly adhered to the notion that canonical authors such as Augustine or Maximus the Confessor presented appropriate evidence for a particular doctrinal truth. His relatively modest defence of reason – especially when considered from a modern perspective – was distinctive as a matter of principle but also as a method of argumentation in the classic discipline of dialectic. Pound's initial attraction to Eriugena's thought tends to focus on the defence of reason as a partisan blow against slavish obeisance to authority: Pound's is an inherently political stance, regardless of the specific ideological hues it may (or may not) demonstrate.

But what forms might the appeal to authority take in a Carolingian context? It was commonplace to follow certain rules and conventions in citing patristic and classical texts as evidence for a particular argument, as examples from the Predestination controversy show below. But numerous works to have survived from this time exhibit nuanced and strategic attitudes towards citation and elaboration of such sources, especially in the conventions of glossing and annotating. Evidence embodied in glosses 'can show both how much of an ancient text a medieval thinker understood, and how many of its arguments he accepted' (Marenbon 1981, 8). Glossing was a critical activity, by which a glossator might introduce elements of his own argument or seek to augment that of the source text: 'Early medieval philosophers thought *through* the ancient texts they studied, but their ideas were not bounded by their sources' (8). Consequently, it is not sufficient for modern scholars merely to transcribe glosses from a single manuscript without considering their provenance and transcriptional contexts: glosses were themselves often transcribed into subsequent copies of a text, as important textual matter in their own right, or as instructional tools to be shared among centres of learning. Equally, a set of glosses is not necessarily a stable object in itself, nor often the work of one author, but can display signs of composite authorship and change across time. Eriugena's glosses on Martianus Capella's *De nuptiis Philologiae et Mercurii*, Boethius's *Opuscula Sacra* and the Aristotelian *Categoriae Decem* display his critical facility: not only is he credited with inventing the line-by-line commentary (Moran 41), Eriugena's treatment of secular texts inaugurated the method of commentary that came to dominate in the medieval universities (Schrimpf 39).

An especially apposite example of this textual phenomenon is in the various glosses found in manuscripts of Eriugena's *Periphyseon*: the nineteenth-century palaeographer Ludwig Traube attributed the glosses and marginal additions made in an Irish hand in various manuscript copies of the *Periphyseon* to Eriugena himself. Traube's student E. K. Rand proposed two hands, i[1] and i[2], neither of which belonged to Eriugena, to account for marginalia in the R manuscript (*Reims 875*). More recently, scholars have argued for i[1] (T. A. M. Bishop) or i[2] (Édouard Jeauneau, Bernhard Bischoff) as Eriugena's hand, without compelling evidence for either view (Marenbon 1981, 89–91).[7] Detailed scholarly arguments account for the authority of various hands in manuscripts containing Eriugena's texts, and particularly the authorship of marginal revisions, many of which are very probably Irish and Carolingian scribes writing under Eriugena's instruction. These details might seem slight at first, but they grow in significance when establishing the nature of Eriugena's workshop, his scholarly networks and the possibility of a functioning scriptorium in Laon.

A persistent myth of Carolingian scholarship (and one that Pound absorbed) is that Eriugena functioned largely in isolation as an authentic intellectual figure. While this fallacy is explored further below, it is worth demonstrating here the utility of the gloss as evidence for or against this kind of assumption. The myth of the isolated philosopher rests largely upon the unusual extent to which Eriugena relied upon and cited Eastern sources – particularly Maximus, Gregory of Nyssa, Gregory Nazianzus and Pseudo-Dionysius. But close inspection of the R manuscript – upon which Traube and Rand based their arguments both for and against Eriugena's hand – demonstrates the kind of intellectual sociality within which Eriugena functioned: 'two pupils, who were also scribes, and a number of other copyists, are employed to help him revise a manuscript which cannot have been the first text of his work to have been made' (Marenbon 1981, 97). Three recensions of the text are known to have been produced in Eriugena's lifetime, one of which exists in multiple manuscripts probably produced at Corbie, and whose erroneous additions suggest hands other than that of Eriugena himself (John J. O'Meara 1987, 16). Ninth- and tenth-century manuscript witnesses of the *Periphyseon* (or parts thereof) comprise a moderately complex provenance, with three major phases of revision in evidence. The R manuscript is the most significant text in the stemmatic line of descent, forming the basis for later witnesses as well as two significant florilegia: the so-called X (*Valenciennes 167*) and Y (*Paris BN 13953*) texts. These manuscripts provide valuable information regarding the learning of Greek in Carolingian France, their compilers demonstrating 'an enthusiasm for definitions [as] a guiding principle in their choice of extracts' (Marenbon 1981, 104). They also excerpt passages in order to give the appearance of a definition, as in the two misleading 'entries' for ἐνέργεια: 'A fascination for Greek terms, especially theological ones, is linked to this taste for definition; the compilers are keener on no type of extract more than one which takes the form of a gloss on a Greek theological term' (104). The varying patterns of glossing and excerpting, and the Irish and Carolingian hands that mediate the text material, all indicate a much wider study of the *Periphyseon* during Eriugena's lifetime and in the following century than had been assumed.[8]

Glossing practices provide a crucial evidentiary source for the distribution of texts and knowledge in the Carolingian era: Eriugena's glosses of Greek terms, the glossing of his texts by other major scholars such as Martin Hiberniensis (Master of the Laon cathedral school during Eriugena's tenure at the court of Charles the Bald), and the glosses of his texts in subsequent centuries, allows scholars to trace, at least partially, the distribution and use of Eriugenian manuscripts. The text of the *Categoriae Decem* – a work central to Carolingian learning and erroneously attributed to Aristotle – is a useful index to the utility of glosses as measures of scholarly influence and networks of text production and commentary. The glosses concerning the primary Category of *ousia* is especially of significance, not least for its role in the *Periphyseon*: 'The treatment of *Usia* in the glosses to the *Categoriae Decem*, the *De nuptiis* and Boethius's *Opuscula Sacra* reflects the development which has been traced from Aristotle, through his antique and patristic commentators and users, to Ratramnus of Corbie and John Scottus' (Marenbon 1981, 123). Similarly, glosses on Category IV in the *Categoriae Decem* in the manuscripts M (*Milano Ambrosiana B 71 sup.*), G (*Sankt Gallen 274*) and H (*Paris BN 12949*), and thought to be by Heiric of Auxerre, draw heavily on Eriugena's cosmology:

> Having distinguished between a *fantaston*, an object of sense-perception, a *fantasia*, a sense-datum, and a *fantasma*, a sense-impression stored in the memory, the glossator proceeds to parallel these three concepts to the three heavens, the third of which Paul was to take to in his ecstasy. The first heaven is those things that are, that is, which have bodies (*fantasta*); the second heaven

is *mentuale* and consists of those things that are perceived (*fantasia*). The third
heaven is made up of those things that are said (*fantasma*) and is 'intellectual'.
(134–35)

These glosses demonstrate Eriugena's influence on the next generation of
scholars, but they also indicate the ubiquity of specific philosophical problems:
the analogy of the three types of perception with the Trinity suggests the influence
of Neoplatonist thought (specifically the hypostases) as well as that of the
Eastern patristic tradition more generally. These structures of perception arise
in Pound's commentary on Cavalcanti's 'Donna mi prega', where he ties them to
thirteenth-century interpretations of the Islamic commentators on Aristotle. An
intellectual link exists between Cavalcanti's poem – *fantasia, memoria* – and the
Categoriae Decem, tracing a line from the emergence of rigorous philosophy in
the early Middle Ages to the Tuscan poet.

Pound's knowledge of medieval textual practice may not have been
particularly honed to the minutiae of Carolingian intellectual culture. But
he was sensitive to general matters of manuscript annotation, glossing, and
patterns of excerption in his work on the Troubadours and especially Cavalcanti
from his university days. His annotations of texts in philosophy (Fiorentino)
and Byzantine Studies (Michael Psellus) provide ample evidence of this acute,
if not strictly specialist, textual awareness. In the case of Carolingian texts,
manuscript sources are rare, and offer dispersed, scant information in the form
of glosses and annotations from which certain inductive postulates of influence,
filiation and philosophical advancement might be made. The dissolution of
the monasteries in France following the Revolution of 1789 severely affected
the study of Carolingian texts, and thus its history, but the nineteenth-century
publication of both the Monumenta Germaniae Historica and the Patrologia
Latina fundamentally changed the landscape, even accounting for the flawed
and fragmented nature of many texts in both series. The newly available
manuscripts shed light on the scholarly and teaching practices at Laon and
among cultural centres nearby such as Liège, Corbie, and Reims. The existence
of a functioning scriptorium at Laon must be considered by careful attention to
the physical traits of manuscripts: 'The origins of Laon's manuscripts not only
help to determine whether a scriptorium operated at Laon during the ninth and
tenth centuries, they also provide a clearer picture of the most important centers
with which Laon had intellectual contacts' (Contreni 1978, 40).

Evidence for the material production and distribution of manuscripts tells
a great deal about the intellectual culture in which Eriugena lived. But the
texts copied and distributed, glossed and annotated, also provide clues as to

contemporary pedagogical priorities and intellectual endeavours. The early fifth-century *De nuptiis Philologiae et Mercurii* of Martianus Capella was extremely influential in the early Middle Ages and afterwards as the foundation text of the *trivium* (grammar, logic and rhetoric) and the *quadrivium* (arithmetic, geometry, music and astronomy), and was widely copied, glossed and annotated. Eriugena was long thought to have produced a commentary on this text, although it is now considered to be the work of his countryman Dunshad.[9] The existence of this commentary points to the way education and theology coexisted in the cathedral schools from which the early universities emerged. The argument for the arts as innate human faculties, and thus education as a process of recollection, clearly absorbs Platonic and Neoplatonic traditions. But this tradition is profoundly 'Christianized' by having the student progress toward a prelapsarian condition: 'No longer simply a propaedeutic in Alcuin's sense, the arts are man's link with the Divine, their cultivation a means to salvation' (Contreni 113–14). Manno, a student of Martin's, entered the court in the early 870s to receive an education befitting a future bishop. In his *Life of Bishop Radbod* of Utrecht, Manno writes that Radbod came to the court of Charles the Bald not to pursue courtly honours but to study the 'seven-fold wisdom' that flourished there (138). There are obvious thematic and structural links to Pound's pedagogy and paideuma. If one were to replace the Christianized God with a more general (and more Platonic) metaphysics, inflected by Confucian cosmology, one gets a sense of the world to which Pound might have been drawn more profoundly had he completed the projected 'Note on Eriugena'; one in which a liberal education is not merely a civic obligation and preparatory to the betterment of society, but the realization of an innate faculty threading back to the divine: in short, the *paradiso terrestre*. The Carolingian combination of the liberal arts curriculum and Irish masters did not always pass uncontested, however. Hincmar of Laon was a student of Martin's, but his uncle, Hincmar, Archbishop of Reims, disapproved of his education, accusing him of 'cluttering his words with bad Greek, Irish, and other "barbarisms"' (136). Similarly, Eriugena's texts were described by Hincmar of Reims as 'pultes Scotorum' (Irish porridge) at the Council of Valence in 855.

Whilst the context of court and cathedral school education is of direct relevance to the fate of Eriugena's texts, and of his reputation, the point at issue here is that several features of that milieu parallel quite closely some of Pound's cherished notions of a discerning education of wide reading, linguistic competency and particular attention to the provenance and material transmission of core texts. These features come into sharp focus in Pound's own reading and annotative practices, as will be demonstrated in some detail in the annotated transcription of his manuscript material pertaining to the 'Eriugena Note' in the next chapter. There exists now a clearer picture of Eriugena's cultural and intellectual milieu than was available to Pound via his sources. Pound's note-taking, working by careful transcription, hunches and informed hypotheses, demonstrates an uncanny sympathy for the kinds of pressures that bear upon Carolingian sources and their reception. These two pictures combine to produce the groundwork from which to imagine where Pound might have taken his Eriugena materials.

The Predestination controversy

From his earliest reference to Eriugena, Pound was aware of the serial condemnations suffered by the Hibernian. Pound speculates that Eriugena's persecution may have been the result of his 'talking nonsense on some issue' (*GK* 333) or 'some fuss about the trinity' (*SL* 304). It is clear from the context of his writing in *Guide to Kulchur* and his correspondence with Otto Bird that Pound refers to the thirteenth-century condemnations of the Averroists and their interpretations of Aristotle at the University of Paris in which Eriugena's texts were implicated. But the condemnations in Eriugena's lifetime, at Valence in 855 and Langres in 859, were reactions to disputes of pivotal importance to Church doctrine, the Predestination dispute with Gottschalk of Orbais foremost among them. This event propelled Eriugena into public view of ecclesiastical authority for the first time: it marks a significant point of difference in interpretations of Augustine's writing on the subject in *De uera religione* (*On True Religion*), *De libero arbitrio* (*On Free Will*) and other texts. The dispute split Carolingian ecclesiastical authority and Gottschalk suffered a heavy penalty of lifelong monastic confinement at Hautvillers for his beliefs. Eriugena also came under attack for his rebuttal, and his protection in the court of Charles the Bald also appealed to Pound as a model for a cultivated centre of political power and enlightened rule. There is insufficient direct evidence to know how well Pound knew Eriugena's views on Predestination and human agency in questions of good and evil: his so-called anthropology.[10] In his reading of Patrologia Latina 122 in 1939–1940 Pound confirmed his own affinities with the Hibernian philosopher in the Carolingian court.

The following outline of the dispute and its consequences is a necessary step in establishing what was at stake in theological terms, and the ways in which it may have proved useful to Pound had he taken his studies further.

The controversy reignited the conflict between Augustine's doctrine of total depravity (that humans are necessarily fallen and rely on the proper exercise of free will and God's grace for redemption) and the Pelagian heresy in which the exercise of free will is the determining factor in salvation. In the fifth century it was established that Augustine's doctrine was orthodoxy and that of Pelagius heretical.[11] Despite this ecclesiastical *summa*, the numerous ambiguities in Augustine's texts on matters of free will, divine grace, predestination and foreknowledge continued to cause doctrinal disputes throughout the Middle Ages and beyond. In addition to his dispute with Hincmar on matters of predestination, Gottschalk was simultaneously engaged in a Trinitarian controversy, about which Pound knew little, but the details of which resonate with Pound's interests in divine participation and immanence by way of his Neoplatonic sources, including Eriugena.

It is telling how many of Eriugena's known scholarly habits resonate with those Pound developed prior to his having any direct knowledge of the Irishman's life or work: Eriugena preferred interlinear Latin glosses in his Greek texts (Priscius, Pseudo-Dionysius) rather than the parallel translations preferred by such contemporaries as Sedulius; Eriugena's strenuous promotion of Greek studies in the royal court and its school must also have appealed to a modern writer famous for his urgent exhortations to take up the study of erstwhile difficult or abstruse topics and languages; Eriugena broached political topics in his poetry, and his tenure as poet in Charles's court implied a political dimension; and as one of very few scholars with competence in Greek for centuries before and after, Eriugena bore an appeal to Pound as a lone beacon of ancient wisdom in a benighted milieu (a misleading portrait upheld in scholarship even into Pound's lifetime). Eriugena is an unusual figure of Carolingian scholarship in many ways – as a scholar, poet, wit, personality and theologian – but he functioned within a court which took learning very seriously: Charles himself commissioned Eriugena's response to Gottschalk in the *De praedestinatione*, as well as many of the translations from Greek texts including the Pseudo-Dionysian corpus.

The Predestination controversy implies a tradition of contested thought reaching back to Augustine, implicating other late-classical thinkers such as Boethius. In the more immediate context of the ninth-century Carolingian world, the philosophical contributions of Alcuin's circle at the court of Charlemagne two generations previously are pivotal. Alcuin's revision of Augustine's view of the human relation to divinity directly shaped both the Predestination and Trinitarian controversies that would explode in Eriugena's lifetime. Augustine saw a parallel between the three Persons of the Trinity and the three faculties of the human mind: *intellectus, voluntas,* and *memoria* (intellect, will and memory). For Augustine, human *likeness* to divinity is a general condition, a sub-class of which is the image-relation: the notion of the human being made in God's *image*. This image-relation implies a direct process of creation and thus an unbroken bond with God's goodness: 'Consequently, it was not open to Augustine to interpret Man's likeness to God as something for the individual to attain by good behaviour, in contrast to his innate image of God: for Augustine, Man's creation in the image of his maker implies his Godliness' (Marenbon 1981, 45). Alcuin inverts this hierarchy, where the human image-relation is innate, part of the structure of the soul and that reflects the Trinity. The likeness-relation is a matter of human potential and therefore subject to loss and recovery, a notion that Alcuin adapts from the Greek patristic tradition (45).[12] Previously, Ambrose had adopted this notion of human Godliness as a condition attainable by the operation of human faculties, stemming from the unfallen state of human nature.

It is unclear how much Pound knew of this complex network of problems, but there are numerous direct echoes in his writing on related subjects.[13] Pound correctly assumes that the Greek tendency to a doctrine of participation – where human agency occupies a role within a system of divine emanation – caused problems for Eriugena's reception, namely the accusations of pantheism in the thirteenth century. Pound sustains an interest in the tripartite division of the soul through his reading of Richard of St Victor. *Memoria* plays a pivotal part in the Averroist structure of emanations Pound discerns in Cavalcanti's philosophical canzone, to which he gives ample attention in his translation of Canto XXXVI and the essay 'Cavalcanti'. This tripartite concept is a staple of both Neoplatonic thought and Western Christian doctrine, largely the result of Augustine's influence. To this might be added the Augustinian–Alcuinian debate over image and likeness. Pound deploys these terms within a Neoplatonic discourse, strictly beyond the Christian remit, in his translation of 'Donna mi prega', but there is at least an indirect influence of Christian doctrinal controversy. Pound's reasons for splicing Eriugena's alleged heresies into the canto are consistent with his preoccupations with the long-established discourse of doctrinal controversy.

Gottschalk and the Predestination controversy

Gottschalk's life and doctrines inform Eriugena's response to his views on predestination, as well as to Pound's subsequent (if imperfect) interest in Eriugena's role in the dispute. Although marginalized doctrinally and historically, Gottschalk drew the attention of the French Jansenists in the seventeenth-century, as well as a number of religious scholars in the nineteenth and twentieth centuries. Although Pound shows no awareness of this renewed attention, its timing is significant, arising in a period when Latin gave way to vernacular languages as the medium of scholarship (Genke 2010, 8). There was an efflorescence of German interest, as well as French, in the figure of Dom Maïeul Cappuyns, 'who wrote on various aspects of the controversy before 1931, when Dom Germain Morin discovered a rich collection of Gottschalk's theological texts in the library of Bern' (9). Soon after this discovery, Gottschalk's grammatical treatises came to light: 'The largest part of these materials was published in 1945, yet other texts by the rebellious Benedictine appeared until 1958' (9). The uncanny parallels with Eriugena's career – contemporary recognition of his brilliance, condemnation, occlusion from the tradition, then latter-day revival – makes Gottschalk a fascinating case study in the context of Pound's Carolingian sources.

Gottschalk was born probably in 804 and forced by his father into monkhood at Fulda under the Benedictine abbot Rabanus Maurus, who later became Archbishop of Mainz. After resisting this coerced induction he was released from Fulda for a time, but was subsequently recalled. He travelled to Italy in defiance of the oath of sedentariness (taken in addition to the three vows of chastity, poverty and obedience) although it is unclear whether he was released from his order at the time. Gottschalk developed ideas in eschatology in the context of proselytizing and missionary work in Scandinavia under Louis the Pious. This work formed a critical element of the identity of the monastery at Corbie which Gottschalk joined: 'Scandinavia was the end of the known earth; when Christ is proclaimed there, the end of the world will come' (Genke 22). Gottschalk was required to appear before the Synod at Mainz in 848, presided over by Louis the German, to defend texts he wrote on the subject of predestination. He presented two treatises confessing his faith and refuting the accusations of Rabanus (37). Hincmar, Archbishop of Reims, then presided over a small council at Quierzy in 849, submitting Gottschalk's thinking as heretical: 'Gottschalk presented to the assembly presided over by Charles the Bald a collection of scriptural and patristic quotations, designed to prove the orthodoxy of his doctrine, but it was found heretical' (39). He was publicly flogged (for the second time) and imprisoned, and his books were also burned. The symbolic force of such punishment functions as a kind of displaced violence on the body of Gottschalk: 'Death was inflicted as if the books acted as an effigy of Gottschalk, with destruction and purification by fire' (McKitterick 2004, 219).

Hincmar was forced to enlist the services of Eriugena to rebut his critics following the wholesale rejection of his letter 'Ad simplices' ('To Simple Believers') following the Quierzy condemnation of Gottschalk. Prudentius, Bishop of Troyes, and Ratramnus of Corbie rejected Hincmar's viewpoint, and Rabanus Maurus had since retired into silence, unwilling to be implicated in the controversy. On the request of Charles, Lupus of Ferrières wrote *De tribus quaestionibus*, joining Hincmar's critics (Wohlman, in Eriugena 2003, xxiv). In such an environment of beleaguered authority, Bishop Pardulus of Laon requested that 'the Scot from the king's palace' be called on to refute Gottschalk, the product of which was the even more controversial *De praedestinatione* (c. 850–51). Florus, Archbishop of Lyons, wrote a rebuttal of Eriugena's position, *Book against the Erroneous Definitions of John Scot Erigena* (PL 119, 101–250). There were further councils at Quierzy (853) and Valence (855): 'On 8 January 855, at Valence, Lothar convened a council where the bishops of Lyons, Vienne and Arles were present [and where] the six chapters (*capitula*) concerning predestination enacted there openly attacked those of Quierzy and Erigena's nineteen statements' (Genke 2010, 50).

Given the difficulties in acquiring volumes of the Patrologia Latina during wartime, Pound narrowly missed a wealth of relevant texts concerning Eriugena's role in the Predestination controversy – the central theme of his interest in Eriugena in the first instance – in volumes adjacent to that containing Eriugena's works.[14] Ironically Gottschalk's notions of double predestination fit, aesthetically, into Pound's quasi-Manichaean division of the world's political and ethical actors, going back to his London days and associations with *BLAST!* One example from the *Confessio* or *Shorter Confession* concerns the twofold nature of predestination (being a single thing): 'The omnipotent and immutable God has gratuitously foreknown and predestined the holy angels and elect human beings to eternal life, and [...] he equally predestined the devil himself, the head of all the demons, with all of his apostate angels and also with all reprobate human beings, namely, his members, to rightly eternal death' (Genke and Gumerlock 2010, 54–5). Another resonant element in Gottschalk's theology pertains to the way he enlists Plato as a counterpoint to the anthropology of Augustine (and in more radical form, Eriugena): 'The immutable God fascinated him, very much in line with certain views of Plato, whom the rebellious Benedictine highly esteemed, and he wrote that God's wisdom spoke through this pagan' (61). In a sense, Gottschalk's heresy was a function of geographical displacement: there was limited knowledge of Augustine in the north, and in centres in the south such as Lyon there was a long-standing proneness to doctrines of semi-Pelagianism (Laistner 1957, 295) with which Augustine himself disputed vigorously (Wetzel 51–2).

Perhaps the most surprising aspect of Gottschalk's intellectual work to have elided Pound was his pioneering facility in early vernacular lyric. Gottschalk composed a series of penitential poems in his ostracism following the predestination controversy. For Dronke they constitute a newly emergent 'fully-fledged lyrical stanzaic form' in Latin:

> Gottschalk, persecuted at his own monastery, Fulda, lives on the island
> Reichenau, where he feels himself an exile, and a young boy asks him for a
> 'pretty song' (*carmen dulce*). The poet refuses: his melancholy is too great:
>
>
>
> Magis mihi, miserule,
> flere libet, puerile –
> plus plorare   quam cantare
> carmen tale   iubis quale,
> amore care.
> O cur iubes canere?
>
>
>
> Poor little lad, I would sooner weep, sooner lament than sing such a song as you,
> dearly beloved, demand. Oh, why do you ask me to sing? (Dronke 2002, 35)

The rhetorical-poetic flourish of refusal is a venerable classical and biblical topos, evident in such texts as Psalm 137. Instead of applying it to an orthodox religious theme from the New Testament (its usual application in the medieval period), Gottschalk applies the topos of refusal to himself in a daring appropriation of poetic authority. Gottschalk epitomizes the poetry of exile that was to become a critical aspect of Pound's poetic in the Seven Lakes Canto and especially *The Pisan Cantos*. This, compounded with his poetic innovations and subsequent invisibility in the canon, makes Gottschalk an eminently suitable model for Pound, despite his fundamental opposition with Eriugena in the Predestination controversy.

Eriugena's contribution to the Predestination controversy

Eriugena's contribution to the Predestination dispute only intensified doctrinal problems for the church. Rather than settling the dispute in favour of an orthodox Augustinian reading of the matter (putting aside the ambiguities of Augustine's texts), Eriugena's document was troublesome not only for its conclusion but in its very methods in his argument by dialectic:

> Reason (*ratio*) is given a hearing on an equal footing with the time-honoured
> authorities (*auctoritates*) of Scripture and the Fathers; this balancing of reason
> and authority was to be greatly elaborated in the *Periphyseon*. The secular
> language of the liberal arts is applied in theological discussion, a procedure duly
> and formally anathematized by Prudentius of Troyes and Florus of Lyon in their
> rebuttal. (Brennan, in Eriugena 2003, xi)

Eriugena was requested to provide a reasoned rebuttal to Gottschalk's thesis:
it is difficult to determine whether Eriugena overstepped his remit in making
this argument for reason over authority. However, a close examination of *De
praedestinatione* shows that he draws very extensively on Church authority,
principally Augustine.[15] Both Eriugena and Gottschalk were outsiders to the
system to which they found themselves answerable, perhaps allowing them
'to consider the question of predestination – one of those which elicited most
passion in the third generation of the Carolingian Renaissance – in so highly
personal a fashion' (Wohlman, in Eriugena 2003, xvii). The controversy went to
the heart of the nature of learning in the Carolingian epoch: Gottschalk's radical
use of syllogism (after Jerome's commentary on the Galatians) as a central device
of argumentation was forcibly met by Eriugena's use of dialectic bearing the hues
of Augustine's early works (Ganz 353).

   De praedestinatione provides an epitome of Eriugena's early thought: it is
not heavily invested in the learning of the Greek patristic tradition, unlike his
later texts in which Pound took greatest interest, but many of his characteristic
doctrines and concepts are established in this early commissioned work. The
following study of the structure of Eriugena's argument therefore establishes
the groundwork for a general appraisal of his thought, including the relation
between humanity and God in the *Periphyseon*, and the impact of Greek learning
in his poetry and in his work generally. In the Preface to *De praedestinatione*,
Eriugena dedicates his argument in terms of the first chapter of Pseudo-
Dionysius's *Celestial Hierarchy*, as Pound was to identify in his notes: 'To the
most illustrious lords Hincmar and Pardulus worthy and preeminent guardians
of the Christian faith and endowed from above by the father of lights with the
divine gift of Episcopal grace, John your devoted servant offers greetings in the
Lord' (Eriugena 2003, 3). Eriugena establishes the terms of his argument not
within the discourse of theology, but of philosophy: 'Every true and complete
doctrinal system by which the theory of all things is most assiduously inquired
into and most clearly ascertained is established within that discipline which
the Greeks usually call *philosophia*' (7). He does not claim autonomy from all
temporal authority, however, but instead proclaims the canonical role of Charles

and his responsibility to the Church: 'We have, too, the particular approval of the most orthodox prince and venerable lord, Charles, whose greatest concern is to harbour devout and proper sentiments towards God, to refute the distorted teachings of heretics by true reasonings and the authority of the holy Fathers, and to root them out utterly to the last one' (8).

Although Eriugena makes a claim for reason in his dialectical approach, authority is a necessary precondition for his rhetorical performance: ideally, the two combine in the course of arguing from reasoned authority. Eriugena gives priority to authority in setting out the grave nature of Gottschalk's transgression: 'This foolish and merciless lunacy is in the first place refuted by divine authority; secondly it is annulled by the rules of right reason' (10). Eriugena introduces the metaphor of light for knowledge of the divine,[16] stating that heretics are useful in alerting true believers to the 'light of truth': 'For that reason it is through heretics that many people are roused from sleep to look upon God's daylight and rejoice' (9). He inverts this figuration of light in the accusation that Satan (Lucifer the 'light-bringer') works through Gottschalk, who 'tries to deny the most equitable rewards of justice and the most merciful gifts of grace' (10). Eriugena employs a dialectical method strikingly prescient of its codification by Thomas Aquinas in the twelfth century: this is particularly true of the argument by contrariety, which functions as a dialectical counterpart to his apophatic theology. Eriugena proceeds to show by systematic argumentation that double predestination is absurd and countermanded by authority, namely Augustine. This is a highly risky approach, given that Augustine is ambiguous on precisely these matters, shifting between attacks on Pelagianism and on Manichaeism at different times. Eriugena begins by defining divine will: 'God made all that he made out of his own will and out of no necessity' (11). Virtues of the soul are effects of the divine will, manifested individually but stemming from the unified essence (and primary category) – *ousia*, which is 'number without number [yet] in itself one, undivided and inseparable' (14). *Ousia* reflects the super-essential characteristic of the divine – that is, being more than essence. Conversely, evil is a matter of negative absence, 'experienced as punishment by those for whom, according to their just desserts, the just judge has prepared eternal torments' (15). These concepts of apophasis and superessentialism drive *De praedestinatione*, but also underpin the entire schema of the four divisions of nature in the *Periphyseon*.

Eriugena applies logical argument to questions of first principles: the existence of God, the nature of divine will, the nature of number (crucial for an exposition of unified or double predestination), and the understanding of divine superessence by way of negative theology (i.e. if God is beyond essence then he can only be described by what he is not). The question of evil is central to this logic: God predestines, which is the same as willing, but as this is a unified act it does not permit of two predestinations. If evil is not from God, can it then be said to exist, rendering God's creative power limited in scope? The answer to the existence of evil comes by way of *enthymeme* (argument by opposition):

> God cannot be both the cause of things that are and the cause of things that are nothing. But God is the cause of things that are. Therefore he is not the cause of things that are not. Sin and its effect, death, to which unhappiness is conjoined, are not. Of them, therefore, neither God nor his predestination, which is what he himself is, can be the cause. (19)

This is a powerful expression of meontology: God is predestination, and given that evil falls outside of creation, it properly doesn't exist, and is absence by privation. By straying from the will of God, human commission of sin is the expression of this negative, and is thus not part of the predestined plan. Although sin is known by God, it is not predestined, being nothing and not part of creation. As with other patristic expressions of evil-as-negation (namely Augustine), Eriugena struggles to provide a compelling rational case for this argument, proceeding by carefully weighted meanings of specific words. He is especially careful to negotiate the apparent paradox between divine unity and the multiplicity of genera and created forms in which that divinity is wholly contained: this problematic recurs in the Trinitarian controversies in which Gottschalk was also embroiled at the time.

Eriugena situates Gottschalk's thesis as a modulation of two heresies: that of Pelagianism (that human will is paramount in determining salvation or damnation, thus seen as a disparagement of divine will, *contra* Augustine), and the converse heresy of claiming that divine will disparages human will, which effectively rejects both free will and divine grace (25–6). Eriugena systematically refutes Gottschalk's double predestination – inherited at least in part from Isodore of Seville (Moran 30) – which seeks to deny both Pelagianism and the doctrine of divine grace. Eriugena comes close to a denial of predestination altogether: 'If [...] wherever there is freedom of choice with the gift of grace, there the necessity of predestination cannot be, it follows conversely that where there is the necessity of predestination, there neither free choice or the gift of grace can be' (28). Drawing on Augustine's *Enchiridion ad Laurentium* (*The Manual for Laurentius*), Eriugena asserts that the human likeness to God ('made in his image') requires a faculty of free will also in the image of God: 'By the misuse of free choice man lost both himself and it' (30). Crucially, Eriugena figures free will in images of light, first in terms of the privative 'shadow' of original sin, then the 'light of divine mercy' which dissipates night and sin, and purifies human will by opening its 'eyes' (31). Free will means no one is compelled to good or evil by foreknowledge and predestination, but instead impels a choice between evil, as an absence of grace, and good bestowed by grace and act of free will (38). Eriugena again quotes Augustine's *De uera religione* (*On True Religion*), citing an argument for the separation of foreknowledge and predestination. The bestowal of free will is no guarantee of its virtuous use, in this case quoting Augustine's *De libero arbitrio* (*On Free Choice*) in a chain of descent: 'The will, therefore, cleaving to the universal and unchangeable good, obtains man's first and great goods, although it is itself a sort of intermediate good; but a will sins that is turned away from the unchangeable and universal good and is turned towards the individual good or to something external or to something inferior' (Aug. *De lib. arb.* II, 19, qtd at 47). The turning away from good and God is sin, not authored by God, therefore nothing and thus beyond knowledge: this argument is almost entirely Augustine's, but the germ of Eriugena's fully developed negative theology can be viewed in this most reputable of Western Christian authorities.

Despite this heavy reliance on Augustine, Eriugena misattributes an important argument found nowhere in the patriarch's writings: 'As indeed Augustine many times very clearly impresses upon us, it is our belief that the substantial trinity of the interior man is composed of [...] being, will and knowledge' (51). Free will too bears a Trinitarian morphology for Eriugena, being 'free, moved, intelligent', 'Yet it is evident that every sin and the punishment for sin have drawn their origin from its perverse use, and that it thrives in every sinner, leading to an evil way of life' (57). In a move that will reach its full expression in Book I of the *Periphyseon*, Eriugena calls on Aristotle's ten categories in a catalogue of God's goodness: 'Those things that are made by his goodness are made substantially with all the accidents which naturally adhere to them, which are qualities, quantities, relations, situations, conditions, places, times, action and passion; within that ten in number all created substance as well as all accidentals to it can be included' (52). The rationality in human nature means it is logical that humans also possess free will (53).

Eriugena's deployment of negative theology in his dialectic provides a powerful structure by which to define and differentiate between divine foreknowledge and predestination. These terms are not to be taken literally but to be understood by way of an argument from contrariety:

In the first place it is to be noted – since no expression is adequate to God – that almost no speech-signs, whether nouns or verbs or other parts of speech, can be properly affirmed of God. How could sensory signs, that is signs

connected with bodies, signify with clarity that nature which is far removed
from all corporeal sense and scarcely attainable to even the purest mind since it
transcends all understanding? (59)

This manouevre entails a twofold structure of language when speaking of God:
the Aristotelian language of substance and accidents, on the one hand, and the
fungible language of metaphors (likeness, contrariety, difference) on the other:
'nothing is contrary to God except non-being, because he alone it is who said:
"I am who am"; but other things also that are said to exist do not entirely exist,
because they are not what he is, and they do not entirely not exist, because they
are from him who alone is being' (61). This dynamic, dialectical use of being and
non-being as relative ontological terms – God is Being, but is also superessential
and therefore not being; worldly things possess being, but pale into partial being
in the view of divine light – anticipates the fully-fledged notion of *multiplex
theoria* in the *Periphyseon*. The concepts of foreknowledge and predestination
are applied to God metaphorically, as a kataphatic function of speech: that is, to
speak of God in positive terms is strictly false, but humans require some positive
means of reference, which is supplied by metaphor and figures of speech and
are not to be taken literally. Divine foreknowledge of sin and punishment is also
argued by way of contrariety, to mitigate the attribution of perversity to God. The
punishment for sin is embodied in the turning away from God and the absence
of grace: 'the perverse movement of a will that is free and changeable turning
itself away from the creator and misusing the creation' suspended between the
limits of sin and punishment (66). Punishment, as a manifestation of sin, allows
for the claim that God does not know corruption: 'And for this reason, just as
God is not the author of evil, so has he not foreknowledge of evil nor does he
predestine it' (67). This complex dialectical argument utterly refutes Gottschalk:
sin and punishment are absolutely negative, are not known by God and could
therefore hardly be authorized by God. Divine perfection is maintained by
positing punishment as the absence of God's grace, which originates in and
eventuates from the sinful act itself.

  Eriugena's argument then enumerates a physiology of evil by a similar
process of privative negation, whereby 'in the ensouled body the corruption of
health is pain and disease, the corruption of energy weariness, the corruption
of rest toil' (67), just as negative physical attributes are corruptions of their
virtuous complements. This privative model for sin, as deficiency rather than
efficiency, draws directly on *City of God* XII for authority (68). Eriugena uses
the distinction between genus and species to distinguish foreknowledge from
predestination: all predestination is foreknowledge but not all foreknowledge is

predestination, in that God has foreknowledge of the things he will not make, i.e. evil things, sin and punishment, but predestination is always geared to the good, and effects divine grace. To speak of Augustine's phrase, 'the predestination of punishments', is a figure of speech arguing from contrariety, thus making this phrase intelligible (78). But Eriugena appears to waver on this point: God predestines none to punishment (according to his Augustinian source), but 'foreknew within the damnable mass' (91) (*massa perditionis*). Those not given grace of election are foreknown to be damned but not predestined, although (in a particularly oblique passage) punishment itself is predestined by virtue of it being foreknown: those who reject the faith of salvation and are 'given over to depraved thoughts to practise what is not decent' (Romans 1.28) are sinners who 'in their own wickedness are in the world foreknown only, not predestined; but that punishment is predestined because of the fact that they are foreknown' (91). Eriugena establishes that sinners are not predestined by God for punishment, but 'by their own deserts condign punishments that have been predestined for them by him' (91). The distinction seems to turn on fine semantics and a kataphatic theology made manifest in figurative language. Eriugena provides a lesson on the rhetorical uses of negativity, drawing on his proficiency in Greek: he provides examples of subalternation or *hypallage* (υπαλλαγη) as a variety of contrariety as well as κατ αντιφρασιν or *antiphrasis* (96–7). Eriugena sums up the nature of negative entities of sin, death, and punishment: 'the highest essence in no way brings about things that are not: sin, death, punishment are a deficiency of justice, life, happiness; therefore they are not from him who is; and hence, if they are not from him, who would dare to say that there is anything in them?' (98).

Eriugena effects a dialectical move in his argument related to the problem of the one and many in God; that is, divine unity and divine presence in the multiplicity of forms and genera. He cites Augustine's *De ciuitate Dei* (XIII, 14) and *Enarrationes in Psalmos* (84, 7) to pose the argument that Adam sins and contains all men, and thus all men sin: 'In him [Adam], therefore, it was not the generality of nature that sinned but the individual will of each one, because if that nature offended, since it is one, the whole would certainly perish' (103). Eriugena also draws upon Augustine's commentary on Psalm VII, in which he states that punishment does not emanate from the 'ineffable light of God' but is meted out by the sinner in the act of sinning (107). Sinners are cast into the outer darkness, their sin being not of God nor known by God, and this comprises the ultimate punishment and a consequence of the ultimate sin, which is the turning away from God. The argument seems to double back on itself at this point: 'It is established by reason and authority that it must be firmly held that God, in a word, is not in any way the author of the punishments by which proud wickedness will be racked by eternal torment, that is to say he is in no way their maker, in no way their predestinator' (111). Eriugena concludes his discourse on Augustine with a Trinitarian division of creation: the condemnation of sinners, the testing of the just and the perfecting of the blessed (quoting *De uera religione*, at 114).

Eriugena calls upon his knowledge of Greek as a lynchpin in his argument for orthodoxy. This argument is contestible, not least for the way in which the Eastern Fathers considered the Trinity, which was often regarded as heretical in the West. He cautions that the tendency to distort patristic sources ('and for the most part Saint Augustine') to serve a doctrinal viewpoint is compounded by a general 'ignorance [...] of Greek writings in which the interpretation of predestination generates no mist of ambiguity' (117). In tune with late-classical and Carolingian scholarly practices, Eriugena produces a glossary of examples:

> There is, then, a word among the Greeks ΩΡΩ which among the Latins is expressed by three words: for ΩΡΩ is interpreted as 'I see' (*uideo*) and 'I define' (*diffinio*) and 'I destine' (*destino*): similarly its composite ΠΡΟΩΡΩ 'I foresee' (*praeuideo*), 'I predefine' (*praediffinio*), 'I predestine' (*praedestino*). This is very easily deduced from the constructions of holy scripture [...] Hence that noun ΩΡΟCΙΑ or ΠΡΟΩΡΟCΙΑ which for them is derived from the verb ΩΡΩ or ΠΡΟΩΡΩ among us is called 'vison' (*uisio*) or 'definition' (*diffinitio*) or 'determining' (*destinatio*), and their composites 'foresight,' 'predefinition,' 'predestination,' come from the Greek compound, which is ΠΡΟΩΡΟCΙΑ. From this it is clearly shown that in these three words there is either the same sense or so great a closeness in meaning that any one of them can be put in the place of the other. (118)

The difficulties in separating the meaning of foreknowledge from predestination are evident not merely for the fact that both are tied to metaphors of sight and foresight. The linguistic hazards of translating 'predestination' from Greek are obvious to Eriugena, but may not appear so starkly, or at all, to scholars not conversant in Greek or otherwise skilled in the arts of translation. He is almost uniquely equipped to make such a claim, providing his argument with an almost irrefutable authority on matters of the definition of words. This sharp focus on the polysemic character of terms underpinning central doctrines of the church comes into play in the Trinitarian controversy in which Gottschalk was also embroiled.

Eriugena's radical rebuttal of predestination rests upon a finely tuned sense of the negative. Knowledge of God is expressible only within the terms of negative theology: a superessentiality expressed only in terms of absence or metaphor. The definition of sin and punishment is that it is privative of divine grace by virtue of the sinful act:

> Given that God is eternal, we cannot say that He foresees or predetermines. Beyond that, to think that God foresees sin and punishment is silly: evil does not exist, being a pure absence, so one cannot know it. To think that God has prepared hell from the beginning of time for human beings is a pitiful anthropomorphism. God is the Good above all goods and the source of all good. The only punishment is immanent to sin itself, confining sinners in the prison of their own conscience. (Brennan, in Eriugena 2003, xxv)

The deployment of an intensively syllogistic dialectic must have done little to engender sympathy to his position. The apparent inevitability of his position on predestination is produced in a rational argument, revolving on the pivot of presence and absence:

> Therefore the death of the soul is sin; God did not make sin for the soul, since he it is who frees it from sin; and so life did not make the death of life. The penalty for sin is death; God did not make death; therefore he did not make the penalty. Torment is a penalty; God did not make a penalty; therefore he did not make torment. The penalty for sin is death; the death of life is sin; therefore the penalty for sin is sin. Penalty is suffering; therefore the suffering of sin is sin. (120)

The consequences of Eriugena's refutation of predestination *per se* were stark and immediate: Prudentius wrote *De praedestinatione contra Joannem Scotum* in 852, accusing Eriugena of reviving Pelagianism (the heresy of man's free will in his redemption), and Ratramnus, Lupus and Prudentius defended Gottschalk against what they saw as Eriugena's contrariety to Augustinian doctrine.[17] Pope Nicholas I confirmed the Prudentian doctrine of double predestination in 859 (xxvii). Eriugena escaped from further sanction beyond the condemnations of Valance and Langres by virtue of his protection in Charles's court.

Gottschalk and the Trinitarian controversy

Pound's question to Otto Bird in 1938 – whether Eriugena was embroiled in 'some fuss about the trinity' – was prescient. The complex disputes of the early church over the definition of the Trinity were apparently settled at the

Council of Nicaea in 325 with the defeat of the Arian doctrine that God had made the Son *ex nihilo* as a separate being, rather than begetting the Son as part of Himself. But the concept of the Trinity had not resolved by the ninth century, turning on 'precise definition' in the translation of the Greek term *trina deitas*. Gottschalk and Hincmar also brought this issue to a head, into which Eriugena inadvertently waded. The Eastern Church was more heavily invested in the concept of the Trinity, and bore the added dimension of a strongly Neoplatonist heritage. Eriugena's familiarity with Eastern patristic texts afforded him an unparalleled advantage in negotiating the doctrinal and linguistic differences at stake in the controversy. Hincmar argued, with varying success and support, that *trina deitas* implied, heretically, a three-personed God, against which the orthodox concept of a triune God (one God in three Persons) was posed. Again the Augustinian texts are ambiguous, but the role of translation from Greek is pivotal. Aristotle's categories also play a crucial role, especially the definition of *ousia* as essence/substance. Eriugena's involvement in this controversy extended to his predicating God in three persons, wholly within each. This he extended to the whole of humanity and other species in his doctrine of participation (all men are in Adam, all tokens of a type exist in all tokens), leading him into further difficulties including the charge of heresy. Pound was right to guess at the controversy at issue, but knew little of the doctrinal and political circumstances of the dispute. At issue are the Neoplatonic proclivities of the Eastern patristic tradition, which allows for a notion of the Trinity considered to be suspect in the Latin West, by virtue of its analogies with the three hypostases of the One, Nous and the Soul. The formula of the Cappadocian Fathers became: 'three hypostases in one ousia', in the form of God, the Word and Wisdom (*deus, logos, sophia*) for the Father, Son and Holy Spirit.

Pound's reading of the controversies

Eriugena's contributions to the Predestination and Trinitarian controversies of his day risked imperilling his livelihood. He was able to flourish, and to write his masterwork the *Periphyseon*, due to royal patronage borne from a common stock of intellectual interests. Charles the Bald not only enlisted Eriugena to write *De praedestinatione*, he also commissioned the complete translation of Pseudo-Dionysius. The cultivation of *hilaritas* in the court is evident in Eriugena's poetry and the circumstantial evidence of interlinguistic puns and comedic set-pieces, of which 'tabula tantam' is the most celebrated example.[18] That his involvement in the Trinitarian controversy hinged upon the meaning of specific doctrinal translations from Greek aligns with Pound's demands for the 'precise definition of terms' in his *Confucius* and elsewhere. Eriugena's deployment of light imagery as the vehicle for theophany draws on long-standing traditions both within and outside of the Church: Pound folds Eriugena into the 'ideogram' of light that also includes the emblematic *cheng* 誠 ideogram, interpreted to depict 'the precise meaning of words', where 'the sun's lance strikes the precise spot verbally' (*CON* 20). The controversial nature of Eriugena's doctrines – the theory of participation, divine superessentialism, apophatic theology, his anthropology (all humans sin because we are all Adam and he is each of us) – provides Pound with abundant material by which to see Eriugena as ahead of his time, the one true clear thinker sidelined by political jealousy and ignorance. The tantalizing question remains: what might Pound have made of Gottschalk, had he known of his intellectual attributes as thinker and poet, as well as his persecution by plodding archiepiscopal interests?

Eriugena's posthumous career gripped Pound's imagination, especially in how his texts might intersect with the Averroist commentaries on Aristotle at the University of Paris in the thirteenth century and their subsequent influence on Cavalcanti. Questions of heresy circulated around the reception of Aristotle's *De Anima*, specifically the relation of divine wisdom and its intersection with the possible intellect, resulting in a series of condemnations erroneously implicating Eriugena as a source text for Siger of Brabant and David of Dinant, among others. Pound's reading in Eriugena was intensive with regard to the Pseudo-Dionysian texts and commentaries, but was otherwise cursory. His attention was held mostly by the reception of Eriugena in the thirteenth century, given that the minutiae of Predestination or Trinitarian controversies of centuries before were not well understood at the time. Eriugena's tenure as Palatine scholar and court poet presented an image of political agency of great allure to Pound, especially from the mid-1930s when his own activities in Fascist Italy and his correspondence with members of the United States legislature was building to a frenetic peak. Eriugena's asylum at court and Gottschalk's severe punishment following from the Predestination controversy both resonate with a model of rustication given expression in Pound's poetry, from the Seven Lakes canto of the mid-1930s to *The Pisan Cantos* composed in the final months of World War Two. The importance of light as a metaphor and intellectual lifeline sharpens considerably at these moments: bereft of liberty as well as an intellectual milieu, Pound produces a consolatory poetics in the form of the gossamer thread joining Neoplatonism, Confucianism, the composition of poetry and respect for the definitions of words.

Pseudo-Dionysius: Translations and commentaries

The treatises of Pseudo-Dionysius fulfil a crucial function in Eriugena's career in theology: they provide a strong basis for his apophatic and kataphatic theology; they delineate the hyperphatic concept of superessentialism upon which the *Periphyseon* hinges in its schema of *processio* and *reditus*; and in their Neoplatonic affirmation of triadic structures, they provide Eriugena with a powerful dialectical hermeneutic that reflects the triadic structure of the dynamic cosmos and divinity. Each of these virtues indicates how fruitful Eriugena found Eastern patristic thought. Eriugena gives Pseudo-Dionysius pride of place among his other Greek theological sources: Maximus the Confessor, Gregory of Nyssa, Gregory Nazianzus and Basil of Caesaria.[19] Pound's Eriugena notes, fully transcribed and annotated in the following chapter, show significant interest in Eriugena's translation of the Pseudo-Dionysian corpus. These notes almost exclusively concern *The Celestial Hierarchy*, as well as Eriugena's commentary on that text, *Expositiones Super Ierarchiam Caelestiam*, with an occasional gloss on the *Expositiones Super Ierarchiam Ecclesiaticam*. This intensive focus on a significant if pseudonymous Eastern Christian theologian compels a brief overview of the texts, if only to demarcate the themes to which Pound gives his attention when glossing his edition of Patrologia Latina 122 in 1939–1940.

Medieval scholars regarded Pseudo-Dionysius to be the authoritative starting point of the patristic tradition (75).[20] The Pseudo-Dionysian corpus was composed in the early sixth century[21] in Syria or Anatolia, only several decades after the Council of Chalcedon in 451. This event settled the Christological controversies of the patristic era,[22] and was considered to be the final efflorescence of early Christian thought (Louth 2). The texts were long attributed to the Areopagite converted by Paul's sermon to the Athenians on the 'Unknown God' in Acts 17: 22–34, but were written under a hagionym by an unknown author. Dionysius stood symbolically 'at the point where Christ and Plato meet' (Louth 11). The texts were composed as a unity: 'The author's apparent intention was that the treatises be encountered together and treated as a discovery from the first century' (Rorem 1993, 6).[23] This unity confers a sequential conceptual and reading order: *The Celestial Hierarchy, The Ecclesiastical Hierarchy, On the Divine Names* followed by *The Mystical Theology*. Maximus the Confessor defended the orthodoxy of the Pseudo-Dionysian texts in his *Ambigua* later in the sixth century, following which their canonicity in the Eastern Church was assured (15). The texts blend late fifth-century Syrian Christianity and Athenian Neoplatonism (18) and codify a world picture arranged along a vertical axis, a 'Great Chain of Being'.[24]

The Celestial Hierarchy and *The Ecclesiastical Hierarchy* were the texts to which Pound gave most attention by virtue of their schematic theology. The thread uniting heaven and earth, and reflected in the orders of the church, resonates with Pound's appropriation of the Confucian *Chung Yung* or 'Unwobbling Pivot' that combines celestial and temporal hierarchies. Pound's emphasis on 'right naming' and the definitions of words naturally drew him to the treatise *On the Divine Names. The Mystical Theology* introduces the phrase 'the darkness of unknowing' into theological discourse, from which the phrase 'the cloud of unknowing' derives (Rorem 1993, 8). The fourteenth-century mystical text of that name demonstrates the persistent influence of the Pseudo-Dionysian corpus on theological thought generally: 'That the Pseudo-Dionysian corpus seems best known for its contributions to the theme of unknowing and apophatic theology might well please the author, who probably chose the pen-name Dionysius to help make this very point' (214). The texts were often invoked to support diametrically opposed viewpoints in significant disputes, such as that between the papalists and the royalists at the turn of the fourteenth century in Rome on the issue of papal and secular authority, or the dispute between the mendicants and the secular bishops regarding their symbolic position in the ecclesiastical hierarchy (Rorem 1993, 34–8). This doctrinal flexibility epitomizes Alan of Lille's witty observation of the dexterous uses to which Platonic texts were often put in his *De fide catholica*: *Sed quia auctoritas cereum habet nasum, id est in diversum potest flecti sensum, rationibus roborandum est* (authority has a wax nose, it can be bent in diverse directions) (Patrologia Latina 210, 333A, qtd in Rorem 1993, 38). Pound could not have known precisely how fitting it was that Eriugena chose to translate these hagionymic texts, given the controversies that were to embroil his early career at court. That Eriugena introduced the word *hierarchy* into the Latin West in his transliteration from the Pseudo-Dionysian Greek only makes this network of associations the more serendipitous.

The Celestial Hierarchy adopts a Neoplatonist triadic structure for its schema of the nine angelic orders: the first hierarchy of seraphim, cherubim and thrones; the second of dominions, powers and authorities; and the third of principalities, archangels and angels. Higher orders contain all the powers of lower orders within them, providing a template for Eriugena's concept of participation (33). This structure draws from Plotinus in the metaphysical triad of the One, Intellect and the Soul. Porphyry arranged the *Enneads* (nines) into a similar assemblage. Proclus adapts the Plotinian triad of procession, rest and return into a dynamic theology: one that Eriugena (via Pseudo-Dionysius) adopts into the structure of *processio* and *reditus* in the *Periphyseon*.[25] Proclus formalizes the system of procession and return – not a temporal or spatial relation, but one relating cause to effect – that governs his whole philosophy: cause, procession from the cause and reversion to the cause as a system of identity, difference and overcoming difference in identity (52). *The Celestial Hierarchy* begins with the quotation from James 1:17 that was to capture Pound's attention when he read Eriugena's translation and commentary: 'Every perfect gift is from above, coming down from the Father of lights' (Patrologia Graeca 3, 120B, quoted in Rorem 1993, 50). This immediately turns to the structure of procession and return: 'Each procession of the Light spreads itself generously toward us, and, in its power to unify, it stirs us by lifting us up. It returns us back to the oneness and deifying simplicity of the Father who gathers us in' (*PG* 3, 120B). Eriugena recognized the way this text combined a Neoplatonic triadic structure with the dynamism of creation that was reflected in a dialectical method. This stems from Plotinus, who introduces a logic of mediation between the One and the many, where the mediating device is the hinge holding all of creation together. For Eriugena, this role is fulfilled by humanity, both the proper end of creation and the hinging point that initiates the *reditus*, and is embodied in the act of Christ's crucifixion (and thus creation is a reflection of the Trinity).

Chapter 2 of *The Celestial Hierarchy* describes a scriptural hermeneutics where symbols are not to be taken literally, but are signs acting to initiate and uplift those who know how to read them: 'symbols have a double rationale: to reveal and to conceal, to accommodate revelation to the capacity of the receivers and to keep it secret from the outsiders' (54). This mode of reading not only aligns with Eriugena's kataphatic theology, by which God is described metaphorically to enable a crude reckoning with what passes understanding, but also goes to the heart of his view of scripture. Francesco Fiorentino notes in the *Manuale di Storia della Filosofia* that Eriugena considered scripture to be in service to the 'infantile senses', constrained to a kind of 'Alexandrian allegory' in order to convey its intended meaning (Fiorentino 1921, 216). But this hermeneutics provides an anagogical thread to the perceptive human agent seeking to uplift themselves towards divinity: 'In the Dionysian universe [...] [t]he material world of sense perception is symbolic of a spiritual world of conceptions, and of God' (Rorem 1993, 77). The logic of concealment and revelation also bears obvious affinities with the esoteric philosophical schema Pound discerned in Cavalcanti's 'Donna mi prega'.

The Celestial Hierarchy generates a method of interpreting symbols that became very influential in the Middle Ages, stemming from the first Latin translations of Hilduin and Eriugena. To understand the sacred order where all things are images of God was to begin to make one's way up the hierarchy, in a process of uplifting towards divinity (58). This hermeneutics found its corollary in Gothic architecture, 'eventually incorporated into Abbot Suger's rationale for the uplifting beauty of the new church at the Abbey of Saint-Denis in the twelfth century, long regarded the first Gothic building' (74).[26] This link between Abbey and hagionym was accepted in Eriugena's time and served as a powerful symbol of church and state for Charles. Eriugena shows restraint when referring to Dionysius as the French patron saint Denis, although he accepts Hilduin's popularization of this story in his *Life of Saint Denis*, the *Post beatum ac salutiferam*. Eriugena also writes a number of poems for his patron, to commemorate such holy days as Easter which Charles often spent at the (then-Romanesque) Abbey of Saint Denis: 'The poems were intended for a context in which the Parisian career of Dionysius the Areopagite was not only assumed but indeed central to the spiritual self-understanding of the king himself' (Rorem 2005, 11).

Eriugena composed his commentary on *The Celestial Hierarchy* several years after completing his translation of the text, following the composition of the *Periphyseon*. Yet the two texts are profoundly intertwined: 'Eriugena's translation of *The Celestial Hierarchy* is thoroughly interwoven with his *Expositiones*, both in format and in substance […] [A]ny exposition presupposes a prior translation, just as any translation reflects an understanding of the text' (Rorem 2005, 47).[27] The *Expositiones* conducts a complex process of transliteration, paraphrase and translation of each sentence. This results in a great deal of repetition but is designed to mitigate the difficulties of the 'decal' approach of word-for-word translation which resulted in awkward syntax and obscured meaning. Rorem sees this as a likely rationale, drawing on the model of Boethius's translation/exposition of Porphyry – a text known to Eriugena (54).[28] Despite his unmatched facility in Greek, Eriugena struggles to translate the idiomatic prose of Pseudo-Dionysius (47–75).[29] He systematically interprets the prefix α- as an intensifier rather than privative, the result of which is to have his text 'hinge on negations, as do many other textual and grammatical issues in Eriugena's translation (not to mention apophatic theology itself), and […] reinforce the impression of a powerful interpretive mind triumphing over minor errors' (Rorem 2005, 74). The *Expositiones* contains patristic citations – including Jerome, Ambrose, Epiphanius and Augustine, as well as citations conflating Gregory of Nyssa and Gregory Nazianzius – but no reference to Maximus exists, despite the influence of this thinker upon Eriugena's understanding of the Pseudo-Dionysian corpus (Rorem 2005, 77).

Early in the *Expositiones*, Eriugena interprets James 1:17 in terms of a cosmic framework of descending plurality and ascending unification or anagogy: 'the procession of the divine illumination abundantly multiplies us into infinity, it enfolds and unites and restores us again to the simple unity of the gathering and deifying Father' (Rorem 2005, 79). The function of light that so catches Pound's eye in Eriugena is a kataphatic figure for the *processio* and *reditus* at the heart of Dionysian theology.

Pound pays scant attention to the other treatises in his notes, but several features of those texts deserve a brief comment. *On the Divine Names* contains a long chapter on the nature of evil, which is uncharacteristically rigorous and exhaustive in its argumentation. The treatise concludes that evil is privative, not being of God or known by God (PL 122, 716A–725B), illustrated in an imagery of light and darkness, where evil is akin to a deficiency of light (728A) (Rorem 152). This formulation clearly resonates with Eriugena's discourse in *De praedestinatione*, composed prior to his Pseudo-Dionysian translations. The influence of this schema of privative sin is also apparent in Aquinas's systematic theology, as well as that of the fourteenth-century Byzantine theologian Gregory Palamas (167).[30] This treatise also elaborates a symbology of light as a way of explaining God as both transcendent and immanent, and which functions in concert with the dialectical structure of God as both all things (plenum) and no thing (the superessential). The divine name of the Beautiful is the essential principle of being for Pseudo-Dionysius, following Plotinus, Gregory of Nyssa and Augustine (Perl 2010, 775).

The Pseudo-Dionysian treatises function within a conceptual sequence that Eriugena was to adopt in his *Periphyseon*: from creation, to matters of anthropology, to Christ and ultimately salvation. Eriugena reflects this order in the *Expositiones*. The strength of his systematic theology can be found in the way he harmonizes the Dionysian structure of procession and return (and its triadic implications), and the Augustinian structure of nature and grace (Rorem 2005, 99). The *Expositiones* produces a systematic synthesis of Dionysian and Augustinian concepts, and as such can be viewed as a work that unifies all of his writing in a nutshell, especially *De praedestinatione* and the *Periphyseon*. The concept of hierarchy structures each of the four treatises and their relation to each other, and goes to the heart of the Pseudo-Dionysian epistemology and metaphysics: 'The hierarchies are actually *theophanies*, that is, revelations of God understood in the perceiving mind' (Moran 95). The concept of *theophany* is another of several pivotal terms Eriugena transliterates from the Greek philosophical vocabulary (*theosis, meontology, apokatastasis*) that fundamentally reshapes his theological and metaphysical vision of human reunification with God. This theological tradition is suggestive of a potential paradise realized in the human in the process of *theosis*, a concept to which Pound was drawn in his project to compose his poetic *paradiso terrestre*. He clearly found much in *The Celestial Hierarchy* and Eriugena's commentary to mediate his thinking on Neoplatonism more generally, as well as on fertile points of contact with the intellectual and symbolic structures in the Confucian Four Books he was translating in the years leading up to his detention at Pisa.

The *Periphyseon*

Eriugena composed his masterwork, the *Periphyseon* or *De divisione naturae*, in the years immediately following his translations of and commentaries on Pseudo-Dionysius, perhaps partly as a consequence of that work. The text is a monument to early medieval philosophy: it functions not merely as a work of instruction but as an *inquisitio veritatis* – a vehicle for spiritual enlightenment and divine reunification (Moran 68). Its subject matter concerns the nature of God and the stages of creation. Book I assumes the form of a philosophical inquiry into the nature of Aristotelian categories, knowledge of which was disseminated in the Carolingian era in the *Categoria Decem*. The *hexaemeron* occupying Books II–V develops the schema of creation – *processio* and *reditus* – that turns on the role of humanity as the lynchpin: both a generalized humanity contained in the first man, Adam, and the divine embodiment in the human in the figure of Christ. This creation narrative is thus also an eschatology, in which the human process of *theosis* is linked to the Neoplatonic role applied to the liberal arts in realizing innate divine knowledge that became occluded in the Fall. Consequently, 'the *Periphyseon*'s epistemological and ontological aspects are effectively interrelated' (Otten 1994, 71). The dialectical relationship between light and darkness, knowledge and ignorance, and being and nothingness applies not only to the human perspective from which the discourse of the *Periphyseon* is situated, but also enfolds the notion of the divine nothing and mystical darkness that is the superessence of being, light and wisdom. This apparent paradox, adapted from the Pseudo-Dionysian corpus, provides Eriugena a potent mechanism by which to develop a general theory of theophany, both positive (kataphasis) and negative (apophasis). The extent of Eriugena's achievement must be measured in relation to the intellectual tradition from which the *Periphyseon* emerges, and to which it responds.

The *Periphyseon* stands out as an original contribution to philosophical discourse begun in the court of Charlemagne two generations earlier. His *Admonitio generalis* of 789 'advised that all cathedrals and monasteries were to open schools dedicated to the study of the psalms, musical notation, chant, computistics, and grammar' (Carabine 2000, 6). Alcuin of York turned to reason and dialectical method in his arguments, and introduced a systematic approach to learning to Charlemagne and his circle of students. He asserts in his *Disputatio de uera philosphia* that the House of Wisdom is erected on the seven pillars of the liberal arts: these are not merely propaedeutic but are the means to salvation, recalling (in orthodox Neoplatonic fashion) what had sunk into obscurity upon the sins of the first man (O'Meara 1988, 17). The central texts of Alcuin's circle were the *dicta Albini* composed by Alcuin himself and the *dicta Candidi*, probably written by his student Witto. These texts – collected in the so-called Munich Passages in the V manuscript, *Munich clm 6407* – gloss many of the central patristic texts. As with the general practice of glossing during the Carolingian age, these collections demonstrate scholarly motivations in their practices of selection. The contents of the Munich Passages show decisively that a philosophical agenda buttressed the scriptural hermeneutics and doctrinal controversies that comprise its subject matter:

> The *dicta Albini* is a commentary on Genesis 1:26: 'Faciamus hominem ad imaginem et similitudinem nostram.' In part, the *dicta* is based on Augustine's *De Trinitate*, from which Alcuin took the parallel between the persons of the Trinity and the *intellectus, uoluntas*, and *memoria* which constitute the mind. (Marenbon 1981, 44)

The agenda-setting is unmissable: not only does Alcuin's intellectual milieu develop interests in precisely the issues that were to erupt in dispute during Eriugena's lifetime, but the preoccupation with the Aristotelian Categories and with the syllogistic method establishes the ground upon which Eriugena was to construct his philosophical edifice. Further evidence of this emergent philosophical agenda in the Carolingian world is the *Liber de anima ad Odonem Bellovacensem* by Ratramunus of Corbie, composed earlier in the same decade as the *Periphyseon*. This text responds to Augustine's *De quantitate animae*, in which three views on the human soul are advanced: all souls are one, each soul is separate, or souls are both one and many. Ratramnus used this theme as a way to think through the notions of individuals and classes, turning an ostensibly theological exercise into an ontological study (67–9). The text also anticipates Eriugena's contentious thesis of *hyper-realism*, wherein each individual member of a class contains every other member of that class. Eriugena deployed this notion in *De praedestinatione*, adapted from Augustine's *De ciuitate Dei* and *Enarrationes in Psalmos*, to argue for the agency of individual will.

The *Periphyseon* brings together many aspects of Eriugena's thought on metaphysics, matters of doctrine, the relative merits of patristic sources, as well as rhetoric and dialectic – all of which were heavily mediated by the intensifying influence of Greek sources on his thinking (Otten 1994, 72). These themes are governed by the special role of humanity in the *exitus* and *reditus* of creation, who functions as the 'workshop' (*officina*) of creation, joining the higher world of spiritual things with the lower world of bodily things (McEvoy 1987, 218): 'Whereas the universe of man [*sic*] longs for the realization of the return in the same manner as the whole of the universe, including God, it is still man whose rational nature must guarantee its success' (Otten 1990, 212). The *Periphyseon* displays astonishing ambition in attempting a philosophical meditation of the utmost generality: an investigation into all things existing (ontology), and all things that do not exist (meontology), beyond which is divine nature, the 'nothingness by excellence' (*Peri.* I, 681A; Hankey and Gershon 829). The text combines a thorough study of the problem of universals in Book I, principally in the interrogation of the first Aristotelian Category, *ousia*. Marenbon identifies the problem of universals as the central preoccupation of all philosophy in the Middle Ages, enabling 'the observer to trace an important line of development which ran from the work of Alcuin's circle, by way of John Scottus (Eriugena), to the School of Auxerre' (1981, 6).[31] As an extended commentary on the *Categoriae Decem*, Book I of Eriugena's text might be seen in the same spirit as his earlier commentaries on such writers as Martianus Capella.[32] The hexaemeron comprising Books II–V rehearses the *exitus* of creation and the eschatological vision of the *reditus* (the return of creation to the godhead) as a way of exploring the fourfold division of nature: that which is not created and creates (God); that which is created and creates (the primary Categories); that which is created and does not create (the sensible world and all constituent elements of it, including humanity); and that which is not created and does not create (God in the phase of the *reditus*). These divisons of nature are not to be understood as fixed metaphysical levels but instead 'a set of *theoriae*, or mental acts of intellectual contemplation, which allow human subjectivity to enter into the infinite divine subjectivity and nothingness' (Moran 245).[33]

The structure of the text, as a dialogue between a master (Nutritor) and his pupil (Alumnus), supports its function as schematic theology: it remains open to a variety of physical theories (taking its cues from Augustine's *Genesi ad litteram*) provided no conflict occurs with scripture (Moran 69). This structure may have suggested itself to Eriugena via his student Wulfad, who he describes as his 'collaborator in philosophical pursuits' (*in studiis sapientiae cooperator*) and to whom he dedicated the *Periphyseon*. Wulfad was made Archbishop of Bourges by Charles in 866, and edited the text at Eriugena's request (Marenbon 1981, 112). The argument proceeds dialectically, with Alumnus asking for elaboration on specific points and positing his own views on particular topics. But this dialectical structure also provides Eriugena with the opportunity to work through notions of identity and difference (for example, in discussions of the nature of the Trinity), as well as the concept of nothingness, of which there are two radically different kinds: the privative nothing, that which does not exist (such as sin and punishment in *De praedestinatione*), and the super-essential not-being of God, who exceeds being in its imperfections, and therefore is not by being more-than-being. The modal apprehension of God is thus conducted by way of kataphatic theology (metaphor, figures of speech) and apophatic theology (a 'turning away' from representation in recognition of the divine superiority over any attribute). This structure confirms the perspectival nature of Eriugena's meontology: what might remain invisible from one viewpoint manifests itself in another. Divine nature, being invisible and incomprehensible, manifests itself by creating itself as other (i.e. theophany), just as invisible air is illuminated by light (*Peri.* I, 450A). The operations of the *reditus* in Book V comprise a complete reversal of creation, including the genderless nature of the risen Christ (*Peri.* IV, 894A; Mooney 168–69), the reincorporation of the deceased in an emulation of Christ's resurrection, and the ascension into the pure spiritual body made subordinate to the mortal body as a consequence of the Fall (*Peri.* IV, 798A–800B), before complete union with God. This entire structure of procession and return is heavily indebted to the Eastern Christian Platonists Gregory of Nyssa, Pseudo-Dionysius and Maximus the Confessor.

The Aristotelian Categories and *ousia*

The Aristotelian Categories is the unifying problem of all early medieval philosophy. A paraphrase thought to derive from Augustine, and known as the *Categoriae Decem*, circulated widely in the eighth and ninth centuries – 19 copies have survived from that time – and became ubiquitous: 'Ratramnus of Corbie, John Scottus, Heiric and Remigius of Auxerre, all knew the *Categories* through the *Categoriae Decem'* (Marenbon 1981, 16). Book I of the *Periphyseon* is a logical investigation of the ten primary Categories and the way they relate to God, who transcends them. Eriugena anchors his discussion in patristic authority, asserting from Augustine that the categories are not applicable to God but embrace 'all things that can be discovered in created nature or imagined by the mind' (72). The focus on the primary category of *ousia* however, has Eriugena depart from Augustine who identifies *ousia* with God. Instead, Eriugena follows the apophatic sensibility of the Eastern Fathers, and particularly Pseudo-Dionysius, who asserts that 'the being of all things is God, who more-than-is' (73). In this sense, '*usia* has no genus since it sustains all things (*ipsa autem usia genus habet cum omnia ipsa ustineat)'* (22–3). The notion of *diairetic descent* is taken from Porphyry and Pseudo-Dionysius, in which a chain of being descends from the highest genera to the individual species, then to individuals, in an ontological analogy to the creation. Eriugena's theory of *hyper-realism* takes its form in his anthropology in which Adam contains all men, and which extends to Christ's hypostatic union: 'Similarly, Christ's redemptive mission became less an article of faith than a consequence of logic, since by his incarnation Jesus became all men, and all men were thus saved by him' (77). This notion is adapted from Boethius, who postulated that in the realm of mathematics, the mental image of a number is the individual assimilation of a universal. Similarly, *ousia* is both universal and individual. It is characterised by its immutability and unknowability, known only by virtue of the way the other categories manifest themselves in objects: the human mind cannot know *what* ousia is, only *that* it is, and is thus restricted to a series of perspectival views or *theoriae* (Moran 145). This is a subtle point, where the Category of *substantia* is not identical with *ousia*: 'the *universalis essentia*, which is not subject to accidents, is distinguished from *substantia*, the first of the Categories, which is finite and subject to accidents' (79). This model bears a distinct morphological analogy to the theory of emanations later developed by Avicenna and Averroes, especially in the workings of the active and passive intellects. Pound saw this analogy, evident in his discussion of the Categories in his notes on Eriugena (for example, see YCAL MSS 43 76/3383, 5.10–11; YCAL MSS 43 77/3406, 22A.10–16).

Eriugena develops three versions of *ousia* in Book I of the *Periphyseon*: the first entails species and genera, which do not relate to the corporeal. The essential form is the species, whilst the qualitative form is the matter (*Peri.* I, 493C). Secondly, quality and quantity are all invisible, '[b]ut when these […] come together to form a sensible body, quantity brings forth a perceptible *quantum* and quality a perceptible *quale'* (Marenbon 1981, 80). Bodies return to the four elements but *ousia* is immutable (*Peri.* I, 494A–D). Thirdly, natural bodies have *ousiae* but geometrical ones do not, making *ousia* and matter codependent, whereas elsewhere in Eriugena's work they are opposing ends of the spectrum of being (*Peri.* I, 493B). The primordial causes are created in unity by the divine Word and are thus above order and number. Eriugena complicates his schema of primordial causes by making reference to them by different names and in different quantities. There are several lists throughout the *Periphyseon*: 'John lists in order Goodness, Essence, Life, Reason, Intelligence, Wisdom, Virtue (*virtus*), Beatitude, Truth, Eternity, Magnitude, Love, Peace, Unity and Perfection – a strange medley which seems to have been inspired by the various descriptions of God listed by the Pseudo-Dionysius' (82). These causes may be spoken of as kataphatically as attributes of God: '*Usia*, treated as a *genus generalissimum* having real existence, could be used both to forge links and to point contrasts between God and his creation' (140). Eriugena draws on Augustinian Trinitarian theology in positing the creative power of the Son, and the Holy Spirit's division of the things of creation into forms, genera, and individuals. His attempts to reconcile this schema with the four divisions of nature in the *Periphyseon* create difficulties in keeping the ontology coherent and consistent (Booth 1983, 80–1).

Anthropology

Books II–IV of the *Periphyseon* concern the *hexaemeron*, or the six days of creation, as a framing device by which to explore the essence of divinity and the human role in creation. These books explore the divisions of nature in the *exitus*: the production and power of the primordial cause, the Categories, and other essences, and the role of the human at the centre of the divine plan. Human nature descends from the realm of angels as a consequence of the Fall, but retains the potential to inhabit this perfected state again in the process of *theosis*. The human thus mediates the spiritual and physical realms, and contains all of physical creation by way of participation: 'all lower creatures were made in man initially in the sense that he possessed "concepts" (*notiones*) of them ontologically prior to their unfolding in physical extension' (Gersh 1990, 124). Eriugena derives his concept of participation from Gregory of Nyssa, who, in his *De hominis opificio* (titled *De imagine* in Eriugena's c.863 translation) asserts the central role of humanity as *imago Dei* in the great chain of being (Moran 51). This is a kind of idealist mentalism: the notion that the human mind has the capacity to contain all things in their essence as ideas (82). It is 'a dignity not afforded to angelic natures' (97), thus marking out the unique role of humanity in creation, including the Fall: 'Just as God became not God through manifestation and self-creation in theophany while remaining God, so in the process of being embodied in the material world, human being becomes not-human through its own self-creation, that is, through its willingness to turn away from its original nature' (Carabine 2000, 68). Human reason also emulates the divine mind in being able to articulate the hierarchy of being: an anthropology blending aspects of Augustine's thought with that of Gregory of Nyssa and Maximus the Confessor, but 'in radical opposition to the Latin realist tradition' (Moran 97). The human mind thus 'produces the world which it knows through intellect' (144), and 'has the power to order infinite reality according to its own free inclination and also in accordance with divine theophany' (267). Eriugena's innovative concept of *natura* is predicated on the human mind, even extending to those parts beyond the mind's grasp (Carabine 2000, 30). Book IV, which concentrates on the sixth day of creation, develops a series of complex arguments for the status of human nature as both that which it is and is not intended to be, by virtue of the dialectical perspectivism by which the *natura* of any thing can be said to exist or not, depending on the mode by which it is apprehended. This hermeneutic method is the thread that unites the application of philosophy and the liberal arts as innate human faculties (and divine gifts) with the process of *theosis*. Modal perspectivism includes all stages of development – from the Fall into ignorance to the wisdom of learning to the blessed ignorance that demarcates divine reunification. Humanity participates in both the *exitus* and the *reditus*, and as such, is central to the divine plan of creation.

Meontology and superessentialism

In the *Periphyseon* Eriugena develops the concepts of kataphatic and apophatic theology by which to navigate human apprehension of divine nature as represented in theophany or else understood as beyond being and non-being. He produces an exhaustive analysis of divine superessentialism: the negative theology he draws from Pseudo-Dionysius to distinguish privative negation (that which is not) from divine negation by virtue of being 'more-than' (the more-than-goodness that produces the good; the invisible more-than-light that produces the light signifying divinity). Book III (634A–690A) contains what Sheldon-Williams has called a 'little treatise' (1981, 5 n.1) on the nature of divine nothing as superessential rather than privative, which extends Eriugena's thinking on this subject first broached in *De praedestinatione*. The passage reconciles creation *ex nihilo* with creation *de Dio* or *ex se ipsa*, where the 'nothing' from which created matter derives[34] is the superlative divine Nothing: Eriugena explicitly attributes this concept to Pseudo-Dionysius (*Peri*. III, 644A and 644B) and returns to this theme in Chapter 4 of the *Expositiones*. It bears implications for the idea of theophany, or divine self-expression in creation, in which 'God, beyond being, becomes the being of all' (Rorem 2005, 111). This marks out a radical departure from the primacy of being which underwrites Western metaphysics, and develops the modal perspectivism that indicates the various stages of human *natura* and *theosis*. But this notion extends beyond the human – central as its role in creation may be – and is applied to the whole of creation as the *universalis natura* or το παν (*Peri*. II, 529A). This *universitas* of created nature is dynamic, a *multiplex theoria* which bears multiple meanings in the dialectical flux of human cognition (*Peri*. III, 621A).

Eriugena's articulation of theophany in the *Periphyseon* is informed both by apophatic theology and by superessentialism, but in its positive or kataphatic manifestation it often takes the form of light imagery: thus Pound's natural attachment to the poetic formula *omnia quae sunt, lumina sunt*. The process of divine manifestation in light finds its human complement in the ascent from the darkness of ignorance to the light of truth, but the metaphor of light cannot 'be employed usefully in terms of apophatic utterances unless it is adapted, if not indeed fully reversed' (Carabine 1994, 142). While the Exodus story of Moses ascending Mount Sinai may be understood allegorically as the soul's ascent to the *deus absconditus*, the vision of theosis must instead be figured in terms of the *lux inaccesibilis* drawn from 1 Timothy 6:16. In his letter to Dorotheus, Pseudo-Dionysius figures the *lux inaccessibilis* of divine nature as both cloud and darkness: Eriugena quotes this letter and adopts these figures in Book V (920A). These images might appear contrary to the notion of divine light, but they deftly express the notion that the resurrected soul knows *that* God is, just not *what* God is (Carabine 1994, 148): the distinction between *quia est* and *quid est*. The divine ray may shine on all things, from the modal perspective of the created human mind, but it does not illuminate (except by exceeding light in ineffable darkness) the realm of things that are not, or that exceed being, such as the uncreated divine *natura*.

Reditus

Book V turns to the *reditus* in which all of creation is transmuted from corporeal to incorporeal being and returns in unity to God. Combined with the thesis that all of creation is present in the human (*Peri.* IV, 755B), and that the human body is ideal before the Fall into a material and corruptible condition, the *reditus* transforms this radical anthropology into a fully-fledged *theosis*: 'Eriugena offers a provocative and original account of man becoming God interwoven with his exegesis of biblical symbols' (Dietrich and Duclow 1986, 30). The *reditus* entails all of creation, but at its centre is the human shift from physical being to pure intellection, and the unity of all people into one ur-person:

> The initial restoration applies to the entire *genus* of man; it is a *grant* conferred by *nature*, and symbolized by entrance into the outer porticoes of the temple of Solomon and re-entry into the garden of paradise. The *special* return of the elect is the *gift* of deification bestowed by *grace*, and symbolized by access to the Holy of Holies or eating the fruit of the Tree of Life. The first movement is 'the restoration of human nature as a whole to Christ' while the second refers to the bliss and deification of those who are to ascend to God himself. (31–2)

The distinction between the resurrection of humankind, on the one hand, and the transformation of the elect, on the other, retains the Augustinian distinction between the *datum* (gift) and the *donum* (grace), allowing all to be raised into the unity of divine bliss but only the elect to be deified. Sinners are punished by the privative nature of their sins: they engage in phantasies reflecting their sins, manufactured not by God – who knows nothing of sin – but by their own wills. God saves sinners' natures, but not their wills, and thus they are denied the union with God enjoyed by the elect.[35] The dyad of *datum* and *donum* is derived from James 1:17 by Augustine and Pseudo-Dionysius.[36] Pound takes an intensive interest in this verse, dealing with the 'Father of Lights,' as a touchstone of divine light not only in the Neoplatonic tradition but as a method by which to align it with Confucian light symbolism, especially in the *Da Xue* or *Great Learning*, to be treated in the final chapter of this study.

Early in Book V Nutritor provides Alumnus with a precise schema of the stages of the *reditus*, precisely reversing the process of *exitus* with which the Books II–IV were occupied:

> The first step in the Return of our human nature is taken when the body suffers dissolution and turns back into the four elements of the sensible world from which it was composed.

The second is fulfilled at the Resurrection when each shall take his own body out of the common fund of the four elements.

The third when body is changed into soul.

The fourth when soul, and in fact the whole human nature, shall revert to its Primordial Causes, which ever and immutably abide in God.

The fifth when that spirit with its Causes is absorbed into God as air is absorbed into light. For when there is nothing but God alone, God will be all things in all things. (876A–B) (Sheldon-Williams and O'Meara 1987, 541)

By placing the human experience at the centre of the *reditus*, Eriugena shows how his conception of salvation is intimately bound with his anthropology: 'Because all things were created in human nature, they cannot return except with it' (Carabine 2000, 97). The notion of the human is 'a certain intellectual idea made in the Divine Mind' and the essence of the human soul is in the intellect, in its circular motion around God: 'John identifies deification with the contemplative vision of and union with god; *theosis* and *theoria* coincide' (Dietrich and Duclow 1986, 35). This architecture is reflected rhetorically in the text, where recapitulation echoes the divine *recollectio* in the *reditus* (Moran 74). The geometrical arrangement of the human-God relation resonates with Pound: in *The Pisan Cantos* the idea of circular motion around a celestial object is expressed in Greek – ''HΛION ΠEPI 'HLION' (LXXIV/451) – and this geometrical figure also becomes a powerful expression of the Confucian ruler-sage, evident most explicitly in Pound's Italian title for *The Unwobbling Pivot* as *L'Asse che non vacilla* (*The Axis Never Wavers*) and the central role of the 中 (*zhong*) character in the later poetry.

Eriugena deploys the image of the Tree of Life in his vision of the *reditus*, specifically as the world's *omphalos*. Scholars have likened this usage to the sixth *De Pascha Homilia*, variously attributed to Hippolytus of Rome – probably the most important theologian of the third century – or to Pseudo-Chrystostom (Dietrich and Duclow 1986, 39), where the Tree of Life is not only the fulcrum or fixed pivot of the universe, but also the tree of the crucifixion and the means of transit between earth and heaven:

The features implicit in the iconography of the cosmic tree: the tree as symbol of ascension, microcosm and macrocosm, a cosmic theophany, fount of immortality, the *axis mundi*, resurrection – all are rooted in the paradisal garden as source and setting of the tree. John's account of the Tree of Life indicates his reading of Genesis as an eschatological document. The biblical cosmogony is also an apocalypse. (39)

The *Periphyseon* is thus not only a work of dialectic and biblical exegesis, but also a mystical theology driven to an eschatological vision. Genesis, especially in the creation and fall of humanity on the sixth day, functions as an *auspicium* of the *reditus* (48). Since human nature fell as soon as it was created, paradise is not structured with a past, and thus instead becomes an eschatological hope (Carabine 2000, 86). Eriugena draws on patristic authority in the *Periphyseon*, but in the case of Augustine he chooses *City of God* and *de Genesi ad litteram* over the *Confessions*, despite the latter's intensive focus on Genesis. This has to do with the rhetorical equipoise for which Eriugena aims: the *Confessions* combine passion and action, whereas the *City of God* is more in keeping with the precise rhetorical balance sought in his own work (O'Meara 1986, 117). *City of God* also deals with eternal beatitude following the judgement, unifying time's arrow with the circularity of creation. Eriugena's use of Eastern sources also treads a careful path through divergent views of the nature of theodicy:

> being itself […], life itself and thought itself in Proclus were subordinated emanations from the One, Pseudo-Dionysius identified them with God; thus returning to the position of Aristotle which Proclus had rejected. God is the one who gives substance, the substantifier of every single existing thing, giving it total existence; everything pre-exists in him, who is the exemplar of everything. (Booth 1983, 77–8)

Eriugena follows Pseudo-Dionysius in viewing God as the origin of all creation, but is careful to distinguish between God and the elements of creation by way of the distinction between kataphatic and apophatic theology.

Despite its devotional subject matter, the *Periphyseon* aroused suspicions concerning its doctrinal rectitude, and was included in the condemnations of 1050, 1059, 1210 and 1225. Following its first modern publication in 1685 by Thomas Gale, the text was placed upon the Vatican's Index Librorum Prohibitorum Sanctissimi until the Index itself became defunct in 1948.[37] Its role in consolidating Eriugena's doctrine of participation – where all humans participate in Adam's sin and are coexistent with him, and where all are saved in the single unitive process of the *reditus* – and his heavy reliance on Pseudo-Dionysius clearly made his text a doctrinal target. Added to this vexed history of reception is the rhetorical challenge laid down to the reader: the persistent use of *amplificatio*, which has the effect of radically deferring the main clause of a sentence; and the use of inversion, 'of putting phrases in an order which even by the standard of hyperbaton used in Latin styles of various kinds is unusual' (Marenbon 1981, 120). The problem of accounting for, and translating, the unusual combination of Greek and Latin in Eriugena's text has been likened to 'carrying the cargo across the river of time on the bridge of style' (O'Meara 1986, 117). The unsatisfactory state of published editions of the *Periphyseon* exacerbates these impediments to reading the text. Whilst Sheldon-Williams's parallel text translation attempts to establish a genetic edition, it fails to account accurately for the relation between several important manuscript sources, and the translation employs numerous archaisms. Sheldon-Williams did not live to produce the parallel text of Book V. O'Meara's single-volume translation follows Sheldon-Williams for Books I-IV, and produces its own translation for Book V: the text is explicitly presented as a service to scholars as a reading text, with no claim to philological integrity or significant editorial intervention. The edition of record is Édouard Jeauneau's five-volume Latin edition in the Corpus Christianorum Continuatio Mediaeualis series, with apparatus in French, but without a parallel translation into a modern European language. This edition takes into account widely divergent manuscript versions attributed to Eriugena himself, and represents the *Periphyseon* not as a final, unified theological statement, but as 'a text in perpetual becoming' (Jeauneau 1996, xix): perhaps a fitting textual reflection of the modal perspectivism it espouses for human *natura* and the division of nature generally.

Quid distat inter sottum et Scottum?
Eriugena as Carolingian court poet

In *The Pisan Cantos* Pound makes reference to Eriugena's verses 'stitched' (στίχος) in the company of Charles and Irmintrude, occupied with stitching her own *textus* (LXXXIII/548).[38] This apparently casual reference, occurring after Pound had viewed volume 122 of the Patrologia Latina, celebrates the *hilaritas* shared by king and poet, and bears witness to the spirit in which precious cultural knowledge is transmitted through history. Beneath its surface reside specific kinds of historical information: 'The *Liber pontificalis* relates that Charles presented a garment to [Pope] Nicholas made of gold and gems and we know that Ermintrude worked on one such robe given to Nicholas, since its dedicatory verses have been preserved. In Eriugena's poem, Ermintrude is praised as skilful in the art of Athena, that is, weaving' (Dutton 1986, 67–8). Eriugena transmits his Greek learning in poetry in praise of his king, providing insight into this corner of enlightened and decorous relationship between Carolingian king and courtier: '[t]he *carmina* show him to have been an intensively partisan poet, an "écrivain engagé," for he chiefly sang songs for his King' (51). Although Eriugena's poetry has been largely sidelined in Carolingian scholarship, it formed a central part of his intellectual endeavours at court:

> The writing of Latin poetry can no longer be viewed as a 'leisure-time activity' in the life of a busy philosopher/theologian and teacher. Rather, poetry was for John a central occupation in which he was engaged for most of his known career. (Herren 1993, 11)

Pound makes reference to Eriugena's 'tags' as though his use of Greek is a matter of clever adornment, whereas its deployment is carefully motivated, and its use extensive, from single words to entire poems: 'John loved Greek and believed that the Greek language had greater authority than Latin' (12). The relative novelty of Greek verse contributed to the Eriugenian legend, which took extravagant form. Ludwig Noack (1876) and Reginald Poole (1920) likened Eriugena to a meteor, and Joseph Marie de Gerando's Ozymandian image of 1823 – 'like encountering a monument of art standing in the middle of the sands of a desert' – was repeated often (Dutton 1986, 52). Such an antiquated view persisted well into the twentieth century: 'He was thought a lonely genius, a man outside his time, a thinker without real intellectual contemporaries, a brooding embodiment of pure mind adrift in a dull and unreceptive age' (53). Pound's suspicions concerning the wider ideological implications of Eriugena's serial condemnations align with this view of Eriugena as a solitary beacon of reason, but investigates beyond complacent stereotypes to discern precisely what was at stake in Eriugena's thought to arouse such ecclesiastical antipathy. In this sense, Pound moves against the intellectual current of his times – Cappuyns being the notable exception – and anticipates the general reappraisal of the Carolingian age later in the century.

Despite the relative obscurity of Eriugena's poetry in the field of scholarship, there existed three editions of Eriugena's poetry prior to Michael Herren's authoritative edition for the series Scriptores Latini Hiberniae. The first was by Angelo Mai (1833–1838); Henry Joseph Floss then produced 'largely a retrograde effort' (Herren 12) that was used as the base text for Pound's source, the Patrologia Latina; and thirdly Ludwig Traube produced an edition (1896), which is considered to be exemplary. The erratic and erroneous treatment of Greek in prior editions was a principal rationale for Herren's new edition, as well as providing the chance to include previous omissions and subsequent discoveries to the corpus. Herren's stylistic and codicological analyses also provide a better understanding of poems that were previously supposed to be merely Greek fragments but that actually form part of larger poems (14). Each of the three major manuscript collections underpinning all editions contain extraneous material, as well as Greek excerpts, some of which link back to their poems, whilst others do not: Greek fragments are therefore not always able to be given strict attribution. In addition to the reconstructed ω manuscript that comprises the larger portion of his edition, Herren notes: 'John wrote groups of prefatory poems to his translations of the pseudo-Dionysian corpus and the *Ambigua* of Maximus the Confessor [...] These groups have separate traditions' (20). Whilst there were other Irish scholars in Charles's kingdom with a facility for Greek – notably Sedulius Scottus, Martin Hiberniensis and Fergus of Laon – the boast of Greek proficiency and the promotion of its study are specifically Eriugenian *topoi* (34). One can imagine Pound finding this kind of bravura suitable to his own temperament. He shows little sign of having worked through the poems in any detail, however, and by describing them as 'excellent verses' (LXXXIII/548) he goes against the grain of most scholarly opinion up to his time, probably without knowing it.

Eriugena's poems can be classified into three discrete types: firstly the 'long poems' addressed to the king on the occasion of an important feast or event, usually Easter (the most important day on the Christian calendar), which often skilfully interweave theological themes with topics of current interest; secondly a series of metrical prefaces, colophons and *tituli* meant to accompany John's own writings and translations and perhaps manuscript illustrations; and thirdly, short poems in Greek, Latin or a mixture thereof, often in epigrammatic form, addressed to or dealing with a variety of individuals such as the king, pupils, teachers, or one or both Hincmars (the Archbishop of Reims and his nephew, the Bishop of Laon) (Herren 1993, 25). There are no long poems in Greek, but instead there are words and phrases and the occasional distich, and a suite of short poems ranging up to 14 lines: 'Although John did attempt to deal with serious themes in Greek [...] it would appear that he was most effective when using this language for satirical or witty themes' (26). However, he took the prosodic challenges of Greek metre seriously, attempting to compose parallel hexameters in both Greek and Latin.

Like many of his earlier poems, Eriugena's longest poem, *Aulae siderae*, is an occasional poem addressed to Charles: 'It connects the foundation of Charles's new church (at Compiègne) in 870 with the mysteries of Christmas and depicts the king enthroned in the new church' (26). Other poems deal mostly with theological themes, but occasionally, political themes arise: Eriugena champions Charles in one of his several fraternal wars, criticizes Charles's pro-Jewish policies, provides a critique of Hincmar of Laon, and issues a vindication of Charles's taking the additional crown of Lotharingia on death of Lothar (27). Eriugena was able to deploy his abilities in Greek to adorn Charles with titles that were not appropriate in a purely Latin context:

> While Eriugena frequently calls Charles a 'rex', his chief innovation was in the use of Greek titles for his ruler: Charles is ΑΝΑΞ or king, and he is ΚΥΡΡΙΟC or lord. John also addressed his ruler as ΒΑCΙΛΕΥC, the term so often applied to Byzantine rulers, as CEBACTOC or Caesar, and ΑΚΡΟC ΤΕ ΜΟΝΑΡΧΟC, the pinnacle of monarchs. Moreover, one finds combinations of Greek and Latin words, and lines of acclamation rendered in both Greek and Latin. (Dutton 1986, 69–70)

Charles's royal authority is founded in his heritage and in the figure of Christ: as grandson of the first Holy Roman Emperor, Charles came from a line of kings or *stemmate regum*. This auspicious heritage meant two things for Eriugena: the stemma as royal ancestry and stemma as the garland worn on the head of the king (71–2). Eriugena's experiments in punning and wordplay extended to the head of a poem composed entirely in Greek, where the first letters of each line spell out in acrostic fashion, 'KAROLVS REX'.[39] Eriugena urged Charles to further his study of Greek (evident in poem 20.6: 'be not reluctant to take up Attic training'), transforming these aspects of his poetry from a general challenge to the culture of learning in which he circulated, to a specific entreaty to his king to enter into specialist knowledge. Eriugena's Greek verses thus 'stand as living proof that a westerner might attain a command of the Greek language such as to enable him to think and write in it – however harshly our scholarly predecessors may have judged the fruits of this effort' (47).[40] Eriugena's Greek mixes its idioms, advertising the direct influence of his sources in the Greek gospels, Maximus the Confessor, Gregory of Nyssa, and Pseudo-Dionysius, as well as secondary sources such as Martianus Capella and Macrobius. The tone of this linguistic challenge, and its obvious novelty in the Carolingian context, presents an alluring example of how Eriugena's temperament resonated with Pound, whose own linguistic efforts in Greek, Provençal and Chinese place him in an analogously propaedeutic position.

Much as in the classical tradition, the shorter poems tend to be scathing and pithy, and broach such topics as drinking or long-winded teachers. Eriugena's doctrine is that of man as self-willing agent of misery, and God as agent of mercy towards those with good will. This is evidence of his anthropology – a radical expression of human free will, and the tying of divine mysteries to human individuality – and is consistent with his refutation of Gottschalk's double predestination. Eriugena's poetic productivity during the 860s might be attributed to his intensive interest in the liberal arts, especially rhetoric and dialectic, consistent with his interest in Martianus Capella. He considered poetry to be an intellectual activity equal to philosophy, rather than merely propaedeutic to it (Herren 1993, 42). There is evidence of influence by Latin poets such as Virgil (both the *Aeneid* and the *Georgics*), Ovid and Lucretius: Eriugena borrows the phrase '*machinae mundi*' in one poem (3.5), from *De rerum natura* (Book V line 96). Eriugena was also informed by his immediate predecessors such as Alcuin (45). Several poems begin with an invitation to meditate on a symbol such as a cross or a word: 'All such symbols lead the reader directly to the contemplation of the *mysteria Christi* – his Incarnation, birth, death, Resurrection, and descent into hell – which provide the only proper matter of true Christian poetry' (54). Numerous poems address the role of Charles as benevolent ruler facing hostilities and warfare (not least from Louis the German):

> In the letter-preface to the translated works of the pseudo-Dionysius from a few years later, Eriugena speaks of the great and persistent disturbances of civil wars and more than civil wars. The phrase 'ciuilia plusque quam ciuilai bella' is a rather famous one, since it derives from Lucan's *Pharsalia*, another poem on a civil war. A king, as the saying suggests, faces several different kinds of assault: civil wars like the one caused by Louis, a more generalized state of disorder brought about by criminals and disloyal subjects, and finally the invasion of the barbarians. (Dutton 1986, 75)

Eriugena draws on the classical tradition in supporting a king at risk from malevolent forces both internal and external to his kingdom. He frames the very fact of such disorder as an attack on reason. Charlemagne had been lauded as a warrior-king: Eriugena wisely chooses not to frame Charles the Bald within such a discourse but instead as a *rex sapiens*. Thus political instability and military threat do not signal the king's failure to maintain control of his lands, but imply a redoubled commitment to enlightened discourse and the defence of culture. Whilst Pound may have had only a passing awareness of this historical context, he seemed to intuit the ideological role Eriugena established as poet within the Carolingian court.[41]

Closer examination of Eriugena's use of imagery reveals a number of innovations amidst the conventions of religious poetry he inherits from the late classical tradition. His use of light as metaphor of divine emanation is conventional, drawing from long-standing usage in prose texts from both the Eastern and Western Churches. However its specifically poetic use foregrounds certain aspects of the late-classical lyrical tradition. Ambrose's composition of hymns in the fourth century was ground-breaking in the history of lyric, and was motivated as an exercise in congregational solidarity in the face of Emperor Valentian and the threat of the Arian heresy he represented. Ambrose also composed the *Exulset*: 'a fourth-century prose-poem that plays with the imagery of light almost symphonically, the praises of light mounting until they embrace even the world of darkness, the "blessed night," which is transfigured and made radiant by Christ overcoming death' (Dronke 2002, 33). The tropological force of light imagery undergirds *The Celestial Hierarchy* of Pseudo-Dionysius, in which Eriugena took intensive interest: as a kataphatic representation of divine will, it also functions in analogous fashion as evidence of Eriugena's right-thinking in an epoch otherwise darkened by the eclipse of intellect. Eriugena also draws on Ambrose's innovative use of *figura*: the transfiguration of the poetic image by its union of divine and human aspects that shows a 'human moment in a divine pattern' (34). This kind of continuity is precisely what Pound values in Eriugena, especially in the context of the 'magic moment' in *The Cantos*, as well as his focus on Cavalcanti's 'Donna mi prega' as a thirteenth-century cognate exercise, the whole poem producing an extended figure of the human-divine continuum. In Eriugena's poetry, the axis joining heaven and the divine mysteries to earth (with Charles as a protected and privileged recipient of divine grace) produces a view of 'human history [as] *sub specie aeternitatis*' (Herren 1993, 55). In essence, 'Eriugena's entire philosophy of nature is really a light metaphysics of manifestation and concealment, darkness and illumination' (Moran 267). This outlook makes Eriugena unique in all Carolingian poetry, but it also resonates very clearly with Pound's own attempts to amalgamate Neoplatonic thought with the Confucian worldview to which he had devoted a great deal of attention in the later 1930s. In more than one sense, the time was absolutely ripe for his discovery of Eriugena, and his continual rediscovery thenceforth.

***

Pound's awareness of the major philosophical and doctrinal themes of Eriugena's texts was initially directed by his reading in secondary works. The prominence given by Francesco Fiorentino and Étienne Gilson to matters of Eriugena's ecclesiastical condemnation and his sponsorship in the Carolingian court play a large part in Pound's interest in Eriugena's historical context, and his eagerness to acquire and work through the primary texts themselves. The consequences for Pound's Eriugenian negotiations following his acquisition of Patrologia Latina 122 are borne out in his two sets of notes made in the course of his reading that volume. As the closely annotated 'edition' of Pound's notes shows, his attention sharpens considerably with regard to Eriugena's translations of and commentaries upon the texts of Pseudo-Dionysius, aspects of the *Periphyseon* relating to the nature of divine emanations and their kataphatic representations in light imagery, and the aspects of Eriugena's poetry concerning his use of Greek and his exhibition of *hilaritas* in the court of Charles the Bald. This study has Pound's Eriugena notes at its heart: for what they tell of Pound's specific interests in the Hibernian scholar-poet, but also in how he mediates these interests in the paradisal poetry on which he intended to embark, and after a significant wartime delay, that became instead the famous *canti nel carceri, The Pisan Cantos*.

Notes

1 David Ganz points out that the various participants in the Predestination controversy were also authors of treatises on canon law, royal annals and panegyric and were thus active shapers of social discourse: 'Because it is through the source which they wrote that we see the reign of Charles the Bald, their theological preconceptions are directly relevant to our interpretation of this reign' (Ganz 353). Ganz also notes the intensification of synod activity in Charles's kingdom – including those at which Eriugena's work was condemned – coincided with the political instability of Carolingian confraternal rule, viking invasion, and aristocratic unrest.

2 John J. Contreni contests that the copy of the *Periphyseon* in Paris Bibliotheque Nationale lat. 12964 came from Laon: see Contreni 1972, 7, note 8.

3 The glosses thought to be from Heiric are found in M (*Milano Ambrosiana B 71 sup.*), H (*Paris BN 12949*) and G (*Sankt Gallen 274*): 'It does not seem probable that Heiric had a set of Eriugena's own glosses to follow: the glosses in M seem to be the work of an imaginative thinker who has read the *Periphyseon*; they lack the logical thrust of John's own work and his characteristic traits of expression' (Marenbon 1981, 123).

4 The *Libri Carolini* helped inflame the *Filioque* controversy, in which the Nicene Creed was emended to state that the Holy Spirit descended from the Father and the Son: this assertion was present in neither the text stemming from the First Council of Nicaea of 325 nor that of the First Council of Constantinople of 381. The Eastern Church never admitted the legitimacy of the change, which eventually helped lead to the East-West Schism of 1054. See Davis, especially Chapter 2, 33–80 and Chapter 3, 81–133.

5 On the subject of Charlemagne's court as a seat of learning, see McCormick 20, Brown 28–44, and Garrison 111–140.

6   The question of how much Greek learning took place in Ireland is long disputed: Maïuel Cappuyns asserts that little Greek learning took place there, whilst Ludwig Bieler maintains the opposite view. For further details see Carabine 2000, 14.

7   For an exhaustive examination of the question of Eriugena's hand in extant manuscripts of his work, see Édouard Jeauneau and Paul Dutton 1996.

8   To these early *florilegia* might be added two twelfth-century manuscripts: the edition produced at Malmesbury by several scribal hands that came into William's possession and is now housed at Trinity College Cambridge (*Trin. Coll. 0.5.20*); and *Clavis physicae*, an important if flawed *liber excerptus* by Honorius Augustodunensis, a modern edition of which Paolo Lucentini has prepared.

9   See Cora Lutz 1944. Several scholars question this attribution, thinking it more likely the work of another Irish contemporary, Martin Hiberniensis: see Jean G. Préaux 1953, 437–59.

10 Eriugena's case for human agency in *De praedestinatione* overstepped the bounds of orthodoxy of his time, which was heavily inflected by (a far from unambiguous) Augustinian doctrine. Later, in the *Periphyseon* (predominantly in Book IV), Eriugena makes a radical case for human nature 'in which the whole of creation is brought together in an ineffable harmony' (Carabine 2000, 67). As both animal and spiritual, the human in its fallen state is conditioned to seek a return to its original status as a primordial cause equal to that of angelic intellects. For a detailed study of Eriugena's anthropology, including its negative manifestation and its function as *multiplex theoria* (given to various perspectives) and *officina omnium* (the 'workshop' of all things), see Otten 1991a and Moran 154–85.

11 The condemnation of Pelagianism was ratified at the Third Ecumenical Council at Ephesus in 431 (see Davis 134–68). For a discussion of Augustine's equivocal theology on this point, see Wetzel; for a detailed historical account of Pelagianism see Bonner 1992 and 1993.

12 Marenbon also demonstrates that the *Dicta Albini* (often attributed to Alcuin) gives the *imago-similitudo* discourse proper philosophical treatment. See also Moran 8–11. Another critical element in this discourse is the thought of Marius Victorinus, a Roman grammarian who brought Greek philosophy into the Latin world in the fourth century (Markus 332), including Plotinus and Porphyry. He developed a philosophical vocabulary of enormous influence upon metaphysics in the Middle Ages, and Alcuin copied numerous passages of his work in *De fide* (Clark 3). Victorinus considered the soul's likeness to God to be accidental and thus able to be lost and recovered, whereas its image-relation to God is essential and cannot be lost (337).

13 In *After Strange Gods*, T. S. Eliot notes the disappearance of the notion of original sin in Pound's poetry (Eliot 1934, 42).

14 See for example Hincmar's *On Predestination* (PL 125, 55–474); Prudentius of Troyes, *On Predestination against John the Scot* (*De predestinatione contra Joannem*

Scotum) (PL 115, 1009–1366); Ratramnus of Corbie, *De praedestinatione Dei, ad Carolum Calvum libri duo* (PL 121, 12–30); and Florus of Lyon, *Liber adversus Joannem Scotum* (PL 119, 101–248). Gottschalk's three works on predestination, *Confessio, Confessio prolixior,* and *Epistola Gotteschalci ad Ratramnum,* appear in the same volume as those of Ratramnus (PL 121, 347–70).

15   In this sense Eriugena's subsequent exposure to Pseudo-Dionysius transforms his thinking on reason and authority. Whilst both are products of divine wisdom, for the Areopagite, apophatic theology is superior to kataphatic theology. 'On the basis of scriptural authority, man learns what can be said of God; on the basis of right reason, man learns what should be denied' (Marler 102): thus reason precedes authority. Alternately, D'Onofrio quotes the famous passage 'authority proceeds from true reason, but reason does not proceed from authority' (*Periphyseon* I, 513B) as evidence for Eriugena's identification of patristic authority and true reason (115–16).

16   In *Periphyseon* I, 511CD Eriugena distinguishes between true reason and authority as two paths to wisdom, the role of the liberal arts in directing the mind to higher things, as well as the concept of God as *lux mentium.* Although he was to draw much of his light metaphysics from Pseudo-Dionysius in later texts, in *De praedestinatione* Eriugena follows Augustine's treatment of light and reason in *De ordine,* as an expression of orthodoxy in the context of disputation (Moran 111).

17   Prudentius extended his critique of Eriugena – 'calling him a *vaniloquus et garrulus homo*' (Moran 33) – for developing a novel way of reading the scriptures based on the quadrivium.

18   William of Malmesbury (586) reports this apocryphal story of Charles scolding Eriugena's manners at table with the well-worn insult: *Quid distat inter sottum et Scottum?* ('What separates a sot from a Scot' [i.e. Irishman]?). Eriugena's response: *tabula tantam* (Just this table).

19   Eriugena also found much to recommend Eastern patristic thought in such doctrinal dilemmas as the *filioque* question: that is, whether the Holy Spirit proceeds from the Son as well as the Father. This formulation was never accepted by the Eastern Church with whom Eriugena sympathized in this matter (see *Periphyseon* II, 613A–615C). The *filioque* formula seems to have first appeared at the First Council of Constantinople in 381 and became customary in the Western Church, although adopted by the papacy only in 1014. Eriugena also manifests the Eastern tradition of *theosis* or deification of humanity in the *reditus,* a concept poorly understood in the Western Church during (and after) his lifetime (Meyendorff 56).

20   For an excellent overview of the Pseudo-Dionysian corpus, see Perl 2010. The standard English translation of the texts is that of Colm Luibheid, from Patrologia Graeca 3, edited by B. Corderius. Eriugena's translation into Latin is incompletely represented in PL 122, but some sections have been retrieved from other manuscript sources and translated in Rorem 2005, 174–225; part of Chapter 7 of

Eriugena's text appears in Chase, 166–86. See Rolt for a translation of *On the Divine Names* and *The Mystical Theology.*

21 In his *History of Saint Dionysius* (c.835–40) Hilduin conflated Dionysius with the martyr Denys, the patron saint of France. In the twelfth century Peter Abelard refuted this claim while serving as a monk at the Abbey of Saint-Denis. Nicholas of Cusa was the first to question the authenticity of the texts (Moran 49), followed in the sixteenth century by Lorenzo Valla. Hugo Koch and Josef Stiglmayr finally resolved the matter, negatively, at the turn of the twentieth century, when they independently verified that phrases in the corpus were taken from the fifth-century texts of the Neoplatonist Proclus (Rorem 1993, 16–17). Severus of Antioch is the first to cite Pseudo-Dionysius in a letter in the first quarter of the sixth century (O'Meara 1988, 57–8); John of Scythopolis produced a Prologue to the Pseudo-Dionysian corpus as well as *scholia* in the first half of the sixth century. René Roques and John J. O'Meara settle on a *floruit* date of c. 510.

22 The Alexandrian doctrine of Christ's unified nature (*monophysitism*) was set against the Antiochene doctrine of Christ's fully divine nature and fully human nature in hypostatic union (*dyophysitism*, of which Nestorianism is a variety), through which human redemption is conducted. This doctrinal division held hermeneutic implications: the Alexandrians tended to read scripture spiritually, whilst the Antiochenes tended towards historicist interpretation. It also led to the permanent schism between the Oriental Orthodox Church, which took the Alexandrian position, and the Western and Eastern Orthodox Churches, which took the Antiochene, or Chalcedonian position. For a fuller explanation of the controversy and its implications, see Davis *passim.*

23 Schäfer notes that the Pseudo-Dionysian corpus of ten letters and four treatises shows astonishing integrity over time: their content and arrangement bears an irreproachable internal logic, no sign of revision, redaction, multiple authorship or emendation is in evidence, nor have any new discoveries come to light (11). The author goes to some lengths to situate the works in the first century: each of the four treatises is dedicated to 'Timothy,' an associate of Paul's, and the letters are addressed to a variety of first-century bishops and deacons. One is even addressed to John the Evangelist. The seventh letter claims that its author witnessed the lunar eclipse at the crucifixion, and *The Divine Names* also claims that the author was present at the dormition of the Virgin Mary with the Apostles James and Peter. Eriugena assimilates this tradition in his dedicatory poem to Dionysius, 'Lumine siderio,' which introduces his translation of *The Celestial Hierarchy* (PL 122, 1037–38) and begins: 'Lumine siderio Dionysius auxit Athenas/Areopagites, magnificusque σοφός' (Dionysius the Areopagite and brilliant sage/adorned Athens with his stellar light [21.1–2 in Herren 1993, 111]). The poem imagines Dionysius, 'radiant with the light of heavenly wisdom' (21.9), following Paul into the 'third heaven' where he witnesses the ninefold hierarchy of angelic beings.

24 This cosmological figure stems from such earlier instances as the golden chain (*catena aurea*) in Homer's *Iliad* (Book VIII, 18–20) as well as Macrobius and Boethius (Rorem 1993, 168).

25 Eriugena also derives this structure from the Neoplatonic journey of the soul described in the *Commentarii in somnium Scipionis* (*Commentary on the Dream of Scipio*) by Macrobius.

26 For a fuller account of the relation between Pseudo-Dionysius, Eriugena and Gothic architecture, see Palusińska.

27 For a discussion of the complex interweaving of translation, paraphrase and exposition in Eriugena's treatment of Pseudo-Dionysius, see 'Traduction ou interprétation? Brèves remarques sur Jean Scot traducteur de Denys' in Roques, 99–130.

28 This reticulated process bears an uncanny resemblance to Pound's work with the Fenollosa notebooks, where he effectively performs a poetical paraphrase of Fenollosa's 'decal' transliteration of individual characters.

29 Eriugena makes the point in Book I of the *Periphyseon* (509C) that because 'the theologian St. Dionysius […] expresses himself in an involved and distorted language, and therefore many find him extremely obscure and difficult to understand, I have decided to present his opinion […] by arranging his words in an order easier to understand than that in which they are written' (Sheldon-Williams in Eriugena 1968, 189).

30 Perhaps surprisingly, Pseudo-Dionysius exerted a profound influence upon Aquinas: there are 1702 individual citations in his works, matched in number only by Augustine and Aristotle. Aquinas also wrote a commentary on *The Divine Names*, the only full-length commentary he wrote aside from his commentary on Boethius (Rorem 1993, 169).

31 Marenbon adapts this argument from Barthélémy Hauréau's *Histoire de la philosophie scolastique*, but asserts that it is the question of the nature of the first Category, *ousia*, specifically, that generates the essence of medieval philosophy (Marenbon 1981, 6).

32 This might account for Sheldon-Williams's hypothesis that Book I began separately as a study in dialectic: Édouard Jeauneau has proven this to be false in his stemmatic and codicological analyses of the extant manuscripts in his Corpus Christianorum edition of the *Periphyseon*. Moran points out that Book I can be read as a typical Neoplatonic proof that God is beyond being and thus human understanding, but that to consider Book I as an exercise in dialectic and the rest of Eriugena's text to be an outgrowth of this study of the *Categories* would be erroneous (59).

33 Otten provides a similar argument to Moran, whereby Eriugena's methodology creates 'an open platform for discussing the totality of all things' rather than

circumscribing the subject by way of definition (1990, 204). In the Homily on the Gospel of St. John, Eriugena draws analogy between the four levels of the intelligible world of the scriptures and the four levels of the sensible world: historical, literal, ethical, and theological (Carabine 2000, 18). This strategy provides Eriugena with a dialectical rationale for reading scripture as analogy, allegory or even as negation.

34 Augustine remains the conventional authority on creation ex nihilo, 'made of nothing, not of God' in his *On Marriage and Concupiscence* (Book II, Chapter 28, paragraph 48). For a full exploration of Augustine's assessment, see Torchia; for a critical evaluation of this doctrine as a response to Platonism, see May.

35 Eriugena's allegorical approach to sin and punishment in Book IV raises a complication in the conceptualization of paradise: on the last day of creation paradise is equated with human nature, but the presence of sin within paradise precipitates the act of expulsion. Eriugena resolves this dilemma by a dialectical reading of Genesis as allegorical, whereby historical time and literal order may be elided in two creation narratives: the first has humanity created as *imago Dei* in paradise as a spiritual entity; the second narrative describes the Fall into corporeal being and the division of the sexes (as per Gregory of Nyssa), within paradise, thus indicating that humanity can recover its graced state by the exercise of rationality (Otten 1994, 209–10). Paradise is thus a future condition toward which humanity aspires.

36 Eriugena's interpretation of *datum* (the gift of substantiation) and *donum* (the bestowal of grace) became standard, and was recorded in the *Glossa Ordinaria*: the compendium of patristic Biblical glosses first assembled in the Carolingian era and popularized in a twelfth-century edition from Laon. Although it fell into disuse after the fourteenth century, the *Glossa* was fundamentally influential as a propaedeutic throughout the Middle Ages. See Smith for an account of its history; see Salomon for an innovative interpretation of its textual structure.

37 For one example, see the 1843 Index: 'Erigena Iohannes Scotus. De Divisione naturae libri V. Accedit Appendix ex Ambiguis S. Maximi Graece, et Latine dec. 3 Aprilis 1685,' in *Index Librorum Prohibitorum Sanctissimi Domini Nostri Gregorii XVI* (Rome 1843) 157.

38 Eriugena's poem 'Haec nostram dominam Yrmindrudis nomine claram' (All these adornments grace Queen Irmintrudis) is dedicated to the Queen, likening her artful weaving to the talents of Athena, of which the spider is justly envious (Herren 1993, 72–5). See Pound's notes on this poem, to which his numerous references apply, at YCAL MSS 43, 76/3383, 21.5–14 and 22.2–7 in Chapter 3 below.

39 There is evidence that Eriugena's intensive experimentalism saw occasional emulation. A disciple at Laon, Hucbald, composed the 'Ecloga de calvis' (Ecologue on baldness) containing the line: '*Carmina, clarisonae, calvis cantate, Camenae*'

(Poetry, clear-cut, sing baldly, Goddesses). Note that Camena is the singular for a goddess of poetry, or muse, but it can also refer directly to the poem itself, thus making one possible translation: 'Thou Poetry, poetic, sing baldly, Poems!' or perhaps even 'Song, striking, sing baldly, Songs!' The potential redundancy in transliteration is offset by the subtleties of grammar: Carmina (noun: poetry), clarisona (adjective: clear-cut), cantate (verb: enchant, sing), Camenae (noun, feminine plural, first declension: Goddesses, Muses). The line is quoted from *MGH*, Poet., iv, 1, 267 et seq. in Laistner 1957, 186.

40   Until recently criticism of Eriugena's Greek has been harsh, but several material factors must be considered in weighing up his relative proficiency: the rarity of Greek lexicons in the ninth century, the likelihood of textual corruption, and the problem of Greek vowel quantities (confusions of H and E, O and W) (Herren 1993, 48). There was very limited opportunity to study the language outside of the Irish 'colonies' of Francia and the Alemmanian centres of Reicheneu and Saint Gallen. Despite these limitations, '[w]hile John's prosody is somewhat shaky, his command of the techniques of alliteration and assonance show a high degree of verbal artistry' (53).

41   Further study into the role of poets in Charlemagne's court, especially Theodulf of Orleans, may offer insights into Eriugena's status as an innovator or as part of a nascent tradition of Carolingian court poetry. Eriugena's poem *Aulae sidereae*, for example, departs fundamentally from other Carolingian poetry in fusing religious exegesis – the Nativity and Incarnation – with political symbolism – Charles enthroned and invested with the royal insignia (Godman 173). For Theodulf's connection with the *Libri Carolini*, see Ann Freeman 1957, 1965 and 1971; see also Greeley, and Godman *passim*.

The Missing Book of the Trilogy

The source materials available to Pound directly shaped the way he conceived of Eriugena in his intellectual schema. Chapter 1 outlined how his reliance on authoritative secondary sources led him to view Eriugena through the lens of wrongful ecclesiastical condemnation: a figure misunderstood in the Latin West by virtue of his Neoplatonic Christianity, and in his wilful engagement in doctrinal disputation that crossed the most powerful ecclesiastical figures of his time. But for Pound, Eriugena demonstrated an investment in the Great Chain of Being he saw as a structural model for *The Cantos*: the affinities with the theory of emanations the great medieval Islamic philosophers drew from Aristotle; the notion of divinity indwelling in the human agent; and the fourfold division of nature orchestrating divinity, the categories, sensory experience and a return of creation to the godhead. Pound drew this portrait into the frame of perhaps the most important lyric influence upon his poetic development, Guido Cavalcanti's canzone 'Donna mi prega'. Canto XXXVI brings together this complex field of Aristotelian ontology, Neoplatonic hypostases, the Troubadour cult of amor and the culmination of medieval lyric in the poetry of trecento Tuscany. Pound's poetic and philosophical intuition was acute, although his knowledge of the particularities of Eriugena's textual production – the context of the Predestination controversy, the provenance of texts he translated or on which he produced commentaries, the transmission of Eriugena's own texts by way of scribal copying, the production of glosses, florilegia, and so on – hampered aspects of his initial understanding of Eriugena's thought.

This changed significantly upon Pound's acquisition of Patrologia Latina 122 – the volume containing all of Eriugena's extant works. Pound read over the entire volume, and it is instructive to note his predilections for and emphases upon certain texts – namely the material pertaining to Pseudo-Dionysius, sections of the *Periphyseon*, and the *Versus*. Pound's evident haste came at the expense of the more substantial representation of Eriugena's originality, especially in the schematic argument of the five-book *Periphyseon*: both an *hexaemeron* and eschatology. Pound's attitude towards totalizing systems also changed through the course of World War II, reflected in the cognate project of translating the Four Books of Confucianism. By the time of composition of *The Pisan Cantos*, Pound had shifted to a rhetoric of personal consolation and 'paradise postponed', emblematized in his citations of Eriugenian *hilaritas* in the court of Charles the Bald, the 'Greek tags' in Eriugena's poetry and the ascetic vision of transcendence in Neoplatonic light.

The circumstances leading up to Pound's acquisition of Patrologia Latina 122 in 1939 illustrate the shifting priorities in Pound's Eriugenian deployments. Nearly two years earlier, on 9 January 1938, Pound had written to Otto Bird, then a graduate student under Étienne Gilson at the University of Toronto:

> In return for my answers to whatever you don't know and I might, I suggest you gather any available information re Scotus Erigena, trial of Scotus Erig., and his condemnation. Was it merely for some fuss about the trinity? Does Gilson know aught abaht it?? Where *is* Gilson, if he ain't in Toronto? (*SL* 304)

Pound's tone is brimming with a comic urgency over matters of nearly 1100 years standing: the precise circumstances of Eriugena's 'trial' and condemnation (presuming Pound refers to the direct fallout of the Predestination controversy: he may mean instead the condemnations of the thirteenth century, matters of perhaps very slightly more urgency). Pound was partially correct. There was a Trinitarian element to the disputation with Gottschalk, with direct implications for the interpretation of patristic sources, especially Augustine. However, there is no evidence that Pound had read the relevant documents in proximate volumes of the Patrologia Latina.[1] His attempts to engage Gilson on this topic appear to have come to nothing, and no further correspondence on the issue of Eriugena appears for nearly two years. During this time Pound was also trading philosophical viewpoints with George Santayana, to whom he wrote on 8 December 1939:

> Nuisance not to have Migne on the premises as mere reports of Erigena look as if the interest may have been painted on by the writers of the reports [i.e. Fiorentino, Renan, Gilson]. Gemisthus Plethon's polytheism evaporated when one got near it. (*SL* 331)

This tone of scepticism concerning Eriugena's originality, and the substance of the reports of heresy, indicates Pound had made little headway in his investigations.

Pound did finally locate a copy of PL 122 in the Biblioteca Marciana during a visit to Venice in late 1939, and then was presented with the Genoese library copy by Ubaldo degli Uberti either in late December or the first days of 1940. In a flurry of letters in the weeks following, Pound shows every indication of having glanced through the entire volume, although any detailed account of the contents is not forthcoming. He writes again to Otto Bird on 12 January 1940, two years after his earlier inquiry:

> Dear Bird: If you are still plugging at that thesis, I think you will find a good deal of interest in J. Scotus Erigena, vol. 122 of Migne.
>
> No use my bothering you with partic. refs. until I know what you are doing. Also one ought to read the whole thing esp. the commentary of the pseudo-Dionysius. So far I don't find the text backs up various statements I have read *about* Erigena. I want corroborations on various points. Often a hurried reading fails to find a 'denegat' at the end of passage. A lot of nice ideas start in one's own head that can't be attributed to J. S. E.
>
> …
>
> Re Cavalcanti: Erigena certainly throws doubt on various readings: *for*mato and *infor*mato, etc. I wonder whether lots of copyists didn't each emend the text to suit their own views.
>
> I at any rate have got to digest Erigena and then review the whole 'Donna mi Prega.' And I shd. like a fellow-traveller. (*SL* 332)

In this revealing letter Pound immediately identifies Eriugena's *Expositiones super Ierarchiam caelestem S. Dionysii* as the centre of his focus. This is reflected in both sets of notes he took during the earlier phases of drafting the Italian suite of cantos in Rapallo during the war, and which demonstrate significant attention to the *Expositiones* (PL 122 col. 126–254). Pound's scepticism concerning the claims made of Eriugena (in Fiorentino, Renan and Gilson) is shaped by his ignorance of the controversies of the Carolingian era documented in associated volumes of the Patrologia Latina, and the fact that he seems to have made only a very preliminary reading of the *Periphyseon*. This text explicates the doctrines of positive and negative theology, participation and the *reditus*, and is the fullest explication of Eriugena's philosophical vision. Pound is sensitive to the affinities Eriugena's texts might share with Cavalcanti's vocabulary (the agent and possible intellects) and the design of his famous canzone, and he shows awareness of the codicological contingencies of early medieval textual transmission and scribal error. This perceptive sense informs his own annotative and glossatory techniques in the notes.

Pound writes to Santayana four days later, on 16 January 1940, complaining about Eriugena's Neoplatonic tendencies and his grapplings with Aristotelian categories:

> Have I indicated my letch toward *teXne*, and do I manage to indicate what I conceive as kindred tendency? From the *thing* to the grouped things, thence to

a more real knowledge than in our friend Erigena (whose text I have wheedled
out of Genova) – nice mind but mucking about in the unknown. *Damn* all these
citations of Hebrew impertinence or whatever. Erig. *had* a nice mind, full of light
and had perceived quite a lot. It's the fussing with nomenclature by absolutely
ignorant arguers that gets my goat. (*SL* 333)

The scholastic predilection for nomenclature is double-edged for Pound: his
long-standing endorsement of 'precise definition' is blunted by the style and kind
of scholastic wrangling over terms, but such controversies were at the very heart
of doctrinal disputation throughout the patristic era as well as throughout the
middle ages. In fact, the Predestination controversy can be seen as the inevitable
consequence of scholastic attempts to explicate Augustine's notoriously knotty
text, *De Trinitate*. Definition of words runs through the entire self-conception
of the Church, as well as marking out the exercise of its agency in possessing the
ecclesiastical power to condemn and excommunicate on the basis of wayward
interpretation of terms. The significance of the Word takes on special meaning
in the Church's absorption of the Neoplatonic *logos*, as well as the opening verses
of the Gospel of St John.

Pound reprises his complaint in a letter to T. S. Eliot two days later, on 18
January 1940:

I shd. start rev. of mod. esp. of Erig. with Schlueter's Latin comment, dated
Westphalia 1838. A bit special but *non*-political. Johnny Scot. 'Pietate insignia
atque hilaritate.' Johnny had a nice mind. Omnia quae sunt lumina sunt. I haven't
yet found anything that fits what I had read about what he thought, but it may be
in the 600 pages double col. Migne, vol. 122. (*SL* 334)

Pound did read Schlueter's prefatory comment to the *Periphyseon* in PL
122, evident in his notes containing the quotation in Latin: '[Eriugena]
balanced piety and good humour' (77/3406, 21.A3–4). Schlueter, the 'prete'
mentioned in Canto LXXXIII, discusses the virtue of *hilaritas* and addresses
the spurious claims of 'Manichean' tendencies in Eriugena's thought. Michaels
sees this preface as the motivation for Pound's proposed essay on Eriugena
(Michaels 1972, 46). Whilst there may be limited scholarly virtue in Schlueter's
commentary, it is evident that Pound drew some of his abiding concerns from
the apparatus to Eriugena's texts. The tone of his letter to Eliot suggests he
is fishing for specific political scandal to attach to Eriugena's texts but finds
instead an intelligent and discreet courtier. The famous formula – 'Omnia quae
sunt, lumina sunt' – appears in this letter, notably displaced from its original
form as question (*Exp. Cel. Hier.* 128C; see 76/3383, 1.13–14). Pound returns

to this theme continuously throughout the Eriugena notes (see especially 76/3383, 1.13–14; 77/3406, 2.15–16; 18.13–14; 22B.7; 36.8–10 in the following annotated edition). This letter also contains Pound's proposal for a 'note' on Eriugena: the wording is ambiguous, in that the 'Trilogy' would be 'about twice the size' of the *Ta Hio* text by itself, but would also contain the *Mencius* and the Eriugena 'note'.

An annotated edition of Pound's Eriugena notes, with commentary

The following pages comprise complete annotated transcriptions of the two major series of notes on Eriugena in the Ezra Pound archive in the Beinecke Library at Yale University: the annotations comprise matters of information and preliminary critical commentary. The first set (YCAL MSS 43 Box 76 Folder 3383) consists of 26 pages of notes inserted in early drafts of *The Pisan Cantos*, dated 1941–1945. The second set (YCAL MSS 43 Box 77 Folder 3406) consists of 38 pages of notes – some pages containing two columns – which gradually shift into original verse composition interspersed with occasional quotations from Eriugena.

Editorial principles

The following diplomatic and topographic transcriptions are as complete as comprehension allows: the notes on pages 14, 15, 17 and 21–35 in YCAL MSS 43 Box 77 Folder 3406 appear in two columns. These leaves are transcribed diplomatically, with apparatus recording Columns A and B. Sources for most of the material have been located and recorded. No attempt has been made to correct eccentric spelling, although these notes display a high degree of fidelity to Pound's major source, Volume 122 of the Patrologia Latina, ed. Jacques-Paul Migne (Paris 1853). The provenances of the PL texts are complex, and often more than one layer of editorial apparatus pertains to any single work in the volume, as well as to the volume itself. Readers interested in such matters of textual transmission are directed to the PL volume for further information, although it should be noted that Pound makes reference to such editors as Thomas Gale (who first published *De Divisione naturae* in Oxford in 1681), Henry Joseph Floss (who edited the text of Eriugena's *Opera* in 1853, now printed in the PL), and the 'prete' C. B. Schlueter (who adapted Floss's edition of the *Periphyseon* and appended a ''Praefatio' in 1855).

Pound's notes are annotated primarily to facilitate further scholarly research: annotations provide the immediate context for Pound's often very fragmentary quotations of Eriugena's writings, and outline limited historical context and hermeneutic evaluation of them. This annotative edition does not pretend to the expertise required for a philologically precise evaluation of Pound's sources and his mediation of them: authoritative translations from Greek and Latin are provided wherever possible, and I have provided my best attempts at translation (or transliteration) where no alternative text could readily be found. The annotations themselves take a hybrid form, combining scholia with limited textual-philological matter, but with an emphasis on guiding the reader interested in the provenance and context of Pound's note-taking. The commentary provides a brief running overview of both sets of notes, making some general observations concerning the thematic and textual patterns and tendencies in Pound's citations, as well as some account of how they might radiate into the wider sphere of his writing and thought.

Key to abbreviations:

PL 122	*Joannis Scoti Opera*, ed. Henry Joseph Floss, Patrologia Latina Volume 122, second series, gen. ed. Jacques-Paul Migne (Paris 1853)
Ambig. S. Max.	*Versio Ambiguorum S. Maximi*, PL 122, 1193–222
Cel. Hier.	Pseudo-Dionysius, *De caelesti Ierarchia*, PL 122, 1035–68
Epi. Cel. Hier.	*Epigramma in beatum Dionysium de caelesti Ierarchia*, PL 122, 1037–38
Exp. Cel. Hier.	*Expositiones Super Ierarchiam Caelestiam S. Dionysii*, PL 122, 126–264
Exp. Myst. Theol.	*Expositiones in Mysticam Theologiam S. Dionysii*, PL 122, 267–84
Herren	Michael W. Herren, ed., *Iohannis Scotti Erivgenae: Carmina*, Scriptores Latini Hiberniae XII (Dublin: Dublin Institute of Advanced Studies, 1993)
Peri.	*Periphyseon/De divisione naturae*, PL 122, 439–1022
Versus	*Versus*, PL 122, 1221–42

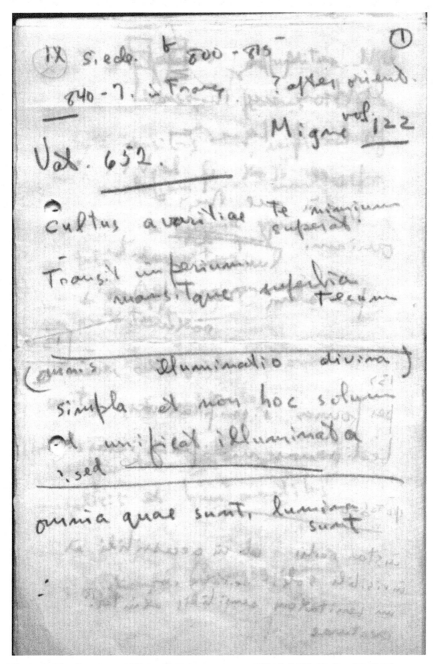

Plate 1 The first page of Pound's Eriugena notes: YCAL MSS 43, Box 76, Folder 3383, l.1. Courtesy of the Ezra Pound Trust and the Beinecke Rare Book and Manuscript Library.

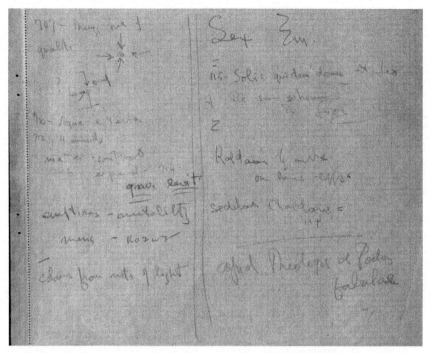

Plate 2 Pound's Eriugena notes: YCAL MSS 43, Box 77, Folder 3406, l.25. Courtesy of the Ezra Pound Trust and the Beinecke Rare Book and Manuscript Library.

Eriugena notes, Set One, 26 pp.
(YCAL MSS 43 Box 76 Folder 3383)

1

IX siècle. b 800–815

840–7 in France   ? after orient.

——

Vat. 652   Migne vol 122

————

cultus avaritiae te minimum

5   superat

Transit imperium

     mansitque superbia

          tecum

————————

(omnis illuminatio divina)

10   simpla et non hoc solum
       [sed] unificat illuminata
       ? sed _____

---

       omnia quae sunt, lumina
                  sunt

1–2 *IX siècle… orient*] general biographical details on the life of Eriugena, from the *Prooemium* of Henry Joseph Floss, PL 122, i–xxviii, and the anonymous *Vita et Praeceptis Joannis Scoti Erigenae*, PL 122, 1–87; Eriugena was believed to have arrived at the court of Charles the Bald from earlier scholarly employment in the Rhine Valley (for a more recent recapitulation of this hypothesis, see Contreni 1978, 86).

3 *Vat. 652*] Codex Vaticanus 652, the first of three sources for Floss's recension of the *Expositiones Super Ierarchian Caelestiam S. Dionysii*, in PL 122 (Pound's citation isolates one work by Eriugena, the *Commentary* on *The Celestial Hierarchy* of Pseudo-Dionysius, but may be taken to function as generally indicative of PL 122).

4–8 *cultus avaritae… tecum*] these lines comprise part of a poem Eriugena allegedly appended to his translation of Pseudo-Dionysius, praising the wisdom of the Eastern Church over that of Rome. The poem first appears in a letter allegedly written by Pope Nicholas I to Charles the Bald several years after the Predestination controversy: see *Sancti Dionysii Areopagitae: Epistolae Diversae*, PL 122, 1194BC. The veracity of this attribution is not settled: Bett (11–12) makes the attribution; Whittaker is dubious (124–125). Floss cites the poem in full in *Prooemium* xxiii, several lines of which (ll. 5–8) are as follows:

> Constantinopolis florens nova Roma vocatur:
> Moribus et muris Roma vetusta cadis.
> Transiit imperium, mansitque superbia tecum,
> Cultus avaritiae te nimium superat.
> (Constantinople is called the flourishing new Rome:
> whose ways and old walls fall.
> Glorious rule has passed, but pride remains,
> Overcome with the worship of greed.)

9 *(omnis illuminatio divina)*] *Exp. Cel. Hier.* 125C–127A: 'Sancti Dionysii Areopagitae primus liber, qui inscribitur de caelesti ierarchia, xv capitulorum

serie contextitur, quorum primi titulus est: *Quoniam omnis divina illuminatio secundum bonitatem varie in ea, quae praevisa sunt, proveniens*, hoc est, quoniam divinae bonitatis omnis illuminatio …' This is the opening sentence of Eriugena's exposition on *The Celestial Hierarchy*, which begins with the italicized section above: 'Even though in various ways every divine enlightenment proceeds, out of its goodness, towards those provided for, it not only remains simple in itself but also unifies those it enlightens'. (Luibheid 145)

10–12 *simpla… illuminata/sed*] *Exp. Cel. Hier.* 127B: 'Et hoc est quod ait: manet simpla et non hoc solum, sed unificat illuminata'; cf. Pseudo-Dionysius, *Patrologia Graeca* Volume 3, 120A: 'it [divine enlightenment] not only remains simple in itself but also unifies those it enlightens' (Luibheid 1987, 145).

13–14 *omnia quae sunt, lumina sunt*] Pound's favourite formula for Eriugena's kataphatic theophany of light occurs early in the *Exp. Cel. Hier.* at 128C, but in the form of a question: 'Sed fortasse quis dixerit: Quomodo omnia, quae sunt, lumina sunt?' (But perhaps someone will say: all things that are, in what ways are they "lights"? (Rorem 2005, 182)). See Gilson: 'Ainsi conçues, tous les êtres créés sont des lumières – omnia quae sunt, lumina sunt. (*Sup. Hier.* Col. I,1)' (213) and Baumann (250).

2

      light as of day 明 =
      lighten all thought
      Father of lights
      & all that of lights =
5   that is all things =
      omnium ~~lux et~~
         lumina sunt
      partaking that father's
            nature.
10   130C
      137
      per formas signifiativus
      beatissimus manifestat ierarchias

      φότοδοσια

15   instar radii ab in accessibili et
      invisibili sole, i.e. Patre, in
      universitatem sensibilis et intel.is
      creaturae

1–9 *light as of day… nature.*] Pound's paraphrase and adaptation of Eriugena's translation of Chapter 1 of *The Celestial Hierarchy*, PG 3, 120B–121A: 'Inspired by the Father, each procession of the Light spreads itself generously toward us, and, in its power to unify, it stirs us by lifting us up. It returns us back to the oneness and deifying simplicity of the Father who gathers us in. For, as the sacred Word says, "from him and to him are all things"' (Luibheid 1987, 145). Pound associates ming^2 明 (light = 'sun and moon') with the Pseudo-Dionysian/ Eriugenian light emblem, 'sunt lumina'. This phrase-character dyad appears in the typescripts and early published versions of Canto LXXIV alongside 'Erigena Scotus' and 'Mt Taishan', until replaced by hsien^3 顯 in the 1958 New Directions *Cantos* and (by virtue of the adoption of the New Directions text) the 1975 Faber *Cantos*.

10 *130C*] no passage in PL 122 is identified here

11–13 *137 per… ierarchias*] *Exp. Cel. Hier.* 133BC: 'et restituimur iterum, ex ipsa videlicet multiplici datione, in simplum ipsius radium, dum recipimus immaterialibus et non trementibus mentis oculis, sed spritualibus et infirmis simul theoriae obtutibus, principalem et superprincipalem, hoc est, plusquam principalem divini Patris claritatem, id est, ex divino Patre datam illuminationem, quae angelorum nobis in figuratis symbolis, hoc est, per formas significativas, beatissimus manifestat ierarchias'

> And we are restored again (namely, from this multiple giving of the lights) to its simple ray, when we receive, with the immaterial eyes of the mind, not wavering but with the direct and spiritual gaze of contemplation, the original and super-original (that is, the more than original) brightness of the divine Father (that is, the illumination given out of the divine Father), which manifests the most blessed hierarchies of angels to us in figurative symbols (that is, through signifying forms). (Rorem 2005, 187)

Cf. *Cel. Hier.* 121B: 'We must lift up the immaterial and steady eyes of our minds to that outpouring of Light which is so primal, indeed much more so, and which comes from that source of divinity, I mean the Father. This is the light which, by way of representative symbols, makes known to us the most blessed hierarchies among the angels' (Luibheid 145–46). Note that Pound misnumbers this citation as PL 122, 137 rather than 133BC.

14 φότοδοσια] 133C: 'φωτοδοσία vero est *luminum datio*, quae specialiter ad Patrem retertur, qui omnium luminum dater est' ('φωτοδοσία is indeed the giving of lights, which refers especially to the Father, who is the giver of all lights' (Rorem 2005, 187)). Cf. *Cel. Hier.* 120B: 'Every good endowment and every perfect gift is from above, coming down from the Father of lights' (Luibheid 1987, 145). Note Pound introduces an omicron in place of the (correct) omega in φωτοδοσία.

15–18 *instar… creaturae*] *Exp. Cel. Hier.* 134B: 'Like a ray from an inaccessible and invisible sun (that is, the Father) it [the divine ray] is poured into the totality of sensible and intelligible creation' (Rorem 2005, 188).

3

princ^tr in intellectus diffunditur …
penetrans obstrusa … formans visiones
in intr^bs sensibus; seipsum
sec.^dm analogian … manifestans.
5 neque … a propria singularis
unitate deseritus.
    – in simplum suum radium
nos restituit …

–

never relinquishes its own
10 unity, & simplicitas.

–

multiformitas omnm et max^e in
angelicis et hum^is mentibus

–

? simiglianza anagogicam ?

1–8 *princ^tr … restituit*] *Exp. Cel. Hier.* 134B:

et maxime ac principaliter in angelicos et humanos intellectus diffunditur, implens omnia, perficiens imperfecta, penetrans obstrusa, illuminans mysteria, formans visiones in interioribus sensibus theologorum, aperiens intellectus eas visiones quarere et intelligere volentium, et seipsum secundum analogiam uniuscujusque omnibus in se intuentibus manifestans. Quod ex consequentia praesentis capituli facillime quis potest approbare. Nam sequitur: *Etenim neque ipse usquam unquam a propria singulari sua unitate deseritur*, hoc est, ipsa patris luminum claritas pure a nobis ac firmiter intellecta in simplum suum radium nos restituit, quoniam ipse radius nullo loco, nullo tempore, a propria et singulari sua unitate, id est simplicitate, relinquitur

and mostly and principally into angelic and human intellects: filling all, perfecting the imperfect, penetrating the closed, illumining the mysteries, forming visions in the interior senses of theologians, opening the intellects of those willing to seek these visions and to understand them, and manifesting itself to all who gaze upon it, according to the proportion of each one. This anyone can easily confirm from the rest of this chapter. For there follows: *and indeed it is not ever anywhere deprived of its own singular unity*. That is, this brightness of the Father of lights purely and firmly understood by us restores us into its simple ray, since this ray itself in no place and at no time is forsaken by its own singular unity (that is, its simplicity). (Rorem 2005, 188)

This passage follows on directly from that cited in 2.15–18 above.

9–10 *never… simplicitas*] Pound's translation of the direct quote from Pseudo-Dionysius, *Cel. Hier.* 121C, quoted in italics in Eriugena's text above.

11–12 *multiformitas… mentibus*] *Exp. Cel. Hier.* 134CD: 'multiformis omnium, et maxime in angelicis et humanis mentibus' ([the manifestations of divine creation] are in the manifold of all things, especially in the minds of humans and angels) (my translation).

13? *simiglianza anagogicam?*] 'analogue of anagogy?': Pound expresses uncertainty in the usage, where Eriugena uses 'analogiam' in *Exp. Cel. Hier.* 134B, but the word 'anagogicam' is used in the corresponding phrase from Ps.-Dionysius *Cel. Hier.* 1038CD.

4

manetque intra se in
incommutabili similitudine
uniformitas fixus

–

Ad anagogicam vero et unificam
5   eorum quae provisa sunt.
contemporantiam opt^e et
pulchre multiplicantur et

provenit, manet.
et in se quantum fos [?] est.
10   respicientes proportionaliter
in se extendit et
unificat secundum
simplicem sui unitatem

1–3 *manetque…fitus*] *Exp. Cel. Hier.* 134CD: this phrase is excerpted from the longer sentence of ll. 4–13, quoted below.

4–13 *Ad anagogicam…unitatem*] *Exp. Cel. Hier.* 134CD: 'Ed hoc aperte declarat dicens: *Ad anagogicam vero et unificam eorum, quae provisa sunt, contemperantiam optime et pulchre multiplicatur et provenit, manetque intra se in incommutabili simititudine uniformiter fixus, et in se, quantum fas est, respicientes proportionaliter in se extendit et unificat secundum simplicem sui unitatem'*. Eriugena quotes his translation of *Cel. Hier.* 1038CD, corresponding to PG 3 *Cel. Hier.* 121BC:

Even though it [the ray of the Father] works itself outward to multiplicity and proceeds outside of itself as befits its generosity, doing so to lift upward and to unify those beings for which it has a providential responsibility, nevertheless it remains inherently stable and it is forever one with its own unchanging identity. And it grants to creatures the power to rise up, so far as they may, toward itself and it unifies them by way of its own simplified unity. (Luibheid 1987, 146)

Parts of this quotation appear elsewhere in Pound's notes: YCAL MSS 43, 77/3406, 2.1–13. Rorem provides a different translation:

And this he openly declares, saying but it is excellently and beautifully multiplied and comes forth for the anagogical and unifying melding of what has been foreseen, and yet it remains uniformly fixed within itself in an unchangeable sameness, and proportionately to them extends those looking on it, as far as permitted, and unifies (them) in a manner consistent with its simple unity. (2005, 188–89)

5

135.
unificat ad similitudinem
— suae simplicis unitatis.
ray incomprenabl.

5   nisi per quondam velamina

–

in memoria conformatae sunt

–

full contemplation of
virum perfectum

---

not a one ball'd frump

---

10   136.   bonitas, essentia, vita,
sapeintia, veritas, virtus et sim.

–

all species etc allegoriae.
in fac. in dic. are velamina
of divine rays

1 *135*] *Exp. Cel. Hier.* 135, the column in PL 122 from which the following quotations derive

2–5 *unificat… velamina*] *Exp. Cel. Hier.* 135BC: 'ad se ipsum erigit et unificat eos ad similitudinem suae simplicis unitatis. Sed quia ipse radius, per se ipsum incomprehensibilis, invisibilis, inaccessibilis est omni creaturae, siquidem sensus omnes omnesque superat intellectus, non potuit omnibus, in quibus multiplicatur, apparere, nisi per quaedam velamina nobis connaturalia, quibus sese adhuc in hac carne constitutis quoquomodo manifestare voluit.'

> [the Divine ray] raises them [all things] to itself and unifies them to a likeness of its simple unity. But because this ray is in itself incomprehensible, invisible, inaccessible to every creature, indeed transcends all senses and all intellects, it has not been able to appear to all those in whom it is multiplied, except through certain veils co-natural to us to whom, still constituted in this flesh, it wished to manifest itself in some way, as if someone had said, for what reason and how is the simple multiplied? (Rorem 2005, 189)

6 *in memoria conformatae sunt*] *Exp. Cel. Hier.* 135D: 'in theologorum memoria conformatae sunt' (shaped in the memory of the theologians), i.e. the conformities of heaven, sensory experience and theological institutions are evidence of an harmonious ordering. Pound's omission of *theologorum* (theologians) generalizes the statement, and is more in keeping with such formulae as Cavalcanti's 'dove sta memoria'/'where memory liveth'. This is

deployed by Pound as evidence of the Arab and medieval European inheritance of the Aristotelian distinction between the active intellect (νοῦς ποιητικός) and the potential intellect (νοῦς δυνάμει).

7–8 *full… perfectum*] *Exp. Cel. Hier.* 136A 'quibus per actionem et scientiam rationalis anima crescit, donec occuramus in virum perfectum, hoc est, in plenissimam Christi, qui est finis perfectionis nostrae, contemplationem, et in ipso et cum ipso perfectissimum adunationem' (by the action of the rational soul and its developing knowledge, unto human perfection, that is, Christ in his plenitude, who is the culmination of our perfection, contemplation, and with Him and in Him, being united together in the highest perfection). In Eriugena's text this passage follows on from the short quotation of l.6 above.

9 *not a one ball'd frump*] uncertain transcription, potentially scurrilous praise for the Pseudo-Dionysian anagogy, and by extension, Eriugena's devoted attention to the text.

10–11 *136. bonitas… sim.*] *Exp. Cel. Hier.* 136C: 'In eo vero, qui est de divinis nominibus, peripetesmata radii sunt principales causae, verbi gratia bonitas, essentia, vita, sapientia, veritas, virtus, et similia' (But in that which is *The Divine Names*, the peripetasmata [veils] of the ray are the primordial causes of all things, for example, goodness, essence, life, wisdom, truth, power, and similar things (Rorem 2005, 190)). Eriugena elsewhere provides lists of divine attributes (e.g. *Periphyseon* Book II), demonstrating how Aristotelian ontology of essence/*ousia* and the ten Categories was adopted in late-classical and early-medieval theology as the primordial causes stemming from the First Principle of God.

12–14 *all species… divine rays*] Pound transliterates excerpts from the next sentence at *Exp. Cel. Hier.* 136C: 'Et ut breviter dicam, omnes species visibilis et invisibilis creaturae, omnesque allegoriae, sive in factis, sive in dictis, per omnem sanctam utriusque Testamenti Scripturam, velamina paterni radii sunt' (And, to speak briefly, all types of the visible and invisible creation and all allegories, whether in acts or in words, through the entire holy scripture of both testaments, are the veils of the paternal ray (Rorem 2005, 190)).

6

ΦΥΣΕΟΣ

Sine dilatione ~~com~~

        mutatis solemniter
            comburendum.

————————————————

5   within 15 days
     ~~10ᵗʰ Feb in lateran~~
            1225.
     Decimo Rabendas Feb.
     Chronicon Alberici.
10   no mention till Th. Calei. ed. 1681
     –
     1050
     attica vela sequor
     –
     forsan vistutem
            vilia verba tenent
15   nodosae vitis sumitur
            uva ferax

1 ΦΥΣΕΩΣ] *physeos*, nature: this word signals the shift in Pound's note-taking from *Exp. Cel. Hier.* to the *Periphyseon*. The word bears significance for Eriugena (if not overtly for Pound) in its connection to works by Anaxagoras, Heraclitus and Empedocles titled ΠΕΡΙ ΦΥΣΕΩΣ / *Peri Physeos* (*On Nature*), and also recalling the Latin text of Lucretius, *De rerum naturae*. Note that Eriugena's elder contemporary, Rabanus Maurus (see 12.7 below) also wrote a text titled *De rerum naturis*. Eriugena's appropriation of the term absorbs ontology into theology, and more specifically, theogony.

2–4 *Sine… comburendum*] 'sine dilatione mittatis solemniter comburendum' (solemnly burn without delay): this phrase is quoted from the letter from Pope Honorius III of 10 February 1225, instructing the church authorities in Paris to burn, among other texts, the *Periphyseon*. It is quoted in Floss's 'Monitum ad Lectorem' (Advice to Reader), which precedes Eriugena's text in PL 122, 439–442.

5–10 *within… 1681*] further excerpts from Honorius's letter: 'qui ultra quindecim dies', 'Datum Laterani decimo Kalendas Februarii' and the letter's textual provenance in 'Chronicon Alberici ad a. 1225, ed. Leibnitz, Lipsaic MDCIIC p. 511'. The letter was not republished until the edition of Thomas Gale of 1681, which provides the base text for the PL edition: 'Lata hac sententia acerbissima, nulla medio aevo illorum librorum amplius mentro fit. Anno demum 1681 pro ierunt typis excusi cura Thomae Galei, Angli. Statim repetitur censura Ecclesia' (441–42).

11–16 *1050 … uva ferax*] The number 1050 is a pagination error: Eriugena's Prefatorial poem to his translation of the works of Pseudo-Dionysius is at PL 122 1029–30. The fragments quoted are significant in furthering Pound's view of Eriugena as a pioneering Greek translator and (at one remove) thinker: 'Attica vela sequor' (l.12 of the *Praefatio*) is translated as 'I pursue Attic ends' by Herren in the *Carmina* (109); 'forsan virtutem vilia verba tenent' (l.22) is 'words purchased cheaply retain their power perchance'; and the poem's final line, 'nodosae vitis sumitur uva ferax' (l.24) is 'a copius cluster is taken from a knotty vine' (Herren 1993, 109). Note that this final image of grape harvesting bears an august classical heritage as a figure for scribal activity and reading, and functions as a central image in the *Didascalicon* of Hugh of St Victor, a pivotal text of the twelfth-century Renaissance: 'Pliny had already noted that the word *pagina*, page, can refer to rows of vines joined together. The lines on the page were the threads of a trellis that supported the vines' (Illich 57). Further, the etymology of 'reading' leads to the Latin *legere* and German *lesen*, both of which refer to bundles or harvests: thus to read is to bundle alphabetic units into syllabic harvests, materially, on the page (58).

7

φυσεως
444. pars generalis animae
corpus nutrit et auget.

–

angelus est essentialis motus
5   intellectualis circa Deum
rerumque causas.

–

450. Maximus cum vero
solare lumen aeri misceatur, tunc
incipit apparere.

=

10   Καταφατικην, αποφατικην
intentionem, repulsion.
Cicero   461.   περι φυσεος
ΜΕΡΙδΗου

Erig. affirmation, negation

=

15   de ουσια nemo dubitat. 470

1 φυσεως] See 6.1 above.

2–3 *444. ... auget.*] *Peri. I* 444AB: 'ad extremam rationabilis irrationalibisque animae partem, nutritavam dico et auctivam vitam. Quae pars generalis animae ultima est, quae corpus nutri et auget' (the furthermost element of the rational and irrational soul – I mean the nutritive and growth-giving life-principle, which is the least part of the soul in the general acceptance of the term because it nourishes the body and makes it grow (Eriugena 1968, 41)). This section, early in Book I, describes the second mode of being and not being (the Aristotelian Categories), which establishes 'orders and differences of created nature': ranging from 'intellectual power', i.e. the highest angels, to the 'nutritive element' of the human soul to which Pound refers.

4–6 *angelus ... causas*] *Peri. I* 444BC: 'Item si angelus est essentialis motus intellectualis circa Deum rerumque causas, profecto homo non est essentialis motus intellectualis circa Deum et rerum causas' (Likewise, if an angel is an essential intellectual motion about God and the causes of things, then man is certainly not an essential intellectual motion about God and the causes of things (Eriugena 1968, 41)).

7–9 *450. Maximus ... apparer*] quotation from Maximus the Confessor at *Peri. I* 450B: 'Cum vero solare lumen eari misceatur, tunc incipit apparere' (But when the sunlight mingles with air, then it begins to appear (Eriugena 1968, 55)). Eriugena employs the *Ambigua* of Maximus to draw an analogy between the way air appears to be pure light in sunshine, and the way human nature appears to be entirely divine when illuminated by divinity.

10–11 *Καταφατικην ... repulsion*] *Peri. I* 461B: 'S. Dionysii Areopagitae [...] bipertitam Theologiam asserit esse, id est, Καταφατικην et αποφατικην quae Cicero in *intentionem* et *repulsionem* transfert' (St. Dionysius the Areopagite [...] asserts that theology is divide into two parts, that is, Καταφατικην and αποφατικην which Cicero translates into 'intentio' and 'repulsio' (Eriugena 1968, 81)). This is Eriugena's famous formulation of positive (kataphatic) and negative (apophatic) theology: Pseudo-Dionysius is used as an authority here, but this division is generally widespread in the Eastern Fathers. This dualism became a sharp point of contention between the two branches of the late antique and medieval church.

12–13 *Cicero…ΜΕΡΙδΗου*] Source unknown: *Peri.* I 461 does not make reference to Cicero, nor does the Greek text appear.

14 *Erig.…negation*] Eriugena's preferred theological division into *affirmationem* and *negationem* over Cicero's division into *intentio* and *repulsio*.

15 *de ουσια nemo dubitat. 470*] *Peri.* I 470BC: 'Nam de οὐσία, id est essentia, nemo dubitat, quod nullius indiget ad subsistendum' (For concerning οὐσία, that is, essence, no one doubts but that it does not require anything in order to subsist (Eriugena 1968, 101)). For an extended discussion on ουσια as the philosophical concept from antiquity that enables early medieval philosophy, see Marenbon 1981.

8

488
per formam movetur materia,
sine forma immobilis est.

────────────────

status finis motionis

5   ousia, δυναμις, ενεργεια
essence, vintus, operatio materialis.

–

intellectualis
        much above rationalis.

–

nulla natura sive r. sive
10   L. est quae ignoret se esse;
quamvis nesciat, quid sit.

–

intellego me esse.   490.

–

519 Amor
nat. motus of all things.
15   Dion. 'unitive & continuative virtus.

1–4 *488…motionis*] *Peri. I* 488B: 'Nam per formam movetur materia; sine forma immobilis est, ut Graeci volunt. […] Status siquidem finis motionis est' (for it is through form that matter is moved; without form it is immobile, according to the Greeks [...] For rest is the end of motion (Eriugena 1968, 141)). Theory of matter: matter alone is inert, neither at rest nor in motion, and is thus an example of definition by negation (a crucial concept in Eriugena's prior work, *De Praedestinatione*).

5–12 *ousia ... me esse*] *Peri. I* 490B:

> Haec enim tria in omni creatura, sive corporea sive incorporea, ut ipse certissimis argumentationibus edocet, incorruptibilia sunt et inseparabilia, οὐσία ut saepe diximus, δύναμις, μνέργεια hoc est, essentia, virtus, operatio naturalis. Disc. Horum trium exemplum posco. Mag. Nulla natura, sive rationalis sive intellectualis, est, quae ignoret se esse, quamvis nesciat, quid sit. Disc. Hoc non ambigo. Mag. Dum ergo dico, intelligo me esse, nonne in hoc uno verbo, quod est intelligo, tria significo a se inseparabilia? Nam et me esse, et posse intelligere me esse, et intelligero me esse demonstro
>
> For there are these three things which in every creature, whether corporeal or incorporeal, as he himself demonstrates by the surest arguments, are incorruptible and inseparable: οὐσία, as we have often said, δύναμις, μνέργεια, that is, Essence, Power, its natural Operation. A. I request an illustration of these three. N. There is no nature, whether rational or intellectual, which does not know that it is, although it may not know what it is. A. This I do not doubt. N. Thus, when I say, 'I understand that I am,' do I not imply in this single verb, 'understand,' three meanings which cannot be separated from each other? For I show that I am, and that I can understand that I am, and that I do understand that I am. (Eriugena 1968, 145)

13–14 *519 Amor ... things*] *Peri. I* 519BC: 'Amor est naturalis motus omnium rerum, quae in motu sunt, finis quietaque station, ultra quam nullus creaturae progreditur motus' (Love is the end and quiet resting place of the natural motion of all things that are in motion, beyond which no motion of the creature extends (Eriugena 1968, 211)). This sentence extends the discussion of motion and rest in formed matter at 7.15 above into the realm of love, posited at 519C to include 'divine or angelic or intellectual or psychic or natural love' (Eriugena 1968, 211).

15 *Dion. ... virtus*] *Peri. I* 519D: 'in unum congregantes dicamus, quia una quaedam est simplex virtus, seipsam movens ad unitivam quandam temperantiam ex optimum usque existentium novissimum, et ab illo iterum consequenter per omnia usque ad optimum' (again into one, let us say that there is one simple virtue which moves itself to a unitive mingling (of all things) from the Best to the lowest of beings and back from that through all things in order to be the Best again (Eriugena 1968, 213)). Pound is sharpening his suite of

citations on unifying virtues binding the most exalted and the humblest forms. Cf. light, 'the sun's cord unspotted', and the diminutive agents of the natural world in *The Pisan Cantos* for a poetic expression of the chain of being.

                            9

        'seipsam movens ad
                unitatem'

        –

        ipsiusque pultritudo
        omnia ad se attrahit.

   5   solus summa ac vera
        bonitas et pulchritude est.

        –

        ad seipsum reducit,
        sime ullo sui motu, sed sole
        suae pulchtritudinis virtute.

        –

   10   lux ista sensibilis –
        semper immobilis.   520

        –

        moveri tamen in mentibus
        sapientum videantur

1–2 *seipsam…unitatem*] See 8.15: 'moves to a unitive mingling'. Note Pound's transcription error: 'unitatem'.

3–4 *ipsiusque…attrahit*] *Peri. I* 520B: 'His beauty draws all things to Himself' (Eriugena 1968, 213). God's perfection drawing all of creation to Him: this is a proleptic gesture to the return of creation to God in the *reditus* in Book V, making the *Periphyseon* simultaneously a theogony and eschatology.

5–6 *solus…est*] *Peri. I* 520 B: Ipse enim solus vere amabilis est, quia solus summa ac vera bonitas et pulchritudo est' (For He alone is truly lovable because He alone is the supreme and real Goodness and Beauty (Eriugena 1968, 213)).

7–9 *ad seipsum…virtute*] *Peri. I* 520C: 'ita rerum omnium causa omnia, quae ex se sunt, ad seipsam reducit, sine ullo sui motu, sed sola suae pulchritudinis virtute' (so the Cause of all things leads back to itself all things that derive from it without any motion of its own but solely by the power of its beauty (Eriugena 1968, 213–15)).

10–11 *lux... immobilis*] *Peri. I* 520D: 'Nam et lux ista sensibilis, quae totum visibilem mundum implet, dum sit semper immobilis, quamvis vehiculum ejus, quod solare corpus dicimus, per media aetheris spatial circa terram aeterno motu volvatur [...]' (For even this sensible light which fills the whole visible world, while it remains forever immutable although its vehicle, which we call the solar body, revolves in an eternal motion through the intermediate spaces of ether about the earth [...] (Eriugena 1968, 215)). This is part of a long sentence describing the unchanging and immutable nature of (metaphysical) light due to its absolute pervasion in all things, despite the presence of the sun as a moving object.

12–13 *moveri... videantur*] *Peri. I* 521BC: 'ad se considerandas attrahunt, ita ut et ipsae, dum per se, ut diximus, immutabiles sunt, moveri tamen in mentibus sapientum videantur, cum eas moveant?' ([What is to be said of the Liberal Arts, which] attract [the mind] to consider them, so that they too, although, as we said, they are immutable in themselves, yet seem to be moved in the minds of the wise because they move them? (Eriugena 1968, 217)). Eriugena shifts from cosmogony to matters of education and the liberal arts: these are not merely lessons or metaphors of theological principles, but are consitutent elements of the human soul to be recollected in education.

10

super omnem similitudinem
–   521.
noun & verb,
amor & amare.
5   also the passive.

584   vita fragile   – lib III

Vos qui Romuleas nescitis
Temnere τέχνας
Attica ne pigeat sumere
10   Gymnasia

–

Usibus Ausoniis si libet,
         aspicite.

1–2 *super… 521*] *Peri. I* 521: 'Ipsa enim est super omnem similitudinem, omneque excellit exemplum' (For [Divine Power] itself is above every likeness and surpasses every example (Eriugena 1968, 217)).

3–5 *noun… passive*] A digest of several complex sentences in which Eriugena outlines his notion of God's hyper-realism: 'Therefore God by Himself is Love, by Himself is Vision, by Himself is Motion; and yet he is neither motion nor vision or love, but More-than-love, More-than-vision, More-than-motion' (*Peri. I* 521D; Eriugena 1968, 217). This doctrine of hyper-realism, along with his ontology of participation – where, for example, all humans identify in their being with Adam and are thus each proponents of original sin – drew the attention of ecclesiastical authorities in Eriugena's time, and for several centuries to follow.

6 *584 vita… lib III*] Presumably an erroneous reference to the opening of Book III of the *Periphyseon*, which occurs at 619.

7–12 *Vos… aspicite*] Lines 5–6 and 8 of the *Praefatio* to *Op. S. Dionysii* 1029:

> You may not know how to scorn the arts of Romulus
> be not reluctant to take up Attic training.
> Observe, if you please, whether some spark of these
> flashes through me to the profit of Latin studies. (ll.5–8, Herren 1993, 109)

Eriugena's reputation as an isolated proponent of Greek in the Carolingian Age, whilst profoundly misleading, is buttressed by the propaedeutic tone of the poem: a tone to which Pound lends his own sensitive ear. Note the self-conscious use of τέχνας: it is both a reference to Greek learning and a material embodiment of it, 'stitched into' Eriugena's verse.

11

Ierugina   Grajugena
Carolum calvum

–

Roma
cultus avaritiae te
5   nimium superat.–

–

Ingenuique tua suna
          pelasga colunt
Truncasti vivos crudeli

vulnere santos.
10   Verdere nunc horum mortua
            membra soles.

Alfredi=allectus venit in
Angliam. to
Malmsbury,? stabbed
15   by students.

1–2 *Ierugina … calvus*] Variant spellings of Eriugena's name, designating Ireland as his country of birth: Schlueter provides an exhaustive account of the various spelling over time in his *Prooemium* to PL 122. Most Carolingian and later medieval sources used variant forms of John Scottus, but the early manuscripts of his translations of the works of Pseudo-Dionysius carried the form Ieruguna: *Berne 19, Berlin Phill. 1668, Cologne Dombibliothek 30, Florence Gadd. Pl. 89, Cambridge Trin. Coll. B.2.31* and *Cambridge Corp. Christ. D9* (Sheldon-Williams in Eriugena 1968, 1). Sheldon-Williams suggests that the form Grajugena in one of Eriugena's poems emulates a Virgilian formula, but it is also found in older texts such as the *Ad Fidolum* of Columbanus (although the authorship of this poem is contested: see Lapidge 1997b, 277). Carolum calvum or Carolus calvus is rendered as Charles the Bald in English.

3–11 *Roma … soles*] Three lines from a poem of uncertain authorship quoted in full in the *Prooemium*: 'De mutata Romae fortuna' (On the Changing Fortunes of Rome), in *Poetae Latini Minori*, Vol. 4, ed. N. E. Lamaire (Paris 1825), 537–38. The poem laments the fall of Rome to the Goths, and observes the rise of Constantinople as the new imperial centre. The context here is clear: the deep influence of Greek writers upon Eriugena, not least Pseudo-Dionysius. The lines, roughly translated, are: '[Roma], the cult of avarice has led to your downfall' (l.8), and 'your own sons tend Greek lands./You cruelly maimed your living saints/and now trade in the parts of their corpses' (ll.12–14). Note line 8 reads as 'Truncasti vivos crudely funere santos' in Lamaire's edition.

12–15 *Alfredi … students*] *Prooemium* xxv: 'Hic succedentibus annis munificentia Alfredi allectus venit in Angliam, et apud monasterium Malmesberiense a pueris, quos docebat, graphiis, ut fertur, perforatus, et martyr aestimatus est' (Subsequently, Alfred's generosity lured Eriugena to England, where he taught in the monastery of Malmesbury. It is thought he was martyred when his students stabbed him with their styli). These invented biographical details of Eriugena's death first appeared in the *Gesta Regum* of William of Malmesbury (Sheldon-Williams in Eriugena 1968, 5)

                    12
          grafhiis ut fertur
                         perforates.

                 –

          1223. ab errox
                 Berengarii
    5   by Leo IX
          Bede's pupils,
          Alcuin, Rabanus, Claudius
          & J. S.

          J. Mailrosius
    10   J. Patris
          etc.

                 –

          Scotum qui est in palatio
                         regis.

1–2 *grafhiis … perforates*] See 11.12–15

3–5 *1223 … Leo IX*] *Prooemium* xxv: 'Unde liber ejus de Eucharistia lectus est et damnatus in synodo Vercellensi, celebrata sub Papa Leone IX, eodem anno, quo se Lanfrancus ab errore Berengarii purgavit' ([Eriugena's] book on the Eucharist was read and condemned at the synod of Vercelli conducted by Pope Leo IX, in the same year in which he purified Berengar and Lanfranc from the error [of heresy attributed to Eriugena's text]). The dispute between Berengar of Tours (who belonged to the School of Chartres) and Lanfranc of Normandy concerned a treatise on the body of Christ: Berengar wrongfully attributed authorship to Eriugena but it was written by the Carolingian cleric Ratramnus. Leo IX excommunicated Berengar at the synod of Vercelli in 1050 (see Holopainen 2012, 105–122).

6–8 *Bede's … J. S.*] *Prooemium* xxv: 'Bedae discipuli, scilicet Rabanus et Alcuinus, Claudius et Joannes Scotus.' This designates Bede's Carolingian intellectual legacy generally, as none of the figures mentioned were contemporaries of Bede.

9–11 *J. Mailrosius…etc*] *Prooemium* xxvi: details from the *Illustrium majoris Brittaniae scriptorum summarium* of Joannes Baleus (c.1560), in which Joannes Mailrosius Scotus and Joannes Patricius Erigena are erroneously identified with Eriugena. These accounts combine authoritative historical data, such as Eriugena's major works, with more fanciful claims, such as his teaching in Britain and his knowledge of Chaldean and Arabic (xxvii).

12–13 *Scotum…Regis*] Auctore Anonymo, *De Joanne Scoto Erigena Commentatio*, PL 122 1C: 'Nicolaus quidem I. Pont.Max. in epistola de Nostro ad Carolum Calvum scribit: «Joannes, genere Scotus». Pardulus, episcopus Laudunensis, qui item Nostri mentionem facit, «Scotum illum», ait, «qui est in palatio regis (Caroli Calvi) Joannem nomine scribere coegimus»' (Indeed, Pope Nicholas I writes in a letter to Charles the Bald, of John, of whom Pardulus, bishop of Laon, also mentions: "We compelled Scotus, of the palace of the king (Charles the Bald), to write"). Pound cites these early mentions of Eriugena in papal and episcopal correspondence, in which Eriugena was requested to respond to Gottschalk's treatise on predestination.

13

    magnam partem
    quos (lat. author) ipse legit.
    –

    IV. 26
    introd

5   nothing compells good prob.
    men to virtue, but did.
    gratia cui cooperantus sua
    libertate humana
    –

    vin Ω νους

10   fin Ω αἴσθεσις
    –

    21. hell in pelluta sua
    conscientia
    not in time & space.
    Judas. late useless repentance,
15   ava semper usitur

1–2 *magnam ... legit*] PL 122, *De Vita et Praeceptis J. Scoti* 9AB: 'Primum igitur satis magnam in eo deprehendimus latinarum litterarum cognitionem. Laudat Boethium, Plinium, Virgilium, Ciceronem, alios; quos magnam partem ipse legit' (Firstly, we find in [Eriugena's writing] an extensive knowledge of Latin literature. He praises Boethius, Pliny, Virgil, Cicero, and others, whom he read extensively).

3–8 *IV. 26 ... humana*] *De Vita* 26D: 'IV. « Boni probique homines nulla neccessitate ad virtutem compelluntur: adjuvantur autem gratia divina, cui cooperantur sua libertate humana»' (Good men are not compelled to virtue: aided by divine grace, they work towards human liberty). This articulates Eriugena's doctrine of human will: the notion of grace (*donum*) recalls his use of Augustine in distinguishing between the resurrection of humanity and the deification of the elect at the Last Judgement.

9–10 *vin ... αἴσθεσις*] No source has been established for these references.

11–15 *21. Hell ... usitur*] *De Vita* 81B: 'Diversas suppliciorum fromas neque in loco neque in tempore ullo esse credimus. [....] Ubi Judas proditor torquetur? – Nusquam, nisi in polluta sua conscientia! – Qualem poenam partitur? Seram poenitentiam et inutilem, qua semper uritur' (Torment takes place nowhere in space and time. [...] Where was the traitor Judas chastised? Nowhere, except in his defiled conscience! What kind of punishment does he receive? Belated and ineffectual penance, which burns him forever). This paraphrase from Book V of the *Periphyseon* 937B alludes to the non-existence of sin and punishment: they do not stem from God, the source of all things, but are one and the same and endured negatively: see Eriugena, *Periphyseon* 1987, 613.

14

    giorgias
    1v Pefub
    Philebas

    Eikos
5   of Socrates

1–5 *giorgias ... Socrates*] These notes refer to two Platonic dialogues: the *Gorgias* and the *Philebus*. The *Gorgias* concerns the separation of philosophy, as an art, from rhetoric, which is a 'knack'. Pound may be drawn to this text for its myth of Tartarus, the place where Cronos sent damned souls for their punishment in the afterlife, in contrast to the Isle of the Blessed. The context here is clear, following from Eriugena's negative formulation of Judas's sin and punishment and as banishment from being, space and time. The *Philebus* was alternatively known as *Peri Hedones* or *Concerning Pleasure*. Given Pound's citation of the nature of sin and punishment in Eriugena's cosmogony, these texts may serve as classical counterpoints to his absolute division of creation into being and non-being in Part V of the *Periphyseon* (and elsewhere). Note: εικος is defined as 'probable truth' or 'likelihood' in Liddell and Scott (416).

[Sheets 15 and 16 are missing, or were not included in this sequence of notes. There is no evidence of removal from the sequence.]

17

246. C 145
73610. vol 122
Pat. Lat. Migne
Joannis Scot.

5   1037.
Pneumatis excelsi forte
     renatus erat
nec mora; perfulgens caelestis
     luce sophiae
10   Ατθιδα edocuit, de quibus
     ortus est
Namque ferunt Paulum qui Cristum
     sparsit in orbem
Ipsi felices imposuisee manus
15   Empyrei caeli tertia regna
     videt.

–

aetherios thronos, quo sedet
     ipse Deus

1–4 *246. … Scot*] Accession information for the copy of Volume 122 of the *Patrologia Latina* that Pound was able to access from the library in Genoa. The presence of such information at this point in the notes suggests that pages 1–14 may be the result of his earlier consultation of a copy of PL 122 in Venice.

5 *1037*] The column location in PL 122 from which the following quotations derive, from Eriugena's verse epigram to his translation of *The Celestial Hierarchy*.

6–18 *Pneumatis…Deus*] *Epi. Cel. Hier.* 1037B–1038B, ll.8–12, 16 and 18: the poem expresses praise for Dionysius the Areopagite and functions as a précis of the entire work. The lines (accurately) transcribed by Pound are translated as:

> [Dionysius] soon was reborn at the fount of the Spirit on high.
> Sans delay Dionysius, radiant with the light of heavenly wisdom,
> Began to teach the Athenians, from whom he sprang;
> For they say that Paul, who spread Christ to the world,
> Imposed his blessed hands upon him. […]
> [Dionysius, having followed Paul to the Empyrion]
> gazes upon the third kingdom of heaven […]
> [and sees] the heavenly Thrones where God himself is seated. (Herren 1993, 111)

That Pound excerpts l.18 of the poem is telling: whilst perhaps not his first citation of the division of Thrones in the Celestial Hierarchy, Pound is clearly drawn here to its significant place in the first triad in the architecture of heaven. The word, and all it represents, becomes an abiding theme in Pound's later career, not least in the decad of *cantos* bearing this name first published in 1959.

18

Αρχων, ἀρχανγέλως τε χορῶν
ἀνγελως τε
τηναυγων

–

mentibus uraniis tertia
5   ταξις inest

–

varietate socrorum reburimum
anagogice circumvelatum.

–

immaterialis luculentiae
imaginem materialia lumina.

10   1039
        conrationalibem theosin
        misericors perfectionis
        principium.

_____

per sensibilia in intellectualia

1–5 *Αρχων... in est*] *Epi. Cel. Hier.* 1038B, ll.21–22:

Αρχων, ἀρχαγγέλως τε χορῶν ἀνγελως τε τηναυγων
Mentibus uraniis tertia ταξις inest.
'Principalities, archangels, and Choirs of far-gleaming angels;
the third order partakes of the heavenly intellect'. (Herren 1993, 111)

The function of this third order resonates with Pound's earlier work on the motions of the soul in Cavalcanti's 'Donna mi prega', which hinges on the way love/*amor*, as an 'accidente', touches on or 'grazes' the potential intellect (νοῦς δυνάμει) and provides the subject with an insight into the active intellect (νοῦς ποιητικός) of God.

6–7 *varietate... circumvelatem*] *Exp. Cel. Hier.* 135BC: '*Et enim neque possibile est, aliter nobis lucere divinum radium, nisi varietate sacrorum velaminum anagogice circumvelatum, et his, quae secundum nos sunt, per providentiam paternam connaturaliter et proprie praeparatum*' (*For it is not possible for the Divine ray to enlighten us in any other way, except anagogically enveiled by a variety of sacred veils, co-naturally and appropriately prepared from them by the paternal providence for the things which exist in a manner consistent with us* (Rorem 2005, 189)).

8–9 *immaterialis... lumina*] *Exp. Cel. Hier.* 139B: '*Et immaterialis luculentiae imaginem materialia lumina*, subaudis similiter a superioribus: arbitrans' (*And the likeness of immaterial splendour illuminates matter*, which we consider to sound similar to higher understanding).

11–13 *conrationalibem... principium*] *Cel. Hier.* 1039B: 'Propter hanc ergo nostram conrationabilem theosin misericors perfectionis principium, et caelestes Ierarchias nobis manifestans' ('The source of spiritual perfection provided us with perceptible images of these heavenly minds' (Luibheid 1987, 147)). This quotation expresses Eriugena's kataphatic theology which extends to his biblical hermeneutics.

14 *per… intellectualia*] *Cel. Hier.* 1039C: 'sensibilibus imaginibus supercaelestes descripsit intellectus in sacroscriptis eloquiorum compositionibus, quatenus nos reduceret per sensibilia in intellectualia, et ex sacre figuratis symbolis in simplas caelestium Ierarchiarum summitates' (He revealed all this to us in the sacred pictures of the scriptures so that he might lift us in spirit up through the perceptible to the conceptual, from sacred shapes and symbols to the simple peaks of the hierarchies of heaven (Luibheid 1987, 147)).

19

et sac. fig. symbolis
in simplas cael. hier.
summitates.

_____

pulchre … informium formae 1040

_____

5   invisibilem et formificam
pulchritudinem aeternae
vere et invisibilis societalis
1090.
Quod enim Deum imitatur agalma
10   ad illam invis.^{m} et beneolentam
aspiciens formam.

Dom. glos. pl.^{mo} div. prov. @ adj.
grat. reg. Carolo Johannis
ext^{mus} serv^{n} Vestrorem perpet
15   in C^{to} salutem.

1–3 *et sac. … summitates*] *Cel. Hier.* 1039C: the second half of the sentence begun at 18.14. See above for translation.

4 *pulchre… 1040*] *Cel. Hier.* 1040D: 'Quia quidem enim pulchre procuratae sunt informium formae, et figurae carentium figures' (Now there are reasons for creating types for the typeless, for giving shape to what is actually without shape (Luibheid 1987, 149)).

5–7 *invisibilem … societalis*] *Ciel. Hier.* 1042D: 'Cum vero dissimiles similitudines intellectualibus circumponentes, concupiscentiam eis circumformemus, amorem divinum ipsam intelligere oportet super rationem et intellectum immaterialitatis, et inflexibile, et non indigens desiderium superessentialiter castae et impassibilis contemplationis, et ad illam puram et sublimissimam claritatem, et invisibilem et formicam pulchritudinem aeternae vere et invisibilis societatis' (Now when we apply dissimilar similarities to intelligent beings, we say of them that they experience desire, but this has to be interpreted as a divine yearning for that immaterial reality which is beyond all reason and all intelligence. It is a strong and sure desire for the clear and impassable contemplation of the transcendent. It is a hunger for an unending, conceptual, and true communion with the spotless and sublime light, of clear and splendid beauty (Luibheid 1987, 151)).

8–11 *Quod…formam*] *Eccl. Hier.* 1090A: 'Quod enim Deum imitatur agalma, ad illam invisibilem et beneolentem aspiciens formam, sic seipsum figurat et effingit ad formosissimam imitationem' (Hence virtuous conformity to God can only appear as an authentic image of its object when it rivets its attention on that conceptual and fragrant beauty (Luibheid 1987, 225)).

12–15 *Dom.…salutem*] *Ambig. S. Max.* (*The Ambigua of Maximus the Confessor*) 1193D: 'Domino gloriosissimo piissimoque divina providente atque adjuvante gratia regi CAROLO JOANNES extremus servorum Vestrorum perpetuam in Christo salutem' (Glorious Lord who bestows divine grace and aid, may you provide King Carolus eternal salvation in Christ). Eriugena's dedication of the *Ambigua* to Charles the Bald by way of a prayer of intercession.

20

nimbus Ω adumbrans passiv.
velamen Ω error
secundum sensum.

–

motions of soul. sec. animum
5   rationem
                          sensum
a caritate docuerunt
1219

1220

10   et intellectum cum
                    intellectuali passibilem
         quem etiam phantasiam vocant
                    animalis
         imaginata arbitrio et motu

1–3 *nimbus…sensum*] *Ambig. S. Max.* 1218D: 'Cur autem *nimbum* esse et *velamen carnem* dicit Magister' (But why be there a *halo covering flesh*, says the Master). Chapter VI of Eriugena's text is titled 'Quomodo est Nimbus et Velamen Caro' (On the Spirit's Halo Covering the Body).

4–7 *motions… docuerunt*] *Ambig. S. Max.* 1219C: 'Tres enim universales motus habere animam in unum collectos, a caritate docuerunt; unum secundum animam, alterum secundum rationem, tertium secundum sensum' (The three universal movements of the soul, to return to unity by way of the love bestowed: one movement according to the soul, the second according to reason, and the third according to sense). This triad structure, familiar from Plotinian Neoplatonism and Pseudo-Dionysius, is adapted by Maximus the Confessor to develop his notion of the human microcosm. See Thunberg, 107–13.

10–13 *et intellectum… animalis*] *Ambig. S. Max.* 1220CD: 'et intellectum cum intellectuali passibilem, quem etiam phantasiam vocant animalis' (in the intellect there is the conception of suffering, which is also in the animal).

14 *imaginata… motu*] *Ambig. S. Max.* 1220D–1221A: 'et duos quidem extremos a solo Deo habitos ut a causa, alium vero medium et nostro pendentem arbitrio et motu' (at the other extreme God alone can be the origin of causation, while on the other hand we tread a middle way, reliant upon our judgement in motion).

                    21

         naturale ratione –
         extremis admixtum –   1221
         –

         Ch. Bald. s. Lud. pius.
         gradio C. magne

              – –

5   Yrmindrudis –
        perfecta Palladis arte
        auro subtili serica fila parans

        actibus eximiis conlucent
                pepla mariti.

                –

10   ἀράχνη

        –

        orans. ac legitans libros,
                manibusque laborans.

        –

        christicolis plebis
                oc choris

                –

1–2 [*naturale... admixtum*] *Ambig. S. Max.* 1221AB: a continuation of 20.14
concerning the mixture of soul, rational intellect and animal response in the
human agent.

3–4 *Ch. Bald... magne*] *Versus* PL 122 1221–22: 'Versus Joannis Sapientissimi
ad Carolum Calvum Filium Ludouuici Pii Cujus Avus Fuit Carolus Magnus'
(Poems of the Wisest John, to Charles the Bald, Son of Louis the Pious and
whose Grandfather was Charlemagne). The dedication of Eriugena's poetry
to Charles the Bald, adduced from marginal notes in various manuscripts (see
note: PL 122, 1221–22).

5–9 *Yrmindrudis... mariti*] *Versus* 1227B: 'Ingens ingenium, perfecta Palladis
arte/Auro subtili serica fila parans./Actibus eximiis conlucent pepla mariti'
(ll.7–9) (Her great skill, nay mast'ry, in the art of Athena –/she prepares the silk
threads intermixed with fine gold./The cloaks of her spouse are resplendent
(Herren 1993, 73)). The poem is dedicated to Charles's wife, Irmintrude
('Laudes Yrmindrudis Caroli Calvi uxoris'), and is placed fourth in the PL
edition, after three important long religious poems: 'De Christo crucifixo',
'De cruce', and 'De paschate'. Its prominence is reflected in the significance
Pound placed in the figure of Irmintrude, who 'stiches' clothing (textus) as
Eriugena 'stitches' Greek into his poetry (στιχοι). Eriugena's verse is famous
for this kind of trans-linguistic punning, which no doubt appealed to Pound
in his admiration of Eriugena's '*hilaritas*' (LXXXIII/548). The poem 'may

have been written in 864 to compliment the queen in helping her husband in a negotiation with Pope Nicholas I, to whom was given a garment made of gold and gems, woven, in all likelihood, by Irmintrude herself' (Herren 1993, 140). Massimo Bacigalupo also notes the association between Irmintrude and arachne in Eriugena's 'Greek tags' (*L'Ultimo Pound*, 189–90).

10 ἀράχνη] *Versus* 1227B: 'Miratur fugitans numquamque propinquat ἀράχνη' (l.11) (The fleet spider admires her, can never approach her (Herren 1993, 73)).

11–12 *orans. … laborans*] *Versus* 1227C: Orans, ac leg'tans libros, manibusque laborans' (l.19) (praying and reading, making books with her hands (Herren 1993, 73)). Eriugena extends the text/poetry/stitching pun into a literal fusion of these activities.

13–14 *christicolis… choris*] *Versus* 1227D: 'Dignum christicolis plebibus atque choris' (l.28) (a king worthy of Christians and heavenly choirs (Herren 1993, 73)).

22

1227
Da pacem populo
chirstigenis floreat quies

–

paganos piratas vastantes
5   regna per orbem
consumptos gladio gurgite
merge maris.

–

Βασιλέει Καρόλιο ἡμῶν
ου χριστε βοῆθει

10   VIII verbo incarnato
Si vis οὐρανιας sursum
volitare per auras
Empyriosque polos mentis
sulcare meatu

2–7 *Da pacem… maris*] *Versus* 1228A: the penultimate quatrain in the poem to Irmintrude:

> Da pacem populo, qui tibi servit ubique,
> Omnibus christigenis floreat alma quies.
> Paganos piratas vistantes regna per orbem,
> Consumptos gladio gurgite merge maris. (ll.45–48)
> 'Grant peace to your people who everywhere serve you,
> let peace yield her bounty to all born in Christ.
> Slay and submerge in the surge of the ocean
> piratical pagans laying waste the earth's realms'. (Herren 1993, 75)

8–9 *Βασιλέει… βοῆθει*] *Versus* 1229A: 'Βασιλεει Καρολιο ημων ου χριστε βοηθει,/Ως κληιουσθαι ξοροις δυναμις ουρανιους' (You, O Christ, help our king Charles/obtain a place in the heavenly choir (Herren 1993, 79)). This is the final couplet of 'De Christi resurrectione', a major poem in which Eriugena rehearses some of his theological principles – the Trinity, light as an image of God's profusion in creation and in human being, and episodes from the Old Testament – and crucially ties these in with Charles's rule. This tactic, common in Eriugena's poetry, must be seen in the context of Charles's precarious reign, especially with regard to his half-siblings and fellow Carolingian kings, Louis the German and Lothar. Eriugena's Greek gesture is especially political, fusing by linguistic association Charles's legitimacy to rule with the powers of the Eastern Roman Empire in Byzantium.

10–14 *VIII verbo… meatu*] *Versus* 1230C: the title and first three lines (two on this leaf and the third at 23.1) of 'De Verbo incarnato' (The Word incarnate):

> If you wish to fly through the heavenly aether above
> And plough through the Empyrion along the path of the mind,
> With gleaming eye you will course the temples of wisdom (Herren 1993, 85)

23

> Ommate glaucivido
>   lustrabis templa sophiae
>
> –
>
> Quae stant, quae vario
>   volvuntur praedita motu
> 5 pneumata ventorum, vis
>   ignea,

lucidus aether

———————————

chorus et ~~aspring~~
     astrigeriae
10   perpuri luminis
      αἴγλη

Palladis. hinc gemmis
     septem redimita
       corona
15   φιοβη και Στιλθων
     και Φος, και Ηλιος,
      ʿAres

1–2 *Ommate… sophiae*] See 22.10–14

3–17 *Quae… ʿAres*] *Versus* 1231AB: lines 16–20 of 'De Verbo incarnato', transcribed faithfully except in line 20 where Pound has the Latin for Αρης:

> The things that rest and those that move, being endowed with different motions,
> The breath of winds, the force of fire, the bright aether,
> The chorus and radiant stars of Pallas's most pure light,
> The crown with her girdle of seven jewels,
> The moon, Mercury, Lucifer, the sun and Mars (Herren 1993, 85)

24

Εξης του κοσμον
     Κεντρον θετις
       ασχετος αχας
Caelestis motus
5   Modulaminis
       εννεαφθογγυς
Summa chelys vocum
     mortales effugit
       ωτας

     –

10   Cristum
    ars. lex. consilium, ξωη ζωη,
       sapientia, virtus

1–9 *Εξης … αχας*] *Versus* 1231B: lines 22–25 of 'De Verbo incarnato':

> Next unbounded Tethis, the salt-sea, the centre of the universe.
>
> (The motion of the heavens makes a harmony nine-toned;
>
> The highest pitch of its voices escapes our mortal ears.) (Herren 1993, 85)

10–12 Cristum … virtus] *Versus* 1231B: 'Cristum' is the final word in line 25, 'Rerum principium primum cognoscite Christum' (Know that Christ is the first principle of the universe (Herren 1993, 87)); line 27 reads: 'He is art, law, counsel, Life, wisdom, power' (Herren 1993, 87).

25

Fons.. de lumine lumen

Est. non est. super est.

–

    qui nullis partibus
      haeret

–

5   cunctorum subitans
        essentia simplex

Ὧν τελος, ων αρχη
    παντοων,
    ων οντα τα εισιν

10   Ὧν αγαθος και καλὸς,
    κάλλος, μιορφων
      τε χαρακτηρ

1 *Fons … lumen*] *Versus* 1231B, l.28: 'Fons medium finis, genitum de lumine lumen' (The source, the middle, and the end, light begotten of light (Herren 1993, 87)). This image of the Word as light begotten of light (cf. the Nicene Creed) both adheres to Trinitarian orthodoxy and neatly suggests the participation of the Son in the Father (Word = Light) that is extrapolated in the *Periphyseon* to all creation. See especially Book IV (PL 122, 778B) and, for human participation in the divine (*theosis*), see Book V (879C–880A).

2 *Est. … superset*] *Versus* 1231B, l.29: 'Est, non est, super est, qui praestitit omnibus esse' (He is being, non-being, supra-being, he excels all things in respect of being

[Herren 1993, 87]). This line neatly captures Eriugena's notion that God exceeds Being, essence and other attributes. See Marenbon 1981, 67–87.

3–6 *qui … simplex*] *Versus* 1231BC, fragments of ll.31–32:

> Totus per totum, qui nullis partibus haeret,
> Cum sit cunctorum substans essentia simplex.
> 'Himself being whole in wholeness, adhering to no divisions,
> Although he is their simple and substantial essence' (Herren 1993, 87)

7–12 *Ὢν … χαρακτήρ*] *Versus* 1231C, ll.33–34:

> He is the end and beginning of all that has being;
> He is good and beautiful, beauty itself and the seal set upon forms (Herren 1993, 87)

26

Fi.
Cavalli
    giasone

---

anf parasso Pound
5   Bartoli =
       @ Trieste
       circ. 1897.

1–3 *Fi. … giasone*] Francesco Cavalli's opera *Giasone* on the subject of the Golden Fleece, which premièred in Venice in 1649. It was perhaps the most popular opera in the seventeenth century.

4–7 *anf … 1897*] No source has been located for this note. This leaf is unnumbered.

27

F. Caffé
stor. mus. Teat. Ver.

1–2 *F. Caffé … Ver*] No source has been located for this note.

Eriugena notes, set 2, 38pp.
(YCAL MSS 43 Box 77 Folder 3406)

1

134. last – largir simiglianza

Φοτοδοσία
      origins of light   133

      –

      god father giver of lights
5   clarity of the father =
                 θεῖον πατέρα
                 That is the father
                 of gods
      Ƕ φοτοδοσια λαμπρίαν
10   radius ille simplex   paternae
                        claritatis
      the inaccessible invisible sun
      penetrans obstrusa
      illuminans mysteria

1 *134. … simiglianza*] The final line of the second stanza in Guido Cavalcanti's canzone 'Donna mi prega': 'Sì che non pote larger simiglianza' ('Nor can [Love] leave his true likeness otherwhere', *The Cantos*, XXXVI/177). The themes of amor, the active and passive intellects, and memoria in Cavalcanti's poem directly intersect with Eriugena's philosophical negotiations, especially his Aristotelian concerns of essence, *ousia*, and the Categories, and Neoplatonic theories of light and theogony. Pound includes the Arab commentators on Aristotle's *De Anima* in this system, and in *Make It New* he sees the controversies in Paris in 1209, 1225 and 1270 as emblematic assaults on the thinking of Eriugena, Averroes, Cavalcanti and their intellectual fellow-travellers.

2–3 *Φοτοδοσία … light*] *Exp. Cel. Hier.* 133C: 'Et notandum, quod hic quoque, sicut superius, simplicia pro compositis transtulimus verba. Pro eo enim, quod est θεαρχιικοῦ πατρὸς, *divini Patris*, et φωτοδοσίαν, *claritatem* posuimus' (And it should be noted that here, as above, we have translated simple words for compound ones. We have put 'of the divine Father' for θεαρχιικοῦ πατρὸς' and 'φωτοδοσίαν brightness for φωτοδοσιαν (Rorem 2005, 187)).

4–9 *god… λαμπρίαν*] *Exp. Cel. Hier*. 134A: 'Ipse quippe pro θεαρχεκῶ Patre θιεον πατέρα, id est divinum Patrem, et pro φωτοδοσια λαμπρίαν, id est claritatem, frequentissime ponunt' (They [the Greeks] themselves very frequently put θιεον πατέρα (that is, divine Father) for θεαρχεκῶ Father, and λαμπριαν (that is, brightness) for φωτοδοσία (Rorem 2005, 188)). The precise definition of terms: here, Eriugena's careful parsing of the terminology of Pseudo-Dionysius with regard to the light and clarity of God the Father.

10–11 *radius… claritatis*] *Exp. Cel. Hier*. 134A: 'Quis est autem radius ille simplex paternae claritatis, in cujus conspectu ab ipsa claritate immaterialibus et non titubantibus mentis oculis intellecta reponimus, merito quaeritur' (Now it may rightly be asked what is this simple ray of fatherly brightness, into whose sight we are brought back by that brightness which is known by the immaterial and non-trembling eyes of the mind? (Rorem 2005, 188)).

12 *the inaccessible… sun*] *Exp. Cel. Hier*. 134A: 'Et mihi quaerenti nihil probabilius occurrit ad credendum et inteligendum, quam Dei Patris Verbum, quod instar radii ab inaccessibili et invisibili sole, id est Patre, in universitatem sensibilis et intelligibilis creaturae' (In asking this, nothing more probable occurs to me to believe and understand than that this is the Word of God the Father. Like a ray from an inaccessible and invisible sun (that is, the Father) it is poured into the totality of sensible and intelligible creation (Rorem 2005, 188)).

13–14 *penetrans… mysteria*] *Exp. Cel. Hier*. 134B: 'implens omnia, perficiens imperfecta, penetrans obstrusa, illuminans mysteria, formans visiones in interioribus sensibus theologorum, aperiens intellectus eas visiones quaerere et intelligere volentium, et seipsum secundum analogiam uniuscujusque omnibus in se intuentibus manifestans' (filling all, perfecting the imperfect, penetrating the closed, illumining the mysteries, forming visions in the interior senses of theologians, opening the intellects of those willing to seek these visions and to understand them, and manifesting itself to all who gaze upon it, according to the proportion of each one (Rorem 2005, 188)). These passages combine to form a long sentence at 134AB in which a catalogue of the powers of the Word are given in mystical terms, suggesting a negative theology (cf. 'invisible sun').

2

formans visionem

–

awake the mind to see

```
             visions
        to ask & to know

             –

5                    intuentibus
        in commutabili
             similitudine inuformiter
                       fixus.
        respicientes
10             in se proportionaliter extendit
        & unificat secundum
             simplicem sui
                  unitatem.
        losing not its own unity

             –

15             unifies all things
        all things that are, are lights
```

1–4 *formans vision*] *Exp. Cel. Hier.* 134B: 'formans visionem' or 'creative vision' – this phrase continues immediately from 1.13–14 above, followed by Pound's paraphrase at 2–4.

5 *intuentibus*] *Exp. Cel. Hier.* 135C: 'beholders' of the divine vision, the kataphatic manifestation of Divine Light.

6–14 *in commutabili… unity*] *Exp. Cel. Hier.* 134D: Pound draws extensively from these sentences in YCAL MSS 73, 76/3383, 4.1–13 (for which a translation is provided).

15–16 *unifies… lights*] Pound's epitome of the anagogical passages quoted extensively here: note that he shifts from the mystical contemplation of divine unity to the formula he adapts from *Exp. Cel. Hier.* 1328CD: 'Quomodo omnia quae sunt, lumina sunt?' See YCAL MSS 43 76/3383, 1.13–14.

```
        3

        prepared us by appointing
        =
        found in theologians'
                  memory       135
                  for our teaching –
```

5   rationalis anima crescit –
                  by <u>action</u>, by knowing,
         Xt. virum perfectum

                  –

         in pristinam naturae mostras
                  simplicitatem

                  –

10   above all natural figures

                  –

         purgatur in actione
         5th or dimension of stillness

1 *prepared… appointing*] a further fragmented transliteration of 134D–135A.

2–7 *found… perfectum*] *Exp. Cel. Hier.* 135D–136A:

> In hoc itaque libro velamina, quibus divinus circumvelatur radius, et per
> paternam providentiam propter nos praeparatur, propheticae visiones sunt, quae
> per angelicas virtutes in similitudinem rerum senisbilium, infirmitati nostrae
> adhuc sensibus corporeis succubenti naturaliter congruentium, in theologorum
> memoria conformatae sunt, ad eruditionem nostram, et ab infantilitate nostra,
> qua rebus sensibilibus adhaeremus, reductionem per intelligibiles aetates,
> quibus per actionem et scientiam rationalis anima crescit, donec occurramus in
> virum perfectum, hoc est, in plenissimam Christi.
>
> (Thus, in this book, the veils by which the divine ray is enveiled and prepared
> for us by the paternal providence are the prophetic visions, shaped in the
> memory of the theologians through the angelic powers into the similitude of
> sensible things that are naturally congruent to our weakness as still burdened by
> sensible bodies. [This is done] for our instruction and for leading us back from
> our infancy in which we adhere to sensible things, [up] through intelligible ages
> in which the rational soul grows through action and knowledge 'until we come
> into complete manhood' [Eph. 4.13] (that is, into the fullest contemplation of
> Christ). (Rorem 2005, 189–90))

8–9 *in pristinams… simplicitatem*] *Exp. Cel. Hier.* 137A: 'ut nos merito peccati
originalis dispersos in pristinam naturae nostrae simplicitatem, in qua facti
sumus ad imaginem divinae unitatis' (bathed in the glow of Divine providence,
we are made in the image of Divine unity and are saved from original sin). This
expression of the concept of *imago Dei* is crucial in Eriugena's anthropology:
whilst it occurs in Augustine and elsewhere, Eriugena especially draws on the
De hominis opificio of Gregory of Nyssa.

10 *above…figures*] Pound's annotation to the extended discussion at 137AB concerning the reflection of Divine providence in nature, evident in the passage above at 3.8–9.

11 *purgatur in actione*] *Exp. Cel. Hier.* 138A: 'est omnium sacrorum mysteriorum, quibus nostra rationabilis natura eruditur in doctrina, purgatur in actione, illuminatur scientia, deificationis virtute perficitur, primum et immobile firmamentum' (of all of the sacred mysteries, by which the doctrines of reason instruct our nature, purged in action, enlightened by knowledge, perfected deific power, the fundamental immobile firmament).

12 *5th… stillness*] Pound's annotative commentary on the doctrine of assimilation in *The Celestial Hierarchy*: an understanding of the sacred orders allows humans to become closest to God, as a reflection of the Divine Wisdom of the Celestial Hierarchies themselves. The precise wording is significant, as the final lines of the 'Seven Lakes' canto are: 'The fourth: the dimension of stillness./And the power over wild beasts' (XLIX/245). In this note Pound links the Chinese Imperial aesthetic discourse of rustication with the text of Pseudo-Dionysius, providing a nexus between the Confucian and patristic world orders. This is examined in greater depth in Chapter 4.

4

why the celestial substance
by abstract visions

138
simple
5   by holy   not figured
image   heights   138
To simple
unfigured heights

–

visible forms > witness to invisible beauty

10   invisible beauty –
beloved –
of all lovers –
whereth tendeth
all love

The excerpts on this leaf and 5.1–5 below are all Pound's translations taken from *Exp. Cel. Hier.* 137–138: each of these represents Eriugena quoting his own earlier translation of *The Celestial Hierarchy*, from which the Luibheid translations below are thus taken.

1–2 *why... heights*] Cf. *Cel. Hier.* 1030B: 'quaecunque alia caelestibus quidem essentiis supermundane, nobis vero symbolice tradita sunt' (And so it goes for all the gifts transcendently received by the beings of heaven, gifts which are granted to us in symbolic mode (Luibheid 1987, 146)).

9 *visible... beauty*] cf. *Cel. Hier.* 1030AB: 'quae secundum ipsum est, meteriali manuductione utatur, visibiles quidem formas invisibilis pulchritudinis imaginations arbitrans' (any thinking person realizes that the appearances of beauty are signs of invisible loveliness (Luibheid 1987, 146)).

10–14 *invisible... love*] cf. *Cel. Hier.* 1042D: 'Cum vero dissimiles similitudines intellectualibus circumponentes, concupiscientiam eis circumformemus, amorem divinam ipsam intelligere oprtet super rationem et intellectum immaterialitatis, et flexibile et non indigens desiderium superessentialiter castae et impassibilis contemplationis' (Now when we apply dissimilar similarities to intelligent beings, we say of them that they experience desire, but this has to be interpreted as a divine yearning for that immaterial reality which is beyond all reason and all intelligence. It is a strong and sure desire for the clear and impassible contemplation of the transcendent (Luibheid 1987, 151)).

5

sensible suavity
  figure of distribution
    invisible

 –

calling all h̶[̶x̶x̶x̶]̶s̶
5   souls to itself

knowing, unknowing

 –

light over light, whereof our light
   is the shadow

 –

7 parts into knowledge
10 7 streams
   angel intellect

free of all carnal

gravity

141

–

15   solum modo

cognoscunt se esse –

1–3 *sensible … invisible*] cf. *Cel. Hier.* 1042D above at 4.10–14

4–5 *calling … itself*] *Cel. Hier.* 1037D: 'iterum ut unifica virtus restituens nos replete et convertit ad congregantis Patris unitatem et deificam simplicitatem' (in its power to unify, [Divine Light] it stirs us by lifting us up. It returns us back to the oneness and deifying simplicity of the Father who gathers us in (Luibheid 1987, 145)).

6 *knowing, unknowing*] Light and other figures of divinity are strictly metaphorical, and thus unknowable in any direct sense, but the morphology Pseudo-Dionysius draws between the Celestial and Ecclesiastic Hierarchies allows indirect knowledge to draw the human toward the divine realm, and by way of metaphor in the condition of theophany.

7–8 *light … shadow*] No direct attribution appears to exist for either *Exp. Cel. Hier.* or *Cel. Hier.* – this is likely a poetic formulation from Pound's reading in Eriugena and Pseudo-Dionysius.

9–10 7 *parts … streams*] There are nine hierarchies of angelic beings, thus '7 parts' or '7 streams' refer elsewhere. No corresponding passage arises in Eriugena or Pseudo-Dionysius, although cf. Isaiah 11.15, 'And the LORD shall utterly destroy the tongue of the Egyptian sea; and with his mighty wind shall he shake his hand over the river, and shall smite it in the seven streams, and make men go over dryshod' (King James Bible). This reference to the Nile River recalls the Crossing of the Red Sea (Exodus 14.21) but is commonly thought to refer here to the Euphrates during the Babylonian Captivity.

11–13 *angel … gravity*] *Exp. Cel. Hier.* 141AB: 'Ac brevi sententia beatus Dionysius docet nos, incunctanter non solum humanos animos adhuc in carne detentos per sensibilia symbola, verum etiam angelicos intellectus omni carnali gravitate absolutos per invisibiles significationes, quas theologia theophanias nominat' (And as the pithy utterances of the blessed Dionysius teaches us, the angelic intellect is filled with sensible symbols, although not of the fleshly kind, but the meaning of the absolute gravity of the flesh, by what he calls theological thoeophanies).

15–16 *solum… esse*] *Exp. Cel. Hier.* 141B: 'sed solummodo cognoscunt se esse, et veritatem superessentialiter esse' (but only know that they exist, and that truth exceeds existence). This passage is an excellent illustration of the Pseudo-Dionysian *via superlationis*, a counterbalance to the *via negationis* that Eriugena subsequently adapted into his *Periphyseon*.

6

misericors
       perfectionis principium   141

–

    φῖλανθροπιαν
         begins of perfect purgation
5   142

     –

by sensible forms setting forth
    minds of divinities

by figured symbols to simple celestial
        virtues
10   Trinity our θεοσις
    per sensibiliter to lift of
        angelical nature

τελεταρχια, perfect purgation

     –

ubi nullus ignis sensibilis est

     –

15   from aetheral & igneus
     nature

1–24 *misericors… purgation*] *Exp. Cel. Hier.* 141D–142A: 'misericors et elementissimum perfectionis principium (nam φιλανθροπίαν quidam vertent in misericordiam, quidam in humanitatem, hoc est, humanitatis amorem, quidam in elementiam; φιλάνθροπιαν autem misericors, vel humanus, vel clemens Deus est, et ipse est τελεταρχια hoc est perfectae purgationis initium)' (the merciful and fundamental principle of perfection (for some people it will become mercy φιλανθροπίαν, for some with regard to humanity, that is, a love of humanity, and for some in principle; φιλάνθροπος, full of human compassion, God is merciful, and he is the τελεταρχια, that is the foundation of a cleansing perfection)). Note: Trinity = τελεταρχια.

6–7 *by sensible… divinities*] *Exp. Cel. Hier.* 142B: 'per sensibiles formas divinos descripsit intellectus'.

8–9 *by figured… virtues*] *Exp. Cel. Hier.* 142B: 'per symbola figurate in simplam caelestium virtutem excelsitudinem subveheret'.

10–12 *trinity… nature*] *Exp. Cel. Hier.* 142BC: 'deificat enim nostram naturam, reducendo eam per sensibilia symbola in altitudinem angelicae naturae'.

13 τελεταρχια… *purgation*] *Exp. Cel. Hier.* 142BC: 'Ipsa est nostra τελεταρχια, hoc est, perfectissimae nostrae purgationis et sanctificationis exordium' (It is our τελεταρχια, that is, the most perfect introduction to our purification and sanctification).

14 *ubi… est*] *Exp. Cel. Hier.* 145C: 'in supercaelestibus essentiis, ubi nullus ignis sensibilis est, et ut non imaginemus ibidem thronos materiales' (the supercelestial essences, where no fire is sensible, and nor imagine the thrones are material).

15–16 *from… nature*] *Exp. Cel. Hier.* 148C: 'ex aetherea videlicet igneaque natura'.

      7

    154   informato   (loco)

sup^r omm^m essentiam et vitam
nullo quidem ipsam lumine
      caracterizante
5   omnique ratione et intellectu
similitudine ipsius
in comparabiliter derelictus

–

negat. statem vera re divine
positive '   metaphorical '

–

10   candid igneus colour
       in our soul   naturally
προσὕλον – all ^ that is inclining ^
       to the likeness of our material
           bodies.
15   158
bent <u>thence</u>

individually
to love of visible things

———

1 *informato (loco)*] Cf. Pound's letter to Otto Bird of 12 January 1940: 'Re Cavalcanti: Erigena certainly throws doubt on various readings: *for*mato and *in*formato, etc. I wonder whether lots of copyists didn't each emend the text to suit their own views' (*SL* 332).

2–7 *sup*ʳ *... derelictus*] *Exp. Cel. Hier.* 154AB: 'Est enim super omnem essentiam et vitam, nullo quidem ipsam lumine caracterizante, hoc est, figurante, seu formante, omnique ratione et intellectu similitudine ipsius incomparabiliter derelictis; id est, dum omnis ratio et intellectu similitudine ipsius alienatur'; cf. Pseudo-Dionysius, *Celestial Hierarchy*: 'these sacred shapes [...] are actually no less defective than [lower forms of imagery], for the Deity is far beyond every manifestation of being and of life; no reference to light can characterize it; every reason or intelligence falls short of similarity to it' (Luibheid 1987, 149).

8–9 *negat... metaphorical*] *Exp. Cel. Hier.* 155C: 'Si vera est negatio in divinis rebus, non autem vera sed metaphorica affirmatio' (If the truth of divine things is negated, it is not a negation of truth but an affirmation of the metaphorical) – this is a neat expression of the cataphatic theology for which Pseudo-Dionysius was renowned, i.e. reference to that which is unknown or unknowable by way of figurative speech.

10 *candid igneus colour*] *Exp. Cel. Hier.* 155C, quoting Pseudo-Dionysius, *Cel. Hier.* 1042A: 'In quidem enim pretiosioribus sacris formationibus consequens est elt seduei auriformes quasdam aestimantes esse caelestes essentias, et quosdam viros fulgureos, decora indutos vestimenta, candide et ignee innocueque resplendentes, et quibuscunque aliis similibus imaginatis formis theologia caelesies figuravit intellectus' (High-flown shapes could well mislead someone into thinking that the heavenly beings are golden or gleaming men, glamorous, wearing lustrous clothing, giving off flames which cause no harm, or that they have other similar beauties with which the word of God has fashioned the heavenly minds (Luibheid 1987, 150)).

11–18 *προσυλον... things*] *Exp. Cel. Hier.* 158C: 'In Graeco scriptum est: προσύλον ἡμῶν, id est, materiale nostrum, omne videlicet, quod in nostra anima ad similitudinem materialis nostri corporis facillime inclinatur, inque amorem rerum visibilium irrationabiliter flectitur' (In the Greek it is written: προσύλον ἡμῶν, that is, in our complete materiality, the soul in its likeness is inclined to the love of material things, and irrationality bent to the love of visible things).

8

```
        mind ever upward
                    ad spiritualia
        is born by natural appetite

        158        phantasiis memoria
5       159        visions etc as stimulus
                            cf Kulch
        cf. qualitato non discendi
                    mat. can go up
                    spir. cant go down
10                  by nat. transmutation
        angelic               ? non seq
        virtues               or what
        distincta from corpora mortalia –
                            –
        circumscribed by
15                  locibus & spaces    denies
        changeable over time
```

1–3 *mind ... appetite*] *Exp. Cel. Hier.* 159A: 'sursum semper ad spiritualia naturali appetitu fertur' (natural appetite always rises to the spiritual) – a continuation of the theme of 7.11–18 above.

4–5 *phantasmis stimulus*] *Exp. Cel. Hier.* 159C: 'sive interius in phantasiis memoriae' (or the inner phantasia of memory): a faculty in which sensible forms may be apprehended, in contrast to perceptions of the material world.

6 *cf Kulch*] reference to *Guide to Kulchur*, on matters of the hierarchies of perception, of the material world and the sensible forms: here is a clear relation to Pound's apprehension of Cavalcanti's project in 'Donna mi prega', to mediate an Averroist interpretation of the possible intellect and its interactions with 'l'accidente' emanating from the active or agent intellect.

7–16 *cf. qualitato … time*] *Exp. Cel. Hier.* 159C: 'Possibile est namque inferiora ad superiora ascendere, descendere vero superiora ad inferiora naturali transmutatione, impossibile est' (It is possible for inferior matter to ascend, but superior spirit cannot transmute and descend); note the fragments of words and phrases appear scattered through 159C, for example, 'Terrena materialique corpora mortalia, corruptibilia, membrorum compositionibus disticta […]' (Material and earthly bodies are mortal, corruptible, made of distinct parts […]).

9

spiritual bodies   simplicia
   by no lineaments of
   sensible form   coartata

   ———

affirms
5   ——— 'mitis enim loc leo
             non est'
  160.C. irascibile

  161   immutabili amore justitiae
        inflexible – love of
10   heavenly virtue

   –

  162   materialis ingenita passibilitas
          assiduously in corporal lusts.
          impatient love of the transcend.
          provo impetus ruere
15   impossible contemplation

   –

love   above reason & willed
         of immateriality

1–3 *spiritual … coartata*] *Exp. Cel. Hier.* 160C: 'ex materiis sensibilus formare' (from sensible matter to form), i.e. the process of transcendence adumbrated in leaves 7 and 8 above, noting that Pound's excerpting choices comprise words commonly found throughout Eriugena's text, except for 'coartata' (narrowed) which does not appear there, or in *The Celestial Hierarchy*, but does appear several times in the *Periphyseon*.

5–6 *mitis ... est*] *Exp. Cel. Hier.* 160D: 'mitis enim leo leo non est' (the gentle lion, [the divine intelligence] is not this); cf. '[the divine intelligences] are not shaped to resemble the brutishness of oxen or to display the wildness of lions' (Luibheid 1987, 147)).

7–10 *irascibile ... virtue*] these words and phrases are scattered across *Exp. Cel. Hier.* 160–62.

11–14 *materialis ... ruere*] *Exp. Cel. Hier.* 162AB: 'materialis ingenita passibilitas' (the inherent vulnerability of the material realm), 'in rerum mutabilium impatienti amore' (changeable impatient love), 'quod est secundum sensum, prono impetus ruere' (driven by the senses to rush into action).

15 *impossible contemplation*] *Exp. Cel. Hier.* 162B: '*non indigens desiderium superessentialiter castae et impassibilis contemplationis*' (The desire not to require pure and passionless contemplation).

16–17 *love ... immateriality*] *Exp. Cel. Hier.* 162B: 'Quid divinus amor? Est laudibilis concupiscientia ipsius immaterialitatis' (This divine love? Laudable desire of the immaterial).

10

162   ? misprint for   eternal
              fornicam   invisible
                               society

–

laudabilis concupiscentia

–

5   ex qua est omnis forma
            et pulchritudo

–

resonances of intellectual beauty   164
echo in hollow of rock
           form seen in a mirror

–

10   sic. imagination of intellect. Beauty
                heav.^{y} virtu
        in
    (vilent mater respond.)
    lead back surely by the resonance

15   to 1st immat forms

        –

    s̶u̶b̶ subindeque splendor of doing
                        practicae   166

1–3 *misprint… society*] two related notes, each composed vertically: *Exp. Cel. Hier.* 162B: 'formicam pulchtritudinem aeterae vere et invisibilis societatis' ([formicam] the beauty of eternal spring and invisible society). Pound questions whether *formicam* (ant) should instead be *fornicam*, thus altering the phrase's meaning to (very roughly) 'the archway to eternal beauty and the true invisible society', a plausible alternative.

4 *laudabilis concupiscientia*] See above, 9.16–17.

5–6 *ex qua… pulchritude*] *Exp. Cel. Hier.* 162CD: 'ex qua omnis forma et pulchritudo facta est, accipere nos opportet' (it [divine love] produces beauty of every form, which we humbly accept).

7–9 *resonances… mirror*] *Exp. Cel. Hier.* 164AB: 'per omnem sat materialem dispositionem resonanitas quasdam intellectualis pulchritudinem habet', cf. 'Matter, after all, owes its subsistence to absolute beauty and keeps, throughout its earthly ranks, some echo of intelligible beauty' (Luibheid 151–52). The latter two lines 8–9 – echoing lines in 'The Burial of the Dead' in *The Waste Land* (l.25, 'There is shadow under this red rock') – appear to be Pound's own composition.

10–13 *sic.… respond*] *Exp. Cel. Hier.* 164C: 'ita intellectualis pulchritudinis caelestium virtutem imaginationes ex omni terrena vilissimaque material respondent' (earthly matter responds to the intellectual beauty in the heavenly virtue of imagination). The meaning of this phrase is complicated by the potential confusion with the names of the members of the second celestial hierarchy: Dominions, Powers, and Authorities/Virtues. Note Pound's preferred spelling of *virtu*, recalling the ascent of the lady's spirit in 'Donna mi prega' (Surette 1993, 52) – cf. 'What is [Love's] virtu and power' (XXXVI/177) and 'He [Love] is not vertu but cometh of that perfection' (XXXVI/178) – as well as anticipating the direct link to Eriugena in Canto LXXIV: 'in the light of light is the *virtù/*"sunt lumina" said Erigena Scotus' (449).

14–15 *lead… forms*] Pound is tracing the way the soul is 'uplifted' from apprehending physical images to immaterial products of intellectual beauty.

16–17 *subindeque...practicae*] *Exp. Cel. Hier.* 166A: 'Deum suum incipit oriri, subindeque pulcherrimus splendor practicae' (We rise up towards God, into the brightness of the most beautiful sacred imagery).

11

166	conversionem to	
	followed by splendor	166
	practicae	

per se ipsum

5   shining by delituale [?]

of intellectual contemplation divine minds

–

sublimity of the air

quintuplex angularitatis

_____

167.

10   168   pantheri – panther

–

To deny ~~po~~ material possibilities

19.20) <u>78</u>

36

175   divina pulchritude

simpla.

15   ut τελταρχικα

–

adhaerare – cf radere

ratio Ω eye of mind, sez. philos.

1–3 *conversionem...practicae*] See 10.16–17 above.

4–6 *per se...minds*] *Exp. Cel. Hier.* 166B: 'per se ipsum in divinis mentibus altitudine intellectualis contemplationis refulgens' ([the light of truth shines] by itself in divine minds, in the height of intellectual contemplation). These phrases pertain to Chapter 7 of *The Celestial Hierarchy*: cf. Luibheid 164–66.

7 *sublimity of the air*] *Exp. Cel. Hier.* 166C: 'sublimitate aeris'.

8 *quintuplex angularitatis*] *Exp. Cel. Hier.* 167C: 'quintuplex ipsius angularitatis a sactis Patribus traditur modus' (the fivefold way of [Christ's] cornered-ness has been handed down by the Holy Fathers) – this image combines the fivefold division and unification of the world that Eriugena deploys in the *Periphyseon*, his readings in Maximus the Confessor (from whom he initially adopted the fivefold image) and the Cappodocian Fathers, Gregory of Nyssa and Gregory Nazianzus.

10 *pantheri – panther*] *Exp. Cel. Hier.* 168AB: 'Mysticus quoquo pantheri est. Pantheri quippe dicitur quasi panther, hoc est bestialissimus; ferocissima enim omnium bestiarum est' (He [Christ] is also the mystical panther. Indeed "panther" is said as if "pan ther" [all beast], namely, most bestial, for it is the most ferocious of all beasts (Rorem 2005, 194)). The panther appears in Chapter 2 of *The Celestial Hierarchy*, with the lion and the bear, as examples of 'low' images, but here there is a suggestion of its potential as divine metaphor. Eriugena considers Pseudo-Dionysius's use of this image for Christ as dialectical: at once a figure of passion and strength, as well as one who 'devours' irrationality. Pound was to provide the image of the panther with an Ovidian inflection in numerous cantos, for example: 'Crouched panthers by fore-hatch' (II/8); 'Zagreus, feeding his panthers' (XVII/77); 'in the caged panther's eyes' (LXXXIII/550); and 'The black panther lies under his rose-tree' (XCIII/648). The 'caged panther' functions, of course, as an autobiographical totem in *The Pisan Cantos*.

11 *To deny… possibilities*] *Exp. Cel. Hier.* 173A: 'et negare materiales passibilitates spiritualibus carnaliter inesse substantii' (to deny that material and mortal things exist carnally in spiritual substances (Rorem 2005, 199)).

13–15 *divina… τελταρχικά*] *Exp. Cel. Hier.* 175BC: '*Divina pulchritudo, ut simpla, ut optima, ut* τελεταρχικά *pura quidem est*' (Divine beauty, as simple, as optimal, so that it is indeed a pure τελεταρχικά).

16–17 *adhaerare… philos.*] *Exp. Cel. Hier.* 175C 'Nam et ipsa simplex et optima divina pulchritudo, cui adhaerare similisque ei fieri omnis vita purgata naturali appetit desiderio' (The simplest and the best among the divine beauties cleave to him, just as life wishes to be purged of all animal desires). No source for the final line has been identified.

12

summa sapienta, quae Deus est
178   impossible immateriality

<pre>
                    sublimissium suggetti
                        for for the S. B to
5   rest on
            in deformity
            defender of similitude 1 div. <u>formositas</u>
            —

            179. pure of every dissimilitude
            180 by anfracts of error = wont is to
10   removed from love & knowl. of truth
                                190 <u>end</u>
                                <u>208</u>
            212 order   harmony
            221 jews
15   225 – purg. ig.
                    lights – know
                    perf. deificatio
            _____

            270 – not <u>atasal</u>, Transmutatio
                    deificatio
20   270 – <u>super</u>-i   superdea
</pre>

1 *summa… est*] *Exp. Cel. Hier.* 176D: 'Prius siquidem ipsa summa sapientia, quae Deus est, in eos diffunditur immediate' (Firstly, inasmuch as the highest wisdom, which is God, immediately poured forth upon them).

2–5 *impossible… rest on*] *Exp. Cel. Hier.* 177B: 'divini superadventus in impassibilitate omni et immaterialitate acceptivum et deiferum et famulariter in divinas susceptiones suggestum'

6–7 *in deformity…formositas*] *Exp. Cel. Hier.* 178CD: 'Deum imitanti deiformitate dependentem, id est, quae desuper pendet, originemque ducit ex similitudine divinae formositatis' (Deformity consists in imitating God, that is, is dependent, leading from the divine origin of beauty).

8 *pure… dissimilitude*] *Exp. Cel. Hier.* 179CD: 'Puras igitur, inquit, hoc est, omni dissimilitudine mundas, eas, primas videlicet essentias caelestium ierarchiarum, existimandum' (Pure of any dissimilitude, they are the essences in the first order of the heavenly hierarchy).

9–10 *by anfracts… truth*] *Exp. Cel. Hier.* 180A: 'in rerum temporalium cupidine opprimitur, diversorumque errorum anfractibus seducitur, et quod omnium perniciosissimum est, ab amore et cognitione veritatis elongatur, divina gratia nos revocante recipimur, ipsae recipiuntur' (the world shall be overwhelmed by a love of the temporal, and, most dangerously of all, by diverse errors be seduced from the love of the enduring knowledge of the truth, but are received by the recall of divine grace).

11–14 *end…jews*] concepts of order and harmony occur at *Exp. Cel. Hier.* 212B: 'Si nullus ordo fieret, nulla harmonia' (without order, there be no harmony); and reference to Jewish opinion at 221AB: 'Non secundum, inquit, falsam superbamque Judaicam opinionem'.

15–17 *purg. … deificatio*] *Exp. Cel. Hier.* 222CD: 'Primum quidem, quia sancti angeli nostri praesules sunt, et non aliam ob causam imperant nobis, nisi ut nos revocent nostris erroribus et ignorantiis in unius omnium principii et causae cognitionem, quae sola nostra salus est et purgatio et illuminatio et perfectio et summa beatitudo et deificatio' (Firstly, because the holy angels preside over us, and for the reason that they command us, should we recall our errors and the principle of all things and the causes of ignorance in the knowledge of the one, which alone is our salvation and cleansing and enlightenment, perfection, and happiness, and the greatest deification).

18–19 *not atasal… deificatio*] *Exp. Myst. Theol.* 270A: 'Ibi fit etiam deificatio, id est de humanis in divina transmutatio' (There is also deification, that is, the transformation of the human into the divine). Pound contrasts the prevalent notion of *theosis* in Eriugena's Neoplatonism to Avicenna's concept of *atasal*: *theosis* implies a process of transformation and union with the divine, whilst atasal (*ittisāl*) implies contact or influence. Cf. '[Avicenna] is careful, in importing ideas from the repertoire of Plotinus (205–70), to choose the idea of "contact" (Greek *aphe*, Arabic *ittisāl*) rather than "union" (*ittihad*) with the divine' (Goodman 298). Note also: '…nor is this yet atasal/ nor are here souls, nec personae/neither here in hypostasis' (LXXVI/478). See also Little 1985.

20 *super… superdea*] *Exp. Myst. Theol.* 270B: 'Trinitas supersubstantialis, et superdea, et superbona' (Trinity!! Higher than any being,/any divinity, any goodness! (Luibheid 1987, 135)). These opening lines of the exordium to Pseudo-Dionysius's *Mystical Theology* express the notion of God as more-than-essence, exceeding *ousia* and the Categories, as well as human comprehension and expression. This directly influenced Eriugena's theology, evident in the closing pages of Book I of the *Periphyseon*: see 76/3383 10.3–5 above.

13

280 – amnium causa, at super
omnia exiturs – nec sine
substantia est nec sine vita.
        Dion. (J. S. follows)
5   Text
nec sine ratio. ne sine mente
                aliquid
                materialiter
                substantiatum
10 281 – nec virtus est
        G. C.
                the united & unitive
                cause of all things

———————————

413 anything known to us
15   is an <u>accidens</u>
in conf. per se, of some essence
known by quality, quantity form place
        time, etc.

1–9 *amnium…substantiatum*] *Exp. Myst. Theol.* 280C: 'Dicimus ergo, quod omnium causa, et super omnia existens, nec sine substantia est, nec sine vita, nec sine ratione, nec sine mente, nec corpus est, nec figura, nec formam, nec qualitatem, nec quantitatem, aut pondus habet' (So this is what we say. The Cause of all is above all and is not existent, lifeless, speechless, mindless. It is not a material body, and hence has neither a shape nor form, quality, quantity, or weight (Luibheid 140–41)). Pound annotates this long sentence from Chapter 4 of the *Mystical Theology*, which catalogues the negative divine qualities, with a note that the lines above are 'Text' of 'Dion.' and those to follow comprise the gloss of 'J. S.' which begins, at 280D: '*Sensus talis est. Asserimus quod Deus, qui creavit omnia, est aliquid materialiter substantiatum, sive nec vivens, nec ratione utens, nec mente eminens […]*' (The meaning of which is: To assert that God, who created all things, is not something materially substantiated, not a living thing, nor using reason, nor with a higher mind […]).

10–13 *nec virtus…things*] *Exp. Myst. Theol.* 281 CD: 'nec virtus est' (nor is it power) appears in Chapter 5 in a long list of the qualities negatively held by the Supreme Cause; in the same sentence, at 281A preceding Eriugena's gloss, is the phrase 'unita et unitiva omnium causa' (the perfect and unique cause of all things (Luibheid 1987, 155)).

14–18 *anything… time, etc.*] These lines are Pound's annotations to his reading of Eriugena's gloss and commentary on the *Mystical Theology*, recapitulating the catalogue of negative attributes, and making the distinction between the (impossible) knowledge of God and other forms of knowledge that arise by way of accidents (in the Aristotelian sense).

14

1223. largire l.45.		wheat […]
consumaturma		grain '
	essentium	seed of man '
plures odas		[…]
5	consonat chorus	love
ex. erebo lux		osa[…]y
1229	mundi	
=		
seed of the grain		num pens
own constant others		retinocula leti.
10	fire […] break[…]	
	mountain	
		verses 1 Joh +
443.	Στιχοι Ιωάννου	To baz in gk
	Τω βασιλει	Carolus Τω βασι
15	καρόλῳ	λειον

Column A:

1 *1223. largire l.45*] *Versus* 1223B, 'De Christo crucifixo' l.45: 'Qui tantum largire vides quod rite rogaris' (You who see fit to grant as much as is rightfully asked (Herren 1993, 61)).

2–3 *consumaturma essentium*] No source has been located for this phrase, which may be a mistranscription of *consumatur in essentia* (consumed in essence).

4–5 *plures… chorus*] *Versus* 1226D, 'De paschate' l.66: 'Dum plures odas consonat ipse chorus' (while the choir resounds freely with many hymns (Herren 1993, 71)).

6 *ex. erebo lux*] No source has been located for this phrase, 'light from Erebus'; noting that Canto I contains the lines 'Dark blood flowed in the fosse,/Souls out of Erebus, cadaverous dead' (I/3) which describes the rites performed on Circe's island, Aeaea, leading to the apparition of Elpenor's shade.

7 mundi] *Versus* 1229BC, '*Christi descensus ad inferos et resurectio*' l.15: 'Se I victor mundi praestantior omnibus unus' (Where the prince of the world once sat on high (Herren 1993, 81)): this single word conjoins Erebus from *Odyssey* Book X with the descent of Christ to Hell following the crucifixion.

8–11 *seed... mountain*] These lines appear to be Pound's original composition, initiating a sequence of lines and phrases throughout the notes pertaining to agriculture and the impositions of economic duress upon agrarian life.

13–15 Στίχοι... καρόλω] *Versus* 1237C, 'Joannis Scoti Graeci Versus': 'Στίχοι Ἰωάννου τῶ βασιλεῖ καρόλω' (John's verses for King Charles): a dedication used frequently by Eriugena, particularly in poems bearing Greek words and phrases.

Column B:

1–6 *wheat... osa[...]y*] Lines of Pound's composition on agricultural themes.

8–9 *num... leti*] unidentified phrases.

12–15 *verses... λειον*] Parallel formulae in Romans and Greek scripts: 'John's verses for King Charles'; cf. Column A, 13–15.

15

	S. Max	1251.
	1219 = tangens re G. C	Type.
	aut signis visibi ~~lia~~ lium	———
	rationes ~~ad~~ apud seipsum reformat	1231
5		the antient home of death
	magninimiter per hos secundum	& night profound
		–
	verum et immutalibem	inner light in Chas' mind.
	naturalis motus modum	
	praesens laborum seculum	
10	transcenderunt	
	getting (as much) divine mercy	
	as in proportion as they	

are inserted in God
(Deo inserti)

———————

15   quantum homo
invis.[b] nat. Deus per
virtutes fecit manifestum.

Column A:

1–10 *S. Max... transcenderunt*] *Ambig. S. Max.* 1219D: 'Tertium autem compositum, per quem ea, quae extra sunt, tangens, veluti ex quibusdam signis visibilium rationes apud seipsam reformat, magnanimiter per hos secundum verum et immutabilem naturalis motus modum, praesens laborum seculum transcenderunt' (The third thing [the soul's transcendent state] is a combination of that which is outside of it and its inner reason, showing visible signs of change but remaining true to its natural immutability, to transcend the toils of the present).

11–14 *getting... inserti*] Pound's gloss on the quotation from the *Versio Ambiguorum* of Maximus the Confessor at ll. 1–10: the human soul enters into the divine realm but is not identified with God; 'Deo inserti' follows in Eriugena's translation at 1220A.

15–17 *quantum... manifestum*] *Ambig. S. Max.* 1220AB: 'quantum homo invisibilem natura Deum per virtutes fecit manifestum' (by virtue of God's invisible nature to man, made clear).

Column B:

5–7 *the antient... mind*] *Carmina* 1230–32, '*De Verbo Incarnato*': the poem extols the superessence of God, and engages with Eriugena's customary paradoxes, such as the divine light exceeding 'sense' of the intellect, being thus invisible; Christ's incarnation 'ruined Death, which had devoured all the world' (l. 54) (Herren 1993, 87). Note that the final reference to Charles occurs in Eriugena's poem parenthetically in Greek: '– Lord Charles, may Christ grant you eternal Life forever,/May you live many years revered as you are –' (Herren 1993, 87).

16

1220 whereby the physical
body is necessarily
nobled –

by its inborn natural intelligence

5   ad div. intel. dig.ᶻ et pulch.

ad Deum pervenerunt corpus ut

mundum

        corpus vero sensui

–

om. vint et saf. plenitudo

10   1219 –   delectatio –   Cap. VII

        species sensus in sensivo

per quoddam sensibile formati

        vel modus sensivae operationis

per irratᵐ concupiscᵐ constitutus

–

15   concup. in delect. Ventitur

        addends ei speciem

–

1218. secundum intelligentiam beatitudine

        fruentes

1–3 *whereby… nobled*] *Ambig. S. Max.* 1220B: 'per quam etiam corporis necessario nobilitatur natura' (whereby its necessarily corporeal nature is ennobled), by virtue of rational contemplation availing the philosopher of divine intelligence.

4–8 *by its… sensui*] *Ambig. S. Max.* 1220B: 'per insitas cis naturales ad divina intelligentias digne ac pulchre ad Deum pervenerunt, corpus et mundum militariter pertranseuntes' (by accessing the natural dimension of divine intelligences, worthily and beautifully, God may be reached by passing through the bodily realm).

9 *om. vint. et saf. plenitudo*] *Ambig. S. Max.* 1220C: 'Haec est omnis virtutis et scientiae plenitudo' (This is the whole of virtue and the fullness of knowledge).

10–14 *delectatio… constitutus*] *Ambig. S. Max.* 1219B: 'Neque enim aliud aliquid est delectatio, quam species sensus in sensivo per quoddam sensibile formati, vel modus sensivae operationis per irrationabilem concupiscentiam constitutus' (For pleasure is something else, an attitude or mode of operation constituted of irrational desire).

15–16 *concup.… speciem*] *Ambig. S. Max.* 1219B: 'Concupiscentia enim sensui apposita in delectationem vertitur' (The desire for pleasure turns to the appropriate sense).

17–18 *secundum…fruentes*] *Ambig. S. Max.* 1218C: 'Deo secundum habitum approximantes, et ipsius secundum intelligentiam beatitudine fruentes' (God, according to his closeness, according to his wisdom and blessedness).

17

of the Gk: luminosity	Div. Nat.
order of roman gods	arithmetic　　　651–2
–	
virtute ⇔ libertas animae	
S. Max	–
–	
5　　non magnetic ⇔ not good	So Amb. in Eperemus
1200	705
1204 analogiam multiplicans	
	non ergo allegorizavimus
ie. god making angels	706
10　　　　　B.	
–	φῶς, πυρ-πρεύμα
per pulchrum motuum	_____
suum	

Column A:

1–4 *of the Gk.… max*] Pound's note concerning the figuration of divine light in Roman Pagan and Greek Christian and Neoplatonic sources; the *Ambigua* of Maximus makes no reference to 'libertas animae'.

5–9 *non magnetic… angels*] *Ambig. S. Max.* 1204B: 'singulorum analogiam bene ac pulchre ostendens et multiplicans' (the fine analogy of each shows beautifully and multiplies).

10–13 *per pulchrum… suum*] 'through his beautiful movements' – there is no record of this phrase in Eriugena's commentary on Maximus.

Column B:

1–11 *Div. Nat.… πρεύμα*] These sources have not been identified, but Pound's annotations suggest they derive from Book III of the *Periphyseon*.

18

falleth the sun raiseth the sun
      the sun reigneth
falleth rain, of the earth it
   drink not it
5   fallen

 –

[…] & mist over the
     marshes –

 –

stand narrow –
   A sun in his god head –
10 Creator of the light,
    now from the eyes
      of Creator

 –

all they that are, are of
    light

1–12 *falleth … Creator*] Pound's original composition, fusing natural processes with divine creation as delineated in Eriugena's *hexaemeron*, *Periphyseon* II–V; these lines bear striking affinities with the Chinese poems informing Canto XLIX: the lyrical schema accompanies the Song Dynasty genre of the Eight Views of the Xaio and Xiang Rivers.

13–14 *all … light*] Pound's adapted formula from *Exp. Cel. Hier.* 128CD: 'Quomodo omnia quae sunt, lumina sunt?'

19

all things are drawn
   to these gods

   as to a […]

    =

The δεινος   of light all returns
5   epinox. & spirit
light heat & a flame

_____

        Hoc est
                deificatio
        having left the close home of
10   body –
        Kupris ~~Venus~~ hypertans

        _____

                in the portero

        –

        abert. ogni livore. –
                by the lit. p[...]
15   of the portero
                lean to the
                left hand

1–6 *all things...flame*] Pound's original composition, working through the imagery of light across Eriugena's works, intersecting with pre-Christian Greek theology

7–8 Hoc est deificatio] *Ambig. S. Max.* 1195C–1196A: 'Et quomodo praedicta quidem divina in omnia processio ἀναλυτιχὴ dicitur, hoc est resolutio, reversio vero θἰωσις, hoc est deificatio' (As mentioned, in a truly divine procession ἀναλυτιχὴ all is resolved, but the *reditus* is a true θἰωσις, is deification).

9–10 *having... body*] Pound's paraphrase of the process of the return to God (*reditus*) in *Periphyseon* Book V, in which the corporal state is abandoned and the true human body returns to its pre-fallen state before uniting with God.

12 *Kupris... hypertans*] Reference to 'copper-eyed' Aphrodite, associated with Cyprus on which copper has been mined since the Bronze Age by Phoenecians and others; thus the Latin *cuprum* and the element's symbol Cu.

12–17 *in the portero... left hand*] No source has been found for these lines, most of which appear to be glosses or rough notes.

        20

        in Capricorn [?]   irrationale
                                                  a lumina
                                                  petitur
                                                  sol – radius –

5   radiorum
                                                 splendor
      _____

sensible sa[…]
            bu[…]ed by the sandal
      in brightness –
10   for the air is clear
                        in that place   sum
      Deificatur est   noy &
                                             splendor
                  Hic sunt lumina   when it
15   strkes the
                                             bronze

A–B, 1–16 *in Capricorn … bronze*] These lines appear to be original verse drafts, but clearly draw from the range of light sources Pound brings together in the latter pages of the 77/3406 notes: Greek myth, solar and astrological measurements, the Eriugenian 'sunt lumina', and the 'luminous detail' by which the human may ascend the chain of being toward deification.

              21

      or glass   121   not vainly
           –   at vacuum
      pietate, hilaritas   but on the ON
      insignis   –
5   Throne   θεος can sit
      far from   on & not squeak
      Dualismus
      Tristis   Dominem.   potent in
      et rigor Manichaeorum   virtue of god
10   viriliter
                                            operature

                                 _____

                                 198.   non ex perimentu
                                           sed argumento
                                 199. immediate lucent
15   cui

                                 _____

                          δεινοι Ω sapiente

Column A:

1 *or glass*] No source has been found for this reference. 121 refers to the column in Migne, part of Schlueter's introduction of 1838 from which other citations on this leaf derive.

3–4 *pietate… insignis*] *Praefatio* 121B: 'Quum enim auctor noster tam pietate, quam hilaritate insignis' ([Eriugena] gracefully balanced piety and good humour); see Pound's serial reference to Eriugena's *hilaritas*, and cf. Canto XCVIII, 'By hilaritas' said Gemisto [Plethon], 'by hilaritas: gods;/and by speed in communication.'

6–9 *far… Manichaeorum*] *Praefatio* 121C: Quam ob causam nihil ab eo magis alienum fuit, quam Dualismus iste tristis et rigor Manichaeorum obscurus' (This is why he was in no way aligned with the unfortunate Dualism of the obscure Manicheans).

Column B:

1–11 *not vainly… operature*] Notes on various themes raised in Schlueter's *Praefatio*, with a focus on explicating *The Celestial Hierarchy* (on which Pound concentrates his notes more than any on other text written or translated by Eriugena).

12–13 *non… argumento*] *Exp. Cel. Hier.* 198BC: 'Ac si aperte diceret: Nos homines, qui non experimento, sed argumento divinos exploramus sensus' (And if we were to say plainly: We men, who have not the experience, search out the divine by way of dialectic).

14–15 *immediate… cui*] *Exp. Cel. Hier.* 199AB: 'per se ipsus immediate lucentes plenitudines divinorum intellectuum' (it is the understanding of the totality and directness of the divine light).

16 δεινοι Ω *sapiente*] *Exp. Cel. Hier.* 199B: 'Intuere, ubi posuimus sapientes, ibi in Graeco δεινοι, pro quo potest quis dicere: reverendi vel periti vel sapientes' (Consider where we place the wise men, δεινοι in the Greek, where one might say the wise man is expert in sacred matters).

22

αυχε ειδες   Public
       projective

	a Portal –
nihil per se perfectum	–
5 227	natura praecedit mores
–	
But in participation	
– [deificatio]	omnia quae sunt lumina sunt
–	
air full of light	Deus praecedit naturam
–	
αρχον κολων	essences
10 –	virtues
natura praecedit mores	operations
virtutes motuum	some ineffable larger of
	div. vontatis in every
sequitur	intellectual & natural
15 materialis virtutes 228.	soul
(da nat. divinas)	

Column A:

1–2 αυχε ... *projective*] The source of this note/gloss has not been located, but it likely refers to the *Exp. Cel. Hier.*

4 *nihil per se perfectum*] *Exp. Cel. Hier.* 227B: '*Est enim nihil per se perfectum, indigens universalis perfectionis, nisi vere perfectissimum et anteperfectum*' (For there is nothing perfect in itself but that requires the universal perfection, except the nascent perfection that precedes perfection [anteperfectum]).

6–9 *But in ... κολων*] Annotations pertaining to *Exp. Cel. Hier.* 227–8ff. and pursuing the theme of divine light as effulgent, from which Eriugena develops his notion of participation, i.e. the human absorption into the divine.

10–16 *natura ... divinas*] *Exp. Cel. Hier.* 228AB: '*Ut enim Deus, qui supernaturalis est, praecedit naturam, ita natura praecedit mores. Et quemadmodum virtutes morum sequuntur naturales virtutes, ita naturales sequuntur divinas*' (As God is supernatural [super-essential] he precedes nature and thus precedes any notion of identity. And as we follow the virtues of the natural categories, so nature follows the divine): an expression of Eriugena's famous exposition of God as super-essential, and thus beyond being and existence, and therefore nothing (but nothing understood as superplus, not privation).

Column B:

1–5 *Public… mores*] A recapitulation of Column A, ll. 10–16.

7 *omnia… sunt*] Another repetition of the Eriugenian 'tag' of most appeal to Pound.

8 *Deus… naturam*] See Column A, ll. 10–16.

9–15 *essences… soul*] Pound is working out the schema presented in *The Celestial Hierarchy*, with a focus on the relation between free will, the individual soul and the relation to God: this intersects with his study of Averroes's formulation of the active and potential intellect, and its perceived infuence on Cavalcanti's 'Donna mi prega'.

23

	stubt to 252	intellego me esse	
	deiform souls 256	501 = Informato	G. C
	–		
	regnus –ardere et lucere		
	in aliqua materia	628 essence a species of goodness	
5		or goodness ' ' essence	
	253 πυρ		
	preach nicely by the metaphor	bonitas, essentia	
	–		
	490 long before Descartes	vita genus rationis	629
	–		
	no mature rational or		
10	intellectual is		
	& don't know it – however		
	much it ignores		
	~~but don't know~~ what it is		

Column A:

1 *stubt to 252*] This citation has not been identified but clearly refers to *Exp. Cel. Hier.* 252.

2 *deiform souls*] *Exp. Cel. Hier.* 256A: '*Ergo igneum significare censeo caelestium animorum deiformissimum*' (Therefore fire signifies celestial souls optimally godlike).

3–4 *regnus… materia*] *Exp. Cel. Hier.* 256B: 'Incognitus; propria quippe ignis actio est et ardere et lucere in aliqua materia; siquidem sine aliqua materia est' (Unknown; it is proper for the fire to burn and glow in any matter, given that it is not matter itself); Fire here operates as a divine metaphor, in the kataphatic mode.

6 πυρ] This word, Greek for the element of fire, does not appear at 253.

7 *preach… metaphor*] *Exp. Cel. Hier.* 258B: 'Et un breviter colligam omnia, quae de laude ignis praedicantur, pulchre per metaphoram de Deo praedicari possunt' (And if we swiftly gather everything of which fire may be predicated, it is a beautiful metaphor for God, which it may predicate); see 3–4 above.

8–13 *490… what it is*] *Peri. Liber I* 490BC: 'Dum ergo dico, intellego me esse, none in hoc uno verbo, quod est intelligo, tria significo a se inseparabilia? Nam et me esse, et posse intelligere me esse, et intelligere me esse demonstrato' (Thus when I say, "I understand that I am," do I not imply in this single verb, "understand," three (meanings) which cannot be separated from each other? For I show that I am, and that I can understand that I am, and that I do understand that I am (Eriugena 1968,145)); Pound attends closely to this passage, of understanding and existence implying one another, not latently but in the act of understanding: he notes this anticipates the Cartesian *cogito* by several centuries.

Column B:

1 *intellego me esse*] See A:8–13 above

2 *501 = Informato G. C.*] *Peri. Liber I* 500D–501C: Nutritor conducts a discussion of theories of formless matter, drawing on Plato's *Timaeus*, Augustine's *Confessions*, and Pseudo-Dionysius's *Divine Names*, to arrive at the following conclusion: 'Therefore, whether formless matter is a mutability receptive of forms, as Augustine and Plato say, or a formlessness which lacks participation in species and form and adornment, as Dionysius says, you will not deny, I think, that if it can be understood at all, it is perceived only by the intellect' (Eriugena 1968, 169); Pound refers to Cavalcanti ('G. C.') and 'Donna mi prega', following his letter to Otto Bird of 12 January 1940: 'Re Cavalcanti: Erigena certainly throws doubt on various readings: *for*mato and *in*formato, etc.' (*SL* 332). See also 7.1 above.

4–7 *essence… essentia*] *Peri. Liber III* 628A: 'Non enim per essentiam introducta est bonitas sed per bonitam introducta est essentia' ('For goodness does not come through essence but essence comes through goodness' (Eriugena 1981, 47)); God is Goodness in the kataphatic theology, above even οὐσία, and is the primary diffusion of the primordial causes: gift (*datum*) is the counterpart to the spiritual fire of divine grace (*donum*) at A:3–4, 7 above. 'Goodness bestows not only the gift of being and the grace of well-being, but also […] the gift of eternal being' (Carabine 57).

8 *vita genus rationis*] *Peri. Liber III* 629A: 'Nam vita quoddam genus rationis est' (For life *is* a kind of genus of reason (Eriugena 1981, 49)); reason is the genus from which life itself is a species, in that members of the celestial hierarchy, the categories and God also possess reason, but are not material beings.

24

some think there be	Solar body	
tenuous water 697	dum medium mundi spatiam	
above the chorus	possidet	
of stars (firmamentum)		
–		

5	of sun not a star =	Sun 1/2 way between	
	pale because cold	earth & stars	
	–	ergo color ½ pale	
	Men. nat. ag.	½ auburn [?]	
	~~stad~~ There is vapour	½ pallour	698
10	stand	½ fiery	
	no cold […] dampness 697.	–	
	–	Jove. Mars. Ven. Mec.	
	heat only where sun ray J. S.	pale above sun	
	hits matter	red below it	
		–	
15		no water above heaven.	
		pallor is from lack of color	

Column A:

1–4 *some … firmamentum*] *Peri. Liber III* 697D: 'Ab inferioribus enim naturis corpolentiam quandam, a superioribus uero spiritualem subtilitatem ad subsistentiam sui recipit' (For [the sun] receives for its subsistence a kind of corporeality from the natures that are below it, but a spiritual subtlety from those that are above it (Eriugena 1981, 207)).

5–11 *of sun … dampness*] *Peri. Liber III* 697B: 'Alii uero uavorabiles aquas ac paene incorporeas supra caelum argumentatur ex pallore stellarum. Dicunt enim stellas frigidas esse atque ideo pallidas' (Others […] argue from the paleness of the stars that there are vaporized and almost incorporeal waters above the heavens. For they say that the stars are cold, and that is why they are pale (Eriugena 1981, 205)).

13–14 *heat … matter*] *Peri. Liber III* 697C: 'Descendentes autem ad corpulenti aeris spatia ueluti quadam materia operationis inuenta flagrare incipiunt' (When, however [the sun's rays] descend into the regions of the corporeal air, they find a kind of matter on which to work, and begin to blaze (Eriugena 1981, 205)).

Column B:

1–3 *solar … possidet*] *Peri. Liber III* 697D: 'solare autem corpus, dum medium mundi spatium possidet […] medietatem quandam intelligitur obtinere' (whereas the body of the Sun, since it possesses the middle region of the world […] is understood to occupy a kind of midway position (Eriugena 207)).

5–10 *sun … fiery*] *Peri. Liber III* 698AB: 'Proinde splendidi coloris videtur esse, qui color medius est inter pallidum et rubrum, partem quidem ex palliditate firigdorum siderum supra, partem vero ex rubedine calidorum corporum infra in contemporantiam sui splendoris accipiens' ([the sun] is seen to be of a shining heat and this colour is intermediate between pale and ruddy since it receives into the even temper of its own brightness a part of the paleness of the cold stars above and a part of the ruddiness of the hot bodies below (Eriugena 1981, 207)).

11–13 *Jove … below it*] *Peri. Liber III* 698B: 'Jovem dico, et Martem, Venerem, et Mercurium, quae semper circulos suos circa solem peragunt, sicut Plato in Timaeo edocet. Atque ideo dum supra solem sunt, claros ostendunt vultus, dum vero infra, rubros' (Jupiter and Mars, Venus and Mercury, which always pursue their orbits around the Sun, as Plato teaches in the *Timaeus*; and therefore when they are above the sun they show a bright face, but when below a ruddy face (Eriugena 1981, 207)).

15–16 *no water … colour*] *Peri. Liber III* 698B: 'Non igitur pallor siderum cogit nos intelligere, aquae elementum ullo modo supra caelum esse, dum ipsa palliditas ex caloris absentia nascatur' (So the paleness of the stars does not compel us to understand that the element of water is in any way above the heaven, since that paleness comes from absence of heat (Eriugena 1981, 207)).

25

707 – things out of				Sex. Em.	
quality		⇓		–	
	⇒	⊗	⇐	115. Solis quidem domus est Leo	
		⇑		& the sun shows	
5				its form	
710 – Aqua e terra				–	
712	4 elements			Raldam [?] by more	
	matter – contract			on their cells [?]	
	νους – expand	714			
10	grav. levit.			sedulat Chaldaeus =	
emptiness – mutability				114	
venus – κανον					

–

colours from nat. of light .... Apud Theologos et Poetas
fabulae

Column A:

1–2 *things…quality*] *Peri. Liber III* 706D–707A: 'Re anmque vera non elementorum substantiae, sed qualitates dissentiunt' (for actually it is not the substances of the elements that are in discord but their qualities (Eriugena 1981, 227)).

6 *Aqua e terra*] *Peri. Liber III* 710B: 'Et notandum, quod quomadmodum aquarum collectio per se stare non potest, nisi mole terrae sustineatur' (And be it noted that as the gathering together of the waters cannot stand by itself unless it is sustained by the mass of the earth (Eriugena 1981, 233)).

7–12 *4 elements…κανον*] *Peri. Liber III* 712A–D: this passage concerns the combinations and states of the four elements to form material bodies; Pound's associations with the Roman goddess Venus and (oddly, in Greek script) the Japanese kanon (*guanyin*) probably arise from the lines from Virgil's *Georgic II* (l. 325) quoted at 712C: 'Tum pater omnipotens fecundis imbribus aether/ Conjugis in gremium laete descendit' (The Ether the almighty father descended into the lap of his consort in widespread fertilizing showers (Eriugena 1981, 239)).

13 *colours…light*] *Peri. Liber III* 714C: 'Quid dicam de coloribus, qui de lucis natura absque dubio procedunt?' (What shall I say of colours, which without doubt proceed from the nature of light? (Eriugena 1981, 243)).

Column B:

1 *Sex. Em.*] Sextus Empiricus: second-century physician-philosopher; the reference is unclear

3–5 *Solis…form*] 'The Sun is in the house of Leo': unclear reference

7–10 *Raldam… Chaldaeus*] no source has been found for these phrases

13–14 *Apud…fabulae*] 'the stories of Theologians and Poets'; unclear reference

26

περι απιου και	<u>301</u>	mud's dirges
πασχοντος		& wax's melting
		————————
340 – amor Ω affectio		351.
–		aut enim superficies
5 Athenian altars to <u>Misericordia</u>		est incorporea
dogmatic vs sheer yatter		464.
horders mud, ceram liquefici		gold foe to fecundity
		metal ' ' '
350. causa – (one effect overall)		God sit[…]
10 us. sun. =		~~flayed~~ tho
		un s[…]
		life

Column A:

1–2 περι… πασχοντος] No source has been found for this item.

3 *amor… affectio*] No source has been found for this item.

5 *Athenian… Misericordia*] 'Athenian altars to mercy': Seneca the Elder mentions the Athenian altar to Misericordia (Ελεος) erected in the agora, and Statius provides a lengthy description of it in the *Thebaid*; see Stafford 1998, 43–56.

6–7 *dogmatic… liquefici*] These appear to be Pound's notes mixed with citations.

9–10 *causa… sun*] the singular cause associated with the sun links with excerpts from *Peri. Liber III* on leaf 24 above: perhaps recalling 'the Father of Lights' (James 1:17)

Column B:

1–5 *mud's… incorporea*] No source has been identified for these fragments.

7–12 *gold… life*] Pound's notes, partially legible: their relation to Eriugena's texts is unclear.

27

	J. S.	717. moles Terrae in
	714 – fire – panta in all – light	medio mundi
	aer – in all spirare = odour sound	_____
	water – reflect image	
5	earth – weight	722 circumscribes all sensibilia
	_____	
	gravity = attraction	_____
	–	unskilled in reason
	715. lucidissimorum	rely ratio in
	corporum	authority
10	multiplex Disciple	succumbunt
	circular – intestitiis	_____ 781
	Nullam certam ad	
	rationem	St. Ag. prolixa
	mihi videtur	ac in propatulo
15	deducta	
	715	of max. V inter
	–	causes
	earthly v lunar interstices	
		782. nisi pecat = nat.
20		adum. bio. od.
		sun the earth
		solo rationabili
		contuity

Column A:

1–6 *J. S. … attraction*] *Peri. Liber III* 714B–D: 'siquidem πῦρ ignis propterea dicitur, ut arbitror, quia per poros, hoc est, occultos meatus omnia penetrat […] Aer nominatur, id est, spiritus, quia per omnia spirat […] Ὕδωρ vocatur, id est aqua, quasi εἶδος ὁρώμενον, hoc est, species visa. Nulla siquidem corporea res est, ex cujus superficie, attritu quodam levigata, imago quaedam resultare non valeat. Ἄχθος appellatur terra ex gravitate'

> For πῦρ, fire, is so called, as I think, because it penetrates all things through their pores [...] Air, that is, breath, is (so) called because it breathes through all things [...] Ὕδωρ, that is, water, is (so) called as it were εἶδος ὁρώμενον, that is 'seen form'. For there is no coporeal thing from whose surface when polished by some friction some image cannot be reflected. Earth is called ἄχθος from its weight. (Eriugena 1981, 243)

8–15 *lucidissimorum ... deducta*] *Peri. Liber III* 715D: 'De circulis, deque interstitiis caelestium lucidissimorumque corporum, multiplex variaque sapientum mundi opinio est, et ad nullam certam rationem, quantum mihi videtur, deducta' (Concerning the orbits and intervals between the celestial and very brilliant bodies the opinions of the natural philosophers are many and varied and have never been surely reconciled as far as I can see (Eriugena 1981, 245)).

18 *earthly ... interstices*] Pound's gloss on ll. 8–15 above.

Column B:

1–2 *moles ... mundi*] *Peri. Liber III* 717BC: 'Quod ergo valet moles terrae in medio mundi, hoc valet stylus in medio horologii' (So that which the earth's mass accomplishes in the midst of the universe the rod accomplishes in the midst of the sundial (Eriugena 1981, 249)).

5 *circumscribes all sensibilia*] *Peri. Liber III* 722B: 'Proinde in medio totius spatii, quod est a terra usque ad sublimissimam sphaeram, qua omnia sensisibilia circumscribuntur' (the solar orbit is at the centre of the whole space that extends from the earth to the highest sphere by which all sensibles are circumscribed (Eriugena 1981, 261)).

7–10 *unskilled ... succubunt*] *Peri. Liber IV* 781D: 'non enim sanctorum Patrum sententiae, praesertim si plurimis notae sint, introducendae sunt, nisi ubi summa necessitas roborandae ratiocinationis inscii, plus auctoritati quam rationi succumbunt' (For there is no cause to introduce the opinions of the holy Fathers, especially those that are widely known, except where the gravest necessity requires that reason be supported for the sake of those who, being untrained in it, are more amenable to authority than reason (Eriugena, 97)). Eriugena sets out a rationale for his formula, paraphrased by Pound as 'authority comes from right reason; never the other way on' – the citation of Church

Fathers is permitted only as a discursive aid, to persuade those unschooled in rational thought: the proper role of rhetoric is to support the superior art of dialectic.

13–17 *St. Ag.…causes*] *Peri. Liber IV* 781CD: 'Quisquis autem plenius hunc duplicem intellectum divinissimi magistri nosse velit, ipsius verba in Exemero suo, et in praefato de Civitate Dei volumine studiosus legat; quae quoniam prolixa, et omnibus in propatulo sunt, huic nostraw disputationculae superfluum mihi visum est inserere' (But whoever wishes to learn more of this twofold interpretation of the most holy master [Augustine], let him zealously read his own words in the Hexaemeron and in the aforesaid volume of the *City of God*, which I think it would be redundant to quote in this little discussion of ours, as it is lengthy and available to all (Eriugena 1995, 97)).

19–23 *nisi…continuity*] *Peri. Liber IV* 782C: 'Non enim homo, si non peccaret, inter partes mundi administraretur […] solo rationabili contuitu naturalium et interiorum ejus causarum, facillimo rectae voluntatis usu' (For if man had not sinned he would not be ruled among the parts of the universe […] but would govern […] solely by the rational apprehension of its natural and innate causes and by the easy use of right will (Eriugena 1995, 99)). This quotation cites the prelapsarian state of humanity as one equal with that of the angels, that is, pure rationality. The Fall engendered the material body and (after Origen and Gregory of Nyssa) the division of the sexes.

28

Div. Nat.		Gregory of Nyssea = 854	
by use of right direction of will		proper agnostic	120
	rectae voluntatis usu	ref the unknown	9
			1100
5	785 G. C vis in sensu	at rest @ movement	
	oculorum =		
		789	
	formandas is se in num.	=	
	spec. conf. col. fig.	nature sequitur	
10	quorum phantasiae	~~animum~~	
	per hunc sensum	animum	
	in assembliam in gradicentus	praecipientem	

Column A:

1–3 *Div. Nat. … usu*] Pound's gloss on 27B.19–23 above.

5–12 *G. C. … gradicentus*] *Peri. Liber IV* 785B–C: 'Vide, quanta vis est in sensu oculorum ad lustranda in infinitum lucida spatia, ad formandas in se diversas et innumerabiles species corporum, colorum, figurarum, ceterorumque, quorum phantasiae per hunc sensum memoriam ingrediuntur' (See what power there is in the sense of the eyes which can gaze into light-filled spaces to infinity and can mould within itself the diverse and innumerable species of bodies, colours, shapes, and all other things of which the phantasies enter the memory by means of this sense (Eriugena 1995, 105)).

Column B:

1–4 *Gregory … 1100*] Gregory of Nyssa (c.335–c.395) was one of the Cappadocian Fathers along with his brother Basil of Caesarea and Gregory Nazianzus: it is not clear on what grounds Pound claims agnostic status for Gregory, whose theology was apophatic (God cannot be known directly, and supercedes all categories), was influenced by Neoplatonism, and orthodox in his contributions to the Council of Nicaea. Note that this reference to Gregory arises after Pound's note at 27B.19–23.

5 *at rest @ movement*] The source of this note has not been identified.

9–12 *nature … praecipientem*] *Peri. Liber IV* 792C: 'Imperat enim animus ratione, et non patitur, quod utile est eligens, natura autem e vestigio sequitur praecipientem animum' (For the mind rules the reason, and is not passive, but chooses that which is useful: the mind marches before and nature follows after (Eriugena 1995, 123)).

29

Phantasie aliquid bonum	all thus that are
	are lights
———————	
963.	–
all due to natural causes	omnia lumens
5 is good.	what body of
	light
[bod on shadows.	

umbrae   ]   –

deiformis hierarchon

10   ie. bright image surd [wrong way   justitiae plena
possible]

by the communion

10   20–1 = ascent   by the lights of
the stars

15   vitali motu
body → energy → sense → reason → omnium   light – justitiae
plenum –

Column A:

1 *Phantasie… bonum*] *Peri. Liber V* 963B: 'Phantasia igitur aliquod bonum est, quoniam naturalium rerum imaginatio est' (Phantasy then must be something good, seeing that it is an image of nature (Eriugena 1987, 644)).

3–5 *963… good*] *Peri. Liber V* 963B: 'Illud negare non possum: omne siquidem, quod ex naturalibus causis oritur, bonum esse non denegatur' (I cannot deny that this is so. For it must be accepted that everything which springs from natural causes is good (Eriugena 1987, 644)).

7–8 *bod… umbrae*] *Peri. Liber V* 914A: 'Cujus rationis exemplum est vox ejusque imago, quae a Graecis ἠχώ vocatur, seu corpora ipsorumque umbrae, quae sive in puro aere formatae, sive de aquis, sive de qualicunque re' (We may take as an illustration of this the voice and its image which the Greeks call ἠχώ; or bodies and the shadows which they throw either in the pure air or in water or in any other medium capable of producing them (Eriugena 1987, 587)): the doctrine that material bodies do not exist in the same way as the categories or *ousia*, illustrated by a familiar image from Plato's Cave allegory in the *Republic*.

10–11 *bright… possible*] Pound's gloss on the umbrae imagery at 7–8 above.

15–16 *vitali… omnium*] *Peri. Liber V* 874B: 'Anima quoque quinario numero non dissonat. Subsistit namque intellectu, et ratione, et duplici sensu, interiori profecto et exteriori, vitalique motu, quo corpus administratur' (soul also shows a fivefold nature, for it consists of Mind and Reason and the Two-Fold Sense (interior and exterior), and the Vital Motion by which it administers the body (Eriugena 1987, 538)). The fivefold imagery probably derives from Maximus the Confessor.

Column B:

1–6 *all things… body of light*] Pound repeats again the formula for light as *ousia* and divine emanation: see also 76/3383 1.13–14; 77/3406 2.15–16, 18.13–14, 22B.7 and 36.8.

9–17 *deiformis… plenum*] The source for this note has not been identified: the phrases may simply function as variants on the theme of *omnia quae sunt, lumina sunt,* or else provide reference back to Eriugena's cosmology in *Peri.* III.

30

what body of [xx]　　　　　　　This work by
　　　Marsyas　　　　　　　　　　Dionysius
　　　=
our solubas [?]　　　　　　　　at sundown
Marsyas　　Marsyas
5　　　　Nom ad flagem　　　　set sun on the south
The sun heats the　　　　　　　　hill
　　　ovum –　　　　　　　　　　against sun-glow –
　　　spread on the　　　　　　 –
　~~Th ch~~ Threshing floor　　　　The
10　　　　　　　　　　　　　　 ours, were come to their
　~~Mays~~　　　　　　　　　　　　　　funeral
　　　a stiff […] marsyas　　　what body of god
　　　~~to~~ for Marsyas in　　　　our salvatore
　　　　Celaenae
15　　　　　　　　　　　　　 347 = <u>Introd</u>
　　　　　　　　　　　　　　 nature neither sins nor
　　　　　　　　　　　　　　　　punishes
　　　　　　　　　　　　　　 not all rot in hell
　　　　　　　　　　　　　　 but individual will –
20　　　　　　　　　　　　　 & that alone punishable

Column A:

1–9 *what body… Threshing floor*] The source for these lines has not been established: the tropes of sunlight and fertilization bear affinities with Pound's interest in vegetative myths; the sacrificial figure of Marsyas, flayed alive for the sin of hubris, is eerily proleptic of the Mussolini-Manes compound image in the opening lines of Canto LXXIV.

11–14 *Mays… Celaenae*] Celaenae is the town in Phrygia where Marsyas's flayed hide was put on display in the marketplace by Apollo, on defeating the silenus in a contest of skill (see Herodotus, *Histories* Book VII).

Column B:

1–2 This… Dionysius] Reference to *The Celestial Hierarchy.*

3–7 *at sundown… sun-glow*] Lines of Pound's original composition, on the theme of sunlight.

9–13 *The… salvatore*] Pound is splicing Christian imagery with vegetative themes (Marsyas, Osiris, Manes).

15–20 *Introd… punishable*] Pound's glosses on elements of the *Monitum ad Lectorum* prefacing *De praedestinatione* in PL 122 at 347: nature is a state beyond the activity of sin (*naturam natura non puniri*), and the direction of individual will is decisive in determining damnation or salvation (*omnem perversae voluntatis defectum vel privationem vel peccatum*).

31

	natr is	Rel.	philos	science
	totam animae naturam			
	voluntatem esse	hunch	balance	knowable
			of	
5	every evil is sin & its	A		B
	punishment	———————————————		
	omne malum esse	falcy of superfluous		
	paccatum et ejus	abstractions		
	poenam	=		
10	& haec nihil esse.	[semen est verbum Dei.]		
	———————————————	=		
	continual ports	'ubi necessitas, non est voluntas'		
	false dilemmas to			
	an imagined	voluntas in Dei		
	god.			

Column A:

1–3 *natr… esse*] *Monitum ad Lectorum* 347: 'totam animae naturam voluntatem esse' (the nature of the soul is entirely one of the will); the *Monitum* presents an outline of Eriugena's claims in *De praedestinatione*, including his rejection of any form of predestination, and his placing matters of sin and salvation entirely within the remit of the human will.

5–10 *every evil… nihil esse*] *Monitum* 347: 'omne malum esse peccatum et ejus poenam, *et haec nihil esse*' (every evil is both the sin and its punishment, and is nothing, does not exist); the *nihil esse* in Eriugena's negative theology, where sin is a turning away from God and thus no part of his creation, therefore sin does not properly exist. Its punishment is entailed in its commission, removing the sinner from God and from creation. Cf. *De praed.* 421A: 'Omne peccatum, quia malum est, vitium boni est: omne vitium boni ex bono non est: omne peccatum, quia malum est, ex bono esse non potest'

11–14 *continual… god*] Pound's note or gloss: the source of this reference has not been identified.

Column B:

1–5 *Rel. … B*] Pound's schematic view of religion as intuitive, science as inductive and empirical, and philosophy as a mediating balance.

7–8 *falcy… abstractions*] Pound's impatience with scholastic method is evident here, despite his considerable interest in Pseudo-Dionysius.

10 *semen est Verbum Dei*] Associating semen with the second person of the Trinity, the Word or *logos*, may function as a reminder of the Nicene distinction between the Father as not begotten but begetting, and the Son as begotten; it may also function in the context of participation, that is, in physical procreation humans participate, in some way, in an echo of divine creation.

11–13 *ubi… Dei*] *De praed.* 360B: 'Ubi autem est necessitas, ibi non est voluntas. Atqui in Deo est voluntas' (Where there is necessity, there is no will. But in God there is will).

32

<u>139</u>

	invisible forms	
	swapping, invisible body	amor =
	_____	all that are
5	quod amat –	are

            lights –

 s[…] noscitur

 ad quam tendit   Those that

 omne quod amat   did not

10 deificat nostram naturam embezzle

            Those who

            prevented

            embezzlement

            air

15   bracing

Column A:

1–2 *invisible… body*] *Exp. Cel. Hier.* 139B: Pound appears to draw from Eriugena's gloss on *The Celestial Hierarchy*, concerning the invisible distribution of sensible forms.

5–10 *quod amat… nostram naturam*] The source of these fragments has not been identified.

Column B:

3–6 *all that are are lights*] See 29B.1–6 above.

8–13 *Those… embezzlement*] Pound's original composition on economic themes: perhaps an attempt to link the cosmogony in Pseudo-Dionysius and other sources to good government and sound economics: for example, in the Leopoldine cantos published as *The Fifth Decad of Cantos XLII-LI* in 1937, and which include the Seven Lakes canto.

14–15 *air bracing*] Pound's comment of unknown intent.

33

 as when   Tangent &

 from swamp   cos. ~~falli~~

 but malga –   fall

 into the alpe –   = falling crystaline

5 upland   fugue on

 pastures –   fugue

of free will	of 'witches'
descend to	Agnostic
hell	A = not of 2
10	is the circles
	call

Column A:

1–9 *as when … hell*] Pound's original composition, layering the *topoi* of nature onto Eriugena's doctrine of free will in *De praedestinatione* (that human will provides the agency to sin and to suffer damnation, or otherwise, *pace* Augustine and Gottschalk): in arranging such a topological schema, Pound emulated the geography of Dante's *Inferno*, but also recalls the bucolic genre of Chinese literati painting given ekphrastic treatment in Canto XLIX.

Column B:

1–11 *Tangent … call*] Pound's original composition: the intent of these notes is not entirely clear, but the reference to geometry may refer to Eriugena's discussion of the movement of the planets in *Peri. Liber III* (see leaves 23–27 above).

34

out of	calyx	
invisible	calyx	
light		
over the	crysiphare	
stars.		5
	=	
Sotats'		
& Koyets –	contemplation	
next in gabl[…]	knowledge	
& out of	amor	
numbers	giustizia	10
emerges the		
BBC glow	moon	
	sun	
	venus	
	jov.	15

Column A:

1–5 *out of… stars*] Reference to Eriugena's cosmology in *Peri. Liber III*, in which the light of intelligence is not visible and emanates from the zone above the planets and stars. The image of invisible light also cites *The Celestial Hierarchy* on the divine ray of the Father (in turn quoting James 1:17), which is beyond sense perception. This image also recalls the mystical darkness that is the superessence of being and light and wisdom, developed in the *Periphyseon* from the doctrines of Pseudo-Dionysius, in whose letter to Dorotheus the *lux inaccessibilis* of divine nature is figured as both cloud and darkness (Carabine 1994, 148).

6–12 *Sotats… glow*] Pound's composition of undetermined import.

Column B:

1–4 *calyx… crysiphare*] Calyx is the mother of Endymion, and is also a moon of Jupiter; the significance of crysiphare is unknown, although it may be a misspelling of *cruciferae* ('cross-bearing'), and thus in keeping with the fusion of Christian and classical references.

7–10 *contemplation… giustizia*] A sequence of faculties and virtues, connecting Pound's reading in Pseudo-Dionysius with his poetic interests: for *amor*, see 'Donna mi prega'.

12–15 *moon… jov.*] This short catalogue of celestial bodies may correspond to the list above it: contemplation/moon, knowledge/sun, amor/venus, giustizia/jupiter.

35

	content – moon	Ucelli
	inverse – moon	lui so
	enquiry – sun	propizio
	Amore – mars	–
5	efficiency – venus	Fuga ⇔ justice
	justice – zeus	Son III
	balance – Saturn	
	–	κορη δελια
	παν	Erigena
	–	Taylor of Caroline
10	πριση	[…] did not embezzle
	Bianco shade	' prevented embezzlement

Column A:

1–7 *content… Saturn*] Another schema of faculties and virtues given symbolic celestial associations, although the logic of the list runs counter to convention: justice and Zeus provide a match, but *amor* would normally be joined to Venus, not Mars, and Saturn is arguably the best figuration for imbalance.

8–11 παν *… shade*] The significance of these fragments is not clear: παν as 'all' or the Arcadian satyr; 'white shade' is unclear.

Column B:

1–3 *Ucelli… propizio*] Unclear: perhaps the theme of birdsong in Francesco da Milano's adaptation of Clément Jannequin's *Le chant des oiseaux*, the *Canzone degli uccelli* reproduced in score in Canto LXXV.

5–6 *Fuga… Son III*] Unclear.

7 κορη δελια] Kore or Persephone, Goddess of Hades; Delia or Artemis, Goddess of the Moon.

8 *Erigena*] Eriugena's appearance here seems to signify the virtues of association.

9–11 *Taylor… embezzlement*] John Taylor of Caroline (1753–1824), a United States Senator (Virginia) and proponent of States' Rights. Embezzlement may refer to his opposition to ceding States' powers to a central federal government.

36

τεχνε
epinous   loss of

nulla qua […] deos

---

none
5   ubicity   Technical telescope
         Θεοσις   *lux enim*
         fanatic re unknowable

---

omnia quae sunt, sunt lumina
        That descend from the father of

10   lights

  –

pater et fils – filius

Lux
οδυσσευς

1–3 *τεχνε… deos*] *epinous*: aculeated, armed with a sting or barb.

4–7 *none… unknowable*] *lux enim* derives from Grosseteste, *De Luce*: 'Lux enim per se in omnium partum se ipsam diffindit' (Light of its nature pours itself into every part); see also Canto CX.

8–10 *omnia… lights*] See 29B.1–6 above; Pound includes the provenance of Pseudo-Dionysius's assertion in *The Celestial Hierarchy*, as 'Father of Lights' is from James 1:17.

11–13 *pater… οδυσσευς*] a reprise of the *filioque* controversy, in the relation of Father to Son; the associations with generative light and the importance of filial identification in Book XXIV of the *Odyssey*, when Odysseus reveals his identity to Laertes on returning to Ithaca and disposing of Penelope's suitors.

37

  Napoleon wath a goodth man
    said the parrot tongued
      bloat
 It took uth 20 years
5   to cwuth him
 It will not take us 20
    yearth to
 cwuth Mutholini
 H[…] la difesa dula
10   nulla [?]
 ' a new failing
   in & for […]
 blue nicht chew[…]
   (Imp.)
 15 with the bandits
   Joachim

&[...] with entry
　　　　to Harlow's
& Harlow's mortgage on
20　　　　Iceland

1–8 *Napoleon… Mutholini*] See Canto LXXX/497: 'It will not take uth twenty yearth/to cwuth Mutholini/and the economic war has begun'.

9–20 *H[…]… Iceland*] Fragmentary notes taking up the theme of economic banditry.

38

The shit of this arse was the
　　　　Banker
usura = dark suffering [?]
not wholly se[…]t –
5　　　　not wholly down for Jordan
80 nuller to fish the 'cave'
　　　　100 nuller is not what's
　　　　　　proper

1–8 *The shit… proper*] Fragmentary notes veering into economic themes, with no discernible relation to Eriugena.

Commentary

Pound's two sets of manuscript notes pertaining to PL 122 bear the evidence of the material circumstances of their composition: the first, 76/3383, is divided between Pound's reading at the Biblioteca Marciana in Venice in late 1939 (leaves 1–14) and his reading in Rapallo from December 1939 or early January 1940 (leaves 17–26); the second set, 77/3406, was compiled in Rapallo between 1940 and 1945. The two sets overlap in their subject matter, most explicitly in the case of the *Expositiones Super Ierarchiam Caelestiam S. Dionysii*, the *Versio Ambiguorum S. Maximi* and the *Versus*. Specific sections come in for particular attention in both sets – *Exp. Cel. Hier.* 133–42, 156–66 – and the second set occasionally reproduces quotations from the first, *Exp. Cel. Hier.* 134CD being the most prominent example. Pound draws quotations from most of the texts in the Eriugenian corpus, with some notable exceptions: *De praedestinatione* is cited only once (despite the critical function of its subject matter in shaping Pound's early interest in Eriugena's thought); and the Homily on the Prologue of the Gospel of John (*Vox spiritualis aquilae*) and the Commentary on the Gospel of John (*Commentarius in Ioannem*) are not cited at all. Although Pound quotes from four of the five books of the *Periphyseon* (with the exception of Book II), it is not sufficient to say that he read Eriugena's *capolavoro* closely and entirely.

The order in which Pound approached the texts of PL 122 provides a necessarily limited window into his reading and annotating practices. He begins the first suite of notes with fragments from Floss's *Prooemium*, including information concerning the provenance of Eriugena's texts. Pound rapidly moves into the *Expositiones Super Ierarchiam Caelestiam S. Dionysii*, identifying the source of his favourite Eriugenian epithet (but neglecting its original intent as a rhetorical question): 'omnia quae sunt, lumina sunt' (*Exp. Cel. Hier.* 128C). Intensive attention to this text in leaves 1–6 then shifts to Book I of the *Periphyseon* in leaves 7–10, concerning the nature of the Aristotelian Categories and the function of light as a metaphor of theophany. Pound then shifts back to the *Prooemium* (11–12) and the anonymous *De Vita* (13–14), assembling a series of biographical fragments and general precepts on Eriugena's works. The notes break off at this point, and resume at 17 with a quotation from Eriugena's epigraph to his translation of *The Celestial Hierarchy*. Pound then alternates between Eriugena's translation of and commentary on the Pseudo-Dionysian text (18–19) before a sequence of excerpts from the *Ambigua* of Maximus (19–21). Pound then concentrates his attention upon the *Versus* (21–5). This sequence concludes with small fragments of no direct bearing on Eriugena or on Pound's creative endeavors of the time (26–7).

The second suite of notes returns to the passages elaborating the notion of light as theophany in Chapter 1 of *Exp. Cel. Hier.* (1–3). Note that Pound cites, in English, 'all things that are, are lights' at 2.16. Attention then modulates between *Exp. Cel. Hier.* chapters 2–3 and Eriugena's translation of *The Celestial Hierarchy* (4–12), turning to matters of superessentialism as well as apophatic and kataphatic theology. Pound makes a brief series of notes on the *Expositiones in Mysticam Theologiam S. Dionysii* (12–13), elaborating on the notion of superessentialism. Following some brief notes on the *Versus* (14), the notes turn to the *Ambigua* of

Maximus the Confessor (15–17). From leaf 18 the notes become less schematic, interpellating original poetic fragments of Pound's composition with scattered annotations of PL 122. Pound returns to the volume's anonymous *Praefatio* (21) and chapters 8, 9 and 15 of *Exp. Cel. Hier.* (21–3), before a sustained sequence of annotations from the *Periphyseon* Book I, concerning the nature of *ousia* and the Categories (23); Book III, delineating Eriugena's cosmology (23–7); Book IV, on the balance between ecclesiastical authority and reason (27–8); and Book V, on images of light and the nature of *ousia* in the context of the *reditus* (28–9). Pound turns to the front matter of the *Periphyseon*, citing several phrases from the *Monitum ad Lectorum* (30–1). The remaining leaves (32–8) modulate indirect references to Eriugena's theology – light and theophany, the *filioque* controversy, cosmology – with poetic fragments of Pound's composition, including a fragment that finds its way into *The Pisan Cantos*: 'It will not take uth twenty yearth/to cwuth Mutholini' (LXXX/497).

Pound's intensive focus on *Exp. Cel. Hier.* warrants a brief discussion of the Pseudo-Dionysian text of *The Celestial Hierarchy*, Eriugena's translation and his commentary on it. See Rorem 2005, 21–75 for matters concerning the Greek manuscript of the Pseudo-Dionysian text (Bibliothèque Nationale gr 437), its problems and the consequences for its transmission. Pound was dependent upon the PL 122 text of Eriugena's *Exp. Cel. Hier.*, which was missing chapters 4–6. This section of the text has since been reconstructed by Barbet in the Latin edition of 1975, for which there is no full English translation. Rorem (2005, 201–19) translates Chapter 4 in its entirety, along with excerpts from chapters 1, 2, and 8. Pound pays close attention to the opening three chapters of the text, and the beginning of Chapter 7, but makes only a single note in each of the chapters 8, 9, 10 and 15. It would appear that his interests were to be found in the use of light imagery – especially the 'Father of Lights' (James 1:17) quoted liberally throughout the notes, in published essays and in *The Cantos* – and the function of metaphor as a scriptural hermeneutic, rather than in the detailed constitution and architecture of heaven in Pseudo-Dionysius's *The Celestial Hierarchy*.

Although Pound makes a series of notes on Eriugena's translation of the *Ambigua* of Maximus the Confessor, this does not translate into a sustained interest in any of Pound's published work. Pound quotes the opening lines of the *Praefatio*, a handful of words from Chapter 2 (PL 122, 1204), and a selection of words and phrases from the end of Chapter 5 to Chapter 8 (1218–21). These excerpts concern the relation between body and spirit in humanity, and the human function as a microcosm of the divine order. Interestingly, Pound returns to the same columns in the second set of notes, rather than attending to earlier chapters of Eriugena's text passed over in the first set. Maximus functions as a guiding figure of wisdom in Eastern Christianity, and symbolizes (with Pseudo-Dionysius and the Cappadocian Fathers) Eriugena's heroic attempt to synthesize that theological tradition and its language with the Latin Church.

It is difficult to overstate the significance of the *Periphyseon* in terms of Eriugena's oeuvre, as well as more generally with regard to European intellectual history in each of Carolingian philosophy, medieval Neoplatonism and the study of Aristotelian Categories. Pound attends to some critically important parts of Eriugena's opus, such as the analysis of *ousia* in Book I and the study of cosmology inflected by the theology of the Cappadocian Fathers in Book III. But there is little evidence in the notes, or in Pound's prose and poetry to follow, that he undertook a systematic reading of the text. This must be regarded as a missed opportunity, not only on the merits of the *Periphyseon* itself, but for the fact that it represents possibly the highest achievement in systematic philosophy between Proclus and Abelard. The text bore a profound influence on the theology to issue from the School of Chartres and the Abbey of Saint Victor, and its influences can be seen in the works of Thomas Aquinas, Meister Eckhart, Nicholas Cusanus, Pico della Mirandola and Marsilio Ficino, all of whom were of interest to Pound. As things stand, the *Periphyseon* provides ample resources for Pound, especially pertaining to the light imagery in relation to kataphatic theology and in images of theophany. He was able to deploy these images as synecdochic anchors for a largely occluded systematic theology, and combine them with familiar images of light and δυναμις from classical mythology, as the final leaves in 77/3406 make evident.

Eriugena's poetry becomes an emblem of *hilaritas*, and an index of the civility of the Carolingian court for Pound in *The Pisan Cantos* and beyond. What is perhaps most surprising is that Pound annotates very few poems in the *Versus*: besides poem IV, 'Laudes Yrmindrudis Caroli Calvi uxoris' and poem VIII, 'De Verbo incarnato', only one Greek phrase is noted in the poem 'De Christi resurrectione' (V in PL 122, 1228–29), and one other Greek fragment, 'John's verses for King Charles', is cited (fragment 3 in *Joannis Scoti Graeci Versus*, PL 122, 1237C). No other poems are cited at all, including the many Greek fragments of such thematic significance for Pound. The two poems upon which Pound hones much of his attention are excerpted liberally: whilst poem VIII contains a significant proportion of Greek, poem IV contains only two Greek words, one of which Pound cites. In his enthusiasm for Eriugena's bilingual display of learning, Pound clearly places his stock more in the fact of its existence and less in the hermeneutic and strategic weight of specific words, phrases and lines in Greek. This is despite these works' inherent interest as rare Carolingian examples of original Greek poetic compositions and judicious attempts to calibrate Eriugena's Greek and Latin poetic vocabulary.

Note

1   For example, the *Liber adversus Joannem Scotus* of Florus Diaconus Lugdunensis, PL 119, col. 101–248; the *Confessio*, the *Confessio prolixior* and the *Epistola Gotteschalci ad Ratramnum* of Gotteschalk of Orbais, PL 121, col. 347–70; the *De praedestinatione Dei* of Ratramnus Corbeiensis, PL 121, col. 12–30; and especially the *De una et non trina Deitate* of Hincmarus Rhemensis Archiepiscopus, in PL 125, col. 473–619.

The Poetics of Exile: Laon to Changsha

It is difficult to write a paradiso when all the superficial indications are that you ought to write an apocalypse. It is obviously much easier to find inhabitants for an inferno or even a purgatorio. I am trying to collect the record of the top flights of the mind.

– Ezra Pound to Donald Hall in interview, *Paris Review* (1962)

This study has explored Pound's nascent interest in the philosophy and poetry of John Scottus Eriugena from the late 1920s, and his intensive renewal of that interest in 1939–1940 with the acquisition of Patrologia Latina 122. Direct access to Eriugena's texts – mediated editorially by Henry Joseph Floss – inspired Pound to assemble detailed notes on a number of Eriugena's texts towards an extended study, proposed to T. S. Eliot in 1940 but never realized. The circumstances of Pound's life leading up to and during the Second World War divided his attention in several directions: the frenetic composition of prose texts on literature, culture, politics and economics; the furious production of the China Cantos and the Adams Cantos; the composition and delivery of up to two thousand speeches for radio (including, it appears, many hundred written under several pseudonyms) and still-unaccounted correspondence and propaganda for the Mussolini regime. Pound also translated Confucius during these years, publishing two instalments of the Four Books in Italian during the war. After stalling on new canto composition during most of the war, Pound began Italian drafts of new cantos early in 1945. Following his arrest and incarceration in May of 1945, his drafts of *The Pisan Cantos* reprise some of the Italian material – particularly the mysteries of love (Bush 1997, 188–90) – and concentrate his recent work on the Confucian texts, including his translation-in-progress of Mencius. Pound makes a committed return to Eriugena in these cantos, drawing on the notes he had begun composing more than five years earlier (the second suite of which was written between 1940 and 1945). There may have been a book missing from his proposed 'Trilogy', but the way Pound interweaves Eriugena with other important themes in *The Pisan Cantos* provides a window onto precisely what significance the Hibernian held for him. Further, the network of associations – the metaphysics of light, the uses of reason and precise definition in language, urbane expressions of *hilaritas*, courtly rustication – reaches back to poetic composition of years earlier, folding the iconic 'Seven Lakes' canto (XLIX) into a moment of contemporaneity with *The Pisan Cantos*. This chapter sets out how Eriugena functions as a navigational aid alongside the guiding lights of Neoplatonism, Pound's Confucianism and his installation of pastoral exile in the figure of the rusticated literatus.

Pound's interests in Confucianism intersect at various levels with his reading in Neoplatonism: the affinities of each 'system' with the other extends to the use of light as an ordering principle, hierarchies of being that imply an integration between politics, economics, ethics and metaphysics, and long-standing traditions of textual transmission at the centre of their respective textual cultures. Several scholars have drawn out the way these intersecting *cosmoi* find material expression in Pound's activities as translator, cultural impressario and poet. Feng Lan notes the distinctive way Pound synthesizes the worldviews of Confucianism and Neoplatonic philosophy: 'In an Italian article published in Meridiano di Roma in November 1941, he describes the universe presented by Confucianism as "un mondo di luce" (a world of light) much like the world envisioned by Erigena and Cavalcanti' (176). But as the precise nature of Pound's interests in Eriugena still comes into focus, his role as a lynchpin in this system is yet to be properly explored. This is a principal function of the present chapter: to discern how these zones of knowledge and experience intersect in various ways through Eriugena. Following from the study of Pound's Eriugena notes composed from the beginning of the war, and his deployments of Eriugena's thought in *The Pisan Cantos* and beyond – often by way of repetitions of formulae such as 'omnia quae sunt, lumina sunt' or 'Greek stiched into his verses' – it remains to be shown precisely how the Hibernian functions in *The Cantos* as a whole, with the benefit of much more substantial knowledge of his works and Pound's use of them.

Eriugena in *The Pisan Cantos*

Pound turns again to Eriugena in *The Pisan Cantos*, following two decads of cantos surveying Chinese dynastic history (LII–LXI) and the life of John

Adams (LXII–LXXI), and a brief foray into Fascist themes in two Italian cantos (LXXII–LXXIII). The conditions in which Pound wrote *The Pisan Cantos* are perhaps the most infamous in all of twentieth-century poetry in English, and need only be glossed here. His sustained wartime broadcasts on Italian radio and other activities associated with the Mussolini regime[1] led to his arrest by the Italian *partigiani* in Genoa in May 1945. He was handed over to the Allied Forces and was taken to the US Army Detention Training Center outside of Pisa and incarcerated in a steel cage, until a physical breakdown had him transferred to the camp infirmary. He had begun work on new cantos in Italian before his arrest, but his time in the DTC saw him compose drafts of what became *The Pisan Cantos*. He did so without the benefit of materials beyond his copy of James Legge's edition of the *Four Books* of Confucius, a basic Chinese-English dictionary, a US Army issue Bible and M. E. Speare's *Pocket Book of Verse*, which he is said to have found in the DTC latrine (Carpenter 667; Bush 1999, 114–15).

By this time, Eriugena had functioned as a long-term reference point for Pound and as a gesture towards paradise. In Canto XXXVI Eriugena's thought and legacy functions as a European conduit of late–antique Neoplatonism, as part of a suppressed tradition that runs counter to the dominant Aristotelianism of Thomas Aquinas, and that illuminates the hermetic nature of *amor* implied in Cavalcanti's poem, 'Donna mi prega'. On reading PL 122, Pound came to appreciate Eriugena's negotiation with Aristotelian ontology, an admiration he shared with medieval Arabic philosophers such as Avicenna and Averroes. In the DTC, Eriugena then becomes an emblem of the writing of exile and isolation in *The Pisan Cantos*: a holder of the flame of learning during the Carolingian epoch, and a visionary whose eschatology provides Pound with the means to raise the acute threats to his own being to the register of epic statement. Medieval light philosophy is not, in the end, merely a unifying device for Pound's eclectic sources and interests. Pound's recourse to light and the authority of reason in his intellectual genealogy provides him with more than just simple consolation. It unites the major threads of his thinking into a singular 'ideogram': Eriugena's Neoplatonic eschatology and Aristotelian ontology, the Greek and Latin Christian theological traditions, the divine mystery of *amor*, the poetic heritage of Guido Cavalcanti and Dante, Confucian ethics and metaphysics and what Pound saw as the civilizing forces of American Revolutionary thought and Mussolini's Fascism. He was grievously wrong about at least some of this, perhaps making *The Pisan Cantos* a true consolation in the Boethian sense, as Pound awaited his temporal fate in the ruins of what he calls in the opening line of *The Pisan Cantos*, 'the enormous tragedy of the dream' (LXXIV/445).

Pound faced an end of days in more than one sense: his belief in the Fascist order has crumbled along with Mussolini's government; and he faced the very real prospect of his own mortality, having being indicted by grand jury for the capital offence of treason. His attempts to 'write paradise' in these cantos were put on hold, and instead Pound installed a complex recursive amalgam of personal elegiac memory, pastoral tableaux bearing distinctly transcendental impetus, and remnant political vituperation. Writing in straitened circumstances, it is not surprising that Pound should turn to models of transcendence and eschatology, including Eriugena and particularly aspects of the *Periphyseon*. It is fitting that light should be employed as a major philosophical and poetic device in these cantos. Light offers transcendent certainty, inscribing in the spirit and the cosmos whilst the hand and the typewriter may only offer fragile temporal missives.

Eriugena's 'authority comes from right reason' is strategically important for Pound in writing *The Pisan Cantos*. He draws on this formula repeatedly as an emblem of Eriugena's system of thought, and adapts it as an eschatological device behind which we find Book V of the *Periphyseon* and its governing concept of *reditus* – return of all creation to the godhead. Pound repeatedly deploys another Eriugenian emblem in *The Pisan Cantos*: 'onmia quae sunt lumina sunt' (All things that are are lights) (LXXIV/449). This too functions as a kind of virtual archive, a shorthand encoding of texts to which Pound did not have access and to which he might refer with precarious philological precision. Light can exist without attribute, as Eriugena states in his translation of Pseudo-Dionysius. Rolt translates the corresponding passage as follows: 'godlike minds, angelically entering (according to their powers) unto such states of union and being deified and united, through the ceasing of their natural activities, unto the Light Which surpasseth Deity, can find no more fitting method to celebrate its praises than to deny it every manner of Attribute' (Rolt 1920, 60; qtd in Michaels 1972, 47). Pound's isolation and estrangement in the Pisan DTC has him paraphrase notions of authority from memory. *The Pisan Cantos* locates authority in Neoplatonic light rather than in unblemished citation from the textbooks of the Church Fathers or of literary history.

Pound adumbrates his 'conspiracy of intelligence' by accumulating networks of reference, linking Eriugena and Neoplatonism with his abiding interest in Confucian thought. The first reference to Eriugena as a light philosopher in Canto LXXIV is glossed by an ideogram referring directly to Confucian doctrine – the first American and British publications of *The Pisan Cantos* included the Ming[2] 明 character but this was changed to Hsien[4] 顯 in the 1958 New Directions edition and the 1975 Faber edition.[2] The ideogram is framed by the phrases 'the silk worms early/in tensile', and itself is a gloss to the text which follows: 'in the light of light is the *virtù*/"sunt lumina" said Erigena Scotus/as of Shun on Mt Taishan' (LXXIV/449). On the same page occurs Eriugena's signature phrase for his light philosophy in both Latin and English translation:

> Light tensile immaculata
> > the sun's cord unspotted
> 'sunt lumina' said the Oirishman to King Carolus,
> > 'OMNIA,
> all things that are are lights'
> and they dug him up out of sepulture
> soi disantly looking for Manichaeans.
> Les Albigeois, a problem of history (LXXIV / 449)

As previously noted, the formula 'omnia, quae sunt, lumina sunt' is from Erigena's commentary on *The Celestial Hierarchy* of Pseudo-Dionysius, who in turn is quoting from James 1:17 on the 'Father of Lights'. Pound is citing a fragment of this formula from memory, but it retains its compound provenance, if not its original form as a question in Eriugena's *Expositiones Super Ierarchian Caelestiam S. Dionysii* (PL 122, 128C). The divine act of creation is a self-manifestation or theophany, where God imbues all things but transcends them. Creation cannot be *ex nihilo*, as that would imply movement from nothing to something, which would therefore imply that a part of space lacks divine presence (Makin 1973, 74). Light entails a movement between gods and humanity, a *theanthropic* impulse more appealing to Pound. Makin holds that what 'Pound needed from Erigena was a statement of this god-man continuity' (75), thus allowing for a god *in omnibus* and *supra omnia*, and expressed in a graded theophany of light giving precise measure, rather than the 'metaphysical soup' that the 'Aquinian universe' all too readily degenerates into for Pound.[3] Pound's phrasing of Eriugena's formulae stems from his notes on the *Periphyseon*, whilst the 'light tensile immaculata' refers to the Confucian text, *The Unwobbling Pivot* (*The Doctrine of the Mean*), a translation of which Pound was working through during his detention in Pisa.[4] This concept bears a totalizing social-metaphysical meaning in *The Unwobbling Pivot*: 'order in the empire is what conjoins mankind with heaven and earth and realizes the ultimate vision of endless, "tensile light"' (Cheadle 1997, 131). The passage presents the light philosophy and the 'digging up' of Eriugena (actually the burning of his texts in the aftermath of the 1210 condemnation in Paris) as brushstrokes within an ideogram of wrongful accusation by Church hierarchy and blindness to metaphysical insight.

Eriugena is mentioned again in Canto LXXXIII, which opens with an extended set of images of water, fire and light. Pound draws on the Neoplatonism of Gemisthus Plethon, where Neptune is the prime being from which all else derives: 'ὕδωρ/ HUDOR et Pax/Gemisto stemmed all from Neptune/ hence the Rimini bas reliefs' (LXXXIII/548). Plethon was instrumental in the reintroduction of Platonic thought into Western Europe in the fifteenth century. He attended the Council of Florence in 1438–1439 that sought to reunite the Eastern and Western Churches, and his visit prompted Cosimo de' Medici to open the Platonic Academy in that city. The transmission of ideas from East to West is signified in the changing manifestation on the page in Pound's text: the first word, in Greek, is swiftly transliterated into Roman script and capitalized for emphasis; the word is combined with peace (in Latin), before the canto changes again into English and French. Fire comes to replace light – 'lux enim/ ignis est accidens' – and this is combined with Eriugena's 'Hilaritas the virtue *hilaritas*' (LXXXIII/548). The shift from light philosophy to prime matter – fire and water – is significant for the development of Pound's principle of intelligence and is consistent with Eriugena's cosmology in Book III of the *Periphyseon*. It is significant that Eriugena is cited within this evolved arrangement: his installation at crucial points in the opening and penultimate cantos of *The Pisan Cantos* signifies the degree to which his thought, especially that of eschatological redemption, motivates and transcends Pound's acutely imperilled poetic composition.

The development of Pound's light aesthetic – which is always at least implicitly metaphysical – takes on a new strength in *The Pisan Cantos*. Pound considers his confinement in Canto LXXIV by turning to figures of nature – 'the dwarf morning-glory twines around the grass blade' (LXXIV/436) – only to reflect upon the 'magna NUX animae' or 'great nut of the soul'. Terrell reads this image as the first in a development to the 'GREAT CRYSTAL' (XCI/611) and 'the great ball of crystal [...] the great acorn of light' (CXVI/795): images taken from Grossesteste's *De Luce* and consistent with Pound's statements on Plato and the Neoplatonic notion of νοῦς (Terrell 1984, 548). But there is also a sense of nature as *cosmos*, bringing together Eriugena's masterwork the *Periphyseon* with Confucius: 'In classical Confucianism, nature, or to be more exact, heaven, which Pound sometimes renders a nature, is an entity that is both physical and metaphysical. It combines the material and the spiritual, or phenomenal and noumenal worlds, in such a way that each informs and manifests the other' (Lan 2006, 73). Perhaps the most important role played by Grosseteste in *The Cantos* is that discerned by Michaels in Canto LV, where a passage from the *I Ching* is framed by his words:

> Lux enim per se omnem in partem
> Reason from heaven, said Tcheou-Tun-y
> > enlighteneth all things
> seipsum seipsum diffundit, risplende
> > Is the beginning of all things, et effectu (LV / 298)

This passage bears upon *The Pisan Cantos* in an unexpected way. According to Michaels, this passage marks a movement of 'right reason' from an earthly to a transcendental principle via light philosophy, and thus alters the simply ethical Johannes Scottus Eriugena of Canto XXXVI into the mystical figure of Canto LXXIV (Michaels 1972, 45). Michaels does not account for Pound's changing awareness of Eriugena's thought — particularly his negotiations with Pseudo-Dionysius and Neoplatonism — from the time of his first exposure in Fiorentino up to the two sequences of Eriugena notes preceding *The Pisan Cantos*. Yet Michaels is right to see that Pound inflects his references to Eriugena in *The Pisan Cantos* with a newly sharpened focus on Pseudo-Dionysian metaphysics as one of two central themes (the other being Eriugena's poetry and general *hilaritas* in Charles's court). That Eriugena and Grosseteste should be linked in Pound's mind is not altogether surprising. They are often mentioned together in various catalogues of 'the conspiracy of intelligence' (*GK* 263) or 'the definition of words' (*ABCR* 90). Perhaps as a direct consequence of Pound's acquisition of PL 122 in 1939–1940, Eriugena replaces Grosseteste as Pound's most important early medieval source for light philosophy and 'precise definition'. For Pound, Eriugena's ethics were of use in bearing the formula: *Auctoritas ex vera ratione processi ratio vero nequaquam ex auctoritate* (Fiorentino 1921, 217). Pound's translation in Canto XXXVI, 'Authority comes from right reason/never the other way on' (179) is elsewhere repeated as 'authority comes from right reason'.[5]

Eriugena's 'Greek tags' in *The Cantos*

Canto LXXXIII begins with an extended passage concerning Eriugena and Neoplatonic light. But it is particularly distinctive in making reference to

Eriugena's poetry in the court of Charles the Bald, and especially the Greek
elements in his poetry:

> the queen stitched King Carolus' shirts or whatever
> while Erigena put greek tags in his excellent verses
> > in fact an excellent poet, Paris
> > > toujours Pari'
> > > > (Charles le Chauve)   (LXXXIII / 548)

This domestic scene is a sharp change of focus: the court poet is occupied
with his Greek verses or stichoi (στιχοι), whilst the Carolingian queen is
engaged in her own domestic occupation, stitching cloth (*textus*) in a weave
of creativity (τέχνε). Eriugena's poem in praise of Irmintrude ('Laudes
Yrmindrudis Caroli Calvi uxoris') appears fourth in PL 122 following three
long poems on Christological themes. In that poem Irmintrude is likened to
both Athena and Arachne, and Eriugena employs a number of Greek words
to strengthen these associations (as well as to indulge in his characteristic
translinguistic punning, a sure sign of *hilaritas*). The poem 'may have
been written in 864 to compliment the queen in helping her husband in a
negotiation with Pope Nicholas I, to whom was given a garment made of
gold and gems, woven, in all likelihood, by Irmintrude herself' (Herren
1993, 140).[6] The harmony of domestic activity, the culture of creativity
in poetry and weaving, and the subtle arts of diplomacy suggest a tableau
of a world in balance. The joyful spontaneity suggested in the phrase 'or
whatever' is transformed a few lines later in the repetition of the Eriugenian
formula, 'omnia, quae sunt, lumina sunt, or whatever'. Here poetry and the
embodiment of virtue (*hilaritas*) are displaced in an embittered reminder of
Eriugena's persecution: the (fallacious) issue of Eriugena's 'bones' being dug
'in the time of De Montfort'.

Eriugena's poetry has been largely overlooked by Carolingian scholars due
to the poetic use of Greek, dense allusion and the difficult arrangement of
ideas. Further, it is 'rarely cited as evidence for Eriugena's thought and only
occasionally used for information about the reign and times of Charles the
Bald' (Herren 11). The lack of a consistent manuscript tradition has also
hindered philological research (15). Herren's recent edition of the *Carmina*
amply explains the problems of attribution clouding a good portion of
Eriugena's opus. It is only with an examination of manuscripts and the
collation of dispersed knowledge that some of these have been attributable
to Eriugena at all. As his notes attest, Pound read the poems in PL 122

(76/3393, 21–6) and drew on the poems of most interest in *The Pisan Cantos*, principally those delineating God's superessential nature, as well as the poem 'Laudes Yrmindrudis Caroli Calvi uxoris'. Eriugena wrote not merely 'tags', but entire poems in Greek. Strangely, Pound makes reference to these poems only in general and indirect ways, but discerns their utility in painting a palatine portrait of Hibernian poet and Carolingian king. These poems demonstrate Eriugena's *hilaritas*: despite his serious use of Greek, Eriugena's poetry is distinguished by his satirical wit (Herren 1993, 26). Michaels sees this reference to Eriugena's poetic use of Greek as a multivalent cipher for a rich network of ideas: 'Its mention invokes not only what Eriugena was in history but what he is in the poem, that is, it invokes the *Chung Yung* as well as the Pseudo-Dionysius, Gemisthus Plethon as well as the Albigenses' (Michaels 1972, 51). While this may be true in theory, there is a distinct shortfall in a sustained, thematically rigorous fusion of these disparate topics with Eriugena in *The Pisan Cantos*. Pound might have made much more of this rich material, but at the time of composition did not have access to his moderately detailed notes of the *Versus* in PL 122.

The theme of Eriugena's poetry arises again at several points in *Rock-Drill*. In Canto LXXXVII Eriugena is again identified as both a practitioner of light metaphysics and a repository of Greek in the early Middle Ages: 'Y Yin, Ocellus, Erigena:/"All things are lights."/Greek tags in Erigena's verses' (LXXXVII/571). The figure of Ocellus is linked explicitly with Pound's formula, taken from *The Great Digest* (II.1), 'MAKE IT NEW/ [...] day by day, make it new' (LIII/265) (薪 日 日 薪 *xin ri ri xin*): this bond with Ocellus is confirmed in *Rock-Drill* (LXXXVII/591, XCIII/649, XCIV/662) and *Thrones* (XCVIII/704). *Rock-Drill* repeats the poetic mantra – 'With greek tags in his excellent verses,/Erigena,/ In reign of Carolus Calvus' (LXXXVIII/601) – amid a discussion of economic principles gleaned from such ancient philosophers as Thales, Mencius and Ambrose. The final mention of Eriugena in *Rock-Drill* makes explicit connection between him and the rites of Eleusis: the familiar markers of this discourse (Poitiers, Jacques de Molay) lead to the question, 'was Erigena ours?' (XC/625). This ambiguous question arises in the context of 'Sagetreib [...] tradition' (625) and may be taken as a question of Eriugena's belonging to the 'Mediterranean sanity', the elect fellowship of thinkers who see the thread joining transcendent light and the creation of art and culture.

Given the limited amount of knowledge Pound had concerning the Greek content of Erigena's poetry, what special attraction did the medieval poet hold for the modern? On closer examination it seems that the two writers had similar composition techniques, similar attitudes towards history, their subject matter and the perceived role of poetry. A stylistic tendency in Eriugena's poetry is the use of particular words to open a meditation on the mysteries of creation, incarnation and redemption. These mysteries 'in their turn, are related to the existential situation of particular human beings and times – in this case, the plight of the poet/translator' (Herren 1993, 34). Eriugena's wide reading of classical, late antique and Carolingian poets signals the compatibility of poetry and philosophy: 'the most advanced representative of Carolingian philosophy did not regard the study and commentary of poetry as propaedeutic to philosophy, but rather as a central activity that one continues to pursue alongside philosophy' (42). Eriugena mastered Greek at a time when grammars were of exceedingly poor quality, and when learning was confined to Irish communities in northeastern France and Belgium and such isolated Swiss outposts as St. Gallen.

> Despite these hardships John was an ardent proselytizer of Greek studies. He urged Charles himself to undertake the subject [...]. The Greek in the poems, therefore, was employed to challenge not only his royal patron, but all who came into contact with John's verses. (47)

These strong affinities sharpen the sense of Pound's championing Eriugena as a multilingual poet. They make even more sense in the light of Pound's plight in the years of his interest in Eriugena: including the fulcrum event of this phase in Pound's career in the Pisan DTC, under arrest, writing *The Pisan Cantos*.

Eriugena's postulation of *ratio* as the basis for *auctoritas* is clearly evident in the Pisan context: Pound required a method of reference that was not legitimated by exact quotations from determined sources, but by the *verbum perfectum* combining the orders of earth and the heavens in one unbroken ray of light. Eriugena's philosophical weight within the tradition of the Schoolmen is crucial for the metaphysics of light that Pound also finds in Confucius and Cavalcanti. Medieval light philosophy is a unifying device for Pound's eclectic sources and interests – illustrating the unity of the heavens and gods with nature, writing, human society and governance – and thus precipitating the eclectic agglomeration of sources into a unified ideogram or text. But in addition to this, it is a trope joining the best poetry of Europe, the Confucian classics, and the fragile cargo of the poet's memory. Eriugena thus functions as a long-term reference point for Pound. His role is shifted out of place in *The Cantos* as composition becomes more the writing of exile and isolation in *The*

Pisan Cantos. The history of Pound's interest in Eriugena is encoded in *The Cantos*: Pound's inability to draw on specific sources inscribed inaccuracies and inconsistencies in the poem. Given the conditions of composition of *The Pisan Cantos*, it is perfectly natural that Pound could have confused his sources by misreading Fiorentino, as Moody asserts in the case of Amalric's persecution in thirteenth-century Paris. Pound's 'sun's cord unspotted' is confounded by his own discontinuous process of composition, and the changing significance of that process in the context of Pound's larger project.

Pound's scholarly methods were not entirely consistent and often took the form of highly fragmentary allusions, as the Eriugena notes amply demonstrate. During the Second World War Pound withdrew further from many of his closest allies within his intellectual cohort, and found himself functioning within a largely Italian Fascist cultural frame. During the later 1930s Pound's scholarly errors of omission and commission take on an increasingly exilic hue: this sense of displacement culminates in the composition environment of the Pisan DTC. Eriugena is not only a symbol of textual layering, but one *exemplum* of the text's history unpacking itself and revealing its equivocal status in its composition. The history of Pound's interest in Eriugena is, ironically, contained in the text of *The Cantos* (and the *Guide to Kulchur*) and transmitted through the inaccuracies of information and Pound's inconsistent use of the sources. This appraisal of the role of Eriugena in *The Cantos*, in the sequences of Pound's notes, and in his thought generally, must now be contextualized in *The Pisan Cantos*. Pound situates Eriugena strategically, in relation to Neoplatonism and to the materiality of his text, especially its problematic ideograms, as well as with regard to the cross-pollination with the Confucian classics that instigated Pound's desire for his 'note on Eriugena' in the first place.

Neoplatonic tones towards *The Pisan Cantos*

Pound's use of light philosophy in *The Pisan Cantos* is informed by his intensive study of Eriugena in PL 122 early in the Second World War. This focus signals a preoccupation with textual transmission as much as with the transmission of light: almost without exception, the philosophers that keep Pound's attention are notable for the precarious provenance of their texts. Light philosophy becomes a mediation of the inspired word transmitted through (or in spite of) a fragile and threatened text. Pound was absorbed with uncertain textual provenance throughout his career, evident in such early lyrics as 'Papyrus' in *Lustra*.[7] Yet in *The Pisan Cantos* the issue becomes a properly reticulated one, impinging upon the status and composition of the poetic text. The metaphysical certainties and total reach of light philosophy, when measured against the tenuous textual provenance of its sources, functions as a model and vehicle for textual transmission in *The Pisan Cantos*.

The philosophical material assembled within this suite of cantos stems partly from an earlier phase of interest in Neoplatonism (evident in *A Draft of XXX Cantos*), and partly from the notes Pound composed in Rapallo during the late 1930s and published as *Guide to Kulchur* in 1938. In that text, Aristotle is considered a distraction except for his determination of currency as a measuring principle in the *Nichomachean Ethics* (*GK* 325), and for a mention of the residually Presocratic word ευσαιμονειν:

> It is not to be among good angels. It is to be possessed of one's good DAEMON. It is aperient, in the sense that it lets in all the Arabian commentators, and gives a clue as to why mediaeval theologians took up Aristotle, with their angel-ology, and their ouranology, or demonology = good-daemon-ology. With this word (almost an ideogram) we are down through the blither and yatter, the *Spectator-New-Statesman-Villard-Webbite* weekly choinulism, down onto the pre-Socratic paideuma, into folk-lore. Damn the dictionaries. The bleating lexicographers have not looked at the roots of the ideogram. This word is out of thaumaturgy not out of a print shop. It don't prove that Arry was anything but a Bloomsbury simp, but he used it. (*GK* 307)

Pound cuts through philosophical terminology and the work of misled philologists – the 'bleating lexicographers' – to sense the intelligence of myth behind Aristotle's use of the word, as well as its appeal to Avicenna, Averroes, and above all, Pseudo-Dionysius, via Eriugena (the 'angel-ology' of *The Celestial Hierarchy* and Eriugena's Commentary). Pound seeks out a delicate balance: he is prepared to provide his own definition of ευσαιμονειν against the conventions of philology, and to posit the living use of archaic language as his authority. This puts the passage at odds with the texts upon which it is based. The Greek word is described as an ideogram: not literally, but as a glyph ordering a cluster of ideas. Its origins in myth and lore prompt Pound to discredit its material transmission in the Greek world and down to modernity: 'not out of a print shop'. The word speaks out of an oral culture anterior to the written text, but is dependent upon writing, and ultimately printing, for its transmission down to Pound's day. His argument for thaumaturgy derives from, and is produced in, that very print shop he seeks to discredit.

The specific instances of light in *The Pisan Cantos* refine Pound's use of light philosophers over his poetic career. As expressed in *Guide to Kulchur*, his general attitude to philosophy in the later 1930s and during the war was based on a theory of action (*GK* 43), showing little patience with metaphysical systems not verified against empirical measurement (97). *Guide to Kulchur* treats numerous ancient philosophers, major and minor, in order to validate the system of gradations or hierarchy of values that imbues the politics, ethics, economics and poetry of the best civilizations: Pound's 'Mediterranean state of mind' (*SP* 120). Such a gradation is embodied in the archaic light of intelligence, sustained by the Neoplatonists and transmitted by Eriugena, the Islamic Aristotelian commentators, Grosseteste, Cavalcanti, and then, via Gemisthus Plethon, in the Italian Renaissance by Cosimo de' Medici and Sigismundo Malatesta.

Pound orders his digest of metaphysical systems upon the active principle of light, and establishes a provenance for Neoplatonism in presocratic philosophy. Although Pythagoras (XCI/630) and Ocellus (LXXXVII/591; XCI/630; XCIV/662) are first explicitly mentioned in *Rock-Drill*, they are readily absorbed into Pound's syncretic history. They also happen to share a profoundly tenuous textual provenance: their philosophical fragments survive in the texts of Iamblichus and Diogenes Laertius (Terrell 1984, 492). When writing of the Milesian school, also represented by heavily mediated fragments, Pound says of Anaximenes: 'all is from air, proceeding by condensation and rarefaction, PUKNOSIS and MANOSIS, all of which forms nice background to mediaeval writers on light and diaphana' (*GK* 117). Of his later sources, Pound mentions reading Burnet's *Early Greek Philosophy* and cites Milhaud's *Les Philosophes-Géométres de la Grec* in a letter to Wyndham Lewis of 6 December 1954 (*P/L* 285). He also read the Presocratic fragments in Herman Diels's *Die fragmente der Vorsokratiker* and in Freeman's companion to that volume (Terrell 627).

Despite Pound's philologically-minded pursuits early in his career – his study of Cavalcanti and the adaptation of Stesichorus[8] in Canto XXIII are two prominent examples – he rarely acknowledges the extensive doxographical tradition that accounts for the uncertain provenance of Presocratic fragments. This tradition began with Theophrastus's *On Sensation* and took a variety of forms: ' "opinions" arranged according to subjects, biographies, or somewhat artificial "successions" (διαδοχαι) of philosophers regarded as master and pupil' (Guthrie 1962, xiii). Pound sets aside his natural proclivities for such genealogies – forerunners of the early medieval *accessus ad auctores* which developed in the cathedral school of Laon – and instead uses ancient philosophical texts to signify the precision of thought in the face of degenerating language. Indeed, Pound gives a direct critique of philology and textual decipherment:

> Mechanism, how it works, teleology, what it's aimed at, the soul of the world, the fire of the gods, remembering of course that the 'history of philosophy,' when dealing with the greek start, now flickers about among fragments, and that every word is used, defined, left undefined, wangled and wrangled according to the taste of the wrangler, his temperament, his own bias. (*GK* 119)

This posture expresses Pound's hostility to formal education in the 'beaneries'. Yet it indicates a fundamental crux: how can a text establish its meaning and spirit without attention to precise wording and the history of the language? Pound resorts to an idealist view of meaning, a direct conduit from the 'fire of the gods' to the inspired reader.

Throughout his career Pound seems to find fascination with and to invest authority in the fragmented nature of his chosen texts (Materer 1995, 29). The texts of Plato are not valued for their provenance or linguistic accuracy, but instead for their disclosure 'of the *nous*, of mind, apart from any man's individual mind, of the sea crystalline and enduring, of the bright as it were molten glass that envelops us, full of light' (*GK* 44). When a text is liable to corruption or imbricated composition, Pound takes a keen interest in its transmission history: Canto I uses the Andreas Divus translation of the *Odyssey*, 'In officiana Wecheli, 1538, out of Homer' (I/5); and Canto XCIV uses the first Loeb edition of the *Life of Apollonius of Tyana* by Philostratus, translated by the Oxford theologian Frederick Cornwallis Conybeare, 'no full trans/till 1811,/ remarks F. C. Conybeare, the prelector' (XCIV/657). That Pound should take care to identify the edition of Philostratus's text is significant, since the authority of the text has been greatly disputed since the time of its composition. Pound's inconsistent attitude towards philosophical material is a measure of the value he reads within it: texts within the tradition of the 'light of intelligence' can abide without a clear and settled provenance for their authority. This amnesty ironically includes *The Pisan Cantos*, as it does not quote accurately in every case or include extensive scholarly apparatus due to its author's internal exile during its composition and transmission into print. Philosophical authority is channelled into light philosophy, and the clarity and accuracy of citation and reference function within the medium of light.

Robert Grosseteste is a prominent source for Pound's light philosophy, dating from his 1910 study of the sources for Cavalcanti's vocabulary in the

'Donna mi prega' canzone. Pound's essay 'Cavalcanti' indicates the importance of lineage to Pound's sense of European thought:

> it would seem that Guido had derived certain notions from the Aristotelian commentators, the *'filosofica famiglia'*, Ibn Sina, for the *spiriti, spiriti* of the eyes, of the senses; Ibn Rachd, *che il gran comento feo*, for the demand for intelligence on the part of the recipient; [...] and possibly Grosseteste, *De Luce et de Incohatione Formarum*, although this will need proving. (*MIN* 356)

Pound located Grosseteste in a tradition of thought on light that included Confucius: 'Grosseteste writin' on light, hooks up with the ideogram of the sun and moon at the start of Confucius 'testament'' (*EPS* 374). Pound required a system of thought independent of physical mobility in Pisa: one he produced by drawing out the affinity between Neo-Confucianism and medieval light philosophy in *The Pisan Cantos*. A philosophy of action is gradually replaced by one that manifests volition by a gathering of authority to the enlightened subject in the medium of light. The subject is not so much confined or immobile as having found a centre or balance.

The Pisan Cantos demarcates a transition of light from a 'totalitarian' function in Pound's poetics to one of reflection and inner cultivation. The motif of light gathers and registers the philosophical and mythical thought that Pound finds conducive to his epic poem: the light of Eleusis; the light of myth and ancient philosophy in Pythagoras, his followers and Plato's theory of forms; the tradition of Neoplatonism and the Troubadour cult of *amor*; medieval light philosophy that updated the Neoplatonic tradition, particularly Eriugena, Grosseteste, and Anselm of Canterbury; the Neoplatonic revival in Quattrocento Florence; and finally, the few bright lights of later times (Leibniz, Rabelais, John Adams), who tried to maintain the light of Eleusis against a tide of cultural mediocrity, political mendacity and commercial deceit. Despite Pound's increasingly vituperative attacks on usury, war and bad government, optimism is built into his metaphysics of light (via Shakespeare's *Twelfth Night* IV, ii, 43–4): 'There is no darkness but ignorance' (LXXX/521). Whether Eleusinian, Neoplatonic or Neo-Confucian light overlaid upon the Master's texts,[9] light nearly always registers with reference to authorship, inscription or definition. In this way the dominant image of light asserts a kind of textual certainty that transcends the extreme contingency of the text's composition. Whilst there is a strong temptation to read the light imagery in *The Pisan Cantos* as another manifestation of Pound's attempt 'to write paradise' (CXVII/822), it is the impossibility of attainment that drives the text. The impossible modern epic and its evaporated *paradiso terrestre* is written into the impossibility of a stable text object.

The mythic origin and structure of Pound's light in Eleusis – the Attic ritual cycle ending in the mystical union of the *hieros gamos* (Tryphonopoulos 1992, 30) – modulates the two commonly cited schemata for *The Cantos*: the Odyssean journey, or *nostos*, and the progress of Dante in the *Divina commedia*. The two epics seem to fit Pound's own prescription for the tripartite model of metaphysical progress: descent to the Underworld, the 'repeat in history' and the 'magic moment' of touching divinity (*SL* 210). Natural sources of loci of light (the sun, moon, stars, clouds and water) function with Greek myth as emblems of memory and textual composition. The sun, as Helios or Apollo, cites the culture from which came the Homeric Hymns and the *Odyssey*. The sun is the tensile light descending – what Grosseteste called *lux*, and what Pound identifies in the 明 (*ming*) ideogram – and is the source of all immanent light – the *lumen* of Grosseteste, the formless essence for Eriugena and the ΗΛΙΟΝ ΠΕΡΙ ΗΛΙΟΝ for Pound. The sun aids the navigator in periplus (a voyage oriented by coastal features), and defines the arrested location of the *ego scriptor*, who in turn becomes a kind of gnomon or 'Unwobbling Pivot'. It is also the principle and agent of generation, and thus bears relation to the notion of *amor*. Canto LXXVI opens with a plotting of the sun's course: 'And the sun high over horizon hidden in cloud bank' (LXXVI/472). The echo of accentual or stressed verse here confirms the memory of Canto I. The catalogue of female deities, and reference to 'the sun in his great periplum' introduce the Albigensian Heresy and the Mithraic cult: 'and in Mt Segur there is wind space and rain space/no more an altar to Mithras' (472). The Persian god of light bore ancient associations with Helios and the origins of the Greek pantheon. Yet Pound does not lend support or sympathy to the Mithraic cult – popularized in the Roman Empire into Christian times – but declares a lack of evidence for its existence in medieval Provence. As with authority, economics, linguistic accuracy and *amor*, there is also a wrong kind of light obscuring the good.

Sunsets accompanied by clouds provide the natural light of *The Pisan Cantos*. After rain and wind off the nearby mountain, the clouds appear 'in colour rose-blue before sunset/and carmine and amber' (LXXVI/479). Just below these lines, several lines are arranged on the page as clouds might be suspended in the space of the sky:

and the clouds over the Pisan meadows
            are indubitably as fine as any to be seen
from the peninsula (479)

This cloud motif endures through *The Pisan Cantos* and concludes with a suggestion of hope for enduring beauty: 'Under white clouds, cielo di Pisa/out of all this beauty something must come' (LXXXIV/559). Sunset provokes the working of memory for the *ego scriptor*: Pound recalls the 'soap-smooth stone posts where San Vio/meets with il canal Grande' and the Venetian printing history of *A Lume Spento* (LXXVI/480). The sky and the page share a compositional affinity: one provides 'wind space and rain space'; the other provides a canvas for Pound's ideograms both in alphabetic script and in Chinese characters, and establishes a frame for the typeset text. The light of the sky underwrites Pound's light philosophy and solar imagery as the whiteness of the page embodies and fixes the text.

Shadows complement sunlight and resonate in various ways: 'Hast 'ou found a cloud so light/As seemed neither mist nor shade?' (LXXXI/540). The *ego scriptor* – 'a lone ant from a broken ant hill/from the wreckage of Europe' (LXXVI/478) – turns his attention to the life around him: 'if calm be after tempest/that the ants seem to wobble/as the morning sun catches their shadows' (LXXX/533). The sun and the object's shadow render it unstable to the eye. The afternoon sun brings with it resonances of the underworld (shades), rendered in brackets as an annotation or gloss, or punctuated as an interruption into the text matter: '[Only shadows enter my tent/as men pass between me and the sunset,]' (LXXX/535). The 'sunset grand couturier' (LXXX/536) clothes the natural world and the spiritual world, and is the agent of various grades of shadow or shade. The relation between vision and the sun becomes complicated in Canto LXXXIII: 'the ants seem to stagger/as the dawn sun has trapped their shadows', but now the sun itself observes the process, 'the sun as a golden eye/between dark cloud and the mountain' (LXXXIII/551). Anterior to the sun is 'the full Εἰδὼς' with the power to 'interpass, penetrate/ casting but shade beyond the other lights' (LXXXI/540). The time before dawn, and before the advent of shades, provides a state of transfiguration to counterbalance the limbo of sunset: 'Throughout *The Pisan Cantos*, both the successful invocation of Aphrodite and the whole course of mystic fusion occur before sunrise, that is, before the distinctions between subject and object are sharply marked by the light of day, which revives the painful sights and sounds of the camp enclosure' (Pearlman 1969, 290). The telluric gods of the Pisan landscape also sport before sunrise: 'Zeus lies in Ceres' bosom/Taishan is attended of loves/under Cythera, before sunrise' (LXXXI/537), whereas the *ego scriptor*, ΟΥ ΤΙΣ, is godless, 'a man on whom the sun has gone down' (LXXIV/450).

The moon brings light to the Pisan DTC, and complements the generative power of the sun and its representative gods. The moon above a broken, warring Europe, 'Io son' la luna' (LXXVI/473), outlasts the representation of its goddess Diana, the 'huntress in broken plaster'. Elsewhere it blanches the particulars of the moment, dilating into memory: 'Moon, cloud, tower, a patch of the battistero/all of a whiteness' (LXXIX/504). Whiteness functions as an expression of memory: the white of the moon, metaphysical whiteness of intelligible light, and, recalling Canto LXXIV, the white page.[10] The sun, moon, and stars also form a trivium of light:

> The moon has a swollen cheek
> and when the morning sun lit up the shelves and battalions
> of the West, cloud over cloud
> > Old Ez folded his blankets
> Neither Eos nor Hesperus had suffered wrong at my hands (LXXIX / 508)

The Morning Star's luminosity diminishes with the spread of sunlight. In this moment, sunlight is cast upon the instruments of war and of learning (shelves holding books, and the battalions of the DTC), and those instruments are arranged like the clouds, the blankets and the material states of the text, ply over ply.

During a reminiscence of musicians, artists, and writers known to Pound or renowned in history, Diana appears again in an interlude:

> 'I am the torch' wrote Arthur 'she saith'
> in the moon barge Βροδοδάκτυλος Ἠώς
>
> with the veil of faint cloud before her
> > Κύθερα δεινὰ as a leaf borne in the current
> pale eyes as without fire (LXXX / 531)

The moon barge traces a link between Arthur Addington Symons, from whose poem 'Modern Beauty' the first line derives, and the specific interest Pound took in the Homeric epithet, 'rosy-fingered'. The word Βροδοδάκτυλος is written in Sappho's dialect rather than that of Athens (ῥοδοδάκτυλος) and refers to the moon, not to the Homeric dawn (Kenner 1975, 56). Its presence entails a brief history of poetics and of writing, remembered in Pound's text 30 years after Richard Aldington's translation, where Pound commemorates an elegiac loss at Pisa as Sappho does in Lesbos in the original poem.[11] *The Pisan Cantos* establishes a resolution between sunlight and the moon in the subject who observes them:

A fat moon rises lop-sided over the mountain
The eyes, this time my world,
> But pass and look *from* mine
>> between my lids
>>> sea, sky, and pool
>>> alternate
>>> pool, sky, sea,

morning moon against sunrise
like a bit of the best antient greek coinage (LXXXIII / 555)

The *ego scriptor* regains the agency of reported vision, and the verse structure presents the testing out of this power. Eyes fix the elements as they fix the text: figure (moon, sun, words); ground (sky, sea, paper); and the framing devices unifying figure and ground (vision itself, pool, page).

One source of light in *The Pisan Cantos* derives neither from sun nor moon but from the strength of a culture and from the intelligence of its leaders. The statue of Can Grande della Scala – protector of Dante and Ghibelline lord of Verona – recalls the light of intelligence, and is glossed in the text with a line from Cavalcanti's Sonnet 7: 'E fa di clarità l'aer tremare' (LXXVIII/501; *T* 38–9). The gloss is philologically specific, as the best choice between variants among Cavalcanti's manuscripts, and concern for its durability is expressed in the next line: 'thus writ, and conserved (or was) in Verona'.[12] Light is a principle of intelligence unconstrained by the uncertain fate of material objects. Its expression in Cavalcanti and in *The Pisan Cantos* records a moment when its provenance is crucial for the transmission of the message. Light is textual inasfar as it cannot project without the basis of clear transmission: 'Cassandra your eyes are like tigers'/no light reaches through them' (LXXVIII/502); 'Cassandra, your eyes are like tigers,/with no word written in them' (LXXVIII/497). Pound laments the obscurity of his preferred tradition due to its suffering exactly this fate of poor transmission.

The principle of light is bound up in a complex network of images for Pound: the sun 'in his great periplum' (LXXVI/452), Apollo, Helios, *sinceritas* and the *verbum perfectum* of Eastern Christian Neoplatonism. As water and light become mutually implicated throughout *The Pisan Cantos* – ὕδωρ and *lux* – the periplum orients within sight of, or upon, water. It fuses with light (both *lux* and *lumen*, source and trace) in the sun. The cosmos is steadily mapped in *The Pisan Cantos*, just as Eriugena maps the cosmos in Book III of the *Periphyseon*, describing the movement and arrangement of the stars and planets.

> *Cosmos*, in the Greek, means the right ordering of things. It can apply to personal behaviour, a public occasion, or the conduct of government; and it includes the idea of all things in their right ordering, that is, 'the world' or 'the universe'. (Moody 1982, 135)

The sun as *paideuma* is the 'ΗΛΙΟΝ ΠΕΡΙ ΗΛΙΟΝ' or 'the sun around the sun' (Terrell 1984, 371) that constitutes its own behaviour as it governs all other activity, reflecting the divine 'invisible light' of which sunlight is a pale kataphatic shadow in Pseudo-Dionysius (see 77/3406, 34A.1–5). The cyclic nature of the solar and lunar phases is mitigated by the principle of decorum or *sinceritas*:

> The second century translators of the Bible generally used the word sinceritas to translate the Greek 'Ειλιχρινεια.' The Greek word is ultimately derived from the words 'ειλη,' the sun's ray, and 'χρινω,' to distinguish or decide (mentally or judicially). (Schuldiner 1975, 75)

Sincerity is thus a cosmic principle – the order of things – and the linguistic image sought after by Pound: 'only the total sincerity, the precise definition' (LXXVII/488). Pound's own definition is of course found in the terminology of his *Confucius*: 'The precise definition of the word, pictorially the sun's lance coming to rest on the precise spot verbally. The righthand half of the compound means: to perfect, bring to focus' (*CON* 20). The sun, a divine principle, is also the textual principle. It gives light and reflects its constitution as light, just as *The Cantos*, 'a poem containing history', reflects its constitution as textual history and as an interrogation of that history. The periplum (orientation by way of terrestrial markers) serves to guide the reader through time and space in the narrative and between disjunctive moments of the text: it is a principle of unity in Pound's poem, ordering and authorizing the composition and transmission of his exiled, displaced text.

The space of composition in *The Pisan Cantos*

The book shd. be a ball of light in one's hand. (GK 55)

The composition history of *The Pisan Cantos* is famously complex: following some tentative attempts in Rapallo, Pound composed his manuscript notes under difficult conditions in the Pisan DTC, and parts of the manuscript text did not survive into typescript. Different sets of typescripts were sent to Dorothy Pound, Olga and Mary Rudge, T. S. Eliot and James Laughlin. Some of these typescripts were to be given to Hugh Gordon Porteous so that he could check the ideograms written into the margins and in the body of the poetic text, but most of these ideograms did not survive the transmission into print. Other aspects of these cantos were equally fragile in transmission, such as Gerhard Münch's violin line score of Clément Jannequin's *Le Chant des Oiseaux* that comprises most of Canto LXXV. Pound simply made a note in the typescript where the score was to be inserted, if it could be tracked down from Ronald Duncan, editor of the journal *Townsman* where it had first been published. Poetic space and authorial intention are therefore unusually vexed issues in the case of *The Pisan Cantos*, and offer insights into the utility of disembodied light as a metaphor of transcendence, not only for the incarcerated poet, but for his fragile and vulnerable text.

In his work towards a critical edition of *The Pisan Cantos*, Ronald Bush has conducted a comprehensive study of the loss of ideograms from the final published texts. The matter of their omission is complex, both in terms of the various actors in the transmission of the text to publication, and in terms of the long-term attempts to restore the neglected ideograms:

> About the Chinese characters, there is no written evidence that Pound authorized their omission. On the contrary, in letters whose photocopies are in the Beinecke, he badgered James Laughlin to put them all in and to do them well. Finally, however, New Directions' delays in publication drove Pound wild and seem to have worn him down. At least in a letter to Laughlin of 21 [February? 1947?] he has been reduced to asking that one key ideogram be allowed to remain on page 6 of the *Yale Poetry Review* proofs of Canto 83 in lieu of the 'more' he remembers being there originally. (Bush 1997, 207 n.2)

The ideograms that do survive in Canto LXXIV are 顯 (*xian*) (449) – altered from 明 (*ming*) – and 莫 (*mo*) or the simple negative (450). The typescripts reveal that a large number of ideograms were excised from the text or were simply not included by Faber and New Directions for a number of reasons. The presence of either *ming* ('sun and moon' or 'the intelligence') or *xian* (Pound's Hsien[4], 'tensile light descending') is meaningful in that each ideogram refers, in Pound's usage, to the precision of language. In a further irony, the composition of each ideogram in the published texts of *The Pisan Cantos* is calligraphically imprecise. In the context of 'precise definition' that is at once linguistic, metaphysical and ethical, and follows from the dense historical and ideological matter of the China Cantos, it would seem a heresy to produce such contingent work at this point. It appears that Pound's circumstances led to provisional sketches of ideograms becoming permanent elements of the text. Dorothy Pound composed the ideograms in the typescript she sent to Ronald Duncan in London for copying, as she stated in a letter to James Laughlin on 5 December 1945: 'I have just got the thick batch of Cantos that went via Base Censor: & am doing the characters for [Gordon] Porteous or somebody in London to deal with' (*P/L* 143). She wrote to Pound with similar information on 13 December: 'No. 60 [Olga and Mary Rudge] is typing the copies & putting in Greek – after wh. I am inserting Chinese Characters in legible manner – (but not for printing)' (*E&DP* 217). Dorothy emphasized the provisional status of these ideograms in two separate letters to Laughlin, on 16 and 19 December. The published ideograms were only intended to refer to entries in Chinese dictionaries from which the reproductions were to be made. Several months later, in a letter to James Laughlin on 31 July 1946, Dorothy expressed Pound's concerns about delays in publication, and intimated his forlorn resignation over the diminished role of his ideograms in *The Pisan Cantos*: 'yesterday E. said to photograph his pencilled-in ideograms if it would hurry up the printers of the last cantos – it would at least add an interest anyway' (qtd. in Taylor 1999, 174). Pound invests his ideograms with the precision and authority also found in motifs of light (and light philosophy), the *periplum* and the aesthetic object. These themes ideally converge to reveal in the 'magic moment' the unity of all things and νοῦς or intelligence that can imagine the *paradiso terrestre*. Pound's understanding of ideograms and their component parts – such as his 'pictorial' reading of 誠 (*cheng*) as 'the sun's lance coming to rest on the precise spot verbally' – entails the syncretic and unifying function of the poem's larger structures.

The ideograms of *The Pisan Cantos* are situated somewhere between text and gloss, both in their semantic function and in their sometimes-awkward placement on the page. The ideograms are not merely exotic apparatus to more conventional text material, but in their precarious placement they contribute to the faceting of the text. Seen in this way, the text discerns what is right or fitting (*sinceritas* or the *verbum perfectum*) and encodes a set of discrete histories and compositional processes that contribute to an overall textual effect. Pound presents the ideogram as a hermeneutic device mediating the abstract (its semantic relation to the text material) and the particular (its striking visibility). The ideogram is an exemplar of difference and discrete object-hood contained within a larger frame of metaphysical, linguistic and organic unity.[13]

The *chung* (中 *zhong*) ideogram appears again on the first page of Canto LXXVII (484). It is also represented phonetically in the Roman alphabet, and uneasily inhabits a space within the text frame, functioning iconically as a gloss or rough illustration. Nearer to the ideogram than its transliterated name is its definition, 'in the middle', which is not signified as a quotation but presented as a direct utterance of the poetic voice. The next line qualifies this definition: 'whether upright or horizontal'. The reference to upright or horizontal orientation applies spatially, and describes the *chuan chu* category of ideograms that are rotated either 90 or 180 degrees to render different meanings.[14] The *chung/zhong* ideogram is not one of these. The importance of orientation and stroke-composition of ideograms is not always evident to non-readers of Chinese. Yet the examples above indicate the differences between signification in alphabetic script and the materiality of Chinese writing. The word's form is crucial from the printer's point of view, and the presentation of the word, beyond its spelling, does carry semantic weight. Immediately following the *chung* ideogram, a line of the canto self-consciously represents meaning typographically: 'there is nothing, italics *nothing*, they will not do/to retain 'em' (LXXVII/484). The superfluous 'instruction' for italics, followed by the italicized word, further emphasizes the ideogram – as though Pound had anticipated the trouble inherent in printing such linguistic forms.

Pound's textual ideogram of the 'light of intelligence' or νους gathers the fields of ethical action and precise language together with the notions of *humanitas* and *jen*. The character 仁 (*ren*) – the form of perfect virtue, and also the ontological-social process of person-making (Lan 86) – appears in *The Pisan Cantos* but as an integrated element of the text proper. It not only performs a grammatical function but is the 'thing' the alphabetic text points to:

> and for all that old Ford's conversation was better,
> consisting in *res* non *verba*,
> despite William's anecdotes, in that Fordie
> never dented an idea for a phrase's sake
>
> and had more humanitas 仁 jen (LXXXII/545)

The ideogram is glossed by the words around it rather than acting as a gloss itself.[15] The character is well chosen: Pound defines *jen* in his *Confucius* as the living out of the way of heaven on earth (22). It is a process, but part of the world of things rather than verbal discourse – the italicized Latin words above are significant, since Latin words are naturalized in other parts of the text and are not given distinctive typographic features. Pound draws back from a Yeatsean transcendental impulse, and grounds his principle within the materiality of the alphabetical text space, joining heaven to earth as well as China to Rome and to the Greek world.

Canto LXXXIII recounts (in ideograms) a tale by Mencius of the man who pulled up his corn, anxious to help it grow (552). The parable's moral, 'don't work so hard', is glossed from James Legge (531–32). The presence of ideograms diminishes quite dramatically later in *The Pisan Cantos*, but here it is naturalized into the poetic narrative. An important transition occurs in Canto LXXXIV, where three figures of ethical dissent in Chinese history, 'Wei, Chi and Pi-kan', are attributed with 'humanitas (manhood)/or jên³' (LXXXIV/559). The same equation is made between the Latin and Chinese attributes as that of Canto LXXXIII, but this time both are written alphabetically. The transliteration from the Chinese is accompanied by diacritical marks and the corresponding tone number: Pound uses such textual apparatus consistently only from *Rock-Drill* onwards. Romanized Chinese words does not replace ideograms, for at the bottom of the same page is another equation between (this time) Greek and Chinese moral attributes:

> quand vos venetz al som de l'escalina
>   ἦθος gradations
> These are distinctions in clarity

ming² 明 these are distinctions (LXXXIV / 559)

In these lines, Pound traces the idea of gradations from Dante's rendering of Arnaut Daniel in the *Purgatorio* to the Greek and English words and their glossed annotation, before silence replaces all utterances with the empty line (*tempus loquendi, tempus tacendi*). Finally, the romanized character *ming* is again presented in its ideogrammic form. It is Pound's 'total light' in script and in speech, and encodes his jeremiad against the system that perpetuates war and that fails to exercise its ethical and metaphysical ἦθος. His colourful reading of the character derives from that of Guillaume Pauthier – 'développer et remettre en lumière le principe lumineux de la raison que nous avons reçu du ciel' (45) – bearing its residual Christian iconography and Enlightenment impulse (Lan 24).

The final ideogram to appear in *The Pisan Cantos*, 中 (*zhong*), also entails its pictographic history within its form. Within the same passage as the *ming* ideogram and the raillery against economic bloodshed in war, Pound presents his last ethical man, John Adams:

> there is the norm of spirit

our 中 chung¹ (LXXXIV / 560)

The 'unwobbling pivot' provides the simple ideogrammic ethos with which to repair a culture and a civilization gone wrong (noting that the Faber text prints the ideogram upside-down and without its alphabetic counterpart and tone number). In the fragments of his epic many years later, Pound states:

That I lost my center
          fighting the world.
The dreams clash
          and are shattered –
and that I tried to make a paradiso
                   terrestre. (CXVII / 822)

The attempt to inscribe that *paradiso* articulates the problems of composition and transmission in *The Pisan Cantos*, where the relations between Chinese, Latin, Greek and the modern European languages are measured out on the page. The fate of the ideograms, from typescript to publication, belies the thought Pound had put into their presentation. This is perhaps one of the more radical (and ironic) sign of the text slipping from the reach of its author: a text otherwise so carefully constructed in the distribution of its text space and the relationships between its parts.

Pound's familiarity with several leading sinologists of his era (Guillaume Pauthier, James Legge, Herbert Giles, Arthur Waley and Ernest Fenollosa), and with the history of sinology in the West (Gottfried Leibniz, Alexander von Humboldt, Joseph-Anne-Marie de Moyriac de Mailla and others) is well documented. Pound's tendency early in his career to use ideograms as abstract nouns or as concept placemarkers was a flawed and partial view of the written language, but in certain instances it could be valid nonetheless. In those instances, Pound's working method resembles the notion of Chinese script proffered by Bernhard Karlgren, a leading sinologist who Pound had read by 1950 (*CON* 9): 'On the one hand, Chinese is *monosyllabic*, on the other hand, it is *isolating*, i.e. it treats the words as if they were isolated unities, without modifying them according to their function in the sentence' (Karlgren 1971, 10). The effect of discreteness was attractive to a poet who endorsed 'direct treatment of the thing', since the ideogram approached the status of an 'object' of writing.[16] Pound's understanding of Chinese grammar at the time of composing *The Pisan Cantos* was uneven. His ideographic interpretation of characters, inherited from Fenollosa and untenable for the written language as a whole, proved disarmingly effective in isolated cases, such as the example of 明 *ming*, which recurs in *The Cantos* as well as in a number of prose texts:

Sometimes, e.g. in 明 'bright' (= 'sun' + 'moon') the etymological formation of the character is still, after thousands of years, perfectly clear and consequently assists the memory. But for the most part [one] has no help at all of this kind, but has to hammer in, quite mechanically, the appearance of the character, its meaning, and pronunciation in a particular dialect. (Karlgren 1971, 51; see also Cooper 1985, 10)

By the time of *The Pisan Cantos*, Pound's conception of the Chinese character had developed beyond its function as a pictograph or an abstract noun. Pound considered Chinese a linguistic embodiment of the light of intelligence, and a method of illuminating the message inscribed within nature, government, currency and metaphysics: what Feng Lan calls *etymographic* reading.

Under the scrutiny of the etymographic reader, then, almost every ideogram in the Confucian texts can become a deep container of intellectual deposits. From Pound's point of view, however, it is the intrinsic richness of the ideogram, rather than the intent of the reader, that necessitates the etymographic approach. (31)

The ideograms in *The Pisan Cantos* uneasily inhabit a textual space between gloss, illustration and icon. They are not treated so much as written counterparts to speech as they are proof of Pound's extended argument for the *verbum perfectum*. This bears two important consequences. Firstly, although Pound's ideograms do not indicate relevant tones or pronunciations, they do demonstrate the indispensable role of Chinese script as the only adequate written form of the language (Karlgren 1971, 30). The written language embodies a nuanced and complicated message for those with the requisite conceptual and philosophical literacy. In Pound's text, the page space occupied by the ideogram encounters unanticipated effects, bringing out the text's internal history and inflecting the perceived role of the literary text.

The second major consequence of the ideogram is that the integrity of the script carries something of a national history and authority within it: the emergence of the Chinese people as a distinct nation. Pound's attention to the 'precise definition' of the written form of the language tends to elide differences of dialect. In his consideration of Chinese writing, Pound distinguishes the linguistic integrity of an empire from bordering, hostile populations lacking an integrated and widespread chirographic culture, such as the Mongols and Turkic groups in Western China (Pound fashions a similar relation between the Roman Empire and the Lombards and Huns in *The Cantos*). Further, the mechanics of the script's production on the page imparts its meaning and encodes the history of scripts and writing techniques. The development of small seal script, for example, greatly simplified the elaborate and varied scripts in the

Chou Dynasty (221–206 BCE), and was codified for the nation's scribes in an official catalogue by the minister Li Si (Karlgren 1971, 48). Such an historical resource within language makes Chinese an obvious paradigm for Pound: 'The character of the man is revealed in every brush-stroke (and this does not only apply to ideograms)' ('A Visiting Card', *SP* 293). Yet it is not certain how well he knew the history of Chinese writing, or that he saw his own texts embody their composition histories in complementary ways. Regardless of his intention, a subtle relation exists between his composition processes and the ideograms of *The Pisan Cantos* – a relation prone to the ironic divergence between intention and the uncertain transmission of ideograms into publication.

In his preoccupation with 'precise definition' and the *verbum perfectum*, Pound discovered a utility and ideological base in Chinese writing, the purpose of which 'since antiquity had been to promote good government and foster civilizing influences' (Chen 1988, 2). The *ku-wen* movement preceding the Tang Dynasty sought to correct the corrupting dominance of the parallel prose tradition by training the writer as a pioneer, who works in necessary isolation and without the luxury of being understood: 'Only when society encourages the cultivation of a special talent does the *ch'i* come to life in a writer to produce good literature' (8). The analogy with Pound is striking: it signals his perceived social role as poet earlier in his career and his process of gradual internal exile and estrangement. The compensating immersion in (and translation of) Confucian texts conforms to the idealist turn in Pound's thinking: 'when the *Ta Hio*, Great Learning ("Great Digest") is added [to the *Analects* and the *Mencius*] Confucius becomes systematic, and when the *Chung Yung* is added, the Doctrine of the Mean, what Pound was one day to call "The Unwobbling Pivot," he becomes metaphysical' (Kenner 1975, 446).

Pound's ideal *paideuma* – the coded and abbreviated ciphers of a vast store of knowledge that he tried to assemble in *The Cantos* – bears comparison with dense allusion in Chinese poetry: 'A Chinese author does not write for the *profanum vulgus* but for scholars as well stocked with learning as himself, and the various kinds of allusions are so recondite that the Chinese have found it necessary to compile large dictionaries of quotations and allusions for the help of the student' (Karlgren 1971, 92). The provenance and preservation of Chinese material in *The Pisan Cantos* entails a composition and transmission history of the text. The symbolic and functional status accorded to ideograms and Confucian doctrine was ingrained in Pound's formulation of exilic authority: 'the importance Pound placed on his ideograms in the text of *The Cantos* suggests their emblematic nature as to the force of precise definition, the *verbum perfectum*, and *sinceritas* in language' (Kern 1996, 8). These elements were subject to the contingencies of omission and distortion that the text's coded encyclopaedism tried to circumvent. They demonstrate the way in which Pound's notion of authority was resistant to history and political events. For Pound, it could ensure the integrity of thought and action even if philological correctness was lost in the transmission of the message. In each of these ways Pound's ideograms reflect similar contingencies to those exhibited in Eriugena's texts, providing an elegant counterpart to Pound's Hibernian *literatus*.

Pound's Confucius

Pound combines his Eriugenian and Confucian ideas at several critical points in *The Pisan Cantos*. The shared associations with light – divine light and the theory of emanations from Eriugena; and the 'light tensile immaculata' from Pound's translation of the *Zhong Yong* (*The Unwobbling Pivot*) – establishes a strong bond between ethics and metaphysics, and between political action and the cultivation of the self. The precarious transit of Chinese materials in *The Cantos*, especially that of the ideograms, highlights the fragile nature of material textuality in the case of *The Pisan Cantos* and affirms the attention Pound gives to matters of textual provenance in the form of glosses, citations, translation across languages and particular editions of works. Pound's study of the Eriugenian texts in PL 122 honed his attention to all of these issues, and the gradual but profound shift in his use of Confucian texts can be seen within this context of heightened textual awareness. In particular, Pound's translations of Confucian texts into Italian and then into English during the Second World War affirms a subtle but determined shift from the 'totalitarian' Confucius of *The Unwobbling Pivot* to the contemplative self-cultivation of *The Analects* and the *Classic Anthology* of the postwar years.

Pound's earlier poetic compositions in Italian in 1945 began in the zone of 'writing paradise', and he imported this idea, in part, into the rhetorical framework of *The Pisan Cantos*. Pound saw Eriugena as a model for the ideals of courtly wit, cultural mobility and philosophical acumen. His attunement to those qualities shared by Confucius – or more precisely the Western (and Westernized) portrait of Kung Fu Tzu – presented Pound with ample agency to conflate them in the aspiration to 'write paradise'. Although his notion of paradise was one postponed in the DTC and in the tragedy of war, Pound held to the idea through the sources most important to him: 'Pound was committed to the ideas that Confucianism could help create the earthly paradise that he believed could be achieved – in fact, at certain historical junctures had been achieved – the *paradiso terrestre* he intended to create a vision of in *The Cantos'* (Cheadle 2). Pound's first 'translation' of Confucius in the 1928 edition of *Ta Hio (The Great Learning)* – actually a translated text from Guillaume Pauthier's nineteenth-century French edition – coincided with his reading of Eriugena in Fiorentino's *Manuale di storia della filosofia* and *Compendio di storia della filosofia*. Both Confucius and Eriugena were mediated by other languages and the predilections of other scholarly minds, and it took years before Pound was able to begin breaking down that textual distance in both cases (his reliance on De Maille's *Histoire générale de la Chine* for the China Cantos in the mid-1930s is a case in point). During this phase of Confucian study, Pound made a declaration in 1934 that 'I believe the *Ta Hio*', 'namely the doctrines about the self, family, and social order advocated in the Confucian work *Da xue*' (Lan 2006, 5). Following his second phase of Eriugenian research Pound published a second attempt at translating *The Great Digest*, this time stemming from his own study of the Chinese text: this was published in Italian as *Confucio, Ta S'eu, Dai Gaku, Studio Integrale* in 1942 (also bearing its Japanese title) and in English as *The Great Digest* in 1947. Pound translated that text in the DTC using Legge's edition of the Four Books, acquired in 1937, and a basic Chinese-English dictionary. The preponderance of light imagery in the *Da Xue*, pertaining to the notion of enlightened rule, situates it as cognate with Eriugena's *Periphyseon*, which adapts Neoplatonism in its figuration of divine wisdom as light as well as in the theory of emanations binding human intellect to heaven.

Pound also translated and published *The Unwobbling Pivot* in Italian in February 1945, providing a title unmissable in its morale-boosting intention for the flagging Mussolini regime: *L'Asse che non vacilla* [*The Axis Never Wavers*]. He worked on a translation into English in the Pisan DTC, which was published in 1947. The political intent in these translations is evident in the way Pound establishes what he calls a 'totalitarian' vision for Confucianism in alignment with his views of the Fascist government: the thread joining all aspects of the Confucian world suffuses philosophical meditation with implicit action, working towards the betterment of the social order, and by extension, the cosmic order. Feng Lan is one among several scholars who sees this appellation as a grave misrepresentation of Confucian ideas (9). That Pound was drawn to Eriugena's Pseudo-Dionysian commentaries and translations is in keeping with such totalizing schemas. The *Periphyseon* brings this line of thinking to its apotheosis in rehearsing an *hexaemeron* (with all due deference to the rich Christian tradition, including Augustine, and the varied non-Christian genre of theogony stemming from Hesiod) and an eschatology, accounting for all of creation and all things that exist, as well as providing an exhaustive account of those things that do not exist: the Christian God by way of apophatic theology and superessentialism; and the privative *nihil est* of sin and condemnation, neither issuing from God and thus not properly existent. These sources suggest Pound's compulsion to develop a totalizing worldview during the 1930s and the war.[17] The many shared echoes and morphological resemblances among these texts affirm Pound's world-making project in *The Cantos*. This was all to change in 1945, on the collapse of the Fascist state, the execution of Mussolini and Pound's own arrest.

Some of the most celebrated passages in *The Pisan Cantos* perform tableaux of equanimity: the motions of a katydid, the views of surrounding mountains at sunrise, birds sitting on wires and composing an impromptu musical score, and the extensive operations of memory and textual citation that displace the ego scriptor from the confinements of the present. Whilst Cheadle sees such moments as 'more often Confucian than Neoplatonic' (4–5), several of these textual moments employ Eriugenian citation or allusion in a fusion of the contemplative philosophical virtues of East and West (reprising the blossoms of Canto XIII). But force of personality also brings Confucius and Eriugena together in *The Pisan Cantos*. In his (limited) reading of the ninth-century Predestination and Trinitarian controversies, and the book-bannings in Paris in the thirteenth century, Pound is well aware of the contentious nature of Eriugena's thought, complemented by wit and banter at the Carolingian court. As Pound makes clear in an essay of more than 20 years previously: 'Confucius' constant emphasis is on the value of personality, on the outlines of personality, on the man's right to preserve the outlines of his personality, and of his duty not to interfere with the personalities of others' ('Provincialism the Enemy', *SP* 163). Kung embodies and endorses a similar strength of character in Canto XIII in terms remarkably proleptic of Pound's reading of Eriugena in the court of Charles the Bald:

> And Kung said, and wrote on the bo leaves:
> > If a man have not order within him
> He can not spread order about him;
> And if a man have not order within him
> His family will not act with due order;
> > And if the prince have not order within him
> He can not put order in his dominions. (XIII / 59)

Pound's general knowledge of the political circumstances of Charles's rule was limited, but the pressures of viking incursions, the predations of his elder half-brothers and deep ecclesiastical divisions borne out in several bitter doctrinal disputes weigh Charles in the same scales of political acumen and character as Sigismundo Malatesta, Emperor Justinian II, Archduke Leopold of Tuscany and John Adams.

Pound was attuned to the metaphysical potentialities of Confucianism from the beginning. His Pauthier-inflected translation of *Ta Hio* in 1928 opens with a gesture towards the transcendental realm, perfectly in keeping with Eriugena's mediation of Pseudo-Dionysius: 'The law of the Great Learning, or of practicable philosophy, lies in developing and making visible the luminous principle of reason which we have received from the sky, to renew mankind and to place its ultimate destination in perfection, the sovereign good' (*TH* 7). The divine origins of reason transform in the world of political action as the governance of clear meaning, the 'precise definition of words' as Pound sets out at various points in his prose and in *The Cantos*, and as a series of glosses in the 1938 essay 'Mang Tze (The Ethics of Mencius)' (*SP* 95–111). This takes on a practical, immediate signification in the form of Morrison's dictionary Pound did not have with him in the Pisan DTC, but which was a sharper guide to the Chinese language than even James Legge's translation of the Four Books: 'In the Confucian translations, Morrison is Pound's true Beatrice' (Cheadle 39).

Pound's renewed impetus to translate Confucius during wartime endured difficult working conditions between his many other activities and obligations, reaching a perverse crescendo in the Pisan DTC. This partisan act of translation – the texts were first translated into Italian, not English – carried a burden of responsibility for the accuracy of his transformation of Chinese texts. He did not work in complete intellectual isolation, but relied upon Legge's philologically sound texts, and availed himself of Bernhard Karlgren's authoritative translations, although the conditions of his work must have aroused his sympathies for the lonely portrait of the Greek-speaking Irishman in the Carolingian court. According to Cheadle, matters of linguistic accuracy shift considerably after the war for Pound: his translations of *The Great Digest* (5 October–5 November 1945) and *The Unwobbling Pivot* (also late-1945) tend to espouse precise, unambiguous and direct meanings of characters. In contrast, the postwar translations of the *Analects* and the *Classic Anthology* provide the possibility for multiple readings of characters, as well as a sharper notion of semantic structures of characters in combination.

The value of Pound's Confucian translations lies less in their philological successes or failures than in their power to convey what he believed Confucianism should mean to the West. Where he follows Legge and Karlgren, Pound is orthodox enough. Where he diverges from these cribs, often in passages where he considers Legge's translations too abstract or vague, and often by using Morrison's pictographic definitions as his springboard, he reveals most what he valued in Confucianism (54).

This movement between exacting semantic correspondence and the nuances of Chinese script is most famously illustrated in Pound's reading of 誠 (*cheng*) which adorns the cover of *The Cantos* (or the inside flyleaf of the paperback edition): 'The precise definition of the word, pictorially the sun's lance coming to rest on the precise spot verbally. The righthand half of the compound means: to perfect, to bring to focus' (*CON* 20). Pound's fanciful reading of the Chinese character – an image of the definition of definition, no less – neglects to account for the fact that the right-hand side of the word functions phonetically, not semantically, and nowhere in the radical or the phonetic element is the sun invoked. The concept is given a deific role in Pound's Confucian cosmographia in *The Unwobbling Pivot* XXVI.4: 'With this penetration of the solid it has effects upon things, with this shining from on high, that is with its clarity of comprehension, now here, now yonder, it stands in the emptiness above with the sun, seeing and judging, interminable in space and in time, searching, enduring, and therewith it perfects even external things' (*CON* 181).

Pound's method of reading Chinese characters as residually pictographic and as instruments of unambiguous semantic precision is unorthodox and often misleading in specific cases. However, such esteemed Sinolinguists as Bernhard Karlgren have lent support to Pound's aptitude in translation from Chinese. Pound's pursuit of linguistic 'sincerity' is part of the project of establishing sincerity in action, at the level of individual citizen, ruler or collectively within the state: 'if the Confucian begins with the ethical and social basis of the doctrine of the rectification of names and extends it to logic, Pound began with a logical or at least aesthetic prescription and, under the influence of Confucianism, extended it to the ethical or social order' (Cheadle 67). This fusion of the ethical with the aesthetic, or the metaphysical, is evident in such translations as *The Unwobbling Pivot*: 'Pound's translation […] concludes with a vision of limitless light that merges the Confucian metaphysic with Neoplatonic light philosophy' (86). In that text, the leader's self-discipline entails 'defining himself to himself' (XX.17), which comprises a powerful analogy to the Neoplatonic theophany Eriugena delineates in the *Periphyseon*, where God comes into existence by defining himself to himself, by knowing *that* he is, if not *what* he is (Carabine 2000, 49). These affinities between

Confucian *sinceritas* – as Pound interprets 命 (*ming*), after Pauthier – and the cosmogony/eschatology of the *Periphyseon* delineate the kind of dialectical totalizing vision Pound pursued: 'Developed to the fullest, this "seeing into oneself" or "sincerity" [i.e. 命 (*ming*)] leads the individual to an awareness of the entirety of the universe' (Cheadle 98). It also harmonizes with Pound's Christian sources, demonstrated in Canto LXXIV in the line, 'paraclete or the verbum perfectum: sinceritas' (447): 'Pound deems the "heavenly process" of Sincerity compatible with the Christian Logos because, for him, both identify a similar source of Meaning' (Lan 72).

The shift from the 'totalitarian' translations in Italian in the early 1940s to the later Neoplatonically inflected English version of *The Unwobbling Pivot* of 1945 has been linked directly to the political and military destinies of the Fascist government during the war. Kenner claims that the full force of the 'totalitarian' phase of Pound's Confucian interests is under-represented in *The Cantos* due to the long hiatus between Cantos LII–LXXI, written in 1938, and *The Pisan Cantos* of 1945 (Cheadle 220). The fall of Salò and the arrest and execution of Mussolini in April 1945 weighed heavily on Pound's subsequent work. But this political-historical context is inflected by the earlier shift to Neoplatonism during the time when Pound gained access to Eriugena's texts in *Patrologia Latina* 122: 'The movement in Pound's interest in Erigena from his ethics to his metaphysics, especially to the metaphysics of light, corresponds precisely to a movement that occurred during the first half of the 1940s in Pound's Confucianism' (101). Pound's fanciful pictographic reading of 誠 (*cheng*) infuses Confucianism with a light philosophy on par with that of Pseudo-Dionysius, Eriugena and Grosseteste. This relation is compounded at XXVI.10 in *The Unwobbling Pivot* (*CON* 187), following a lyric concerning 'silky light':

Here the sense is: In this way was Wen perfect.

> The unmixed functions [in time and
> in space] without bourne.
> This unmixed is the tensile light, the
> > Immaculata. There is no end
> > > to its action

Pound deploys the same language in a famous passage early in Canto LXXIV – 'Light tensile immaculata/the sun's cord unspotted' (449) in which Eriugena is directly implicated. The gossamer threads of light, *sinceritas* and the correct principles of language draw Eriugena and Confucius together ever more tightly.

This radiates beyond Pound's English translation of *The Unwobbling Pivot*, however. Pound makes the cosmographical link in his Italian *Ta Hio* translation notes, now in the Beinecke Library (YCAL MSS 43 Box 94 Folder 3955):

> At bottom, or nearly at bottom, or near to the spiritual sphere, we have, it seems to me, a universe in sympathy (not to use stronger terms) with the thought of Scotus Erigena (without the eccentricity of Erigena), of Grosseteste, and of Albertus Magnus. A world of light; perhaps of the diaphanous, which fits with the spirit Guido Cavalcanti was immersed in before writing 'Donna mi Prega'.
> (qtd at Cheadle 101–02; Cheadle's translation)

The implications are clear: Eriugena provides Pound with a powerful cosmographical model, especially in the Pseudo-Dionysian translations and commentary, and in the *Periphyseon*. This model informs Cavalcanti, as we have seen, but also directly shapes the role he saw in Confucius, first as a political philosopher, and then on the collapse of his 'totalitarian' worldview, as a sage worthy of the most subtle Neoplatonists.

Pound's intensive attention to the definitions of words in Confucius demonstrates the valency he placed on this philosophical sympathy between East and West. His primary source for Chinese translation during the war years was his copy of Morrison's dictionary, and this directly shaped his developing terminology: 'He was reading Legge, who, usually translating 仁 (*ren*) as "virtue," notes that another translator suggests the Latin term *humanitas*' (Cheadle 89). On the other hand, the crucial definition of 中 (*zhong*) as circulation around 'l'asse' or the 'unwobbling pivot' seems one of Pound's own making, as there is no analogous definition in Legge, Pauthier, or Mathews (94). The example of 君子 (jun-zi) from the *Analects* is also illustrative of Pound's method: he gives the definition 'proper man', Morrison provides 'wise and virtuous man', for Mathews the word translates as 'princely man', for Pauthier 'l'homme supérieur' and for Legge, a 'student of virtue'. Pound's choice steers away from the implications of nobility or class superiority, and Cheadle sees a direct analogy with the careers of déclassé princelings, who, divested of any inherited political power as junior offspring, instead cultivate the self in their condition of disenfranchisement (121–22). There is great temptation to draw analogy with Pound's radically déclassé circumstances during the war, and profoundly concentrated at Pisa, although it is not clear how much of this historical context was known to Pound or how directly it influenced his choice of linguistic interpretation. The aura of contingency enveloping some of Pound's ideogrammic interpretations reaches a pivotal point in his reading of 正名 *zheng ming* (or, following Morrison, *ching ming*). This phrase identifies Pound's Confucian investments like no other, functioning as his working definition of 'precise definition':

> This is remarkable since these words do not occur at all in *The Great Digest* and *Unwobbling Pivot*, and only once in *The Analects* (XIII.2). For Pound, however, the phrase encapsulates the whole Confucian doctrine of the rectification of names. Enclosed in a letter of 1939 to Pound from Hugh Gordon Porteous was a full page describing how to write and pronounce 正名 (*zheng ming*) (close to 'jung' 'ming,' Porteous writes), and the pictographic etymology of the words. Evidently, Pound had asked Porteous about the character in a previous letter. (251–52)

This textual and linguistic fragility highlights the generally precarious nature of the transmission of knowledge: whilst Pound often uses a rhetoric of robust principles and unambiguous states of affairs – unwobbling pivot, precise definition – the realities of the cultivation and transmission of knowledge are altogether more contingent.

The exiled literatus: From Laon to Changsha

吾 已 矣 夫 *'I've only myself to rely on'* (*CON* 229)

Eriugena is perhaps unique in Pound's pantheon of cultural icons and thinkers: he functions for Pound as a pivot for both the Neoplatonic tradition, from which Pound drew extensively, and Confucianism, with which Eriugena obviously had no direct relation. The affinities Pound discerns between Eriugena's theology and the Confucian worldview expressed in the Four Books are complemented by his proximity to power in the Holy Roman Imperial court of Charles the Bald, and its resonance in Pound's mind with the principles of cosmic and social order in *The Unwobbling Pivot*. But in counterpoint to some of the austere metaphysical and political declarations – the 'precise definition of words' and the 'light tensile immaculata' – Eriugena's role as a victim of doctrinal decree and ecclesiastical hubris has him function as an exponent of *hilaritas* under the protection of his king, just as Pound's postwar Confucian focus begins shifting to the consolatory tones of the *Analects* and the *Classical Anthology*. Eriugena preserves and transmits precious cultural knowledge during darkened times: he inducts Eastern Christian theology and a working knowledge of the Greek language into the Latin West; and he carries over the late-classical Neoplatonist traditions of Plotinus, Porphyry and Proclus to its efflorescence in the twelfth-century Renaissance centred at the School of Chartres, and the Platonic Academy in Quattrocento Florence. He also transmits this knowledge in the form of his texts, and the means by which such knowledge is transmitted by way of glosses, the *accessus ad auctores*, florilegia and other lines of descent beside the scribal copying of monolithic texts. The precarious transit of texts and their contents is something Pound indexes throughout his writing career, and he installs a number of these references in *The Cantos* by his own glossatory practices, self-reflexive marginalia, citation of specific editions and an unusually acute, if eccentric awareness of the interplay of visual and semantic elements in textuality: words, ideograms, alphabets, rebus images, musical scores, footnotes, prose citations, letters and so on.

Eriugena comes to function as a *literatus* figure for Pound: a deterritorialized agent who cultivates aesthetic activity within a context of political displacement, and who waits out adverse circumstances precipitated by public statement (*De praedestinatione*) that contravened temporal (ecclesiastical) authority. Eriugena's case differs from the classical Chinese *literatus* in that he sought imperial protection, rather than anticipating imperial recall in exile. But the affinities with Pound's situation in the years leading to the composition of *The Pisan Cantos* are obvious, especially in Pound's ambiguous relation to power both in Mussolini's Italy and the United States Congress, which was to resolve itself negatively during the war and eventually in Pound's detention. The self-portraiture of the *literatus* in *The Pisan Cantos*, with its Eriugenian inflection, is not the first occurrence of this figure in Pound's poem. Canto XLIX, the 'Seven Lakes' canto, is distinguished for its navigation through such complex textual waters. It comprises an exercise in ekphrasis, across several cultural traditions, scripts and languages, and it occurs as one of Pound's iconic 'still points' in his epic poem. Had Pound kept to his original plan of 100 cantos, this canto would reside almost precisely in the middle, as its unwobbling pivot. The mood of these ekphrastic scenes reflects Daoist and Buddhist themes, and calls upon ancient poetic genres as well as a tradition of painting that stems from the Song Dynasty. This may seem odd at first sight, given Pound's purported antipathies to Daoism and Buddhism,[18] especially as they are rehearsed in the China Cantos that follow *The Fifth Decad of Cantos* in which Canto XLIX appears. But Canto XLIX may also be considered from a Confucian perspective, in the oratorical performance of the exiled *literatus*, the courtier contemplating his future in the southern lakeside country, awaiting recall to the Imperial court.

> The strategy of seeking self-protection in seclusion constitutes an important dimension of the Confucian doctrine of self-cultivation. Although Confucianism always requires one to actualize the values within oneself by participating in social construction, it also insists that one may justifiably retreat into solitude if that is the only way to protect the self from being contaminated or harmed by disruptive social forces. (Lan 130)

The affinities with Pound's image of Eriugena become even sharper within this framework: the exiled thinker whose brilliance has him seek refuge from ecclesiastical censure (the result of the Predestination controversy), and whose intellectual vision transcends his immediate milieu to encompass all of creation, space and time (the Pseudo-Dionysian translations and commentaries; the *Periphyseon*). Eriugena's heroic efforts to harmonize Latin learning with Greek Neoplatonic theology, and to broaden the linguistic and conceptual horizons of his king and fellow scholars, marks him out as a visionary scholar, philosopher and poet.

The 'Seven Lakes' canto momentarily suspends an exposition of eighteenth-century European cultural and economic inquiry of *The Fifth Decad of Cantos XLII–LI* (1937) in favour of an exotic aesthetic meditation. This poem is a collection of poetic translations from an album of painting and calligraphy (*tekagami*) given to Pound by his parents. The meditative pastoral verses comprising the greater part of the canto connect to more significant political and cultural discourses than might at first appear. The complex provenance of this material includes the Japanese album of painting and calligraphy that forms a bridge between its subject matter of Chinese traditions of painting and poetry, and underwrites the poetic experimentations Pound was to perform with Chinese materials in Canto XLIX and later in *The Cantos*. Close consideration of the relationship between the album and Pound's poem helps to identify why he would choose this series of images at this point in his epic, immediately before his concentrated attention to Chinese Dynastic history in the China Cantos to follow. The tone, timing and content of these creative translations in his epic poem provide insight into Pound's idealized view of East Asia as a model of order worth emulating in the immediate context of 1930s Europe, and modulates his alternate model of Neoplatonic sublimation. The complex ways in which Pound mediates word and image, between Chinese and Japanese sources and into an English-language poetic text, demonstrates that there is much more than aesthetic association at stake. Specifically, Pound marshals this material to support an increasingly fraught worldview, which seeks to combine Italian Fascist ideology with the civic vision of the American Founding Fathers, especially John Adams and Thomas Jefferson. More generally, he deploys East Asian aesthetics, and his views on the singular nature of the ideogram, as an aesthetic trope for the unity of ideas beneath the variegated tumult of history. The canto brings the very concept of the *paradiso terrestre* into sharp focus: the very project to which Pound was to turn in his wartime Italian canto composition following his work on Eriugena.

Canto XLIX is a short lyric piece comprising a sequence of translations of Chinese poems framed by several lines of Pound's original composition (XLIX/244–45). The dramatic change in tone and subject matter from the surrounding material gives this canto an aura of quotation, a physical and textual partition from its immediate context. In compiling and composing this canto, Pound draws on his experience in earlier poetic 'translations' or adaptations from Chinese – particularly his early volume *Cathay*. He also installs a strong bucolic sensibility in the canto that reaches across into other important sections of *The Cantos*. The effect of this aesthetic choice is to bridge the 'Eastern' sensibility of this canto with the American pastoral tradition in evidence at specific points in his epic, not least in *The Pisan Cantos*.[19] The effects of orientalism and American pastoralism converge in a suspended moment of contemplation, upon which the vigilant reader is then able to discern the significance of the source materials looming beneath this serene surface, and from which the strategic agency of the *literatus* figures across *The Cantos* may be contemplated.

Pound begins Canto XLIX with a grammatically ambiguous rhetorical statement in the voice of the *ego scriptor*, the narrating persona of *The Cantos*: 'For the seven lakes, and by no man these verses': (XLIX/244). The first word 'for' functions in at least two ways: it embeds a dedication indicating that the verses are 'for' (in homage to) the seven lakes; and it suggests that the following verses are produced by 'no man' (the *literatus* stripped of citizenship and political agency) as a means of illustrating 'thus' the seven lakes in poetry. The final colon in the first line functions deictically, pointing to and ushering in the verses to follow, like a raised curtain upon a stage. This is literally and figuratively a scene-setting which prepares the reader for the suspension of narrative and historical time at this point in the epic poem, and sets a tone for the ephemeral transience of the impressions in the 'verses' to follow. These impressions – scenes from nature intermingled with human activity – fuse visual perception with melancholic contemplation. The conventional schema of the displaced *literatus* ('no man') is invoked by the rhetorical placement of the poem at the interface of word and visual image in the genre of ekphrasis.

The canto does not provide a series of clear internal indications where each of the 'verses' begins and ends, or even what the plural of 'verse' might mean here, aside from the visual cue provided by divisions into verse paragraphs. The attentive reader will detect a change in tone two-thirds of the way through the canto, differentiating the 'Chinese' ekphrastic sections from Pound's own additions and other Chinese lyric materials towards its conclusion. Pound draws on several poetic and linguistic conventions in order to establish an orientalist mood: the brief lines rely on alliteration and assonance rather than on rhyme, and the descriptive mode makes reticent any affective tonality in favour of controlled observation. The preponderance of nouns and adjectives and the paucity of verbs and prepositions have the effect of slowing time and concentrating attention on the physical detail described in the bucolic scene, compounded by the absence of explicit human activity or wildlife until the belated appearance of birds (wild geese, clattering rooks) and young boys fishing for shrimp. This mood of aestheticism is compounded by reference to music – the 'tune amid reeds', for example – even suggesting the paraphernalia of Chinese painting, where the cinnamon spikes and the reeds might stand in for the brush. Pound uses poetic space and punctuation to create a semantic tension: the use of semicolons slows the tempo of reading, reflected semantically in the two semicolons bookending the word 'slowly', which mimics typographically the movement of boats on the river. Pound had the technical and perceptive range to produce the kind of atmospheric poetry demanded of the genre, even if he was entirely unaware of its strong and long-standing links with the poetics of exile.[20] Pound's poetic adaptation in Canto XLIX makes full use of the stock of familiar Chinese imagery at play in the text. His poetic adaptation displays an intuitive sense of the linguistic forms of *wenyan* or classical literary Chinese: a dexterity and suggestiveness prompted by the omission of verbs, conjunctions and prepositions, providing a sense of atmosphere by nuance and polysemy (Yip 2008, 127–28).

The scenes described in Canto XLIX might be seen to fit a stereotypical Chinese aesthetic, as though the speaker turns from one screen painting to the next on a visit to the East Asian Collection at the Boston Museum of Fine Arts,[21] transforming each one into an approximately 'Eastern' lyric. The pictorial origin for these verbal scenes is the album owned by Ezra Pound's parents, given to him in 1928 when he was living in Rapallo, Italy. This album has come to be known as the *Shō-Shō hakkei tekagami*: it is an album comprising eight painted scenes of the Xiao and Xiang rivers in Hunan Province (tributaries of the Yangtze converging near modern-day Changsha) each accompanied in triptych by a Chinese poem on the left and a transliteration into Japanese on the right. Such an album draws on the well-established artistic and poetic traditions of the 'Eight Views' (*hakkei*) of the Xiao and Xiang rivers (*Shō-Shō*), and functions as a primer of Chinese and Japanese calligraphy. This genre comprises a conventional iconographic range to which Canto XLIX closely conforms, and which might be schematized as follows: 'Night Rain', 'Autumn Moon', 'Evening Misty Temple', 'Sailboats Returning', 'Mist over Mountain Town', 'Snowfall over River', 'Wild Geese Returning' and 'Sunset over Fishing Village'. The album (*tekagami*) is thus made up of 24 panels in which each painting is framed by two poetic texts in different scripts. The physical layout of the album in a concertina format invites most Western readers to adapt customary reading patterns, reading from 'front' to 'back', two panels at a time (as in the image below), when instead the album is a series of triptychs, viewed from the 'back' and working to the 'front', then over and back to the point of commencement.[22]

The album in Pound's possession was produced in the late seventeenth century by a Japanese calligrapher of the Edo period (d.1722) by the name of Genryu, whose name appears on the last painting 'Sunset Over Fishing Village', and whose hand produces the calligraphy (although it is not known if he also produced the paintings). Wai-Lim Yip claims that the painter was inspired by painters of the Muromachi period (1336/38–1573), themselves following Chinese models laid down by Chan Buddhist painters of the Song and

Plate 3 (left) Autumn Moon, unidentified Japanese artist, (right) Chinese poem in hand of Genryu, *Shō-Shō Hakkei tekagami*, date unknown (Courtesy Mary de Rachewiltz, Brunnenburg, Italy)

Yuan Dynastic periods (Yip 2008, 132). Several Chinese and Japanese literary scholars (among them Achilles Fang and Sanehide Kodama) assert that Pound's translations comprising the larger part of Canto XLIX are of high quality and capture the spirit of the original poems as recorded in the *tekagami*. Pound had the benefit of informed Chinese guidance when the scholar Pao-sun Tseng visited Rapallo in 1928 and transliterated the Chinese poems for him (Taylor 1993, 338). Pound also drew upon his own intensive study and translation of Chinese texts during this time. Kodama observes that 'it is extremely difficult to decipher [the accompanying Japanese poems] without some historical knowledge of Japanese penmanship', and attributes them to three Edo period courtiers: Asukai Masatoyo (1644–1712), Sono Motokatsu (1663–1713?) and Takakura Eifuku (1657–1725) (Kodama 131, 133–34). Pound makes no mention of the Japanese poetic material, nor of its complex and varied calligraphic presentation.

A long and complex history looms behind this aesthetically refined object that came into Pound's zone of consciousness: a history of which it appears he was largely unaware. The *Shō-Shō hakkei* genre has poetic precedent in the later poems of the Tang poet Du Fu, and perhaps even in the earliest expressions of the archaic poetic *topoi* of exile and mourning.[23] The scenes are taken from geographical points ranging from the confluence of the two rivers near Changsha, north to Lake Dongting and then to the point at which they feed into the Yangtze, further north. The region is noted for its fogs, mists and rains, where mountainous scenery, forests and rivers seem to merge together in an indistinct scene. This haunting topography has inspired mournful, even melancholic poetry and painting, and has often been associated with states of actual or metaphorical exile. Song Di (c.1015–c.1080) executed the first known series of

Plate 4 (centre) *Sunset Over Fishing Village*, unidentified Japanese artist, (left) Japanese calligraphy and (right) Chinese poem in hand of Genryu, *Shō-Shō Hakkei tekagami*, date unknown (Courtesy Mary de Rachewiltz, Brunnenburg, Italy)

paintings of the 'Eight Views' following his dismissal from office and subsequent exile, and Shen Gua (1031–1095) composed the first known accompanying poetic sequence, drawing heavily upon the repertoire of Du Fu (Baker 2010, 10). Wang Hong (fl. 1131–61) painted the oldest known surviving sequence of paintings, now held in the Princeton University Art Museum. Despite the fact that these paintings have faded over the intervening 900 years, they still display the genre's evanescent imagery, where earth and sky blend in mist and fog. Associations of melancholy, and the sense of loss in exile, are easily imagined here. The genre came to Japan in the Kamakura and Muromachi periods when numerous Chan (Zen) Buddhist masters (such as Kenchoji) visited or settled and became abbots of important temples. Many Japanese monks also travelled to famous Buddhist centres in southern China at this time and absorbed the poetic and artistic genres of the region (Yip 2008, 200).

An attentive casual reader of *The Cantos* might not necessarily be aware that an actual album of artworks and poems (and calligraphy) stands behind the text – indeed an entire tradition stretching back a thousand years or more, spanning Chinese and Japanese painting and poetry as well as Buddhist and Daoist quietistic traditions. In addition, the average Western reader may not realise that the album itself demands to be read differently to Western concertina texts: that is, from right to left and in triptych rather than diptych. Yet there is more to the word-image relation being mediated between Eastern and Western sensibilities in Canto XLIX. There are matters of tone and register that alert us to the fact that this canto is a compound text. Following the 'Eight Views' the canto contains two further poetic adaptations and eight lines of Pound's own composition. These additional elements of the poem help clarify Pound's motivations in producing this poetic adaptation and its complex word-image interplay.

Plate 5 Wang Hong, *Sailboats Returning, Eight Views of the Xiao and Xiang Rivers* (*Xiao-Xiang ba jing*), ca. 1150, handscroll, ink and light colors on silk, 23.4 × 90.7 cm, China, Southern Song, Edward L. Elliott Family Collection, Princeton University Art Gallery

Two lines toward the end of the 'Eight Views' section of Canto XLIX refer to the northern and southern skylines. Another line lurks between the two horizons, in which the first named human subject, 'Tsing' comes into view: this figure is meant to portray T'ang Hsi,[24] the second Emperor of the Qing Dynasty, who is said to have visited the region depicted in the poems in 1699 (Kodama 131–38). The effect of this incursion is to break the suspended time and bucolic sensibility of the sequence by introducing the proper name of an Emperor and the appurtenances of the Imperial Court. This telescoping of history confirms the iconic status of the 'Eight Views of the Xiao and Xiang Rivers' throughout history, even drawing an Emperor to see them in person, as well as providing a link of association with the 'Clod Beating Song' to follow. This context, compressed into that one word 'Tsing', prepares the ground for Pound's four-line verse paragraph immediately before Pound's adaptation of two famous Chinese poems:

> State by creating riches shd. thereby get into debt?
> This is infamy; this is Geryon.
> This canal still goes to TenShi
> though the old king built it for pleasure (XLIX / 245)

These lines develop precisely the themes of the *Sacred Edicts* of T'ang Hsi, but by way of negative example, where the twin evils of Usury (interest on unproductive debt) and Geryon (fraud) preside over social decay. Pound provides a stark counterpoint here to the idyllic Buddhist/Daoist *paradiso* in the preceding 'Eight Views'. An Emperor who abuses his power unbalances the empire, the course of nature and the livelihood of all people. His responsibility is to maintain harmony in himself and the empire by acting in accordance with Confucian principles (Qian 2003b, 91).

The governing ekphrastic effect of the canto to this point is modulated by another kind of relation between word and image immediately following the bucolic scenes. The visually striking matrix formation of letters produces an effect where alphabet and ideogram converge:

KEI	MEN	RAN	KEI
KIU	MAN	MAN	KEI
JITSU	GETSU	KO	KWA
TAN	FUKU	TAN	KAI (245)

These letters possess little meaning for the average Anglophone reader, beyond signifying a vague gesture towards the visual dimension of non-alphabetic scripts. These 'words' or 'alphabetic ideograms' in fact constitute a (faulty) romanization of a Japanese transcription of a Chinese poem. The visual effect is intentional: the editor and printers of the first American edition of the poem complained about the author's strict requirement for uniform spatial presentation of each set of letters.[25] The clear message broadcast in these sixteen 'words' – that the spatial dimension of linguistic material is a site of specific hermeneutic intensity, especially in non-alphabetic scripts presented to Western readers of avant-garde poetry – indicates that the ekphrastic burden of the poem as a whole functions as a special kind of translation between artistic and poetic traditions. It is as though by estranging the Roman alphabet sufficiently it might be possible to capture a certain orientalist poetic sensibility. The sixteen 'words' constitute a Chinese poem known as 'Auspicious Clouds', transcribed by Ernest Fenollosa in his notebooks with the aid of Professor Mori. The script in Pound's poem is meant to represent the Japanese pronunciation of characters, but is to be read left to right. There are numerous errors, perhaps the most obvious of which is the 'KAI' word-ideogram at bottom right, which is supposed to be a repetition of 'KEI' above. James Legge's verse translation reads:

> Splendid are the clouds and bright,
> All aglow with various light!
> Grand the sun and moon move on;
> Daily dawn succeeds to dawn. (qtd in Fang 231–32)

Achilles Fang notes, incidentally, that this poem served as the anthem of the First post-Dynastic Chinese Republic in 1911 (Fang 1957, 232). The poem shifts the tone of the canto from the earlier pensive melancholia to an outright celebration of light and progress (the daily succession of dawn), telegraphing clear implications for robust physical activity, and social and political advancement.

The second additional poem follows immediately, and grounds the sensibility of 'Auspicious Clouds' in peasant labour. This is the so-called 'Clod-Beating Song', a traditional verse adapted by Pound into an Imagist poem:

> Sun up; work
> sundown; to rest
> dig well and drink of the water
> dig field field; eat of the grain
> Imperial power is? and to us what is it? (XLIX/245)

He transforms the lyric into a sharp, crystalline form with a terse, direct tone by freeing syntax and grammar. Although the poem might be taken to voice a fatigued resignation to habitual labour, other translations of the same poem by James Legge and Herbert Giles present the poem as a cheerful song celebrating the contentment of peasant life. Human activity is the pivot upon which the poem turns, in direct contrast to the earlier poems: the synchrony of cause and effect in the natural and human worlds serves to reinforce the sense of harmonious dwelling in the world, to the extent that Imperial power, the mechanism driving thousands of years of history, is of no significant consequence to the peasants. A spirit of harmony has reached down from the Emperor to the most humble farmer, leaving everything in its rightful place and in accord with the empire and the cosmos. In fact cause and effect crosses from nature to the human and back again: 'Sun up' (natural element), 'work' (human activity), 'dig well' (human activity) and 'drink of the water' (natural element). This chiasmic movement, back and forth between the human and the natural, sharpens the reader's attention to matters of productive human labour, a principal focus of the entire Leopoldine Cantos sequence in which Canto XLIX appears.

Canto XLIX thus functions effectively as an expression of Pound's endorsement of the Confucian worldview in the immediate historical context of 1930s politics. Balance within the self, on one hand, and balance with the family, social relations and the entire political and metaphysical order up to the Emperor and the cosmos, on the other, comprise twinned virtues just as usury and Geryon are twinned vices. The poem also accords with other cantos in the Leopoldine sequence, extolling centralized political and economic structures in eighteenth-century Tuscany (and, *inter alia*, clearly reflecting Pound's profound deference to Mussolini's political persona and policy action). But why would the poet present his case by way of a Japanese album of painting on Chinese themes and Chinese and Japanese calligraphy, the existence of which is mentioned nowhere in the canto, as well as a picture poem indecipherable to most of his readers? The answer resides in the final two lines of the poem: 'The fourth; the dimension of stillness./And the power over wild beasts.' The fourth dimension, of stillness, is also the dimension of time. This paradox, of time caught still, answers the rhetorical question of Imperial power: it is eternal, memorialized, captured in a visual image (a counterpoint to Keats's Grecian Urn, which reifies the event of animal sacrifice to the Olympian gods), and affords a rare power over nature and its resources, 'the power over wild beasts'. The fourth dimension also circles back to Eriugena and Cavalcanti, the reference sequestered in a preliminary draft of Canto XXXVI, only to re-emerge in this Canto as another 'magic moment', which is also a solitary moment of exile. In that manuscript note held at the Beinecke library, an early draft of Canto XXXVI is preceded by notes on Pseudo-Dionysius, Spinoza, and other matters, and contains the lines: 'The 4th dimension of stillness/the dimensions of/fixed relations' (YCAL MSS 43 Box 73 Folder 3258). Its context and ekphrastic demonstration clarifies what Pound saw in this cluster of Eriugena, Cavalcanti and the Chinese *literatus*, spanning across the surface of *The Cantos*, and across the decades of its composition as a function of textual memory: a compound ideogram of contemplation, *amor* and aesthetics.

But the power over wild beasts also belongs to the poet-musician Orpheus, and to Apollo. This double vision, of Chinese Imperial order and classical Greece myth, is simply a return to the first line and to the establishing voice of the entire poem. 'For the seven lakes, and by no man these verses' – everything that follows is anonymous, by no man. In Homer's epic Odysseus tells the Cyclops Polyphemus that his name is οὐ τις, 'no man', reprised by Pound in *The Pisan Cantos* in the line: 'ΟΎ ΤΙΣ/a man on whom the sun has gone down' (LXXIV/450). Pound authors Canto XLIX by a play at anonymity, simultaneously asserting the classical authority of both the poet-musician Orpheus and the epic wanderer Odysseus. The poem and its speaker thus absorb and assert the cultural authority of the poems and paintings caught in this fourth dimension – this stillness where word and image transmit across time and cultures, from classical Greece, eleventh-century China and seventeenth-century Japan, to the present tense of composition in the 1930s and to the immediate present of the moment of reading. Pound puts on the mask of Odysseus, who is himself masked by anonymity. He reminds the reader in the first and last lines of the poem that the intervening scenes, whilst a picture of a paradise on earth, is only a temporary stillness in his own epic. On turning the page, the reader is returned to the world of corruption, usury, fraud and the threats to political, imperial, natural and divine orders. Canto XLIX operates as a quiet exile from the fray, ironically drawing on the same Buddhist and Daoist aesthetic practices that Pound will consider threatening to Imperial power in the China Cantos to follow.

Canto XLIX demarcates the way in which Pound's Confucian interests converged with his Neoplatonic and Eriugenian interests from the 1930s to after the Second World War, and how each of those zones of interest changed in themselves. In the 1930s, Pound sought out a robust measure of temporal power in Confucian philosophy, legitimized by a metaphysics and ethics in such texts as the *Da Xue* (*The Great Learning*) and the *Zhong Yong* (*The Unwobbling Pivot*). During this time his Eriugenian interests fixed on political-ecclesiastical scandal in the various condemnations and book-burnings of the ninth and thirteenth centuries. The tone alters considerably in *The Pisan Cantos* and afterwards, where Pound shifts his focus to the contemplative and even consolatory tone of the *Analects* and the Confucian Odes. Eriugena too becomes an icon of urbane, courty *hilaritas*, shorn of temporal influence, but through his learning enabled by the same court, fuses Eastern Greek and Western Latin theological traditions into a totalizing vision in the *Periphyseon*, into a future paradisal vision in the *reditus*. Canto XLIX installs this suspension from the immediate temporal order, as it introduces a tableau (the 'fourth dimension') into the Leopoldine cantos: it demarcates a place for the *literatus*, who in exile and in deterritorialized impotence, can still call upon entire traditions of thought and aesthetics to produce a fragile vision of the *paradiso terrestre*.

Coda

The 'Note on Eriugena' never materialized, but Pound's work towards a comprehensive negotiation with the Hibernian pioneer in early medieval philosophy manifests itself in his prose and in *The Cantos*. Whilst wartime activities drew Pound away from writing his *paradiso*, in which Eriugena clearly was to play a prominent role, Eriugena still functions as a touchstone in *The Pisan Cantos*. These cantos represent and perform the acute culmination of Pound's immersion in Fascist politics, Confucian translation and the search to articulate the Neoplatonic chain of being as a means for modern temporal engagement and transcendence. These forces pull Pound in opposing directions, evident in the changing role of Confucian thought as alternatively an expression of 'totalitarian' integration of individual, state and cosmos, or as a mode of self-cultivation in the face of privative coercion and political defeat. Pound saw in Eriugena the expression of several aspects of learning and cultural engagement with which he could identify: the courtly wit, celebrated for his ingenious stitching of Greek into his poetry; the beacon of minority wisdom in bringing Greek learning and the Eastern patristic traditions into the Carolingian world; the unjustly accused defender of reason over blind adherence to authority; and the victim of political passions dressed up as doctrinal disputes. Pound was more correct than he knew about some of these dimensions to the life of Eriugena – indeed, had he known more, he may have divided his allegiance between Eriugena and Gottschalk of Orbais, or explored the minutiae of ecclesiastical politics through Hincmar of Laon. Pound adopts some of the various myths that had grown around Eriugena but questions others: Pound speculates anachronistically with regard to the earlier condemnations directed at Eriugena on the basis of those in thirteenth-century Paris enforced on a much wider scale (and, in the case of the 1277 prohibitions, included none other than Thomas Aquinas himself).

But Pound was right to see a powerful body of thought in Eriugena's translations of and commentaries on Pseudo-Dionysius, his remarkably extensive if imperfect knowledge of Greek in his prose and his poetry, and the monumental importance to subsequent medieval philosophy of Eriugena's masterpiece of dialectic – at once an *hexaemeron* and eschatology – in the *Periphyseon*. Pound's notes are fragmentary, often functioning as no more than mnemonic shards pointing to a larger, partly occluded context. They demonstrate an unfinished aspiration to think through Eriugena comprehensively, and to transform his findings into an ingredient in his poetic *paradiso*. Eriugena shares that level of Pound's pantheon with Confucius and Mencius, with Cavalcanti and with the brightest lights of the Neoplatonic tradition such as Robert Grosseteste and Gemisthus Plethon. These figures serve changing functions at different times – most explicitly in the case of Confucius – but their underlying commonality is their attempts to formulate systems of human action and contemplation, whether by means of theophany, a total social and individual ethical schema, or an access to the permanent world of the gods by way of the Platonic essences or Aristotelian Categories. Pound's later cantos may draw away from a full paradisal vision, but in the shards and fragments of such a vision, Eriugena keeps fleeting company with others in this pantheon. Eriugena is a touchstone for Pound, standing apart from his ideological fate and poetic career. In this sense he is both an ideal image of what might have been, and a consolatory epitome of *hilaritas*, of *humanitas* amidst the chaos of fallen empires. Pound's energetic, ideological activities of the 1930s and during the war may have ended in a certain patent sense of failure, but the divine threads of the Hibernian's thought reach back into Pound's epic, across time and place to its midpoint, the scene of the Seven Lakes Canto and the Chinese Imperial discourse of rustication. From Laon to Changsha, 'How is it far, if you think of it?'

Notes

1   For a recent, groundbreaking reappraisal of the extent of Pound's wartime radio broadcasts, see Feldman 2012.

2   Ming^2 [Mathews number 4534] is usually translated to mean 'light' or 'brightness'. Pound defines it as: 'the sun and moon, the total light process, the radiation, reception and reflection of light; hence the intelligence. Bright, brightness, shining. Refer to Scotus Erigena, Grosseteste and the notes on light in my [essay of 1934]

Cavalcanti' (*CON* 20). Hsien[4] [M2692] is translated as 'manifest' or 'clear' and represents a more general notion of illumination. For further discussion see Byron 2003, 225–38.

3   These last two phrases are taken by Makin from Pound's essay 'Cavalcanti' (*LE* 185) and *Impact* 177.

4   Pound omitted the last seven chapters of *Zhong yong* in his translation, *The Unwobbling Pivot*, and concluded instead with the section adumbrating the 'light tensile immaculata'. By doing so, he 'creates a universally appealing vision by combining the Confucian notion of the Heavenly Dao with the Neoplatonic notion of the divine light' (Lan 2006, 43).

5   This second instance occurs in a discussion of Fiorentino (and his spelling there of Eriugena) in the prose work 'Ecclesiastical History', first published in *The New English Weekly* on 5th July, 1934 (*SP* 61). See also *GK* 74, 164 and 333.

6   Paul Dutton confirms this link between poem and Papal garment, but takes the poem as the documentary evidence confirming the robe's existence: 'The *Liber pontificalis* relates that Charles presented a garment to [Pope] Nicholas made of gold and gems and we know that Ermintrude worked on one such robe given to Nicholas, since its dedicatory verses have been preserved' (Dutton 1986, 67–8).

7   This poem of 1916 encodes a philological trail that leads back to the badly damaged parchment salvaged in Egypt in 1896 and later redacted and published in Berlin (Kenner 1975, 5–6, 54–5). The fragment was redacted by J. M. Edmonds in the *Classical Review* in July 1909 (156). The same parchment contains the poem by Sappho rendered in her dialect (and discussed earlier), recurring in *The Pisan Cantos* at another moment of elegiac loss (56).

8   Tryphonopoulos traces the provenance of Pound's adaptation: he uses Iohannes Schweighaeuser's Greek-Latin bilingual edition of Athenaeus's *Deipnosophistae* and translates from the Latin, in order to check the Greek passages he transcribes into the canto. An emendation from the Athenaeus text inspires Pound to check his Liddell and Scott *Greek-English Lexicon*, in which he finds a Doric equivalent to the Attic word he originally sought, and two other variants of that word. All of this is placed into his text, with the *Lexicon*'s note, 'Derivation uncertain', appearing as a quotation within parentheses, and following this, a translation of the words – 'alixanthos, aliotrephès' (XXIII/107) – that frame the original word, Ἅλιος, in the *Lexicon* (Tryphonopoulos 1992, 128–30). In other words, when the mood arises, Pound can leave a clear trail of his textual and philological investigations.

9   Pound began translating *The Unwobbling Pivot* between 5 October and 5 November 1945, after drafting the larger part of *The Pisan Cantos* (Carpenter 1988, 688), demonstrating his preference for a Confucianism imbued with metaphysics.

10   Pound translates *Analects* XX.1.3 with a similar emphasis on metaphysical whiteness: 'I, the little child Li ("Shoe") ["T'ang"] dare to use the black victim; dare clearly announce to the Whiteness above all Whiteness above all kings, to the Dynasty Overspreading; dare not pardon offences, nor let those who serve the spread cloth of heaven be overgrown; their report roots in the mind of the O'erspreading' (*CON* 286–87).

11   The word derives from a parchment scrap transported from Egypt to Berlin in 1896 after being torn from a book of papyri transcriptions. Professor Schubart published the decipherable fragments in Germany in 1902, and J. M. Edmonds produced a reconsidered deciphering in the *Classical Review* of June 1909 (100–01). Aldington's version of 1912 was given the title, 'To Atthis (*After the Manuscript of Sappho now in Berlin*),' anthologised by Pound in *Des Imagistes* (1914) following Harriet Monroe's rejection of it for *Poetry*. Its exact contents and decipherment remain contentious today (see Kenner 54–9).

12   In a note appending the translation, Pound says, concerning this line: 'This is by far the better reading if the sonnet is spoken, but the other reading: *tremare l'are*, can be sung, and that perhaps explains the persistent divergence between the best manuscripts at this point' (*T* 38). In his Cavalcanti notebooks, Pound shows an unusual degree of interest in weighing up the relative merits of the variant lines among manuscripts in several libraries: see YCAL MSS 43, Box 114, Folder 4889.

13   Both Kenner (224) and Yee (243) identify the essentially taxonomic and static nature of the ideogram in Pound's early usage; Sieburth identifies its potential for change: 'Answering to a *natura naturans*, a nature in process, in the making, Chinese writing thus becomes a *scriptura scribens*, a writing in and of process' (19). Its philosophical suppleness is matched by its textual contingency in *The Cantos*.

14   From Tai T'ung's *History of the Six Writings* or *Liu Shu Ku*; see Hopkins 14–15.

15   This inversion of the conventional text/gloss relationship is symptomatic of what has been described as a redistribution of text material within the reader's frame: 'Like critics' clarifying schemata, the readers' mentally composed, perpetually contingent parallel narratives, each marginal fragment or footnote turns, on examination, into a new center of an endlessly reproportioned text' (Whittier-Ferguson 66). This process is not simply a hermeneutic process, but one enmeshed in the very distribution of the text on the page.

16   Cheadle sees in Pound's creative sino-hermeneutics an effort to ground his view of Confucianism as a practical philosophy buttressed in natural language:

> The elaborate account of Pound's interpretation of 敬 (*jing*) is offered not just as a demonstration of how far Pound could stray from the etymology provided even by the pictographic Morrison, but as a demonstration of how firmly committed

he continued to be to two related areas: the organic, concrete basis of the written Chinese language, and the worldly rather than transcendental orientation of Confucianism (137).

17   Cheadle makes the telling point that Pound's postwar Confucian translations, the *Analects* (1950) and the *Classic Anthology Defined by Confucius* (1954), demonstrate a stark departure from the rhetorical self-certainty of world-making in Pound's earlier efforts. Instead emphasis is placed on ritual and beauty, the precise use of language, and the frailty of human life: 'The closing poems [of the *Classic Anthology*] especially re-establish an aspect of Confucian philosophy that is relatively understated in *The Analects*: the Confucian ideal of social and political order and, ultimately, of a harmony of mankind with the natural and spiritual realms' (3). Pound works through this shift in his poetic composition in the Pisan DTC. The uneasy combination of political defiance, on one hand, and ritual and pastoral vision, on the other, is one of several 'fault-lines' Ronald Bush has identified in *The Pisan Cantos*: see Bush 1991.

18   Pound's negative rhetoric in the China Cantos is adopted whole from his source: in his 13-volume *Histoire Générale de la Chine*, Joseph-Anne-Marie de Moyriac de Mailla combined his Jesuitical suspicions of 'passive' Buddhist and Daoist systems of belief with those of his Chinese Imperial sponsors.

19   Sunsets and clouds predominate in *The Pisan Cantos*: in Canto LXXVI clouds appear 'in colour rose-blue before sunset/and carmine and amber' (479); in a later canto they are explicitly linked to an American pastoral sensibility when the poetic persona exclaims that 'The Pisan clouds are undoubtedly various/ and splendid as any I have seen since/at Scudder's Falls on the Schuylkill' (LXXVII/486).

20   Pound was to make use of this tradition of exile in *The Pisan Cantos*: not only in his recapitulation of imagery associated with the 'Eight Views' (clouds, sky, smoke, birds, etc.), but more completely in binding the pastoral genre with the political discourse of *rustication*, whereupon a court official retreats to the country and a life of fishing, to await invitation to return to the court. The Chinese traditions of painting and poetry are replete with famous examples of political rustication (Du Fu preeminent among them), reflecting its prevalence through history.

21   Ernest Fenollosa's large private collection of Japanese paintings formed the basis for the formidable East Asian Collection at the Boston Museum of Fine Arts (Fenollosa 2007, xxiii–xxv).

22   A facsimile of the *tekagami* comprises part of a box set edition with accompanying monograph (see De Luca 2004).

23   Qian recounts the myth of the daughters of the legendary Emperor Yao, who died on the banks of the Xiang in mourning for their husband Shun. Qian associates

this myth with the sound of rustling bamboo in Canto XLIX, which transforms the speaker into 'a Westerner seeking a way out of political chaos' (Qian 2003a, 136–37).

24　The benevolent rule of T'ang Hsi, second emperor of the Qing Dynasty, is the subject of two of Pound's subsequent China cantos, and his *Sacred Edicts* also provide the subject matter for two later cantos (XCVIII and XCIX) on matters of personal conduct, filial piety and harmonious social relations (Terrell 1984, 191).

25　Richard de la Mare of Faber and Faber wrote to John Easton of Robert Maclehose & Co. (the printers of *The Fifth Decad of Cantos*) on 9 April 1939 complaining of Pound's punctilious demands. The unpublished letter is housed in the Faber and Faber Archive in London (Taylor 1993, 351).

Appendix A

Francesco Fiorentino at Brunnenburg: An Annotated Transcription of Pound's Reading in Eriugena

There are five volumes of Francesco Fiorentino in Pound's library at Brunnenburg:

- (1921), *Manuale di Storia della Filosofia*, a cura di Giuseppe Monticelli, vol. 1. Filosofia Antica e medioevale. Torino: G. B. Paravia. [EP no 577a]
- (1924), *Compendio di Storia della Filosofia*, a cura di Armando Carlini, terza edizione, vol. 1. Filosofia Antica e Filosofia del Medio evo e del Rinascimento. Firenze: Vallecchi Editore. [EP no 574]
- (1929a), *Compendio di Storia della Filosofia*, a cura di Armando Carlini, terza edizione, vol. 2, parte prima (Parte III – La filosofia contemporanea [Bacon to Spencer]). Firenze: Vallecchi Editore. [EP no 575] [HB]
- (1929b), *Compendio di Storia della Filosofia*, a cura di Armando Carlini, terza edizione, vol. 2, parte prima (Parte III – La filosofia contemporanea [Bacon to Spencer]). Firenze: Vallecchi Editore. [EP no 577] [SB]
- (1929c), *Compendio di Storia della Filosofia*, a cura di Armando Carlini, terza edizione, vol. 2, parte seconda (Parte III – La filosofia contemporanea [Wundt to Bergson]). Firenze: Vallecchi Editore. [EP no 576]

The two volumes of the *Compendio*, vol. 2, parte prima, are identical. While all items listed are annotated to some degree, the *Manuale* is the most heavily annotated and will be the focus of this analytic description. Pound's annotative practices are straightforward: he underlines sparsely but strategically, signified in the following transcription by text in bold and underlined. Marginal glosses of Pound's authorship are transcribed within square brackets. The apparatus beneath the transcription provides cursory contextual information, but is not intended to serve a specifically bibliographical purpose (the record of variants, paralipomena and so on).

The initial chapters of Fiorentino (1921) run through the various Presocratic schools of Greece and their major adherents: the Ionic philosophers (Thales, Anaximander, Anaximenes), Eleatics (Xenophanes, Parmenides, Zeno), Pythagoras, Heraclitus, Empedocles, Democritus, Anaxagoras and the Sophists (Protagoras, Georgias). Then a very brief chapter is given to Socrates. Compare the relative scarcity of treatment for both Socrates and Plato (6 pages and 5 pages, although Plato is given another chapter of 10 pages dedicated to his doctrines), with the relatively generous space allotted to Aristotle (a chapter of 30 pages on his life and thought). One might speculate as to why Pound found little to say about the first two (despite his evident interest in Neoplatonism) and has a great deal with which to contend with Aristotle.

Manuale di Storia della Filosofia, a cura di Giuseppe Monticelli, vol. 1 [Filosofia Antica e medioevale] (Torino: G. B. Paravia 1921), 216–21 [EP no 577a]

> Capitolo IX. Prima età della Scolastica. – Giovanni Scoto Eriugena. (1)
>
> La scuola palatina instituita da Carlo Magno, prima vagante con la corte imperiale, poi stabilmente impiantata a Parigi, fu il nocciolo della nuova coltura occidentale: Alcuino, maestro dello stesso Carlo, Rabano Mauro, ne furono maestri; e dopo loro Scoto Eriugena, che fu maggiore di tutti. A tutte le dispute del tempo ei presero parte, richiesti dall'Imperatore; e le dipute erano ancora affatto teleologiche; ma di queste non è nostro compito discorrere, contenti di una breve menzione nell'altro capitolo. Nella filosofia stampò un'orma il solo Eriugena, del quale tocchiamo ora alquanto distesamente, perchè in lui troviamo il primo esempio dove la filosofia greca e la coscienza cristiana si trovano unite in un sistema. Di lunga mano superiore tentative de' sistemi teologici fatti da Giovanni di Damasco e da Isodoro di Saviglia, l'Eriugena si lascia addietro senza paragone le sdrucite raccolte di sentenze scritturali o patristiche intorno a questo o quel domma, alle quali solevasi dare il nome di ᵐειπαι, o di *catenae*.
>
> Giovanni detto Scoto, per accennare all sua origine scozzese, ed Eriugena, perchè Erin era il nome dell'Irlanda, detta allora *Scotia major*, fiorì il nono secolo; dove e quando precisamente fosse nato non si sa: certo che circa **l'anno 843** fu chiamato alla Corte di Carlo il Calvo a Parigi; probabile, secondo l'Haureau, che fosse morto in Francia circa l'877.
>
> Importante sopra tutte le sue opere sono i Cinque libri *De divisione naturae*; or celebrati oltre misura, or abbassati, secondo la varia inclinazione dei critici. Chi ci ha scorto una semplice ripetizione della filosofia neoplatonica cristianeggiata da Dionigi e commentata dal mo-

---

(1) Su Scoto v. E. K. Rand, *Iohannes Scotus*, Monaco, 1906.

Capitolo IX] This short chapter on Eriugena appears early in the medieval phase of the *Manuale*, following the initial chapters dealing with the various Presocratic schools of Greece and their major adherents. On the inside fly-leaf Pound includes the comment '207 Pseud.Dion!!!' – noting a citation of Pseudo-Dionysius in the preceding chapter.

l'anno 843] Fiorentino gives 843 as the year Eriugena was first known to be at the Court of Charles the Bald (although the court spent little time in Paris, and was peripatetic in any event). Note the mention of Eriugena's probable death in Charles's kingdom, not Britain.

> naco Massimo, e chi la prima manifestazione di una riflessione nuova, che non è più greca, ma cristiana e germanica. Il Baur imparzialmente giudica che c'è del vecchio e del nuovo; ch'è ultimo anello di una serie che si chiude; ed il primo di un'altra che incomincia: ma che è più ultimo che primo.
>
> Nell'Eriugena, che fu detto l'Origene occidentale, c'è certamente un ardimento che oltrepassa la misura dei tempi. Ritenendo, secondo l'intuizione fondamentale della Scolastica, l'identità della vera religione con la vera filosofia, egli se ne discosta nel valutare le relazione scambievole fra l'autorità e la ragione. *Auctoritas*, ei dice, ***ex vera ratione processit, ratio vero nequaquam ex auctoritate*. Così il primato della filosofia su la teologia** era propugnato contro all'opinione dominante allora. La Scrittura, per lui, è scritta in servigio de' nostri sensi rozzi ed infantili; bisogna che la ragione sappia intenderla: ci si vede una reliquiae dell'allegoria alessandrina.
>
> Inoltre, mentre a tutti l'intendere pareva un accessorio, e la salute dell'anima consisteva nel credere; a lui l'intendere pare non meno essenziale della fede. «*Animarum salus est... credere, et quae vere creduntur, intelligere*»: Sentenza rilevante ed insolita.
>
> In conformità di queste opinioni, l'Eriugena accoppia insieme la trascendenza di Dio con l'immanenza, quasi allo stesso modo che farà, molto tempo dopo di lui, il Cusano; il solo che gli si possa più da vicino assomigliare.
>
> L'opera *De divisione della natura* è scritta in forma di dialogo fra un maestro ed il suo scolare, ed è ripartita in Cinque libri, il cui contenuto è determinato dal soggetto stesso.
>
> La Fisi, sotto il cui nome egli intende tutto l'essere ed il non essere, è partita in quattro specie: 1° quella che crea e non è creata; **2° quella che crea ed è creata**; 3° quella ch'è ctrata e non crea; 4° quella che nè crea nè vien creata.
>
> Sotto la prima e la quarta s'intende Dio una volta come creatore, un'altra volta come fine di tutte cose. Sotto la seconda s'intende il mondo ideale, o le cause

Auctoritas... teologia] 'Authority, it was said, comes from right reason, but reason is by no means simply from authority. Thus the primacy of philosophy over theology...' This is the source for Pound's famous Eriugenian formula: 'Authority comes from right reason, never the other way on.'

L'opera... stesso] 'The work *De divisione della natura* is written in the form of a dialogue between a master and his pupil, divided into five books, the content of which is determined by the subject itself [i.e. each of the divisions implied in the title].' Note Fiorentino gives the title in a composite of Latin and Italian.

2° quella che crea ed è creata] 'the second [division] concerns that which is created and which creates', i.e. the realm of primordial causes, or from an Aristotelian-Augustinian viewpoint, the Ten Primary Categories.

> Primordiali; sotto la terza, il mondo in quanto apparisce nel tempo e nello spazio, ossia il mondo reale.
>
> I primi quattro libri trattano di queste quattro divisionin della natura, il quinto descrive il ritorno delle cose a Dio.
>
> [Arnaut?] Che cosa è Dio? Eriugena accetta le due teologie del l'Areopagita, l'affermativa, e la negativa, e preferisce pure l'ultima alla prima. A Dio appartiene l'essere, ma appartiene pure il non essere: si può chiamare con entrambi i nomi, ma meglio si direbbe nihilum, che ens, e quando si vuole chiamare con qualche nome positivo, bisogno aggiungere un sopra: **non essenza**, ma sovraessenziale; e così per tutt'i nomi.
>
> **Questa natura così infinita è incomprensibile, non solo agli altri, ma a se stessa: conosce di essere, ma non sa che cosa sia: ogni *quid* è un limite. Questa *divina ignorantia*, che fa pensare alla *docta ignorantia* del Cusano, è però la divina ed incomprensibile scienza.**
>
> Creando le cause primordiali, o il mondo ideale, questa natura infinita crea se stessa, comincia ad apparire nelle sue teofanie; ma non si conosce in nessuna di esse, perchè esse sono finite, ella infinita. Anzi il suo vero essere non comincia, se non in questa distinzione; «*descendens vero in principiis rerum, ac veluti seipsam creans in aliquo inchoat esse*».
>
> **Queste cause primordiali sono create, e creatrici**; le loro operazioni sono le creature realmente esistenti, le quali sono creatie, e non creano.
>
> Tra le cause primordiali e gli effetti loro; ovvero tra il mondo ideale ed il reale qual relazione v'ha?
>
> Sono la stessa natura considerate in due modi diversi (*modi theoriae*): *una eademque rerum natura aliter consideraturin aeternitate Verbi Dei, aliter in temporalitate constituta mundi*.
>
> [p 194 Greg Nissa] **La materia, ch'è la condizione della esistenza reale, è l'unione di qualità incorporee** «*ex incorporeis qualitatibus copulatur*».
>
> Eriugena dà questa dottrina come fondamento razionale della Trinità: la natura increata e creatrice è il

Arnaut?] Fiorentino begins a brief discussion on the first division of nature, that which creates but is not created (i.e. God). Eriugena follows Pseudo-Dionysius in proposing a dual theology: positive and negative, ultimately with a preference for the negative. Pound's annotation naming Arnaut Daniel is perhaps a speculative hint at the potency of apophatic representation: 'that which is not', which precludes describing God in terms of essence, thus 'non essenza'.

Questa… scienza] 'This nature [of God] which is infinite and incomprehensible, not only to others but also to itself: one can know that it is, but not what it is: every thing has a limit. This divine ignorance, that makes us think of the *docta ignorantia* [learned ignorance] of Cusano [Nicholas of Cusa], is, however, the divine and incomprehensible science.' Note Nicholas of Cusa wrote *De docta ignorantia* in 1440, on human insight into divinity.

descendens… esse] Fiorentino quotes from the *Periphyseon* 689B: '[God] descending into the principles of things, and, as it were, creating itself, it begins to know itself in something.' This is the notion of theophany: how God presents himself in sensible form.

Queste… creatrici] 'These primordial causes create, and are created.'

La material… copulatur] 'Material, which is the condition of actual existence, is coupled with incorporeal quality «*ex incorporeis qualitatibus copulatur*».' Pound's marginal note directs to the earlier chapter in the *Manuale* concerning Gregory of Nyssa's Neoplatonic view of 'two natures'.

Padre; la creata e creatrice, il Figlio; la creata e non creatrice, lo Spirito santo.

E poichè questi tre termini equivalgono a tre momenti di uno stesso processo: Dio in sè, mondo ideale, mondo reale; noi vediamo in lui che il processo teogonico della Trinità s'immedesima col processo cosmogonico della creazione. La medesimezza però non è tale che Iddio passi tutto nel mondo; rimane sempre quella indistinta ed inconoscibile sovraessenza, che constituisce il fondo oscuro della transcendenza divina. Eriugena talvolta parla di una conoscenza divina in sè, che non si distinguee, ma sa si attua nel Figlio soltanto, cioè nel mondo ideale, chè poi la stessa cosa del mondo reale: cè una oscillazione, che del resto non può recar maraviglia.

La Dialettica con cui dagli universali si discende agli individui, e viceversa da questi si risale a quelli è un'arte reale formata nella natura del suo autore, e non già escogitata da congegni umani. La vera sostanza, o realtà è l'universale, da cui si procede ai particolari per via di divisione; ed a cui si risale per via di complicazione.

L'uomo è il nodo della creazione, colui dove concorre la creazione invisibile e la visibile; detto perciò officina di tutte le creature, e loro conclusione: in lui tutte nascono, con lui cadono, con lui tornano a Dio, e si salvano.

Il processo divino si scorge nella triplicità delle sue energie: egli è Noo, è Logo, è **Dianoia**, come Iddio è Padre, è Figlio, è Spirito santo: le sue facoltà sono l'immagine della Trinità divina. [Arnaut]

Il Baur nota, che essendo l'essenza divina incomprensibile; e le differenze che noi vi ponghiamo avendo radice nel nostro modo di considerarla; possiamo ben dire che la triplicità delle nostre facoltà cogitative è il modello su cui è fondata la Trinità divina. Il sistema erigeniano qui difatti accenna all'idealismo.

Nè meno valore ha il concetto antropologico nella dottrina del peccato originale, e della redenzione.

L'uomo ideale era perfetto, finchè aderì alla causa primordiale, coiè finchè esistè realmente nel tempo. La

Dianoia] The Trinitarian account of the Nous, the Logos, and Dianoia corresponding to Father, Son and Holy Spirit: the Neoplatonic implications are clear, as are the those of Eriugena's theology of participation, in that human faculties are modeled on this trinitarian structure as a kind of image of divinity. Pound's annotation again refers to Arnaut Daniel, suggesting that the poet too propounds a concept of indwelling divinity in the human form and soul.

caduta non è avvenuta in un dato tempo; peccò, quando uscì dal paradiso, quando **uscì** dal mondo ideale: esistere **realmente è cadere**, la finità è il peccato. Che cosa è la redenzione? La riconciliazione della finità con la infinità. E poichè il peccato non è stato in un tempo, così Cristo, unità del divino e dell'umano, si è sempre incarnato. Se l'incarnazione non fosse avvenuta, sarebbero venute meno le ragioni delle cause che sono eternalmente nel Verbo di Dio: «*Si Dei Sapientia in effectus causarum quae in eternaliter vivunt, non descenderet, causarum ratio periret: pereuntibus enim causarum effectus nulla causa remaneret*». **Il che significa che l'incarnazione non è soltanto necessaria alla salute dell'uomo, ma alla conservazione del mondo ideale, coiè è necessaria allo stesso processo teogonico.**

Questa dottrina della redenzione corrisponde all'altra della creazione del mondo sensibile, la quale, secondo Eriugena, non avrebbe avuto luogo, se Dio non avesse preveduto la caduto del primo uomo: «*mundus iste in varias sensibilesque species... non erumperet, si Deus casum primi hominis, unitatem suae naturae deserentis, non praevideret*».

La caduta dell'uomo e la sua redenzione sono momenti del processo cosmico, e quindi del processo teogonico.

Or qual'è l'unità che l'uomo candendo perdette? L'uomo ideale non aveva divisione di sessi, non divisione di natura sensibile e d'intellettuale; viveva nel paradiso, coiè nelle cause primordiali, nel **Verbo**, e con lui vivevano indivise tutte le creature, di cui egli è centro.

Cadde, e questa unità si sparpagliò: bisogno radunarla da capo: redento l'uomo, le cose torneraqnno a Dio, vale a dire cesserà prima la dualità de' sessi poi la terra si unirà con cielo; poi le creature sensibili e le sprituali faranno tutt'uno, e saranno tutte spirituali; poi le spirituali si raduneranno con le loro cause primordiali; poi queste con Dio: l'appellazione di creature cesserà, Dio sarà tutto in tutti.

L'ardimento di questo pensatore solitario oltrepassa il suo secolo, e parecchi degli altri susseguenti; perciò non

uscì… cadere] Pound underlines phrases in a passage concerning the Fall, where humanity left the 'ideal world' of paradise, where 'to really exist is to fall into sin' as part of the drama of creation, salvation and reditus.

Si Dei… remanaret] *Periphyseon* V, 912B: 'if the Wisdom of God did not descend into the effects of the Causes which enjoy everlasting life in it, the principle of the Causes would perish' (Eriugena 1987, 585).

Il che significa… teogonico] 'This means that the incarnation is necessary not only for human wellbeing, but also for the conservation of the ideal world, and which is necessary for the same process of theogony.'

La caduta… teogonico] 'The Fall of humanity and subsequent redemption are moments in the cosmic process, and thus of the process of theogony.' This sentence is most suggestive of Eriugena's anthropology, that is, his notion of human participation in the divine plan, and the presence of the divine in human agents, a kind of indwelling theophany.

Or qualè… perdette?] 'What is the unity of man [*sic*] who has fallen into sin?'

È da maravigliare se la sua opera fu quasi dimenticata durante la prevalenza della Scolastica. Niccolò I disapprovò certamente l'Eriugena, non sappiamo se per questa, o per altra opera: ***Onorio III***, il 1225, poichè la seppe diseppellita per le ricerche che si facevano contro gli Albigesi, ordinò incontanente si bruciasse (1): la storia della filosofia non pòù a meno di additarla come un primo saggio di speculazione libera in tempi in cui tutti quasi si curvavano sott oil giogo dell'autorità. [fa criare = qualitat non discendo]

_____

(1) Scoto sorpassa il suo secolo per la sua estesa cultura (fatto unico nel sec. XI egli conosce il Greco, ha grande famigliarità coi Padri della Chiesa), per la sua elevatura filosofica che gli rende possible una sintesi, quando appena si balbettava di filosofia. Perciò non è da stupire se non fu subito compreso e se giunse tardi la condanna.

Onorio III] Pope Honorius III (1216–1227) continued the Albigensian Crusade in Languedoc: the preceding sentence notes Nicholas I's condemnation of aspects of Eriugena's thought, linked in theme by Fiorentino, and thus by Pound, to the Cathar suppression.

fa criare = qualitat non discendo] Pound's annotation concerning the eclipse of Eriugena's thought by the rise of Scholasticism (for which we may read Aquinas, as Pound proceeds to do).

Scoto sorpassa … condanna] 'Scottus [Eriugena] surpassed his century in the extent of his learning (he was unique in the ninth century in his proficiency in Greek, and his familiarity with the Church Fathers), for his lofty philosophy that enabled a synthesis, at a time when philosophy was barely more than stammering babble. Thus it is really no surprise that he was not well understood and was eventually condemned.'

Appendix B

YCAL MSS 53 Series II, Box 29 Folder 627 Cantos LXXIV–LXXXIV, Typescript Drafts in Italian

1r

ERIGENA [red pencil]

sure he's over there on the other soide wid dh christians
        but he will be runing off down into the owld pagody
             every now an then
to take a swat at the Florentines: and being at bottom eyetalyan
he looks wid a bad eye suspicious on whatever comes from
outside of there, or at any rate he cant take an ^a rale^ intherest
sure but the owld hook nose meant, well; he had a koind heart in
        him after all/when he cd/ foind it.
        Lo bons reis Corolous, BASILEOS, nella cui corte
Erigena teneva bel discorso
Filava Yrmintruda ^Yrmindruda^ e brodava   al fuso ed al pennocchio
a filo d'oro coi disegni equestre   ^vecchio^ ^specchio^
            auro subtilis serica fila parans
              Palladis arte

Ii nell borgo altro coi cristiani
indugia un po' sul suo gratticiclo
per ciaccherar e per sfogar rancuori
        va anche li a cercar argomento, e di sentir novelle
        cosi fra odia odio ed abitudine, odio nostalgico
del nido suo / or per dar lezion che nessun bada /

Dottor Ilare rispettò la ragione
bontà di Dio ebbe in guiderdone, d'ogni ciclo cittadino
        Omnia lunim lumina sunt /

che tutto è luce ed ogni cosa è ~~luce~~ lume
                              e non specchio
           ciò che esiste e luce e non specchio
                         e non e specchio morto, pur se rifletta
                         anzi in se contiene ~~i~~ luce, quinde esiste
                                   la
~~gaiz~~ gaiezza e splendore   /   rore
                                   rugianda

           Take now his letter to the big BowWow; Can Grande /

1v

fra nubi e nebbia cadon come foglie

2r

                         Erigena

Se prove fisiche e metafisiche avesse
Moise è i sporchi suoi furon ~~su~~ inope /
                 superflui
      e giù tornato ad aspettar bagalio (sbaglio)
           sbaglio; tornar più giù ad aspettar bagaglio
      vede di mal cocchi; tutto che non sia dello suo parocchia
      essendo italiano e toscano
           più ch I cantar / bagaglio / siode /
                      chi mai ha visto un arco con tre corde?
           Bigob oi tink oi putt him on dh roight track wid that translation
of Dionyaius / / He had koindly intentions /
      as in that letter to the big bowwow Can Grande / to t/ and
thought it was useful to the commonweal / non bleatin aesthete /
           qt / episte / C. G.

                 Anti Pius/not from others
                      misfortune
                 Cahou i braos/same bks /
           Brancus /   mais nous/
                 7 to = Kung.

      sure something dat wont sqush when he sits on it

something like a mathematical series /   like two and two equal four
tha wont squash when he leans up ferninst it.
            and dere are udder tings loik that, say Confucius;
      fer instance / things solid
You dont know what dey are / oi dont know what dey are
      but something He can sit down on /
all tings dat are are loights /

                              Dante/ sense/ not the thing but
                  the time

Bibliography

Ezra Pound: Manuscripts

Cavalcanti Notebooks, YCAL MSS 43, Box 114, Folders 4889–4894. Beinecke Rare Book and Manuscript Library, Yale University, New Haven.

Eriugena Notes I (c.1940), YCAL MSS 43, Box 76, Folder 3383, 26pp. Beinecke Rare Book and Manuscript Library, Yale University, New Haven.

Eriugena Notes II (c.1941–1945), YCAL MSS 43, Box 77, Folder 3406, 38pp., English and Italian, inserted within Cantos manuscript drafts in Italian. Beinecke Rare Book and Manuscript Library, Yale University, New Haven.

Eriugena Digression (n.d.), YCAL MSS 53 Series II, Box 29, Folder 627, 2pp., English and Italian. Beinecke Rare Book and Manuscript Library, Yale University, New Haven.

Ezra Pound: Primary Works

Pound, Ezra (1910), *The Spirit of Romance*. New York: New Directions. 1968

—— (1912), *Sonnets and Ballate of Guido Cavalcanti*. Boston: Small, Maynard.

—— (1915), *Cathay*. London: Elkin Mathews.

—— (1916), *Lustra*. London: Elkin Matthews.

—— (1928), *Confucius: Ta Hio*. ed. Glenn Hughes. Seattle: University of Washington Bookstore.

—— (1929), *Complete Works of Guido Cavalcanti*. London: Aquila unpublished.

—— (1932), *Guido Cavalcanti Rime*. Genoa: Marsano.

—— (1934), *Make It New*. London: Faber.

—— (1938a), *Guide to Kulchur*. London: Faber.

—— (1938b), 'Janequin, Francesco da Milano.' *Townsman* 1.1, 18.

—— (1942), 'Canto Proceeding (72 circa).' *Vice Versa* 1.3.5, 1–2.

—— (1945), *L'Asse Che Non Vacilla*. Venezia: Casa Editrice delle Edizioni Popolari.

—— (1948), *The Pisan Cantos*. New York: New Directions.

—— (1949), *The Pisan Cantos*. London: Faber.

—— (Spring 1950), 'The Analects.' *Hudson Review* 3.1, 9–52.

—— (1951), *ABC of Reading*. London: Faber.

—— (1953), *The Translations of Ezra Pound*. 1970 intro. Hugh Kenner. London: Faber.

—— (1954), *Literary Essays of Ezra Pound*. ed. T. S. Eliot. London: Faber.

—— (1958), *Pavannes and Divagations*. Norfolk, CT: New Directions.

—— (1959), *Selected Poems*. ed. and intro. T. S. Eliot. London: Faber.

—— (1960), *Impact: Essays on Ignorance and the Decline of American Civilization*. ed. Noel Stock. Chicago: Henry Regnery.

—— (1969), *Confucius: The Great Digest, The Unwobbling Pivot, The Analects*. New York: New Directions.

—— (1973), *Selected Prose 1909–1965*. ed. and intro. William Cookson. London: Faber.

—— (1978), *Ezra Pound Speaking': Radio Speeches of World War II*. ed. Leonard Doob. Westport and London: Greenwood.

—— (1993), *The Cantos of Ezra Pound*. Fifteenth printing. New York: New Directions.

Ezra Pound: Correspondence

Pound, Ezra (1950), *Selected Letters: 1907–1941*. ed. D. D. Paige. London: Faber.

—— (1985), *Pound/Lewis: The Letters of Ezra Pound and Wyndham Lewis*. ed. Timothy Materer. London: Faber.

—— (1994), *Ezra Pound and James Laughlin: Selected Letters*. ed. David M. Gordon. New York: Norton.

—— (1999), *Ezra and Dorothy Pound: Letters in Captivity, 1945–1946*. ed. Omar Pound and Robert Spoo. New York: Oxford UP.

Primary Works: John Scottus Eriugena

Eriugena, John Scottus (1853), *Opera Omnia quae Supersunt Omnia*. ed. Henry Joseph Floss. Patrologia Latina, vol. 122. ed. Jacques-Paul. Paris: Migne.

—— (1968), *Periphyseon (De divisione naturae)*. ed. I. P. Sheldon-Williams, with Ludwig Bieler. 4 vols. Vol. 1. Dublin: Dublin Institute for Advanced Studies.

—— (1972), *Periphyseon (De divisione naturae)*. ed. I. P. Sheldon-Williams, with Ludwig Bieler. 4 vols. Vol. 2. Dublin: Dublin Institute for Advanced Studies.

—— (1975), *Expositiones in Ierarchiam coelestem Iohannis Scoti Eriugenae*. ed. J. Barbet. Corpus Christianorum Continuatio Mediaevalis XXXI. Turnhout: Brepols.

—— (1981), *Periphyseon (De divisione naturae)*. ed. I. P. Sheldon-Williams, with Ludwig Bieler. 4 vols. Vol. 3. Dublin: Dublin Institute for Advanced Studies.

—— (1987), *Periphyseon: The Division of Nature*. trans. I. P. Sheldon-Williams, rev. John J. O'Meara. Montréal: Bellarmin Washington: Dumbarton Oaks.

—— (1993), *Carmina*. ed. Michael W. Herren. Dublin: Dublin Institute for Advanced Studies.

—— (1995), *Periphyseon (De divisione naturae)*. ed. Édouard Jeauneau, trans. John J. O'Meara and I. P. Sheldon-Williams. 4 vols. Vol. 4. Dublin: Dublin Institute for Advanced Studies.

—— (1997), *Glossae Divinae Historiae: The Biblical Glosses of John Scottus Eriugena*. ed. and intro John J. Contreni and Pádraig P. Ó Néill. Firenze: Sismel.

—— (1996, 1997, 1999, 2000, 2003), *Iohannis Scotti Eriugenae Periphyseon, Liber Primus; Liber Secundus; Liber Tertius; Liber Quartus; Liber Quintus, Editionem nouam a suppositiciis quidem additamentis purgatam, ditatem uero appendice in qua uicissitudines operis synoptice exhibentur*. ed. Édouard Jeauneau. Corpus Christianorum Continuatio Mediaevalis CLXI, CLXII, CLXIII, CLXIV, CLXV. Turnhout: Brepols.

—— (2001), *The Voice of the Eagle*. ed. and trans. Christopher Bamford, intro. Thomas Moore. Great Barrington, MA: Lindisfarne Books.

—— (2002), *Commentary on the Celestial Hierarchy of Saint Dionysius, Chapter VII, in Angelic Spirituality: Medieval Perspectives on the Ways of Angels*. trans. and intro. Steven Chase. Mahwah, NJ: Paulist Press, 166–186.

—— (2003), *Treatise on Divine Predestination*. trans. Mary Brennan, intro. Avital Wohlman. Notre Dame Texts in Medieval Culture. Notre Dame, IN: University of Notre Dame Press.

—— (2006), *Tutti i commenti a Marziano Capella*. intro, notes and critical apparatus Ilaria Ramelli. 1st ed. Milano: Bompiani.

—— (2008), *Homilia super 'In principio erat verbum' et Commentarius in Evangelium Iohannis*. ed. Édouard A. Jeauneau and Andrew J. Hicks. Turnhout: Brepols.

Secondary Works

Ahlqvist, Anders (1988), 'Notes on the Greek Materials in the St. Gall Priscian (Codex 904),' in *The Sacred Nectar of the Greeks: The Study of Greek in the West in the Early Middle Ages*, ed. Michael W. Herren. London: Kings College London Medieval Series, 195–213.

Alexander of Hales (1951), *Glossa in uqatuor Libros Sententiarium Petri Lombardi, in Librum Primum*. ed. V. Doucet, G. Gál et al. Florence: Quaracchi.

Alighieri, Dante (2011), *The Divine Comedy, Paradiso*. ed., intro. and trans. Robert M. Durling. New York: Oxford University Press.

Allard, G.-H., ed. (1986), *Jean Scot écrivain: Actes du IVe colloque international, Montréal, 28 août–2 septembre 1983*. Montréal: Bellarmin; Paris: Vrin.

Anderson, David (1983), *Pound's Cavalcanti: An Edition of the Translations, Notes, and Essays*. Princeton: Princeton University Press.

Bacigalupo, Massimo (1981), *L'Ultimo Pound*. Biblioteca di Studi Americani 26. Roma: Edizioni di Storia e Letteratura.

——— and William Pratt, eds (2008), *Ezra Pound, Language and Persona*. Quaderni di Palazzo Serra 15. Genova: Università degli studi di Genova.

Baker, Jennifer (2010), 'The Eight Views: From its Origin in the Xiao and Xiang Rivers to Hiroshige' MA Thesis. New Zealand: College of Arts at the University of Canterbury.

Baumann, Walter (2008), ' "In Principio Verbum": Seminar on Canto 74, Lines 76–145,' in *Ezra Pound, Language and Persona*, ed. Massimo Bacigalupo and William Pratt. Quaderni di Palazzo Serra 15. Genova: Università degli studi di Genova, 234–56.

Baur, Ludwig (1912), *Die philosophischen Werke des Robert Grosseteste. Beiträge zur Geschichte der Philosophie des Mittelalters*. vol. IX. Munster: Aschendorffsche.

Beierwaltes, Werner (1973), 'The Revaluation of John Scottus Eriugena in German Idealism,' in *The Mind of Eriugena*, ed. John J. O'Meara and Ludwig Bieler. Dublin: Irish University Press, 190–98.

———, ed. (1987), *Eriugena Redivivus: Zur Wirkungsgeschichte seines Denkens in Mittelalter unde im Übergang zur Neuzeit: Vorträge des V. Internationalen Eriugena-Colloquiums Werner-Reimers-Stiftung Bad Homburg 26–30 August 1985*. Heidelberg: Carl Winter.

——— (1990), *Begriff und Metapher: Sprachform des Denkens bei Eriugena. Vorträge des VII. Internationalen Eriugena-Colloquiums, Werner-Reimers-Stiftung Bad Homberg, 26–29 Juli 1989*. Heidelberg: Carl Winter.

——— (1994), 'Unity and Trinity in East and West,' in *Eriugena: East and West*, ed. Bernard McGinn and Willemien Otten. Notre Dame and London: University of Notre Dame Press, 209–31.

Berschin, Walter (1988), *Greek Letters and the Latin Middle Ages: From Jerome to Nicholas of Cusa*. trans. Jerold C. Frakes. Washington, DC: Catholic University of America Press.

Bett, Henry (1925), *Johannes Scotus Erigena: A Study in Mediaeval Philosophy*. Cambridge: Cambridge University Press.

Blumenthal, Uta-Renate, ed. (1983), *Carolingian Essays: Andrew W. Mellon Lectures in Early Christian Studies*. Washington, DC: Catholic University of America Press.

Bogin, Magda (1980), *The Women Troubadours*. New York: Norton.

Bonner, Gerald (1992), 'Augustine and Pelagianism.' *Augustinian Studies* 23, 33–51.

——— (1993), 'Augustine and Pelagianism.' *Augustinian Studies* 24, 27–47.

Booth, Edward (1983), *Aristotelian Aporetic Ontology in Islamic and Christian Thinkers*. Cambridge: Cambridge University Press.

Bornstein, George, ed. (1991), *Representing Modernist Texts: Editing as Interpretation*. Ann Arbor: University of Michigan Press.

Brennan, Mary (1986), 'Materials for the Biography of Johannes Scottus Eriugena.' *Studi Medievali ser* 32.27, 413–60.

——— (1989), *Guide des Études Érigeniennes/A Guide to Eriugenian Studies: A Survey of Publications 1930–1987*. Fribourg: Editions Universitaires Paris: Cerf.

Brown, Giles (1994), 'Introduction: The Carolingian Renaissance,' in *Carolingian Culture: Emulation and Innovation*, ed. Rosamond McKitterick. Cambridge: Cambridge University Press, 1–51.

Bruckner, Mathilda Tomaryn, Laurie Shepard and Sarah White, eds (1985), *Songs of the Women Troubadours*. New York: Garland.

Burch, George Bosworth (1951), *Early Medieval Philosophy*. New York: King's Crown Press.

Burnet, John (1930), *Early Greek Philosophy*. 4th ed. London: A. & C. Black.

Bush, Ronald (1976), *The Genesis of Ezra Pound's Cantos*. Princeton: Princeton University Press.

—— (1991), 'Excavating the Ideological Faultlines of Modernism,' in *Representing Modernist Texts: Editing as Interpretation*, ed. George Bornstein. Ann Arbor: University of Michigan Press, 67–98.

—— (1997), ' "Quiet, Not Scornful"? The Composition of *The Pisan Cantos*,' in *A Poem Containing History: Textual Studies in The Cantos*, ed. Lawrence S. Rainey. Ann Arbor: University of Michigan Press, 169–211.

—— (1999), 'Late Cantos LXXII–CXVII,' in *The Cambridge Companion to Ezra Pound*, ed. Ira B. Nadel. Cambridge: Cambridge University Press, 109–38.

—— (2010), 'La filosofica famiglia: Cavalcanti, Avicenna, and the "Form" of Ezra Pound's *Pisan Cantos*.' *Textual Practice* 24.4, 669–705.

—— (2013), 'Between Religion and Science: Ezra Pound, Scotus Erigena and the Beginnings of a Twentieth-Century Paradise.' *Rivista di Letterature d'America* XXXII.141/42, 95–124.

Byrne, Francis John (1984), 'Introduction,' in *The Irish Hand: Scribes and their Manuscripts from the Earliest Times to the Seventeenth Century, with an Exemplar of Irish Scripts*, ed. Timothy O'Neill. Dolmen Press: Mountrath, xi–xxviii.

Byron, Mark (2003), 'This Thing That Has a Code + Not a Core": The Texts of Pound's *Pisan Cantos*,' in *Ezra Pound and Referentiality*, ed. Hélène Aji. Paris: Presses de l'Université de Paris-Sorbonne, 225–38.

—— (2012), 'In a Station of the *Cantos*: Ezra Pound's "Seven Lakes" Canto and the Shō-Shō Hakkei Tekagami.' *Literature and Aesthetics* 22.2, 138–52.

—— (2013), 'Ezra Pound's "Seven Lakes" Canto: Poetry and Painting, From East to West.' ' *Eibei-Bungaku/The Rikkyo Review* 73, 121–42.

Callus, Daniel (1945), 'The Oxford Career of Robert Grosseteste.' *Oxoniensia* 10, 45–72.

—— (1955), 'Robert Grosseteste as Scholar,' in *Robert Grosseteste, Scholar and Bishop: Essays in Commemoration of the Seventh Centenary of His Death*, ed. Daniel Callus. Oxford: Clarendon, 1–69.

Capelle, Germaine Catherine (1932), *Autour de Décret de 1210: Amaury de Bène. Etude sur son panthéisme formel*, preface Étienne Gilson. Bibliothèque Thomiste 16. Paris: Vrin.

Cappuyns, Maïeul (1969), *Jean Scot Erigène: Sa vie, son oeuvre, sa pensée*. 1933, Bruxelles: Culture et Civilisation.

Carabine, Deirdre (1994), 'Eriugena's Use of the Symbolism of Light, Cloud, and Darkness in the *Periphyseon*,' in *Eriugena: East and West*, ed. Bernard McGinn and Willemien Otten. Notre Dame and London: University of Notre Dame Press, 141–52.

—— (1995), *The Unknown God: Negative Theology in the Platonic Tradition: Plato to Eriugena*. Louvain Theological and Pastoral Monographs 19. Louvain: Peeters Press.

—— (2000), *John Scottus Eriugena*. Great Medieval Thinkers. Oxford: Oxford University Press.

Carpenter, Humphrey (1988), *A Serious Character: The Life of Ezra Pound*. New York: Delta.

Cavanagh, Catherine (2003), 'Eriugenian Developments of Ciceronian Topical Theory,' in *Medieval and Renaissance Humanism: Rhetoric, Representation and Reform*, ed. Stephen Gersh and Bert Roest. Leiden and Boston: Brill, 1–30.

Chase, William (1972), 'The Canto as Cento: XXXIII.' ' *Paideuma* 1.1, 89–100.

Cheadle, Mary Paterson (1997), *Ezra Pound's Confucian Translations*. Ann Arbor: University of Michigan Press.

Chen, Yu-Shih (1988), *Images and Ideas in Classical Chinese Prose*. Stanford: Stanford University Press.

Clark, Mary T. (1978), 'Introduction,' in *Marius Victorinus: Theological Treatises on the Trinity*, trans. Mary T. Clark. Washington, DC: Catholic University of America Press, 3–44.

Contreni, John J. (1972), 'A propos de quelques manuscrits de l'école de Laon au IXe siècle: Découverts et problèmes.' *Le Moyen Age* 78, 5–39.

—— (1976), 'The Biblical Glosses of Haimo of Auxerre and John Scottus Eriugena.' *Speculum* 51.3, 411–34.

—— (1978), *The Cathedral School of Laon from 850 to 930: Its Manuscripts and Masters*. Münchener Beiträge zur Mediävistik und Renaissance-Forschung 29. München: Bei der Arbeo-Gesellschaft.

Cookson, William (1985), *A Guide to the Cantos of Ezra Pound*. London and Sydney: Croom Helm.

Cooper, Adam G. (2005), *The Body in St. Maximus the Confessor: Holy Flesh, Wholly Deified*. Oxford and New York: Oxford University Press.

Cooper, Arthur (1985), *The Creation of the Chinese Script*. 1978, London: China Society.

Courtenay, William J. (1989), 'Inquiry and Inquisition: Academic Freedom in Medieval Universities,' *Church History* 58.2, 168–81.

Crombie, A. C. (1953), *Robert Grosseteste and the Origins of Experimental Science, 1100–1700*. Oxford: Clarendon.

Dales, Richard C. (1982), 'Discussions of the Eternity of the World during the First Half of the Twelfth Century.' *Speculum* 57.3, 495–508.

—— (1990), *Medieval Discussions of the Eternity of the World*. Leiden and New York: Brill.

d'Alverny, Marie-Thérèse (1951), 'Un fragment du procès des Amauriciens.' *Archives d'histoire doctrinale et littéraire du Moyen Age* XVIII, 325–36.

Davenport, Anne Ashley (1999), *Measure of a Different Greatness: The Intensive Infinite, 1250–1650*. Studien und Texte zur Geistesgeschichte des Mittellaters 67. Leiden: Brill.

Davidson, Herbert A. (1992), *Alfarabi, Avicenna, and Averroes on Intellect: Their Cosmologies, Theories of the Active Intellect, and Theories of Human Intellect*. New York: Oxford University Press.

Davis, Leo Donald (1983), *The First Seven Ecumenical Councils (325–787): Their History and Theology*. Collegeville, MN: Liturgical Press.

De Luca, Maria Costanza Ferrero, ed. (2004), *Ezra Pound e il Canto dei Sette Laghi*. Diabasis: Reggio Emilia.

de Rachewiltz, Mary (1980), *The Catalogue of the Poetry Notebooks of Ezra Pound*. New Haven: Yale University Press.

—— (1997), '"Afterword: Ubi Cantos Ibi America," :A Poem Containing History: Textual Studies,' in *The Cantos*, ed. Lawrence S. Rainey. Ann Arbor: University of Michigan Press, 267–73.

Dickson, Gary (1987), 'Joachism and the Amalricians,' *Florensia: Bolettino del Centro Internazionale di Studi Gioachimiti* 1, 35–45.

——(1989), 'The Burning of the Amalricians,' *Journal of Ecclesiastical History* 40.3, 347–69.

Diels, Hermann (1934), *Die Fragmente der Vorsokratiker*. 3 vols. Berlin: Weidmannsche.

Dietrich, Paul A. and Donald F. Duclow (1986), 'Virgins in Paradise: Deification and Exegesis in «Periphyseon V»,' in *Jean Scot Écrivain: Actes du IVe Colloque international Montréal, 28 août – 2 septembre 1983*, ed. G.-H. Allard. Montréal: Bellarmin Paris: Vrin, 29–49.

Dondaine, H.-F. (1953), *Le Corpus dionysien de l'Université de Paris au XIIIe siècle*. Rome: Edizioni di Storia e Letteratura.

d'Onofrio, Giulio (1994), 'The *Concordia* of Augustine and Dionysius: Toward a Hermeneutic of the Disagreement of Patristic Sources in John the Scot's *Periphyseon*,' in *Eriugena: East and West*, ed. Bernard McGinn and Willemien Otten. Notre Dame and London: University of Notre Dame Press, 115–40.

Dronke, Peter (1984), *Women Writers of the Middle Ages*. New York: Cambridge University Press.

—— (1990), 'Eriugena's Earthly Paradise,' in *Begriff und Metapher: Sprachform des Denkens bei Eriugena*, ed. Werner Beierwaltes. Heidelberg: Carl Winter, 213–29.

——, ed. (1992), *A History of Twelfth Century Western Philosophy*. 1988, Cambridge: Cambridge University Press.

—— (2002), *The Medieval Lyric*. 3rd edition. 1968, Cambridge: D. S. Brewer.

Duclow, Donald F. (1977), 'Divine Nothingness and Self-Creation in John Scottus Eriugena.' *Journal of Religion* 57.2, 109–23.

—— (1994), 'Isaiah Meets the Seraph: Breaking Ranks in Dionysius and Eriugena?' in *Eriugena: East and West*, ed. Bernard McGinn and Willemien Otten. Notre Dame and London: University of Notre Dame Press, 233–52.

—— (2006), *Masters of Learned Ignorance: Eriugena, Eckhart, Cusanus*. Aldershot, and Burlington, VT: Ashgate.

Dutton, Paul Edward (1986), 'Eriugena, The Royal Poet,' in *Jean Scot Écrivain: Actes du IVe Colloque international Montréal, 28 août – 2 septembre 1983*, ed. G.-H. Allard. Montréal: Bellarmin Paris: Vrin, 51–80.

Eastman, Barbara C. (1979a), 'The Gap in *The Cantos*: 72 and 73.' *Paideuma* 8.3, 415–27.

—— (1979b), *Ezra Pound's Cantos: The Story of the Text 1948–1975*. intro. Hugh Kenner. Orono, ME: National Poetry Foundation.

Edmonds, J. M. (1909a), 'Three Fragments of Sappho.' *Classical Review* 23.4, 99–104.

—— (1909b), 'More Fragments of Sappho.' *Classical Review* 23.5, 156–58.

Eliot, T. S. (1934), *After Strange Gods: A Primer of Modern Heresy*. London: Faber and Faber.

Elkaisy-Friemuth, Maha and John M. Dillon, eds (2009), *The Afterlife of the Platonic Soul: Reflections of Platonic Psychology in the Monotheistic Religions*. Leiden and Boston: Brill.

Esposito, M. (1918), 'Priscianus Lydus and Johannes Scottus.' *The Classical Review* 32.1–2, 21–23.

Fang, Achilles (1957), 'Fenollosa and Pound.' *Harvard Journal of Asiatic Studies* 20.1–2, 231–32.

Feldman, Matthew (2012), 'The "Pound Case" in Historical Perspective: An Archival Overview.' *Journal of Modern Literature* 35.2, 83–97.

Fenollosa, Ernest (2007), *Epochs of Chinese and Japanese Art: An Outline History of East Asiatic Design*. 1912, Berkeley: Stone Bridge.

Fiorentino, Francesco (1921), *Manuale di Storia della Filosofia*. terza edizione. Vol. 1. Torino: Paravia.

Firmin-Didot, Ambroise (1875), *Alde Manuce et l'Hellénisme à Venise*: Paris: A. Firmin-Didot.

Fisher, Margaret (2002), *Ezra Pound's Radio Operas: The BBC Experiments, 1931–1933*. Cambridge, MA and London: MIT Press.

Frakes, Jerold C. (1988), 'Remigius of Auxerre, Eriugena, and the Greco-Latin *Circumstantiae*-Formula of *Accessus as Auctores*,' in *The Sacred Nectar of the Greeks: The Study of Greek in the West in the Early Middle Ages*, ed. Michael W. Herren. London: University of London King's College, 229–55.

Freeman, Ann (1957), 'Theodulf of Orleans and the *Libri Carolini*.' *Speculum* 32.4, 663–705.

—— (1965), 'Further Studies in the *Libri Carolini*: I. Paleographical Problems in Vaticanus Latinus 7207, II. Patristic Exegesis, Mozarabic Antiphons, and the Vetus Latina.' *Speculum* 40.2, 203–89.

—— (1971), 'Further Studies in the *Libri Carolini* III. The Marignal Notes in Vaticanus Latinus 7207.' *Speculum* 46.4, 597–612.

Freeman, Kathleen, trans. (1948), *Ancilla to the pre-Socratic Philosophers: A Complete Translation of the Fragments in Diels, 'Fragmente der Vorsokratiker.'* Oxford: Blackwell.

Froula, Christine (1984), *To Write Paradise: Style and Error in Pound's Cantos.* New Haven and London: Yale University Press.

Ganz, David (1981), 'The Debate on Predestination,' in *Charles the Bald: Court and Kingdom. Papers based on a Colloquium held in London in April 1979*, ed. Margaret Gibson and Janet Nelson. Oxford: BAR International Series, 353–73.

Gardiner, Alice (1900), *Studies in John the Scot (Erigena): A Philosopher of the Dark Ages.* London: H. Frowde, Oxford University Press.

Garrison, Mary (1994), 'The Emergence of Carolingian Latin Literature and the Court of Charlemagne (780–814),' in *Carolingian Culture: Emulation and Innovation*, ed. Rosamond McKitterick. Cambridge: Cambridge University Press, 111–40.

Géfin, Laszlo K. (1982), *Ideogram: History of a Poetic Method.* Austin: University of Texas Press.

—— (1992), 'So-shu and Picasso: Semiotic/Semantic Aspects of the Poundian Ideogram.' *Papers on Language and Literature* 28.2, 185–205.

Genke, Victor and Francis X. Gumerlock (2010), *Gottschalk and a Medieval Predestination Controversy: Texts Translated from the Latin.* Medieval Philosophical Texts in Translation 47. Milwaukee: Marquette University Press.

Gersh, Stephen (1978), *From Iamblichus to Eriugena: An Investigation of the Prehistory and Evolution of the Pseudo-Dionysian Tradition.* Leiden: Brill.

—— (1986), *Middle Platonism and Neoplatonism: The Latin Tradition.* Notre Dame: University of Notre Dame Press.

—— (1990), 'The Structure of the Return in Eriugena's *Periphyseon*,' in *Begriff und Metapher: Sprachform des Denkens bei Eriugena*, ed. Werner Beierwaltes. Heidelberg: Carl Winter, 108–25.

—— and Charles Kannengiesser, eds (1992), *Platonism in Late Antiquity.* Notre Dame: University of Notre Dame Press.

——, Charles Kannengiesser and Bert Roest, eds (2003), *Medieval and Renaissance Humanism: Rhetoric, Representation and Reform.* Leiden and Boston: Brill.

——, Charles Kannengiesser, Bert Roest and Dermot Moran, eds (2006), *Eriugena, Berkeley and the Idealist Tradition.* Notre Dame: University of Notre Dame Press.

Gibson, Margaret and Janet Nelson, eds (1981), *Charles the Bald: Court and Kingdom. Papers based on a Colloquium held in London in April 1979.* Oxford: BAR International Series.

Gilson, Étienne (1922), *La Philosophie au Moyen Age, I: De Scot Érigène a S. Bonaventure.* Paris: Payot.

Godman, Peter (1986), *Poets and Emperors: Frankish Politics and Carolingian Poetry.* Oxford: Clarendon; New York: Oxford University Press.

Goodman, Lenn E. (1996), 'Ibn Bājjah,' in *History of Islamic Philosophy*, ed. Seyyed Hossein Nasr and Oliver Leaman. London and New York: Routledge, 294–312.

Greeley, June-Ann (2000), *Social Commentary in the Prose and Poetry of Theodulf of Orleans: A Study in Carolingian Humanism*. PhD Dissertation. New York: Fordham University.

Grosseteste, Robert (1942), *On Light (De Luce)*, trans. and intro. Clare C. Riedl. Milwaukee: Marquette University Press.

Guthrie, W. K. C. (1962), *A History of Greek Philosophy, Vol. I: The Earlier Presocratics and the Pythagoreans*. Cambridge: Cambridge University Press.

Hall, Donald (1960), 'The Art of Poetry 5: Interview with Ezra Pound.' *Paris Review* 28, http://www.theparisreview.org/interviews/4598/the-art-of-poetry-no-5-ezra-pound.

Hankey, Wayne and Lloyd P. Gerson (2010), 'John Scotus Eriugena,' in *The Cambridge History of Philosophy in Late Antiquity: Volume II*, ed. Lloyd P. Gerson. Cambridge: Cambridge University Press, 829–40.

Hauréau, Barthélémy (1872), *Histoire de la philosophie scolastique*. 2 vols. Paris: G. Pedone-Lauriel.

Herren, Michael W., ed. (1981), *Insular Latin Studies: Papers on Latin Texts and Manuscripts of the British Isles, 550–1066*. Toronto: Pontifical Institute of Mediaeval Studies.

——, ed. (1988), *The Sacred Nectar of the Greeks: The Study of Greek in the West in the Early Middle Ages*. London: University of London King's College.

——, ed. (1993), *Carmina*. Dublin: Dublin Institute for Advanced Studies.

—— and Shirley Ann Brown (2002), *Christ in Celtic Christianity: Britain and Ireland from the Fifth to the Tenth Century*. Woodbridge, Suffolk; Rochester, NY: Boydell.

Holopainen, Toivo J. (2012), ' "Lanfranc of Bec" and Berengar of Tours.' *Anglo-Norman Studies* 34, 105–22.

Hopkins, L. C. (1954), 'Translator's Prefatory Note,' in *The Six Scripts, or the Principles of Chinese Writing*, ed. Tai T'ung, trans. L. C. Hopkins. Cambridge: Cambridge University Press, 3–16.

Illich, Ivan (1996), *In the Vineyard of the Text: A Commentary on Hugh's Didascalicon*. Chicago: University of Chicago Press.

Jeauneau, Édouard (1979), 'Jean Scot Érigène et le Grec.' *Archivum Latinitatis Medii Aevi (Bulletin du Cange)* XLI, 5–50.

——, ed. (1986), *Johannis Scotti Eriugenae Periphyseon, Liber Primus: Corpus Christianorum Contuniatio Mediaeualis CLXI*. Turnhout: Brepols.

—— (1987), 'La division es sexes chez Grégoire de Nysse et chez Jean Scot Érigène,' in *Études Érigéniennes*, Paris: Institut d'Études augustiniennes, 343–64.

—— (1988), 'Jean Scot: Traducteur de Maxime le Confesseur,' in *The Sacred Nectar of the Greeks: The Study of Greek in the West in the Early Middle Ages*, ed. Michael W. Herren. London: University of London King's College, 257–76.

—— and Paul Edward Dutton (1996), *The Autograph of Eriugena. Vol. 3 of Corpus Christianorum. Autographa Medii Aevi*, dir. Claudio Leonardi, comité coord. G. Cavallo, L. Holtz, and M. Lapidge. Turnhout: Brepols.

Karlgren, Bernhard (1971), *Sound and Symbol in Chinese*. 1923, Hong Kong: Hong Kong University Press.

Kemal, Salim (2003), *The Philosophical Poetics of Alfarabi, Avicenna and Averroës: The Aristotelian Reception*. London and New York: Routledge Curzon.

Kenner, Hugh (1975), *The Pound Era*. 1972, London: Faber.

Kenney, F. (1966), *Sources for the Early History of Ireland: An Introduction and Guide, 1. Ecclesiastical*. 1929, New York: Octagon.

Kern, Robert (1996), *Orientalism, Modernism, and the American Poem*. Cambridge: Cambridge University Press.

Kijewska, Agnieszka, Roman Majeran and Harald Schwaetzer, eds (2011), *Eriugena Cusanus*. Colloquia Mediaevalia Lublinensia 1 Lublin: Wydawnictwo Kul.

Kodama, Sanehide (1977), 'The Eight Views of Sho-Sho.' *Paideuma* 6.2, 131–38.

Laertius, Diogenes (1925), *Lives of Eminent Philosophers*, vol. II, trans. R. D. Hicks. 2 vols. London: Heinemann. New York: G. Putnam's Sons.

Laird, Martin (2004), *Gregory of Nyssa and the Grasp of Faith: Union, Knowledge, and Divine Presence*. Oxford and New York: Oxford University Press.

Laistner, W. M. L. (1924), 'The Revival of Greek in Western Europe in the Carolingian Age.' *History IX* 35, 177–87.

—— (1957), *Thought and Letters in Western Europe, A.D. 500 to 900*. Ithaca: Cornell University Press.

Lamaire, N. E., ed. (1825), *Poetae Latini Minori*. Vol. 4. Paris: Lamaire.

Lan, Feng (2006), *Ezra Pound and Confucianism: Remaking Humanism in the Face of Modernity*. Toronto: University of Toronto Press.

Lapidge, Michael, ed. (1997a), *Columbanus: Studies on His Latin Writings*. Woodbridge: Boydell.

——, ed. (1997b), 'Epilogue: Did Columbanus Compose Metrical Verse?' in *Columbanus: Studies on His Latin Writings*, ed. Michael Lapidge. Woodbridge: Boydell, 274–86.

Legge, James, trans. (1923), *The Four Books*. Shanghai: Chinese Book Company.

Lerner, Robert E. (1992), 'Ecstatic Dissent,' *Speculum* 67.1, 33–57.

Liddell, Henry George and Robert Scott (1883), *A Greek-English Lexicon*. 7th edition New York: Harper and Brothers.

Liebregts, Peter (2004), *Ezra Pound and Neoplatonism*. Madison: Fairleigh Dickinson University Press.

Little, Matthew (1985), ' "Atasal" in Canto LXXVI and Ernst Renan on Sufi Mysticism.' *Paideuma* 14.2–3, 327–29.

Louth, Andrew (1989), *Denys the Areopagite*. London and New York: Continuum.

Lucentini, Paolo, ed. (1974), *Honorii Augustodunensis Clavis physicae*. Temi e Testi 21. Rome: Storia e Litteratura.

—— (1987), 'L'eresia di Amalrico,' in *Eriugena Redivivus*, ed. Werner Beierwaltes. Heidelberg: Carl Winter, 174–91.

Ludlow, Morwenna (2000), *Universal Salvation: Eschatology in the Thought of Gregory of Nyssa and Karl Rahner*. Oxford and New York: Oxford University Press.

Luibheid, Colm (1987), *The Celestial Hierarchy, in Pseudo-Dionysius: The Complete Works,* foreword and notes by Paul Rorem, trans. pref. Rene Roques. New York: Paulist Press.

Lutz, Cora E., ed. (1944), *Dunchad: Glossae in Martianum.* Lancaster, PA: American Philological Association.

McCormick, Michael (1994), 'Diplomacy and the Carolingian Encounter with Byzantium down to the Accession of Charles the Bald,' in *Eriugena: East and West,* ed. Bernard McGinn and Willemien Otten. Notre Dame and London: University of Notre Dame Press, 15–48.

McDermott, John J. (1994), 'Ill-at-Ease: The Natural Travail of Ontological Disconnectedness.' *Proceedings and Addresses of the American Philosophical Association* 67.6, 7–28.

McEvoy, James (1987), 'Ioannes Scottus Eriugena and Robert Grosseteste: An Ambiguous Influence,' in *Eriugena Redivivus,* ed. Werner Beierwaltes. Heidelberg: Carl Winter, 192–223.

—— (1990), 'Metaphors of Light and Metaphysics of Light in Eriugena,' in *Begriff und Metapher: Sprachform des Denkens bei Eriugena,* ed. Werner Beierwaltes. Heidelberg: Carl Winter, 149–67.

—— and Michael Dunne, eds (2002), *History and Eschatology in John Scottus Eriugena and His Time.* Leuven: Leuven University Press.

McGinn, Bernard (1994), 'Ocean and Desert as Symbols of Mystical Absorption in the Christian Tradition.' *Journal of Religion* 74.2, 155–81.

—— and Willemien Otten, eds (1994), *Eriugena: East and West. Papers of the Eighth International Colloquium of the Society for the Promotion of Eriugenian Studies, Chicago and Notre Dame, 18–20 October 1991.* Notre Dame Conferences in Medieval Studies V. Notre Dame and London: University of Notre Dame Press.

McInerny, Ralph (1994), 'Introduction,' in *Thomas Aquinas, Commentary on Aristotle's De Anima,* trans. Kenelm Foster and Sylvester Humphries. Notre Dame, IN: Dumb Ox Books, vii-xxii.

McKeon, Peter R. (1974), 'Archbishop Ebbo of Reims (816–835): A Study in the Carolingian Empire and Church.' *Church History* 43.4, 437–47.

—— (1978), *Hincmar of Laon and Carolingian Politics.* Urbana, Chicago and London: University of Chicago Press.

McKitterick, Rosamond (1980), 'Charles the Bald (823–877) and His Library: The Patronage of Learning.' *English Historical Review* 95.374, 28–47.

—— (1981), 'The Palace School fo Charles the Bald,' in *Charles the Bald: Court and Kingdom. Papers based on a Colloquium held in London in April 1979,* ed. Margaret Gibson and Janet Nelson. Oxford: BAR International Series, 385–400.

——, ed. (1994), *Carolingian Culture: Emulation and Innovation.* Cambridge: Cambridge University Press.

—— (2004), *History and Memory in the Carolingian World.* Cambridge: Cambridge University Press.

—— (2012), 'Glossaries and Other Innovations in Carolingian Book Production,' in *Turning Over a New Leaf: Change and Development in the Medieval Manuscript*, ed. Erik Kwakkel, Rosamond McKitterick and Rodney Thomson. Studies in Medieval and Renaissance Book Culture. Leiden: Leiden University Press, 21–76.

Maccagnolo, Enzo (1992), 'David of Dinant and the Beginnings of Aristotelianism in Paris,' in *The History of Twelfth Century Werstern Philosophy*, ed. Peter Dronke. Cambridge: Cambridge University Press, 429–42.

Madec, Goulven (1988), *Jean Scot et ses auteurs: Annotations érigéniennes*. Paris: Etudes augustiniennes.

Maharaj, Ayon (2010), 'Why Poetry Matters: The Transpersonal Force of Lyric Experience in Ezra Pound's *The Pisan Cantos*.' *Arizona Quarterly* 66.4, 71–92.

Makin, Peter (1973), 'Ezra Pound and Scotus Erigena.' *Comparative Literature Studies* 10, 60–83.

—— (1985), *Pound's Cantos*. London: George Allen and Unwin.

Marenbon, John (1981), *From the Circle of Alcuin to the School of Auxerre: Logic, Theology and Philosophy in the Early Middle Ages*. Cambridge: Cambridge University Press.

—— (1988), *Early Medieval Philosophy (480–1150): An Introduction*. 2nd edition. London: Routledge.

—— (1997), *Aristotelian Logic, Platonism, and the Context of Early Medieval Philosophy in the West*. Aldershot and Burlington, VT: Ashgate/Variorum.

——, ed. (2000), *Routledge History of Philosophy: Vol. 3, Medieval Philosophy*. London: Routledge.

Markus, R. A. (1967), 'Marius Victorinus,' in *The Cambridge History of Later Greek and Early Medieval Philosophy*, ed. A. H. Armstrong. Cambridge: Cambridge University Press, 327–40.

Marler, J. C. (1994), 'Dialectical Use of Authority in the *Periphyseon*,' in *Eriugena: East and West*, ed. Bernard McGinn and Willemien Otten. Notre Dame and London: University of Notre Dame Press, 95–113.

Materer, Timothy (1995), *Modernist Alchemy: Poetry and the Occult*. Ithaca and London: Cornell University Press.

May, Gerhard (1994), *Creatio ex nihilo: The Doctrine of Creation out of Nothing in Early Christian Thought*, trans. A. S. Worrall. Edinburgh: T&T Clark.

Meyendorff, John (1994), 'Remarks on Eastern Patristic Thought in John Scottus Eriugena,' in *Eriugena: East and West*, ed. Bernard McGinn and Willemien Otten. Notre Dame and London: University of Notre Dame Press, 51–68.

Meyvaert, Paul (1977), *Benedict, Gregory, Bede and Others*. London: Variorum Reprints.

Michaels, Walter B. (1972), 'Pound and Erigena.' *Paideuma* 1.1, 37–54.

Milhaud, G. (1900), *Les Philosophes-Géométres de la Grèce, Platon et ses Prédécesseurs*: Paris: Félix Alcan.

Moody, A. D. (1982), '*The Pisan Cantos*: Making Cosmos in the Wreckage of Europe.' *Paideuma* 11.1, 135–46.

—— (1996), ' "They Dug Him Up out of Sepulture": Pound, Erigena, and Fiorentino.' *Paideuma* 25.1-2, 241–47.

—— (2007), *Ezra Pound: Poet: A Portrait of the Man and His Work. Volume I: The Young Genius 1885–1920*. Oxford: Oxford University Press.

Moran, Dermot (1989), *The Philosophy of John Scottus Eriugena: A Study of Idealism in the Middle Ages*. Cambridge and New York: Cambridge University Press.

Nadel, Ira B., ed. (1999), *The Cambridge Companion to Ezra Pound*. Cambridge: Cambridge University Press.

Nelson, Janet L. (1992), *Charles the Bald*. London and New York: Longman.

Nichols, Stephen G. (1980), 'The Light of the Word: Narrative, Image, and Truth.' *New Literary History* 11.3, 535–44.

Norman, Charles (1969), *Ezra Pound*, rev. edition. 1960, New York: Minerva.

Oderman, Kevin (1986), *Ezra Pound and the Erotic Medium*. Durham: Duke University Press.

O'Meara, Dominic J. (1987), 'Eriugena and Aquinas on the Beatific Vision,' in *Eriugena Redivivus*, ed. Werner Beierwaltes. Heidelberg: Carl Winter, 224–36.

O'Meara, John J. (1986), 'Translating Eriugena,' in *Jean Scot Écrivain: Actes du IVe Colloque international Montréal, 28 août – 2 septembre 1983*, ed. G. H. Allard. Montréal: Bellarmin Paris: Vrin, 115–28.

—— (1987), 'Eriugena's Immediate Influence,' in *Eriugena Redivivus*, ed. Werner Beierwaltes. Heidelberg: Carl Winter, 13–25.

—— (1988), *Eriugena*. Oxford: Clarendon; New York: Oxford University Press.

—— and Ludwig Bieler, eds (1973), *The Mind of Eriugena*. Dublin: Irish University Press.

Onéill, Pádraig P. (1986), 'The Old Irish Words in Eriugena's Biblical Glosses,' in *Jean Scot Écrivain: Actes du IVe Colloque international Montréal, 28 août – 2 septembre 1983*, ed. G.-H. Allard. Montréal: Bellarmin; Paris: Vrin, 287–97.

O'Neill, Timothy (1984), *The Irish Hand: Scribes and their Manuscripts from the Earliest Times to the Seventeenth Century, with an Exemplar of Irish Scripts*. Mountrath: Dolmen Press.

O'Rourke, Fran (2005), *Pseudo-Dionysius and the Metaphysics of Aquinas*. Notre Dame: University of Notre Dame Press.

Otten, Willemien (1990), 'The Universe of Nature and the Universe of Man: Difference and Identity,' in *Begriff und Metapher: Sprachform des Denkens bei Eriugena*, ed. Werner Beierwaltes. Heidelberg: Carl Winter, 202–12.

—— (1991a), *The Anthropology of Johannes Scottus Eriugena*. Leiden and New York: E. J. Brill.

—— (1991b), 'The Dialectic of the Return in Eriugena's *Periphyseon*.' *Harvard Theological Review* 84.4, 399–421.

—— (1994), 'Eriugena's *Periphyseon*: A Carolingian Contribution to the Theological Tradition,' in *Eriugena: East and West*, ed. Bernard McGinn and Willemien Otten. Notre Dame and London: University of Notre Dame Press, 69–93.

—— (2004), *From Paradise to Paradigm: A Study of Twelfth-Century Humanism.* Leiden and Boston: Brill.

Palmer, James T. (2004), 'Rimbert's *Vita Anskarii* and Scandinavian Mission in the Ninth Century.' *Journal of Ecclesiastical History* 55.2, 235–56.

Palusińska, Anna (2011), 'Christian Neoplatonism: Denys, Eriugena and Gothic Cathedrals,' in *Eriugena Cusanus,* ed. Agnieszka Kijewska, Roman Majeran and Harald Schwaetzer. Colloquia Mediaevalia Lublinensia 1. Lublin: Wydawnictwo Kul, 49–58.

Pauthier, Guillaume (1846), *Confucius et Mencius:Les quatre livres de philosophie morale et politique de la Chine.* Paris: Charpentier.

Pearlman, Daniel (1969), *The Barb of Time.* New York: Oxford University Press.

Pedersen, Olaf (1997), *The First Universities: Studium Generale and the Origins of University Education in Europe.* Cambridge: Cambridge University Press.

Perl, Eric (1994), 'Metaphysics and Christology in Maximus Confessor and Eriugena,' in *Eriugena: East and West,* ed. Bernard McGinn and Willemien Otten. Notre Dame and London: University of Notre Dame Press, 253–70.

—— (2007), *Theophany: The Neoplatonic Philosophy of Dionysius the Areopagite.* Albany: State University of New York Press.

—— (2010), 'Pseudo-Dionysius the Areopagite,' in *The Cambridge History of Philosophy in Late Antiquity: Volume II,* ed. Lloyd P. Gerson, Cambridge: Cambridge University Press, 767–87.

Philostratus (1912), *The Life of Apollonius of Tyana,* trans. F. C. Conybeare. 2 vols. Loeb Classical Library. London: Heinemann; New York: Macmillan.

Préaux, Jean G. (1953), 'Le commentaire de Martin de Laon sur l'oeuvre de Martianus Capella.' *Latomus* 12, 437–59.

Pryor, Sean (2011), *W. B. Yeats, Ezra Pound, and the Poetics of Paradise.* Farnham and Burlington, VT: Ashgate.

Qian, Zhaoming (1995), *Orientalism and Modernism: The Legacy of China in Pound and Williams.* Durham and London: Duke University Press.

—— (2003a), *The Modernist Response to Chinese Art: Pound, Moore, Stevens.* Charlottesville and London: University of Virginia Press.

—— (2003b), 'Painting into Poetry: Pound's Seven Lakes Canto,' in *Ezra Pound and China,* ed. Zhaoming Qian. Ann Arbor: University of Michigan Press, 72–95.

Quain, Edwin A. (1945), 'The Medieval Accessus ad Auctores.' *Traditio* 3, 215–64.

Rainey, Lawrence S., ed. (1997), *A Poem Containing History: Textual Studies in The Cantos.* Ann Arbor: University of Michigan Press.

Rand, Edward K. (1934), 'The Supposed Commentary of John the Scot on the *Opuscula sacra* of Boethius.' ' *Revue néo-scolastique de philosophie, deuxième série* 41, 67–77.

Redman, Tim (1991), *Ezra Pound and Italian Fascism.* Cambridge: Cambridge University Press.

Renan, Ernest (1861), *Averroès et l'averroïsme.* 2nd edition Paris: Michel Lévy Frères.

Rigord of Saint-Denis and William the Breton (1882), 'Gesta Philippi Augusti,' in *Oeuvres de rigord et de Guillaume le Breton, historiens de Philippe-August, 1*, ed. Henri F. Delaborde. Paris: Renouard.

Rolt, C. E. (1920), *Dionysius the Areopagite on the Divine Names and the Mystical Theology*, ed. and trans. W. J. Sparrow-Simpson. London: SPCK.

Roques, René (1975), *Libres sentiers vers l'érigénisme*. Roma: Edizioni dell'Ateneo.

Rorem, Paul (1993), *Pseudo-Dionysius: A Commentary on the Texts and an Introduction to their Influence*. New York: Oxford University Press.

—— (2005), *Eriugena's Commentary on the Dionysian Celestial Hierarchy*. Studies and Texts 150. Toronto: Pontifical Institute of Mediaeval Studies.

Salomon, David A. (2011), *An Introduction to the Glossa Ordinaria as Medieval Hypertext*. Cardiff: University of Wales Press.

Schäfer, Christian (2006), *Philosophy of Dionysius the Areopagite: An Introduction to the Structure and the Content of the Treatise On the Divine Names*. Philosophia Antiqua XCIX. Leiden and Boston: Brill.

Schrimpf, Gangolf (1982), *Das Werk des Johannes Scottus Eriugena im Rahmen des Wissenschaftverständnisses seiner Zeit: Eine Hinführung zu Periphyseon*. Münster: Aschendorff.

Schuldiner, Michael (1975), 'Pound's Progress: The "Pisan Cantos".' *Paideuma* 4.1, 71–81.

Sells, Michael A. (1994), *Mystical Languages of Unsaying*. Chicago: University of Chicago Press.

Sheldon-Williams, I. P. (1967a), 'The Pseudo-Dionysius,' in *The Cambridge History of Later Greek and Early Medieval Philosophy*, ed. A. H. Armstrong. Cambridge: Cambridge University Press, 457–72.

—— (1967b), 'Johannes Scottus Eriugena,' in *The Cambridge History of Later Greek and Early Medieval Philosophy*, ed. A. H. Armstrong. Cambridge: Cambridge University Press, 518–34.

—— (1968–95), *Periphyseon (De divisione naturae)*. 4 vols ed. with Ludwig Bieler. Dublin: Dublin Institute for Advanced Studies.

Sieburth, Richard (1986), 'Ideograms: Pound/Michaux.' *L'Esprit Createur* 26.3, 15–27.

Smith, Lesley (2009), *The Glossa Ordinaria: The Making of a Medeival Bible Commentary*. Leiden and Boston: Brill.

Stafford, Emma (1998), 'Masculine Values, Feminine Forms: On the Gender of Personified Abstractions,' in *Thinking Men: Masculinity and its Self-Representation in the Classical Tradition*, ed. Lin Foxhall and John Salmon. London: Routledge, 43–56.

Stahl, William Harris and E. L. Burge (1977), *Martianus Capella and the Seven Liberal Arts, Volume II: The Marriage of Philology and Mercury*. New York and Oxford: Columbia University Press.

Stock, Brian (1967), 'Observations on the Use of Augustine by Johannes Scottus Eriugena.' *Harvard Theological Review* 60.2, 213–20.

Stump, Eleonore (2001), 'Augustine on Free Will,' in *The Cambridge Companion to Augustine*, ed. Eleonore Stump and Norman Kretzmann. Cambridge: Cambridge University Press, 124–47.

Sullivan, Richard E. (1953), 'The Carolingian Missionary and the Pagan.' *Speculum* 28.4, 705–40.

Surette, Leon (1979), *A Light from Eleusis: A Study of Ezra Pound's Cantos*. Oxford: Clarendon.

——— (1993), 'Cavalcanti and Pound's Arcanum,' in *Ezra Pound and Europe*, ed. Richard Taylor and Claus Melchior. Rodopi: Amsterdam and Atlanta, 51–60.

Tavard, George H. (1996), *Trina Deitas: The Controversy Between Hincmar and Gottschalk*. Milwaukee: Marquette University Press.

Tay, William (1975), 'Between Kung and Eleusis,' *Paideuma* 4.1, 37–54.

Taylor, Richard (1993), 'Canto XLIX, Futurism, and the Fourth Dimension.' *Neohelicon* 20. 1, 337–56.

——— (1999), 'The Texts of *The Cantos*,' in *The Cambridge Companion to Ezra Pound*, ed. Ira B. Nadel. Cambridge: Cambridge University Press, 161–87.

Terrell, Carroll F. (1973), 'A Commentary on Grosseteste with an English Version of *De Luce*.' *Paideuma* 2. 3, 449–70.

——— (1984), *A Companion to the Cantos of Ezra Pound*. Berkeley, Los Angeles, and London: University of California Press.

Thacker, Eugene (2010), *After Life*. Chicago: University of Chicago Press.

Théry, G. (1925), *Autour de décret de 1210. I. David de Dinant. Etude sur son panthéisme matérialiste*. Paris: Bibliothèque Thomiste.

Thijssen, J. M. M. H. (1996), 'Master Amalric and the Amalricans: Inquisatorial Procedure and the Suppression of Heresy at the University of Paris.' *Speculum* 71.1, 43–65.

——— (1998), *Censure and Heresy at the University of Paris, 1200–1400*. Philadelphia: University of Pennsylvania Press.

Thometz, Joseph (2006), 'Speaking With and Away: What the "Aporia" of Ineffability Has to Say for Buddhist-Christian Dialogue.' *Buddhist-Christian Studies* 26, 119–37.

Thompson, R. M. (2007), *William of Malmesbury, Gesta Pontificum Anglorum: The History of the English Bishops, Volume 2: Commentary*. Oxford: Clarendon.

Thorndike, Lynn (1975), *University Records and Life in the Middle Ages*. 1946, New York: Norton.

Thunberg, Lars (1995), *Microcosm and Mediator: The Theological Anthropology of Maximus the Confessor*, foreword by A. M. Allchin. 2nd edition. Chicago: Open Court.

Tollefsen, Torstein (2008), *The Christocentric Cosmology of St. Maximus the Confessor*. Oxford and New York: Oxford University Press.

Tomasic, Thomas Michael (1988), 'The Logical Function of Metaphor and Oppositional Coincidence in the Pseudo-Dionysius and Johannes Scottus Eriguena.' *Journal of Religion* 68.3, 361–76.

Torchia, Joseph (1999), '*Creatio ex nihilo' and the Theology of St. Augustine.* New York: Peter Lang.

Törönen, Melchisedec (2007), *Union and Distinction in the Thought of St. Maximus the Confessor.* Oxford and New York: Oxford University Press.

Tryphonopoulos, Demetres P. (1992), *The Celestial Tradition: A Study of Ezra Pound's The Cantos.* Waterloo, ON: Wilfrid Laurier University Press.

T'ung, Tai (1954), *The Six Scripts, or the Principles of Chinese Writing.* trans. L. C. Hopkins. Cambridge: Cambridge University Press.

Turcescu, Lucian (2005), *Gregory of Nyssa and the Concept of Divine Persons.* Oxford and New York: Oxford University Press.

Usher, Jonathan (1996), 'Poetry. Part I: Origins and Duecento,' in *The Cambridge History of Italian Literature*, ed. Peter Brand and Lino Pertile. Cambridge: Cambridge University Press, 5–27.

Van Hulle, Dirk (2011), 'Modern Manuscripts and Textual Epigenetics: Samuel Beckett's Works between Completion and Incompletion.' *Modernism/Modernity* 18.4, 801–12.

—— (2013), 'The Extended Mind and Multiple Drafts: Beckett's Models of the Mind and the Postcognitivist Paradigm,' in *Early Modern Beckett/Beckett et le début de l'ère moderne*, ed. Angela Moorjani, Danièle de Ruyter, Dúnlaith Bird and Sjef Houppermans. Samuel Beckett Today/Aujourd'hui 24. Amsterdam and New York: Rodopi, 277–90.

Victorinus, Marius (1978), *Theological Treatises on the Trinity.* trans. Mary T. Clark. Washington DC: Catholic University of America Press.

Westra, Haijo Jan, ed. (1992), *From Athens to Chartres: Neoplatonism and Medieval Thought: Studies in Honour of Édouard Jeauneau.* Leiden and New York: Brill.

Wetzel, James (2001), 'Predestination, Pelagianism, and Foreknowledge,' in *The Cambridge Companion to Augustine*, ed. Eleonore Stump and Norman Kretzmann. Cambridge: Cambridge Uinversity Press, 49–58.

Whittaker, Thomas (1909), *Apollonius of Tyana and Other Essays.* London: Swan Sonnenschein.

Whittier-Ferguson, John (1996), *Framing Pieces: Designs of the Gloss in Joyce, Woolf, and Pound.* New York and Oxford: Oxford University Press.

William of Malmesbury (1998), *Gesta Regum Anglorum/The History of the English Kings*, ed. and trans. R. A. B. Mynors, completed by R. M. Thompson and Michael Winterbottom. 2 vols. Oxford and New York: Clarendon.

Wordsworth, William (2000), 'Lines written a few miles above Tintern Abbey,' in *The Major Works*, ed. Stephen Gill. Oxford: Oxford University Press, 131–35.

Yee, Cordell D. K. (1987), 'Discourse on Ideogrammic Method: Epistemology and Pound's Poetics.' *American Literature* 59.2, 242–56.

Yip, Wai-Lim (1969), *Ezra Pound's Cathay.* Princeton: Princeton University Press.

—— (2008), *Pound and the Eight Views of Xiao Xian.* Taipei: National Taiwan University.

Index of Works by Pound

Note: Locators followed by the letter 'n' refer to notes.

ABC of Reading 22, 213
Analects, The xv, 233, 234, 237, 240–1, 252, 256n. 10, 257n. 17
see also *Confucius*

Cantos, The
  I 173, 220, 222
  XXXVI 1, 4, 6, 9–10, 22, 24–5, 30, 31–45, 48n. 20, 49n. 24, 70, 113, 153, 166, 209, 213, 251
  XXXIX 31
  XL 31
  XLI 31
  XLIX, the 'Seven Lakes' canto 8, 157, 177, 197, 208, 242–53, 258n. 23
  LXXIV 25, 42, 98, 123, 166, 193, 209–13, 223–4, 227, 239, 252, 267
  LXXX 201, 203, 221, 223, 224, 267
  LXXXIII 23, 25–6, 42, 100, 102, 116, 147, 168, 212–14, 223, 225, 230
  LXXXIV 6, 230
  LXXXVII 215, 219
  LXXXVIII 225
  XCVIII 180, 215, 258n. 24
  CXIX 258n. 24
  CV 22
  CX 200
  glossatory practices in 6–8, 10–11, 35, 45, 115, 210–11, 223, 225, 228–32, 234, 237, 242, 256n. 15
'Cavalcanti' 33, 36, 45, 70, 221, 255n. 3
Classic Anthology Definied by Confucius 234, 237, 257n. 17

Complete Works of Guido Cavalcanti 33
Confucius 83, 226, 229, 231, 234–41

'Ezra Pound Speaking' 221

Great Digest, The (Da Xue) 215, 233, 235, 237, 241
see also *Confucius*
Guide to Kulchur 4, 9, 16, 22–3, 28–30, 49n. 29, 68, 163, 213, 217, 218–20, 226, 255n. 5
Guido Cavalcanti Rime 33, 45, 48n. 22

'Immediate Need of Confucius' 28, 29
Impact: Essays on Ignorance and the Decline of American Civilization 255n. 3

Literary Essays of Ezra Pound 255n. 3

Make It New xv, 13, 15–16, 32–8, 41, 43, 48n. 21, 153, 215, 221

Selected Prose 20, 22–4, 28, 29, 46n. 7, 49n. 29, 219, 233, 236, 237, 255n. 5
Sonnets and Ballate of Guido Cavalcanti 32–3
Spirit of Romance, The 32

Ta Hio 117, 233, 235, 237, 240
see also *Confucius; Great Digest*

Unwobbling Pivot, The (Zhong Yong) 85, 98, 211, 233–5, 237–42, 252, 255n. 4, 255n. 9
see also *Confucius*

Index of Works by Eriugena

Note: Locators followed by the letter 'n' refer to notes.

Carmina 11, 20–1, 52, 100–2, 104–5, 109,
    111–13, 130, 136, 142–3, 147–52,
    172–4, 201–2, 214–16

*Epigramma in beatum Dionysium de
    caelesti Ierarchia* 142–3
*Expositiones in Mysticam
    Theologiam S. Dionysii* 170–2, 202
*Expositiones Super Ierarchian Caelestiam
    S. Dionysii* 84–9, 96, 115–16, 121–9,
    143, 153–70, 177, 180–3, 196,
    201–3, 211

Periphyseon / De Divisione naturae xvii,
    4–7, 10–11, 14n. 3, 17–18, 20–2,
    25, 27, 30, 42, 43, 46–7, 49n. 31,
    52, 57–100, 106, 106nn. 2, 3,
    107n. 10, 108, 110nn. 29, 32, 113,
    115–16, 118, 128–9, 131–6, 140–1,
    151, 160, 164, 168, 170, 176–8,
    183–93, 197–8, 202–4, 210–12,
    225, 235, 238–40, 243, 253–4,
    263, 265
    eschatology in 5, 7, 10, 89, 113–14, 134,
        210, 235, 239
    hexaemeron in 5, 113–14
    reditus in 5, 7, 17, 21, 27, 47n. 14, 52,
        84, 86, 88–9, 91–2, 95, 97–100,
        108n. 19, 115, 134, 178, 203, 210,
        253, 265

Pseudo-Dionysius, *De caelesti Ierarchia*
    145

Versio Ambiguorum S. Maximi 145–7,
    174–6, 178, 201

Versus, see *Carmina*

General Index

Note: Locators followed by the letter 'n' refer to notes.

accessus ad auctores 61, 221–2, 242

Albigensians 22–6, 28, 47n. 14, 217, 222, 265

Alcuin of York 55, 61, 67, 69–70, 90–1, 104, 107n. 12, 138, 260

Amalric of Bene 7, 24–6, 42, 46n. 5, 47, 217

amor, medieval theory of 27, 32–8, 41, 44–5, 113, 132, 133, 135, 143, 153, 187, 195, 197–9, 209, 221–2, 252

Apollonius of Tyana 2, 220

apophatic theology 38, 52, 75, 83–7, 92–9, 108n. 15, 131, 191, 202, 236, 263

Aquinas, Thomas 7, 17, 33, 42, 48n. 21, 49n. 26, 75, 88, 110n. 30, 204, 209, 253, 266

Arian heresy 82

Aristotle 26, 32, 34–8, 40, 42, 45, 46n. 5, 48n. 15, 49n. 30, 51, 58, 65–6, 68, 78, 83, 99, 110n. 30, 113, 128, 153, 172, 218–19, 221, 260

  Aquinas on 24, 209, 262

  Categories 21, 27, 58, 61, 64, 77, 82, 89–94, 115, 131, 202, 204, 254

  De Anima 4, 10, 27, 35, 36, 38, 46n. 5, 48n. 15, 83, 153

atasal (also ittiṣāl) 169, 170

Augustine 40, 48n. 17, 49, 51, 63, 68–80, 87–95, 97, 99, 107n. 11, 108n. 16, 110n. 30, 111n. 34, 114, 116, 140, 156, 183, 190, 197, 235

Averroes 10, 17, 22, 27, 32, 35–7, 42–3, 48n. 21, 49n. 30, 51, 68, 70, 83, 93, 153, 163, 182, 209, 218, 221

Avicenna 10, 17, 27, 29, 35–7, 42–3, 51, 93, 170, 209, 218, 221

Bacigalupo, Massimo 12, 148

Bird, Otto 4, 18, 46n. 8, 68, 81, 114, 115, 162, 183

Boethius 13, 16, 20, 48n. 17, 49n. 30, 51, 61–2, 64–5, 69, 87, 93, 110nn. 24, 30, 140, 209

Bush, Ronald 5, 10, 12, 34, 35, 40, 46n. 8, 207, 209, 227, 257n. 17

Capella, Martianus 20, 51, 56–8, 60, 64, 67, 91, 103–4

Cappuyns, Maïuel 6, 18, 61, 71, 101, 107n. 6

Carolingian Age

  political context 4, 6–9, 11, 13, 14n. 3, 30, 45n. 1, 54, 57–61, 63–8, 74, 90, 100–6, 115, 136, 204, 209, 216, 253

  textual culture 52, 57–8, 63–8, 80

Categoriae decem 58, 64–6, 89, 91, 92–3

Cathars 23, 25, 47n. 14, 266

Cavalcanti, Guido 1, 2, 4, 6, 9, 13, 16–17, 24, 27, 29–45, 48n. 20, 66, 70, 83, 86, 105, 113, 115, 127, 143, 153, 162–3, 182–3, 208–9, 216, 219–21, 225, 240, 251–2, 254, 256n. 12

Charlemagne 45n. 1, 53–5, 60, 61, 69, 90, 104, 106n. 5, 112n. 41, 147

Charles the Bald 1, 5, 9, 15, 17–18, 20, 27, 45n. 1, 51–6, 59, 65, 67–8, 71, 82, 104, 106, 114, 121, 137, 139, 145, 147, 214–5, 236, 241, 261

  Palatine School of 1, 6–8, 9, 15, 20, 45n. 1, 56, 83, 215

Clement IV (Pope) 44

Condemnations

  of 1210 46n. 5, 47–8, 99, 212

  of 1225 23–5, 28, 47n. 14, 99, 129, 153, 265

  of 1270 24, 46n. 5, 153

Confucius 7, 207, 209, 212, 216, 221, 229, 234–41, 254, 257n. 17, 269

Constantinople, Council of (381 CE) 106n. 4, 108n. 19

Contreni, John J. 56–62, 66, 106n. 2

Dante, *Divina commedia* 2, 16, 27, 31–2, 42–3, 49n. 27, 197, 209, 222, 230, 269
David of Dinant 26, 47n. 13, 83
de Rachewiltz, Mary 49n. 22
divina ignorantia 27, 262
docta ignorantia 27, 262–3

Ebbo of Reims (Archbishop) 54–5, 59
Eight Views, genre of 8, 177, 241–9, 257n. 20
Eliot, Thomas Stearns 4–5, 18, 46n. 8, 107n. 13, 116, 207, 226
Ephesus, Council of (431 CE) 107n. 11
Eriugena
    authority (comes from right reason) 9, 20, 22–5, 28–30, 42–3, 52, 59, 74–5, 78, 80, 85, 93, 99, 108n. 15, 189, 203, 209–10, 213, 221, 228, 233–4, 242, 252–3, 261–2
    hilaritas 82, 100, 106, 114, 116, 147, 179–80, 204, 208, 212–15, 241, 253–4
    Neoplatonism in 7, 12, 15–45, 51, 59, 61, 66–7, 69–70, 82–6, 89–90, 97, 105, 109–10, 113–16, 146, 170, 176, 191, 204, 208–13, 217–26, 235–6, 238–41, 243, 252–4, 255n. 4, 260, 263–4
    participation, doctrine of 30, 47n. 12, 69–70, 82–5, 94, 99, 115, 136, 151, 181, 195, 264, 265
    superessentialism in 75, 78, 81, 83–4, 88, 95–6, 145, 158, 160, 165, 202, 215, 236

Fenollosa, Ernest 110n. 28, 231, 250, 257n. 21
Fiorentino, Francesco 17, 19, 22–8, 30, 43–4, 47nn. 11, 12, 66, 86, 105, 114–15, 213, 217, 235, 255n. 5, 259–66
florilegia 13, 14n. 3, 15, 51–2, 58, 65, 107n. 8, 113, 242
Floss, Henry Joseph 4, 19, 46n. 9, 99, 101, 117–18, 121, 129, 202, 207

Gale, Thomas 19, 21, 46n. 9, 99, 117, 129–30
Gemisthus Plethon 2, 16, 51, 114, 180, 212, 215, 219, 254
Gilson, Étienne 3–4, 22, 23, 44, 46n. 8, 60, 105, 114–15, 122

glossatory practices, Carolingian 6, 13, 14n. 3, 15, 20–1, 51–2, 57–69, 80, 84, 90, 106n. 3, 111n. 36, 113, 171–2, 196, 242
gnostic thought 27, 29, 32, 36–7
Gottschalk of Orbais 7, 9, 17, 20, 23, 28, 30, 55, 62, 68–78, 80–3, 104, 108n. 14, 114, 139, 197, 253
Gregory Nazianzus 17, 51, 64, 84, 168, 191
Gregory of Nyssa 17, 20, 38, 45, 47n. 10, 48n. 17, 50n. 31, 51, 64, 84, 87, 88, 92, 94–5, 103, 111n. 35, 156, 168, 190, 191, 263
Grosseteste, Robert 4, 22, 29, 37, 40, 43, 48n. 17, 49n. 24, 51, 200, 213, 219–22, 239–40, 254
Guinizelli, Guido 34

Heiric of Auxerre 21, 59–60, 65, 92, 106n. 3
hermeneutics 21, 23, 47n. 11, 86–90, 143, 256n. 16
Herren, Michael 20–1, 101–5, 109n. 23, 111n. 38, 112n. 40, 131, 148, 214–16
Hincmar of Laon (Bishop) 59, 62, 67, 102–3, 253
Hincmar of Reims (Archbishop) 9, 20, 55, 56, 59, 67, 69, 72, 74, 82, 102–3, 107n. 14, 205n. 1
Homer's *Odyssey* 2, 16, 31, 173, 200, 220, 222, 252
Honorius III (Pope) 23–5, 28, 107n. 8, 129, 265
Hugh of St Victor 130

ideogram 3, 15, 52, 83, 209–12, 216–18, 221–3, 227–34, 240, 242, 244, 249–50, 252, 256n. 13
Innocent III (Pope) 47n. 12
intellect, medieval theory of 27–30, 32–41, 44, 48n. 15, 49n. 26, 65–6, 69–70, 83, 85, 90, 93–5, 98, 107n. 10, 115, 124–5, 127–8, 130–1, 133, 143, 153–4, 158, 159, 163, 165–7, 174, 181–3, 235
Irish 'colony' 9, 19, 56
Irmintrude of Orléans, wife of Charles the Bald 6, 100, 147–9, 214
Islamic philosophy 7, 10, 17, 27, 32, 35–8, 40, 42–3, 45, 51, 66, 113, 219

Jannequin, Clément 199, 227
Jeauneau, Edouard 46n. 6, 47n. 10, 61, 64, 100, 107n. 7, 110n. 32

kataphatic theology 30, 37, 52, 78, 79, 84, 86, 88, 92, 94–9, 105–6, 108n. 15, 122, 131, 143, 155, 183–4, 202, 204, 226
Kenner, Hugh 25, 233, 239, 255n. 7, 256

Langres, Council of 20, 24, 68, 81
Laon, Cathedral school of 9, 20, 51, 56–8, 61–2, 65–7, 219
Leo III (Pope) 54
Leo IX (Pope) 138
Libri Carolini 60, 106, 112n. 41
Liebregts, Peter 5, 12
light philosophy 17–18, 45, 209, 211–13, 216–26, 228, 238–9
literatus 11, 208, 241–5, 252, 253
Lothar, Holy Roman Emperor 53–5, 72, 103, 149
Louis the German 53–5, 71, 104, 149
Louis the Pious 53–5, 147

McKitterick, Rosamond 14n. 3, 45n. 1
Makin, Peter 5, 12, 13, 211, 255n. 3
Malatesta, Sigismundo 219, 237
Manichaeism 23–5, 42, 72, 75, 116, 179–80, 211
Marciana, Biblioteca (Venice) 4, 10, 18, 114, 201
Marenbon, John 58, 61, 91, 107n. 12, 110n. 31, 132, 152
Martin Hiberniensis 20, 21, 56–8, 62, 65, 102, 107n. 9
Maximus the Confessor 12, 20, 51, 63, 64, 84, 87, 92, 95, 102, 103, 130–1, 145–6, 168, 174, 176, 192, 202–4
metamorphosis 31
metaphysics 32, 37, 44–5, 48n. 16, 67, 85, 88–91, 96, 105, 108n. 16, 135, 208–9, 211–13, 215–16, 218–19, 221–2, 224, 227–8, 230, 232–4, 237–9, 241, 251–2, 255n. 9
Mithraism 222
Moody, A. David 5, 12, 26, 47n. 14, 217, 226

negative theology 21–2, 27, 39, 73–81, 95, 115, 132, 154, 171–2, 195, 263
Neoplatonism 5, 7, 10–12, 16–18, 27, 29, 32–5, 37–8, 41–3, 51, 59, 61, 66–7, 69–70, 82, 84–6, 89, 97, 105, 110nn. 25, 32, 113–15, 146, 176, 191, 204, 208–13, 217–26, 235, 238–43, 252–4, 260, 264
Nicaea, Council of (325 CE) 82, 106n. 4, 191
    Second Council of (787 CE) 60
Nicholas I (Pope) 28, 60, 81, 100, 121, 139, 148, 214, 255n. 6

Ocellus 2, 215, 219
Origen 47n. 11, 190, 261

paradiso terrestre 16, 38, 44, 67, 89, 222, 228, 231, 235, 244, 253
Paris, University of 3, 4, 7–8, 9–10, 24, 25–6, 30, 32, 35, 42, 46n. 5, 47n. 12, 49n. 30, 68, 83, 129, 153, 212, 217, 236, 253
Pelagianism 69, 73, 75–6, 81, 107n. 11
Pepin of Aquitaine 54
Pisan DTC (Detention Training Center) 6, 7, 12, 42, 89, 209–10, 216–17, 224, 226, 234–5, 237, 257n. 17
Plato / Platonism 20, 62, 67, 72, 84, 85, 92, 111n. 34, 140, 183, 185, 192, 212, 220, 242, 254, 260
Plotinus 85–6, 88, 107n. 12, 146, 170, 241
Porphyry 85, 87, 93, 107n. 12, 241
Pound, Dorothy 226, 228
Predestination controversy 5, 7, 9, 17, 20, 28, 30, 49n. 25, 52, 54, 56, 59, 63, 68–83, 104, 106–8, 113–14, 116, 121, 139, 195, 236, 243
Proclus 16, 85–6, 99, 109n. 21, 204, 241
Psellus, Michael 51, 66
Pseudo-Dionysius 16–20, 27, 35, 38, 42, 48n. 17, 51–3, 58, 60, 64, 69, 74, 82, 84–9, 92–7, 99, 103–6, 108–10, 113, 115, 121–2, 125, 130, 132, 137, 146, 154, 157, 159, 162, 168, 170, 183, 195–6, 198, 200, 203–4, 210–11, 213, 215, 218, 226, 237, 239, 251, 254, 261, 263
    Celestial Hierarchy, The 4, 5, 17, 18, 20, 35, 36, 45n. 3, 48n. 17, 52, 58, 74,

84–7, 89, 105, 109n. 23, 121–3, 142, 157–8, 162–4, 167–8, 180, 182, 194, 196, 198, 200, 202–4, 211, 218
Ecclesiastical Hierarchy, The 20, 84–5
Mystical Theology, The 20, 84–5, 109n. 20, 170, 171, 172

reditus, see *Periphyseon*
Renan, Ernest 22, 44, 114, 115
Richard of St Victor 51, 70
Rorem, Paul 45n. 3, 87, 203

Saint-Médard de Soissons 21, 45n. 1, 54, 57
Santayana, George 18, 46n. 8, 114–15
Schlueter, C. B. 4, 23, 116, 118, 137, 180
scholasticism 17, 20, 28, 33, 35, 38, 42, 116, 195, 266
scripture 23, 50, 59, 74, 80, 86, 92, 108–9, 110n. 33, 128, 144
    New Testament 73
    Old Testament 21, 47n. 11, 149
Sedulius Scottus 21, 56–8, 61, 69, 102
Sheldon-Williams, I. P. 46n. 4, 95, 100, 110n. 32, 137

Socrates 140, 260
    Presocratic philosophy, general 218–19, 260, 261
Sordello da Goito 33, 34, 43–4

Tay, William 5, 12
Ten Eyck, David 7, 46n. 8
Terrell, Carroll 212, 258n. 24
theophany 10, 26, 27, 46n. 5, 52, 83, 88, 89, 92, 95–8, 122, 159, 202–4, 211, 238, 254, 263, 265
Trinitarian controversy 5, 69–70, 76–7, 80–3, 94, 114, 151, 236
Troubadours 13, 16–18, 23–4, 33–4, 41, 43–4, 49n. 23, 66, 113, 221

Uberti, Ubaldo degli 4, 46n. 8, 114

Valence, Council of 20, 24, 67, 68, 72
Vercelli, Synod of 138

William of Malmesbury 21, 46n. 9, 107n. 8, 108n. 18, 137–8

CPSIA information can be obtained
at www.ICGtesting.com
Printed in the USA
LVOW04s1657110316

478796LV00005B/114/P